D1590360

Losing Binh Dinh

Losing Binh Dinh

The Failure of Pacification and Vietnamization, 1969–1971

Kevin M. Boylan

University Press of Kansas

© 2016 by the University Press of Kansas

Published by the University Press of Kansas (Lawrence, Kansas 66045), which was organized by the Kansas Board of Regents and is operated and funded by Emporia State University, Fort Hays State University, Kansas State University, Pittsburg State University, the University of Kansas, and Wichita State University

Library of Congress Cataloging-in-Publication Data

Names: Boylan, Kevin M., author.
Title: Losing Binh Dinh : the failure of pacification and Vietnamization, 1969–1971 / Kevin M. Boylan.
Description: Lawrence, Kansas : University Press of Kansas, [2016] | Series: Modern war studies | Includes bibliographical references and index.
Identifiers: LCCN 2016036373
ISBN 9780700623525 (cloth : alk. paper)
ISBN 9780700623532 (ebook)
Subjects: LCSH: Vietnam War, 1961–1975—Campaigns—Vietnam—Binh Dinh (Province) | Counterinsurgency—Vietnam—Binh Dinh (Province) | United States. Army. Airborne Brigade, 173rd—History. | Binh Dinh (Vietnam : Province)—History.
Classification: LCC DS557.8.B53 B69 2016 | DDC 959.704/342—dc23
LC record available at https://lccn.loc.gov/2016036373.

British Library Cataloguing in Publication Data is available.

Printed in the United States of America

10 9 8 7 6 5 4 3 2 1

The paper used in this publication is recycled and contains 30 percent postconsumer waste. It is acid free and meets the minimum requirements of the American National Standard for Permanence of Paper for Printed Library Materials Z39.48-1992.

Contents

Acknowledgments   *vii*

List of Abbreviations   *viii*

Introduction: Verlorene Siege   1

1. The "Pacified" Province   11

2. Fast and Thin   44

3. The Balance of Forces   71

4. Growing Dependency   97

5. Overextension   133

6. Slowdown   169

7. The Red Queen's Race   206

8. Aftershocks   243

Conclusion: Triumph Mistaken   264

Notes   *301*

Bibliography   *345*

Index   *353*

Acknowledgments

I would like to extend my thanks to all the archivists, veterans, and historians who rendered invaluable assistance to my research over the years. In particular, I would like to thank Richard Boylan (no relation) and Cary Conn at the National Archives in College Park, Maryland, and the staff of the US Military History Institute in Carlisle, Pennsylvania. I am also deeply indebted to Dr. Andrew Birtle, chief of the Military Operations Branch at the US Army Center of Military History in Washington, DC, for his hospitality and assistance. Timothy Mazurek also deserves my sincerest thanks for patiently processing my many requests for the images and maps that have added so much to this study.

I would also like to thank General John W. Barnes (US Army–retired), General Lu Mong Lan (ex–Army of the Republic of Vietnam), both now decesed, Colonel John Waghelstein (US Army–retired), and Colonel Donald Bletz (US Army–retired) for allowing me to interview them. I must also express my appreciation to Michael Cunningham for sharing photos from his father's personal album and graciously granting permission for them to be reprinted here.

I am also indebted to the late Dr. Russell Weigley for the invaluable advice, encouragement, and support he gave me in the earliest stages of this project.

I would like to extend special thanks to Tara Neal for producing the excellent maps included in this book on short notice.

Finally, I must thank my wife, Leslie, for the generous support and encouragement she gave me throughout this project.

Abbreviations

ACAV	armored cavalry assault vehicle
AO	area of operations
APC	Accelerated Pacification Campaign
ARVN	Army of the Republic of Vietnam
AWOL	absent without leave
BAT	Brigade Advisor Team
CAP	Combined Action Platoon (program)
CIA	Central Intelligence Agency
CICV	Combined Intelligence Center—Vietnam
CIDG	Civilian Irregular Defense Group
COIN	counterinsurgency
CORDS	Civil Operations and Revolutionary Development Support
COSVN	Central Office for South Vietnam, Vietnamese Workers' (Communist) Party
DIOCC	District Intelligence and Operations Coordination Center
DSA	district senior advisor
FDC	Fire Direction Center
FSB	Fire Support Base
FSSB	Fire Support Surveillance Base
FWMAF	Free World Military Assistance Forces
GVN	government of (South) Vietnam
H&I	harassing and interdicting
HES	Hamlet Evaluation System
ICEX	Intelligence Coordination and Exploitation (program)
I FFV	I Field Force Vietnam
IPW	prisoner of war interrogation
ISIL	Islamic State of Iraq and the Levant
KIA	killed in action
KIT	Key Inter-Team
LTTT	Land-to-the-Tiller (program)
LZ	landing zone
MACV	Military Assistance Command—Vietnam
MAT	Mobile Advisory Team

MSF	Mobile Strike Force
NCO	noncommissioned officer
NLF	National Liberation Front
NPFF	National Police Field Force
NVA	North Vietnamese Army
OSA	Office of Systems Analysis
PAAS	Pacification Attitude Analysis System
PAVN	People's Army of Vietnam
PF	Popular Forces
PIOCC	Province Intelligence and Operations Coordination Center
POW	prisoner of war
PRG	Provisional Revolutionary Government
PRU	Provincial Reconnaissance Unit
PSA	province senior advisor
PSB	Police Special Branch
PSC	Province Security Committee
PSDF	People's Self-Defense Force
PSG	Pacification Studies Group
RD	revolutionary development (US) or rural development (GVN)
RF	Regional Forces
ROK	Republic of Korea
ROTC	Reserve Officers' Training Corps
RTV	Return-to-Village
RVN	Republic of Vietnam
RVNAF	Republic of Vietnam Armed Forces
SEATO	Southeast Asia Treaty Organization
STAG	Security Training Assistance Group
USMC	United States Marine Corps
VC	Vietcong
VCI	Vietcong Infrastructure
VIP	Voluntary Informant Program
VIS	Vietnamese Information Service
VSD	Village Self-Development
VSSG	Vietnam Special Studies Group

NORTH
VIETNAM

DEMARCATION LINE

QUANGTRI

LAOS

THUATHIEN   Hue   I CTZ

SOUTH CHINA SEA

Da Nang

THAILAND

QUANG NAM

QUANGTIN

QUANG NGAI

KONTUM

BINH DINH

SOUTH
VIETNAM

PLEIKU

CAMBODIA

PHU BON

PHUYEN

Tonle
Sap

DARLAC

II CTZ

KHANH
HOA

QUANG DUC

TUYEN DUC

Da Lat   NINH
THUAN   Cam Ranh

PHUOC
LONG

BINH
LONG

III CTZ

LAM DONG

TAY NINH

BINH
DUONG

LONG
KHANH

BINHTHUAN

BINH
TUY

HAU
NGHIA   BIEN
HOA

SOUTH
CHINA SEA

SAIGON

CHAU
DOC   KIEN PHONG   KIENTUONG   LONG AN   GIA
DINH   PHUOCTUY

AN
GIANG   SA
DEC   DINHTUONG   GO CONG   Vung Tau

KIEN GIANG   VINH LONG   KIEN HOA

PHONG
DINH   VINH BINH

GULF OF
THAILAND   IV CTZ   CHUONG
THIEN   BA XUYEN

BAC LIEU

AN XUYEN

SOUTH VIETNAM
1966–1967

Corps Tactical Zone Boundary

Administrative Boundary

Hue   Autonomous Municipality

0   150 Miles

0   150 Kilometers

Verlorene Siege

Americans have fought two prolonged wars about Vietnam, both of which began in the 1960s. One took place in the jungles and rice paddies of Southeast Asia and ended in 1975. The other was fought at home and continues to this day. The war at home has always been far more important to most Americans, and the side one took was usually determined more by one's stance on domestic social and political issues than by what actually happened in Vietnam. Even now, forty years after the fall of Saigon, both sides are still chiefly concerned with using the lessons of Vietnam as ammunition against their domestic political opponents. The war at home has often spilled over into the halls of academe, duplicating there the deep fissures that sunder American society on this highly divisive issue. In recent decades, this rift within the historical fraternity has been cast in terms of two competing schools of interpretation—the Orthodox and the Revisionist. The former, which argues that the Vietnam War was unnecessary, unduly brutal, and ultimately unwinnable, was established by outspoken critics of US policy in Vietnam such as Frances Fitzgerald and Gabriel Kolko, but it also includes some of those responsible for making that policy, most notably former secretary of defense Robert S. McNamara, whose earnest mea culpa *In Retrospect: The Tragedy and Lessons of Vietnam* was published in 1995. John Prados, author of *Vietnam: The History of an Unwinnable War, 1945–1975* (2009), is currently the Orthodox school's most outspoken champion, but it is supported by a strong consensus among Vietnam War historians.

The Revisionist school began to challenge the Orthodox consensus as early as 1978 with the publication of Guenter Lewy's *America in Vietnam*, and it received a major boost three years later when Harry Summers's *On Strategy: A Critical Analysis of the Vietnam War* first appeared in print. William Colby, who had been the top US pacification official in Vietnam—and later became the director of central intelligence—joined the Revisionist camp in 1989 with his memoir *Lost Victory: A Firsthand Account of America's Sixteen-Year Involvement in Vietnam*. It was not until the late 1990s, however, that Vietnam War revisionism reached maturity with the publication of Mark Moyar's *Phoenix and the Birds of Prey: The CIA's Secret Campaign to Destroy the Viet Cong* (1997), Lewis Sorley's *A Better War: The Unexam-*

1

ined Victories and Final Tragedy of America's Last Years in Vietnam (1999), and Michael Lind's *Vietnam—The Necessary War: A Reinterpretation of America's Most Disastrous Military Conflict* (1999). The Revisionist school gained even greater prominence in the first decade of the twenty-first century thanks to Moyar's controversial *Triumph Forsaken: The Vietnam War, 1954–1965* (2006), which brought a new intensity to the Orthodox-Revisionist debate. This was manifested in *Triumph Revisited: Historians Battle for the Vietnam War* (2010), edited by Andrew Wiest and Michael Doidge.

Despite its great influence, the Revisionist school still counts only a handful of supporters among academic historians. Some claim this continuing minority status reflects an ideological bias within academe that suppresses challenges to the Orthodox premise that the Vietnam War was unnecessary, unjust, and unwinnable. Although this may have been true of some of the earliest Orthodox historians who wrote three or four decades ago, most of the school's current adherents are far less doctrinaire. Moreover, some of the Revisionists are themselves dogmatically committed to a rival creed that insists the conflict was indisputably necessary, just, and winnable, and view all Vietnam War historiography through an ideological lens of their own. Moyar goes so far as to describe several unnamed Orthodox historians as "the VC's American supporters"!¹ Thus, it would be more accurate to characterize the ongoing debate as one between Orthodoxy and Neo-Orthodoxy, though for the sake of clarity, the term "Revisionist" is used throughout this book.

The prominence of the Orthodox-Revisionist debate in recent Vietnam War scholarship also tends to obscure the fact that many works do not fit neatly into either camp. One example is James Willbanks's *Abandoning Vietnam: How America Left and South Vietnam Lost Its War* (2004), which analyzes the final years of the Vietnam War in a commendably evenhanded fashion. Another is Gregory Daddis's *No Sure Victory: Measuring U.S. Army Effectiveness and Progress in the Vietnam War* (2011), which sifts through the "metrics" the United States used to measure progress in Vietnam. There is also David Elliott's two-volume *The Vietnamese War: Revolution and Social Change in the Mekong Delta, 1930–1975* (2001), which dispassionately analyzes the Communist insurgency in a single province in exhaustive detail. Like these authors, many other historians who concentrate on a particular aspect, period, region, unit, battle, or campaign of the Vietnam War steer clear of the contentious questions of whether it was just or necessary.

It is nearly impossible, however, for American historians to avoid the question of whether the war was winnable, since this has always dominated Vietnam War historiography in the United States. Revisionist historians insist that it was winnable, and they engage in contrafactual speculation about how victory might have been achieved if senior US policymakers and military commanders had made different choices at key turning points in the Vietnam saga. However, the Revisionists do not agree on how, when, or even where victory might have been achieved. Moyar believes the best US strategy would have been to "strike at the head of the snake" by invading North Vietnam, whereas Summers and Sorley would have favored permanently cutting the Ho Chi Minh Trail in Laos. However, while Summers argues that combating the Vietcong insurgency within South Vietnam should have been left exclusively to the South Vietnamese, Sorley and Moyar believe that the deep US involvement would have been required in that aspect of the war as well. Yet they disagree fundamentally about how it should have been done. Sorley argues that the strategy of attrition employed by General William C. Westmoreland between 1965 and 1968 was inappropriate and unsuccessful, and dangerously delayed the adoption of a better strategy, while Moyar claims that it was unavoidable and effective, and laid the foundation on which victory could have been built.

This book aims to test the Revisionist school's hypothesis that the Vietnam War was winnable, but needless to say, historical analysis can neither prove nor disprove whether something that did not happen could have. And even if one were inclined to engage in a purely speculative analysis of the Revisionists' alternative history scenarios, testing all the possible permutations of even one of them would be a daunting task. For nested within each, like a set of Russian *matryoshka* dolls, is a whole chain of speculative hypotheses about how the Vietcong insurgents, the North Vietnamese, their Chinese and Soviet patrons, the South Vietnamese people and government, other US allies, and the American public would have responded to a fundamentally different US strategy. The exercise would ultimately prove nothing because, if enough contrafactual assumptions are daisy-chained together, it is conceivable that virtually any alternative strategy could have yielded victory in Vietnam. One is reminded of Groucho Marx's quip: "If we had some ham, we could have eggs and ham . . . if we had some eggs."

Fortunately, the Revisionist school provides us with one historically testable hypothesis. Many Revisionist historians argue not only that the Vietnam War could have been won (at various times and by various means) but that it actually was won in the years following the 1968 Tet Offensive. This victory came about, they claim, due to the success of allied "pacification" operations at securing the South Vietnamese population and defeating the Vietcong insurgency. Sorley puts this case most forthrightly: "There came a time when the war was won. The fighting wasn't over, but the war was won. This achievement can probably best be dated to late 1970, after the Cambodian incursion in the spring of the year. By then the South Vietnamese countryside had been widely pacified, so much so that the term 'pacification' was no longer even used."[2] Moyar concurs, writing: "From 1969 to 1971 the rein-vigorated South Vietnamese forces and their American allies eliminated the remaining South Vietnamese insurgents by killing them, capturing them, or driving them to defect through the national amnesty program. The war ceased to have a significant component of insurgency by the end of 1971, be-coming purely a conventional war between the armed forces of North Viet-nam and South Vietnam."[3] Summers, Colby, and other Revisionists agree that the insurgency was eliminated as a significant factor in the war, and they point to the fact that Saigon ultimately fell to North Vietnamese troops equipped with masses of tanks and heavy artillery—rather than to lightly armed Vietcong guerrillas—as proof of this accomplishment.

The presence of large numbers of North Vietnamese Army (NVA) troops within South Vietnam's borders meant, however, that defeating the internal insurgency was not sufficient to ensure the nation's survival after American troops left. It was also necessary for the South Vietnamese to become capa-ble of defending the country on their own, without the aid of US troops on the ground. Revisionists assert that this goal was also achieved, thanks to the success of President Richard Nixon's policy of "Vietnamization." Sorley writes:

> Not only was the internal war against subversion and the guerrilla threat won, so was that against the external conventional threat—in the terms specified by the United States. Those terms were that South Vietnam should, without help from U.S. ground forces, be capable of resisting ag-gression so long as Americans continued to provide logistical and finan-cial support, and of crucial importance later, once a cease-fire agreement had been negotiated—renewed application of U.S. air and naval power should North Vietnam violate the terms of that agreement.[4]

Under the policy of Vietnamization, the United States vastly enlarged South Vietnam's military forces, greatly enhanced their firepower and mo-bility, provided extensive training and advisory support, and did everything possible to improve their leadership. Of these, the last was undoubtedly the most important, since poor leadership had always been the bane of the South Vietnamese armed forces and was the principal reason why they could not fight the Communists on equal terms even when they possessed superior firepower, mobility, and logistical support. Moyar asserts that, starting in 1968, "South Vietnamese counterinsurgency commanders improved dra-matically in every way."[5] This improvement was primarily due to pressure skillfully applied by Colby and the top US military commander in Vietnam,

General Creighton W. Abrams, which resulted in the replacement of a dozen incompetent South Vietnamese province chiefs and more than eighty district chiefs by the end of 1971. Moyar claims that the superior leadership provided by their replacements had "an electrifying effect" on the South Vietnamese Territorial Forces, which did the lion's share of the fighting on the front lines of pacification. Abrams also managed to secure the replacement of dozens of incompetent and overcautious senior commanders in the South Vietnamese Regular Army. According to Moyar, these "changes of key commanders in the South Vietnamese army worked the same magic as the substitution of district and provincial chiefs did."[6] Not all Revisionists believe that South Vietnam's leadership problems magically disappeared, but there is a strong consensus among them that Vietnamization succeeded—that is, South Vietnam's armed forces became capable of standing on their own if supported by US airpower and generous American financial and material assistance.

These Revisionists therefore affirm that the Vietnam War had effectively been won by January 1973, when the Paris Peace Accords were signed, which soon led to the departure of the last US troops from Vietnam. But victory was subsequently thrown away, they say, by the war-weary and pusillanimous US Congress responding to pressure by vocal antiwar groups and sympathetic elements in the media. The Fulbright-Aiken amendment of August 1973 effectively terminated US air and naval support for the South Vietnamese by prohibiting expenditures for any more American combat operations in Southeast Asia. Motivated in part by escalating budget deficits and runaway inflation sparked by the OPEC oil embargo of October 1973–March 1974, Congress also approved aid to South Vietnam at levels substantially below what Presidents Nixon and Ford requested in 1974 and 1975. This forced the South Vietnamese armed forces to cut their fuel and ammunition consumption, which significantly reduced their firepower, mobility, and overall combat effectiveness. Since Soviet and Chinese military and financial assistance to North Vietnam rose during this same period, the Revisionists assert that the decline in US aid inevitably doomed South Vietnam to the final defeat it suffered in the spring of 1975. Colby wrote: "This refusal to provide the essential logistics and airpower must be considered the final of three major errors of the American performance in Vietnam.[7] The absence of this relatively small increment of assistance made the downfall of South Vietnam certain and rendered futile the years of blood and sacrifice by Vietnamese and Americans leading up to it."[8]

Sorley also identifies several different causes for South Vietnam's collapse (including continuing deficiencies in leadership and the failure to cut the Ho Chi Minh Trail), but he sees the decline in US support as decisive:

One, a simple matter of fact, had to do with the termination of political support, reduction of materiel support, and eventually even denial of fiscal support to the South Vietnamese by their sometime American ally. This was the work of Congress, wrought over the strong and eventually agonized protests of the administration, military leaders, and of course the South Vietnamese. It stood in sharp contrast to the uninterrupted support rendered North Vietnam by her Soviet and Chinese allies. Ambassador [to South Vietnam Ellsworth] Bunker, for one, argued that "we eventually defeated ourselves, but we were not defeated when we signed the Paris peace treaties. We had, I think, then achieved our objective. The fact that it slipped from our grasp was our own doing."[9]

To put it plainly, many—though not all—Revisionists argue that the victory achieved in 1973 came to naught because the South Vietnamese were "stabbed in the back" by the US government itself. This "lost victory" hypothesis had its origins in pro-war commentaries written before Saigon fell and featured prominently in the postwar memoirs of President Richard Nixon and his national security advisor, Henry Kissinger.[10] Thanks to the efforts of the Revisionists, in recent decades it has been embraced by large segments of the US government, armed forces, media, and public—sometimes for partisan reasons—but how true is it? There can be no doubt that waning material and financial assistance weakened the South Vietnamese armed forces and eroded their morale, but was it really decisive? To answer this question, one must look back to the period before the Paris Peace Accords to determine whether pacification and Vietnamization actually succeeded, as the Revisionists claim. If so, then a victory of sorts was won in Vietnam, and Congress must bear most of the blame for subsequently losing it. If these policies failed, however, there was no victory to be lost in the first place, and South Vietnam was abandoned to its fate by Nixon and Kissinger in January 1973 rather than by Congress later on.

The Key Province Approach

Like most Vietnam War historians, the Revisionists favor top-down analyses of the entire conflict written from the Olympian perspectives of senior policymakers and military commanders in Saigon and Washington, DC. This approach can be misleading, however, since insurgencies are inherently decentralized and noncontiguous. Unlike conventional wars, with their clearly delineated front lines and sequence of intricately linked battles and campaigns, "frontless" insurgencies are essentially a multitude of localized conflicts going on simultaneously. Accordingly, they are best studied from the bottom up, since the higher up the chain of command one goes, the more difficult it is to discern what is actually happening on the ground in any given region. Harvey Meyerson, who authored an excellent book about the war in South Vietnam's Mekong Delta, eloquently describes the problem—and identifies the solution:

> So much is happening in Vietnam, simultaneously, at so many differ-ent places, that the panoramic approach—dominant in literature on Vietnam—has the effect of harnessing the observer's senses to a pow-erful centrifugal pull that sends impressions and conclusions spinning outward. The panoramic observer is writing from no context capable of holding a piece of information, fixing it under a light, then moving in more information, comparing, accepting, rejecting, until a measure of understanding can be breathed into his work. . . . A single province provides the missing context. Insights that in the Big Picture environ-ment explode outward now become susceptible to containment, and even dissection. Statistical measurements can be examined critically at the source. The events of yesterday, last week, last month, can be cor-related directly with the events of today, tomorrow and next month. The observer who concentrates on one province develops a mastery of his material not possible on the scale of the Big Picture.[11]

The Vietnam Special Studies Group (VSSG) created by President Nixon came to the same conclusion when it was tasked with analyzing the situation in South Vietnam during the fall of 1969. Instead of using aggregated data to generalize about conditions nationwide, the VSSG staffers chose to pro-duce detailed studies of a relatively small number of key provinces where the stakes were highest and the war was most intense. They wrote, "We consider that the 'key province' approach of this paper is sound and will lead to the best possible assessment of the situation in the countryside and the factors affecting it. Rarely will key facts, relationships, and trends be detected using aggregate data analyzed on a countrywide or Corps basis."[12]

One of the provinces examined by the VSSG was Binh Dinh, situated on the coast at the northern extremity of II Corps (one of the four "corps," or "military regions," into which South Vietnam was divided by the allies—the Communists had different regions of their own). For a variety of reasons, it was a province the allies absolutely had to secure if they were going to win the war. First of all, of South Vietnam's forty-four provinces, only Gia Dinh, the one containing Saigon, had a larger population. In July 1969 Binh Dinh's 931,400 inhabitants represented more than 5 percent of South Vietnam's to-tal populace.[13] Second, although it was relatively poor on a per capita basis, the province contributed substantially to the national economy. Finally, Binh Dinh was of immense strategic importance, since it sat at the point where Highway 1, South Vietnam's only contiguous north-south transportation route, intersected Highway 9, which ran westward into the vital Central Highlands. It also contained Qui Nhon, one of the nation's few major seaports, as well as the huge US Air Force base at Phu Cat. Binh Dinh accordingly witnessed more allied and Communist military activity than all but a handful of other provinces, and the southern part of the province was one of the four National Priority Areas designated in the allies' 1966 Combined Campaign Plan.[14] Two of the US Army's premier combat formations in Vietnam—the 1st Cavalry Division and the 173rd Airborne Brigade—each spent more than two years operating almost exclusively within its borders. As we shall see, these units employed radically different tactics, but between them, their efforts to pacify Binh Dinh were as serious as any the US military made anywhere in South Vietnam.

This book uses Binh Dinh to test the Revisionists' "lost victory" hypothesis on a small scale by determining whether pacification and Vietnamization succeeded in the province. It focuses on the years after the 1968 Tet Offensive—the period during which the Revisionists claim the war was won—and particularly on April 1969 to December 1970, when the 173rd Airborne conducted an operation that was unique in the annals of the US Army in Vietnam. Titled Operation Washington Green, it dispersed the brigade across northern Binh Dinh in detachments of platoon size and smaller; their mission was to secure individual hamlets and facilitate pacification programs implemented by a wide array of South Vietnamese agencies. The US troop detachments were also supposed to aid Vietnamization by giving formal and on-the-job training to South Vietnamese Territorial Forces units (Regional Forces companies and Popular Forces platoons) and People's Self-Defense Forces militia located in the same communities. The intention was for the 173rd Airborne to "work itself out of a job" by improving the Territorial Forces' performance to the point where they could secure the hamlets on their own.

Although the brigade's primary mission of securing the population was essentially a defensive one, Washington Green was an offensive operation that targeted the enemy's "center of gravity" in northern Binh Dinh—the support of the rural population. Counterinsurgency doctrine teaches that access to the population is crucial for insurgents. It is their primary source of recruits, intelligence, and supplies, and their chief advantage—"invisibility"—derives from the ability to conceal themselves among the people. Thus, instead of trying to destroy the enemy guerrillas and regular troops in northern Binh Dinh in direct combat (an approach that had consistently failed in the past), Operation Washington Green attacked them indirectly by striking at the strategic vitals of the Communist revolutionary movement. If it succeeded, the enemy would be reduced to impotence by being denied the popular support he needed to survive.

Washington Green was, in other words, what would nowadays be termed a population-centric counterinsurgency (COIN) operation. After many false starts and failed experiments with other techniques, population-centric COIN was widely adopted by US Army and Marine Corps units in Afghanistan and Iraq—particularly during the Iraq troop surge of 2007. However, in those twenty-first-century conflicts, the enemy did not possess large-scale military units and thus relied almost exclusively on terrorist and guerrilla warfare tactics. In contrast, the Vietcong fielded many regular military units alongside their guerrilla forces and were supported by more than 100,000 NVA troops. American commanders in Vietnam were therefore reluctant to disperse their troops in population-centric COIN missions, for fear that they would be easy targets for the enemy's concentrated regular units. Moreover, dispersing American combat units to guard the population would necessarily surrender the initiative to the enemy and make it exceedingly difficult for those units to mass or maneuver or to surprise the enemy by striking at a time, at a place, or in a manner for which he was unprepared. In short, population-centric COIN violates many of the fundamental principles of war developed by nineteenth-century Prussian military theorist Karl von Clausewitz in his posthumous magnum opus *On War*. In the 1960s and 1970s Clausewitz's maxims did not occupy the same place of honor in US military doctrine that they do today; however, the principles of the offensive, mass, maneuver, and surprise were hardly alien to American commanders of the day.

Not surprisingly, many of those serving in the 173rd Airborne actively disliked Operation Washington Green because it required them to adapt to an uncongenial mission that was radically at odds with both their training and all their prior experience in Vietnam.[15] In particular, it obliged them to live and fight in prolonged and intimate contact with both allied paramilitary units and a civilian population that belonged to a bewilderingly alien culture and were riddled with enemy sympathizers, spies, and guerrilla fighters. Yet, commanders at all levels in the brigade also had to be constantly on guard to ensure that their widely scattered detachments were not overrun by lurking Communist regular units. And since their primary goal was to secure and protect the rural populace, they had to do all this while refraining from the liberal employment of firepower that characterized US Army tactics throughout the Vietnam War. All in all, Washington Green posed a set of daunting and unprecedented challenges for the 173rd Airborne that closely resemble those confronting US troops performing population-centric COIN missions today. Therefore, its lessons are, in many cases, directly applicable to ongoing operations in Afghanistan and Iraq and other potential battlegrounds in the ongoing "war on terrorism."

CHAPTER ONE

The "Pacified" Province

In 1771, as American colonists on the other side of the world were beginning to stir into revolution against the British Empire, three brothers from the village of Tay Son in what is now Binh Dinh Province, Vietnam, led a rebellion against the corrupt Nguyen warlords who dominated the southern half of the country. With the slogan "seize the property of the rich and distribute it to the poor," the brothers raised a rebel army that swept across the country, punishing oppressive landlords and mandarins, redistributing property, sharing out food, and freeing prisoners. By the time the American colonists finally won their independence in 1783, the Tay Son brothers had seized control of all southern Vietnam and driven twenty-one-year-old Nguyen Anh, the last surviving Nguyen heir, into exile.[1]

The Tay Son brothers then came into conflict with the Trinh warlords who dominated the northern half of the country. By 1786, they had overthrown the Trinh and reunified Vietnam for the first time in two centuries. All this was ostensibly done on behalf of Le Hien Tong, reigning emperor of the Le Dynasty, whose ancestors had been reduced to figureheads by the Nguyen and Trinh in the 1530s. But the emperor felt more threatened than empowered by the rebels and fled north to seek the assistance of China's Qing Dynasty in crushing them. The eldest of the Tay Son brothers, Nguyen Nhac, declared himself emperor, but the new dynasty was immediately challenged by a Chinese army that invaded in 1788. Nguyen Hue, the most militarily talented of the brothers, marched out to meet the invaders near what is now Hanoi, the capital of Vietnam.[2] Attacking during the Tet lunar New Year holiday, his troops surprised and routed the Qing army, which fled back to China.[3]

Nguyen Anh had taken advantage of the Chinese invasion by returning to southern Vietnam and launching a revolt against the Tay Son. Nguyen Hue, who had become Emperor Quang Trung, planned to stamp out the Nguyen warlords' resurgence, but he died in 1792 before he could finish the job. Meanwhile, aided by arms, ships, and military advisors procured by the French Jesuit missionary Pigneau de Behaine, Nguyen Anh was embracing Western military technology. Forts, shipyards, and cannon foundries were established; troops were trained and equipped along European lines; and a dozen Western-style frigates were built to form the core of Nguyen Anh's navy. Moving cautiously, Nguyen Anh, now Emperor Gia Long, gradually retook Vietnam from the Tay Son, who were feuding among themselves and whose armies had long since lost their revolutionary fervor. The reconquest would not be completed until 1802, but in 1799 the emperor's armies captured the province that had been the birthplace of the Tay Son movement. Gia Long renamed it Binh Dinh (meaning "pacified") to commemorate this victory.[4]

The emperors who succeeded Gia Long in the new Nguyen Dynasty found it increasingly difficult to resist French imperialism. In a series of wars stretching from 1864 to 1907, all of Indochina (including Cambodia and Laos) became French colonies and protectorates that would survive until the Second World War. The 1940 conquest of France by Nazi Germany ended the illusion of invincibility that had sustained French colonial rule in the Far East, and the Vichy regime's inability to defend Indochina against the Japanese further undermined French prestige among the region's native peoples. In September 1940 the colonial government allowed Japanese troops to enter Vietnam and establish air and naval bases within its territory. Collaboration with the Japanese continued until early 1945, when the Vichy French, recognizing that Allied victory was inevitable, planned to switch sides. The Japanese preempted them by seizing control of all Vietnam in March 1945. French colonial troops put up only slight resistance before being disarmed and imprisoned, along with the entire "European" population of Vietnam. Therefore, when Japan announced its intention to surrender after the atomic bombings of Hiroshima and Nagasaki in August 1945, a power vacuum emerged in Vietnam. It was quickly filled by the Communist-dominated *Việt-Nam Độc-Lập Đồng Minh Hội* (League for the Independence of Vietnam)—better known as the Vietminh. On 14 August, as the Japanese stood by and the French languished in their internment camps, the Vietminh seized power and proclaimed the establishment of the Democratic Republic of Vietnam. However, the French government in Paris responded by sending troops to Indochina to restore colonial rule. After a year of fruitless negotiation and skirmishing, war broke out between the French and the Vietminh in late 1946.

During the First Indochinese War, Binh Dinh formed the heart of Interzone (*Liên-Khu*) 5, a vast Vietminh stronghold that spanned the coastal provinces of central Vietnam from Quang Nam to Phu Yen and was headquartered in the town of Bong Son. The insurgents controlled nearly all of Interzone 5 and its population of about 3 million without interruption for the duration of the war. Lacking sufficient troops to occupy the entire country, the French concentrated their efforts on securing the Red and Mekong Del-

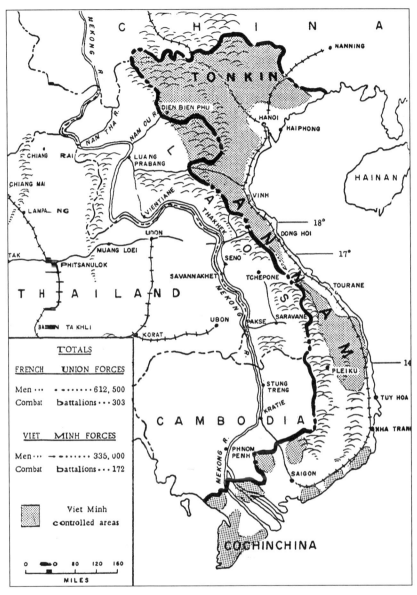

Viet Minh–Controlled Areas (July 1954). *Source: The Pentagon Papers: The Defense Department History of United States Decisionmaking on Vietnam, The Senator Gravel Edition*, 4 vols., (Boston: Beacon Press, 1971), 1:123.

tas, which represented the wealthiest and most populous regions of northern and southern Vietnam, respectively. The only foothold they retained in Binh Dinh was an enclave around the town of An Khe, which was supplied by convoys descending from the French-controlled Central Highlands to the west.[5] French operations in Binh Dinh were limited to amphibious raids for almost the entire war. In 1949 Operation Beta landed a task force built around the 2nd Battalion de Commandos Coloniaux Parachutistes in the northern part of the province to destroy the rolling stock and the maintenance and switching facilities at the Tam Quan rail yard.[6] During January 1953 Operation Toulouse put French troops ashore in Qui Nhon to relieve enemy pressure on An Khe and destroy Vietminh arms factories. The French withdrew a week later, leaving much of the city in ruins.[7]

It was not until the last year of the war that the French made a concerted effort to conquer Interzone 5. In January 1954 the French commander in chief, General Henri-Eugene Navarre, launched Operation Atlante, which began with a pair of amphibious assaults in Phu Yen Province, immediately south of Binh Dinh. Joined by other troops advancing north along the coast from Nha Trang and moving down from the French-controlled Central Highlands to the west, the offensive was to be carried northward into Binh Dinh. The operation's second and third phases envisioned a concentric attack on the northern half of Interzone 5 by the original Atlante force advancing to the north and still more troops pushing south from Da Nang. All told, thirty battalions would be involved in the first phase, thirty-nine in the second, and fifty-three in the third. It was to be a truly massive effort to clean out central Vietnam once and for all.[8] However:

> After . . . [the] initially successful landing . . . the operation bogged down completely. The Vietnamese troops who were to receive their baptism of fire in the beachhead either gave a poor account of themselves or settled down to looting. The Vietnamese civil administrators who began to pour into the liberated areas were, if anything, worse than the military units. Presently, the Viet Minh forces of the Interzone, unimpeded by the French ATLANTE beachhead, went on the offensive on the southern mountain plateau, destroying Regimental Combat Team 100 [aka Mobile Group 100].[9]

The destruction of Mobile Group 100 was the last major action of the First Indochinese War, the outcome of which had been decided by the crushing French defeat at the siege of Dien Bien Phu on 7 May 1954. Fighting was ended by the Geneva Agreement of July 1954, which stipulated that all French forces would be "regrouped" south of the seventeenth parallel, while all Vietminh forces would redeploy north of it.[10] Several hundred thousand North Vietnamese civilians—mostly Catholics—fled to the south, while 60,000 to 90,000 Vietminh troops and civilian supporters moved north. About 85 percent of all Communist regroupees came from Interzone 5, and fully half were from Binh Dinh.[11]

The Final Declaration of the Geneva Conference stipulated that elections would be held in 1956 to establish a single government to rule all of Vietnam, but this clause was a dead letter because the non-Communist State of Vietnam's delegation refused to sign the Final Declaration. When the elections did not take place, the Communist cadres that had stayed behind in the south began agitating for a resumption of the revolutionary struggle, but their comrades in the north—distracted by the task of creating a new nation—held them back for several years. Meanwhile, the "Anti-Communist Denunciation Campaign" launched by South Vietnamese president Ngo Dinh Diem enjoyed considerable success in executing and imprisoning the stay-behind cadres, although it also swept up many former Vietminh who were not Communists.[12] The revolutionary movement survived, however, and fighting broke out anew in Binh Dinh in 1959 when primitive montagnard tribes—which shared a bitter racial animosity with the ethnic Vietnamese—actively resisted government efforts to relocate them from their traditional mountain homes to the plains below. The montagnard uprising was swiftly "captured" by the Communists.[13] However, the "hard core" of the insurgency was formed by veteran "regroupees" infiltrating back from North Vietnam:

They returned, as prudence would dictate, to their home province, whose geography they knew best and where waited relatives and friends to support them. Since numerically most of the southern regroupees were from Binh Dinh, it was to Binh Dinh that most of them went, in all perhaps 25,000. The result was that guerrilla war began earlier in Binh Dinh, more quickly became endemic there, enjoying great popular support. It became a truism, perhaps only slightly exaggerated, that in Binh Dinh if a person was not a Vietcong he was related to one.[14]

The insurgency in Binh Dinh was also fueled by the province's extreme poverty, which was principally the result of overpopulation. Although it was the second largest province in South Vietnam (at eighty by fifty-five miles, Binh Dinh was roughly the size of Connecticut), two-thirds of its territory was covered by rugged mountains. The Annamite Chain (or Truong Son Mountains) stretched along the entire length of the province, rising steeply to the high plateau of the Central Highlands in Kontum and Pleiku Provinces to the west. The narrow An Lao, Kim Son, Suoi Ca, and Vinh Thanh

Valleys cut back into the mountains, creating a series of cul-de-sacs dominated by the surrounding heights. The coastal plain was carved into a series
of compartments by isolated tangles of mountain ridges (the Cay Giep, Nui
Mieu, and Phu Cat Mountains) that rose abruptly on its seaward flank. In
both Vietnam wars, the coastal mountains acted as bases from which the
Communists made forays into the surrounding lowlands.[15]

In 1972 Binh Dinh had 940,000 inhabitants, of whom 190,000 lived in
Qui Nhon, the only major city, and another 40,000 were montagnard tribesmen residing in the mountains. Everyone else was crammed into the narrow
confines of the coastal plain, where the sandy soil was not very fertile and
water resources were often insufficient to produce good rice crops—which
required constant irrigation. According to data from the French colonial period, the population density in some parts of the province had reached 300
persons per square kilometer of cultivated land as early as the 1940s.[16] The
average standard of living was therefore markedly lower than in most other
regions of South Vietnam. Writing in 1972, renowned Vietnam War scholar
Douglas Pike observed:

> Contrary to widespread belief, Vietnam is not a poverty-ridden country,
> but is in fact one of the three or four richest per-capita nations of Asia.
> . . . Particularly in the agricultural sector, all of the requirements and few
> of the handicaps are present for the development of a superb agriculture.
> Virtually the sole exception to this is Binh Dinh Province and parts of
> neighboring Quang Ngai and Phu Yen Provinces. This area is one of the
> few in Vietnam with an endemic kind of grinding poverty of the sort
> found in South Asia. It is a poverty growing out of conditions largely
> beyond the individual: sandy soil, irregular and undependable rainfall,
> too many people and too little land.[17]

Like Appalachia in the United States, poverty, geographic isolation, and
internal compartmentalization bred a strong distrust of outsiders that made
the local inhabitants innately suspicious of the government in Saigon. These
factors also made Binh Dinh's residents particularly receptive to the Communists' redistributive program, which must have evoked primal memories
of the Tay Son rebellion's revolutionary social policies. According to Pike,
the confluence of these economic, cultural, and historical factors with the
large number of returning "regroupees" made Binh Dinh "the Communist
heartland" in South Vietnam. "Here the communist movement has its most
enduring history, its deepest roots, and—because they stem from blood kin-
ship—the strongest ties with the general population."[18]

The Second Indochinese War

In 1960 the Communist-dominated National Liberation Front (NLF) was formed as the political standard-bearer for the expanding insurgency. Better known to history as the Vietcong (VC), the NLF commenced guerrilla warfare with a selective terror campaign targeting government of Vietnam (GVN) officials. Throughout 1960 and 1961 the insurgency enjoyed considerable success as its popular support grew rapidly and fighting spread across South Vietnam. Binh Dinh was predictably one of the provinces where the insurgency was strongest, and by November 1961, the GVN had effectively lost control of its extensive highlands.[19]

The GVN position improved nationwide in 1962 and early 1963, thanks to substantial increases in US advisors, funding, and weaponry (particularly amphibious M-113 armored personnel carriers), as well as direct military intervention in the form of US Air Force pilots covertly flying combat missions in Operation Farm Gate and the overt presence of US Army helicopter units. It would take some time for the Vietcong to adapt to the unprecedented mobility the M-113s and helicopters granted to their foes. The GVN also benefited from the Strategic Hamlet program. Conceived and funded by Americans, this program sought to isolate the Vietcong from the people by concentrating the scattered rural population in fortified communities that were much easier to control. The program often antagonized villagers by forcing them to leave their ancestral homes and failing to provide adequate new ones, and it was implemented far too rapidly for most of the strategic hamlets to become viable. Yet in the short term, it did improve the GVN's position in the countryside. Even in Binh Dinh, where the insurgency was unusually strong, the 9th Division of the Army of the Republic of Vietnam (ARVN) enjoyed some success in restoring government authority in the rural areas.[20]

By early 1963, however, the Vietcong had begun to learn how to deal with the M-113s and helicopters, as demonstrated by the 7th ARVN Division's embarrassing defeat at the Battle of Ap Bac on 2 January. The military situation was overshadowed, however, by President Diem's mounting political difficulties. Starting in May 1963, the Catholic Diem found himself locked in an escalating confrontation with many prominent leaders of South Vietnam's Buddhist population, who accused him of various abuses of power and of displaying favoritism toward the Catholic minority. An effort to end the protests by raiding temples and arresting hundreds of Buddhist monks in August only made things worse and opened a breach between Diem and ARVN commanders, as each blamed the other for the ill-advised raids. Diem was overthrown and killed in November 1963 by a military junta acting in

General Westmoreland Addresses the Troops. *Source:* George L. MacGarrigle, *Combat Operations: Taking the Offensive, October 1966 to October 1977 (The United States Army in Vietnam Series)* (Washington, DC: US Army Center of Military History, 1998), CMH Pub 94-1, 4. [Reprinted by permission of the US Army Center of Military History]

collusion with the Kennedy administration, which had come to believe that the crisis could not be resolved unless Diem stepped down.

Contrary to expectations, the situation only got worse after Diem's assassination, as top ARVN commanders plotted and intrigued to seize and hold the reins of power. Political chaos reigned as coup followed coup in rapid succession, creating a bewildering series of weak, unpopular governments that proved incapable of restoring order. Meanwhile, the Communists ran amok in the countryside, wrecking the strategic hamlets and undoing all the hard-won gains of 1962 and 1963. The situation was particularly dire in Binh Dinh, where, by the fall of 1964, every hamlet had been infiltrated by the Vietcong.[21] At the urging of General William C. Westmoreland, head of US Military Assistance Command–Vietnam (MACV), the ARVN regiments in the province were dispersed so their battalions could help restore GVN control in the countryside. This proved to be their undoing, since the redeployment coincided with the enemy's shift from guerrilla warfare to large-scale operations featuring the 2nd VC Regiment.[22] In December 1964 the Communists launched their first-ever regimental attack in II Corps, wiping out at least 300 GVN Territorial Forces (militia) troops in Binh Dinh's An Lao Valley. An ARVN counterattack retook the lost positions, but enemy pressure was so intense that the valley had to be abandoned—the first area in II Corps to be permanently evacuated (though the Vinh Thanh and Van Canh Valleys in southern Binh Dinh would soon be given up as well).[23]

The Tet Offensive of 1965

Everyone has heard of the 1968 Tet Offensive, in which the Communists failed to win the war at a stroke but managed to start the United States down the road to withdrawal from Vietnam. It is not widely known, however, that a Tet offensive launched three years earlier was also intended to end the war quickly but instead drew the United States much deeper into the conflict. At the start of 1965, the Communists hoped to win a decisive victory in II Corps by using NLF regular troops and the newly infiltrated 325th Division of the North Vietnamese Army (NVA) to cut South Vietnam in two by overrunning Kontum and Pleiku Provinces in the Central Highlands and Binh Dinh along the coast.[24] This would have isolated all of I Corps and probably led to its collapse in short order. And if I Corps had fallen, the damage to GVN morale likely would have proved fatal to the regime. It was precisely this sequence of events that would cause South Vietnam's final collapse a decade later.

After using the Tet holiday truce to move their troops into position, the Communists began the offensive on the night of 6–7 February with simultaneous blows in Pleiku and Binh Dinh. The assault on Pleiku included an attack on Camp Holloway, situated at the city's airfield, where the US Army's 52nd Combat Aviation Battalion was based. Vietcong troops penetrated the perimeter, killed 8 Americans and wounded 108 more, and destroyed ten US aircraft and damaged another fifteen. President Lyndon Johnson was incensed and ordered retaliatory air strikes against North Vietnam, code-named Operation Flaming Dart.[25] In Binh Dinh the 40th ARVN Regiment's widely dispersed battalions were caught flat-footed, and two of them were virtually destroyed within a matter of days. In just the first twenty-four hours, the Communists killed or captured 332 GVN troops in the province and seized 27 crew-served and 275 individual weapons.[26] The official history of the People's Army of Vietnam records: "The 2nd and 10th Regiments ambushed enemy forces at Nhong Pass–Duong Lieu [near the future site of Landing Zone Uplift] in Binh Dinh province, inflicting losses that rendered two battalions and one troop of armored personnel carriers combat ineffective."[27] On 10 February the offensive expanded to Qui Nhon, where guerrillas who had infiltrated the city attacked from within while several VC companies tried to reinforce them by crossing the bay in fishing boats.[28] Although American helicopter gunships smashed the waterborne attack, the infiltrators detonated a massive bomb in the Viet Cuong Hotel, which was being used as bachelor enlisted men's quarters for the US Army's 140th Transportation Detachment. The building collapsed, killing twenty-three Americans and seriously injuring another twenty-two.[29] President Johnson responded with Operation Flaming Dart II, which again sent US aircraft to hit targets in North Vietnam. At the beginning of March it blended seamlessly into Operation Rolling Thunder, a sustained strategic bombing campaign that would continue for another three years.[30] The attacks in Pleiku and Qui Nhon resulted in a dramatic escalation of the war that soon led to the introduction of US ground troops. On 8 March the 3rd Battalion, 9th Marines, would land to secure the air base at Da Nang, and other American units would soon be sent ashore to guard other air bases.

In its first two weeks, the 1965 Tet Offensive conquered much of Kontum and Pleiku and the entire northern half of Binh Dinh, except for isolated ARVN garrisons that held out in the towns of Bong Son and Phu My and were kept tenuously supplied by air. Almost the entire length of Highway 1 from Qui Nhon north to Quang Ngai Province was under enemy control, and on 20 February the enemy also cut Highway 19 near Mang Yang Pass west of An Khe—the same ill-omened spot where the French troops of Mobile Group 100 had met their doom eleven years before.[31] According to General Theodore Mataxis, the senior US advisor in II Corps, ARVN commanders saw so many parallels with 1954 that they began to panic, and

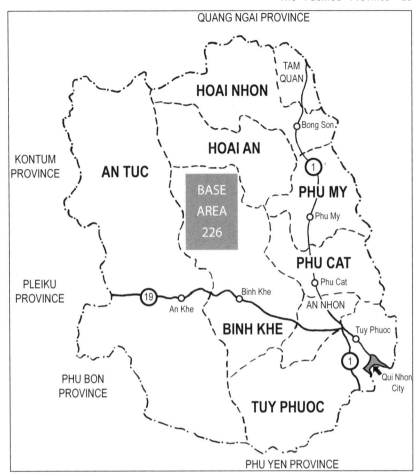

Binh Dinh Province (1969). *Source:* CORDS, Fact Book: Binh Dinh, February 1972, Province Reports II CTZ - Binh Dinh/Kontum Box, Southeast Asia Branch, US Army Center of Military History, Fort McNair, Washington, DC, 1.

"many officers were making arrangements to flee in fishing boats to the Philippine Islands."[32] The South Vietnamese Joint General Staff reported, "The people have lost confidence in the local authorities. The morale of cadre and soldiers is badly depressed. Presently the local authorities only control one fifth of the territory and population in this Sector."[33]

There was good reason to be alarmed, since GVN forces in the Central Highlands could not survive for long if Highway 19 remained closed—and if Pleiku and Kontum fell, what remained of Binh Dinh would soon be lost as

F-100 Fighter-Bombers at Phu Cat Airbase. *Source:* "Untitled [Photograph],"
Virtual Vietnam Archive - Item VA065599, accessed December 17, 2015, http://
www.virtualarchive.vietnam.ttu.edu/starweb/virtual/vva/servlet.starweb
[Reprinted by permission of the Vietnam Center and Archive, Texas Tech
University, Lubbock, TX]

well. When ARVN counterattacks failed to reopen the road, more than 200
montagnard Civilian Irregular Defense Group (CIDG) troops were besieged
in a forward operating base just east of Mang Yang Pass. In this moment of
crisis, President Johnson took the unprecedented step of allowing US Air
Force planes to fly close support missions for ARVN troops. On 24 February
the encircled unit was safely evacuated by US Army helicopters while American B-57 bombers, F-100 fighter-bombers, and helicopter gunships kept the
surrounding area under constant bombardment. Coordinating so many different types of aircraft with different speeds and flight characteristics was
a daunting task that could not have been accomplished without the aid of
American advisors on the ground.[34]

General Westmoreland rushed in US Special Forces detachments from
Okinawa to help reorganize Binh Dinh's shattered Territorial Forces, and
American aircraft flew two elite airborne battalions from the ARVN's general reserve into An Khe. Backed by constant US air support, the airborne
task force pushed westward up Highway 19, reopening the road and maul-

ing a VC battalion in the process. In mid-March the 22nd ARVN Division launched a counterattack northward along Highway 1 that relieved the sieges of Phu My and Bong Son. On 10 April two ARVN Marine battalions from the general reserve were airlifted into the area just below the border with Quang Ngai and began pushing south, while the 22nd ARVN Division drove north from Bong Son. Despite having to repel a counterattack by the 2nd VC Regiment, they succeeded in reopening the full length of Highway 1 by the end of the month.[35]

General Mataxis believed the Tet Offensive of 1965 was far more dangerous than that of 1968; there were only 20,000 US troops in South Vietnam at the time, whereas three years later, there would be 500,000. The 1965 offensive came within an ace of succeeding, and Mataxis was impressed by "how close we came to losing the entire II Corps area."[36] It could not have been defeated without US Air Force combat aircraft and air transports, US Army transport and gunship helicopters, and American military advisors at every level of the South Vietnamese chain of command (including US Army "Green Beret" Special Forces detachments that organized and led the CIDG units). The dramatic escalation of direct US involvement in the war was decisive because it put an end to the mounting panic within the ARVN's ranks. According to Mataxis:

> Initially defeated and driven back by the VC offensive . . . the morale of the ARVN troops sank to a critically low point by mid-February 1965. At this time U.S. air strikes on North Vietnam and the release of [U.S.] jet aircraft to support local engagements . . . gave a shot in the arm to the morale of the South Vietnamese armed forces. President Johnson's dispatch of U.S. Marines to Danang was viewed as the final evidence of our firm determination to stand with the South Vietnamese government.[37]

Yet the Communists had not abandoned their goal of cutting South Vietnam in half. They launched another offensive in II Corps during the summer of 1965, when the persistent rains of the wet monsoon season greatly restricted air operations in the Central Highlands. According to General Mataxis, their attacks were highly successful and "in the highlands cut off every district town from every province town and every province town from each other. We ran into a big problem here running out of food in the isolated towns."[38] Only the arrival of masses of US ground combat troops made it possible to weather the crisis.

Sherman's March

The first American combat unit to arrive in Binh Dinh was the 3rd Battalion, 7th Marines, which landed at Qui Nhon on 30 June 1965.[39] It was the vanguard of what would swiftly become a truly massive US military presence that drastically altered the character of the entire war. Unfortunately, the "Americanization" of the conflict further undermined ARVN performance. General Westmoreland convinced the South Vietnamese Joint General Staff to accept a division of labor in the allied war effort wherein US forces would be employed in mobile offensive operations and most ARVN units would be committed to "area security" (i.e., static defensive) missions in support of pacification. Since the Americans seemed determined to win the war on their own and had, for the moment, eliminated any possibility of a Communist victory, many ARVN units essentially opted out of the war. This reality was obscured by the huge number of carefully choreographed "search and avoid" operations they routinely conducted. One ARVN division notoriously suffered more casualties from traffic accidents than in combat.[40]

The first American combat division sent to Vietnam was the 1st Cavalry Division (Airmobile), a unit designed to exploit the revolutionary new capabilities offered by helicopters. It was the newest division in the US Army, having first taken shape in February 1964 as the 11th Air Assault Division (Test), which was tasked with testing the radically new concept of airmobility and developing an appropriate doctrine. In May 1965 the 1st Cavalry Division was formally constituted, with an official table of organization and equipment that included more than 400 helicopters. Despite the fact that both the division itself and the doctrine it was to employ had barely taken shape, it was hastily dispatched to Binh Dinh for the express purpose of preventing "a military split of South Vietnam by an NVA/VC thrust across the critical east-west Highway 19 from Pleiku to Qui Nhon."[41] Yet even as it began to arrive in the province during August, the enemy countered by forming the 3rd NVA "Yellow Star" Division in Binh Dinh and southern Quang Ngai Province. It comprised the 2nd, 12th, and 22nd VC Regiments, although the latter two were in fact NVA regiments that had been sent south.[42] Indeed, the 12th Regiment was merely the renamed 18th Regiment of the 325th NVA Division, and allied intelligence generally used its original designation. For the sake of clarity, this book refers to them as the 2nd VC and 18th and 22nd NVA Regiments.

The 1st Cavalry Division's principal base, Camp Radcliff, was established at An Khe, a town in western Binh Dinh that was close enough to Qui Nhon (thirty-five miles away) to be resupplied overland along Highway 19, but also far enough west to allow the division's helicopters to range deep into the Central Highlands. The entire division was present and ready for operations by the end of September. Its first major campaign of the Vietnam War took place in Pleiku Province, where the 33rd and 320th NVA Regiments had attacked the Special Forces camp at Plei Me. Intervention by the 1st Cavalry Division led to a series of engagements that culminated in the bloody Battle of the Ia Drang Valley, which ended in a hard-won victory when the battered NVA regiments sought refuge across the border in Cambodia.[43]

In January 1966 the 1st Cavalry Division returned to Binh Dinh and began a prolonged effort to clear the Vietcong and NVA from the province, which General Westmoreland had ranked second in importance only to Saigon.[44] The first operation, code-named Masher, sent the 3rd Brigade searching for a suspected NVA regimental training and logistical center southeast of Bong Son. The operation's name was apropos, because the 1st Cavalry proceeded to pummel the area with huge doses of firepower as it tried to destroy elements of the 3rd NVA Division that had been contacted by its heliborne infantry units. Ironically, the operation was redesignated White Wing in February because President Johnson complained that the original name did not reflect the operation's "pacification emphasis."[45] It progressed through four more phases, each of which expanded the offensive into a new region. By the time the operation came to a close in early March, the entire northern half of the province had been raked over.[46]

> In its combat after-action report, submitted on 28 April, the division reported 1,342 [enemy] killed. Tremendous amounts of firepower were utilized—over 132,000 rounds of artillery alone. Thus, the Army spent, on average, 1,000 rounds of artillery to kill 1 VC, in addition to the fire support received from helicopters and tactical air units. While a satisfactory body count was achieved, the impact on the "other" war [i.e., pacification] was far from beneficial. The lavish use of firepower by the Army contributed toward increasing the refugee population in the town of Bong Son from 7,806 to 27,652. In Hoai An District the total rose from 7,514 to 17,622. . . . These hardships imposed on the population of Binh Dinh might have been accepted more easily had Operation MASHER been the prelude to the introduction of a comprehensive pacification program. It was not. The division quickly moved on to other operations, having improved pacification not a whit while alienating thousands of homeless victims.[47]

The 1st Cavalry Division employed the same tactics in Operations Jim Bowie, Davy Crockett, and Crazy Horse, which lasted into June, inflicted substantial civilian casualties and property damage, and created thousands of new refugees. This "collateral damage" might have been acceptable if these operations had actually succeeded in clearing the province of enemy regular troops, but such was not the case. Instead, units of the Yellow Star Division proved to be extremely difficult to locate and almost impossible to pin down, even when they seemed to be completely surrounded. Since they enjoyed the support of most of the civilian population, the Communists always had superior intelligence and could generally choose whether to accept or refuse battle. The same areas therefore had to be "cleared" again and again, and were progressively devastated in the process.[48] It is difficult to get an accurate view of these operations from the enemy's perspective because Communist accounts are highly propagandistic, mixing stories of exemplary heroism on the part of People's Army soldiers with exaggerated claims about allied personnel and material losses. Setbacks are rarely admitted, and VC and NVA casualties are never enumerated.[49] The 3rd NVA Division's official history, for example, has this to say about the outcome of Operation Masher–White Wing: "The Yellow Star Division and the military and people of Binh Dinh Province removed from combat one third of the American airmobile division's troops and nearly three fourths of its helicopters. Never before had an American division suffered such heavy losses and suffered such a reduction of its fighting power as this pampered child of the Pentagon suffered during its very first round of fighting."[50]

After Operation Crazy Horse concluded, there was a two-month hiatus in Binh Dinh while the 1st Cavalry shifted its attention to Phu Yen Province and then revisited its old haunts in the Ia Drang Valley. It returned to Binh Dinh in September and would remain there for the next seventeen months. On 13 September it launched Operation Thayer in dramatic fashion:

> 120 Hueys and Chinooks lifted five battalions of Col. Archie K. Hyle's 1st Brigade and Col. Marvin J. Berenzweig's 2nd Brigade into a circular configuration on the ridges around the Crow's Foot [i.e., the Kim Son Valley]. The 18th NVA Regiment quickly split up, sidestepped the advance, and slipped away. For the next two weeks the brigades made only scant contact as troop-laden helicopters leap-frogged battalions in airmobile pursuit of the fleeing enemy columns. Several food and clothing caches, a major hospital, and even a grenade and mine factory were uncovered, but the only significant personnel claim was one [NLF] song-and-dance troop specializing in musical propaganda, captured while traveling between villages.[51]

Thayer was followed by Operations Irving and Thayer II, but the name changes did not signify any alteration in objectives, tactics, or area of operations. As before, the goal was to "find, fix and finish" Communist regular

Operation Pershing. *Source:* George L. MacGarrigle, *Combat Operations: Taking the Offensive, October 1966 to October 1977 (The United States Army in Vietnam Series)* (Washington, DC: US Army Center of Military History, 1998), CMH Pub 94-1, 185. [Reprinted by permission of the US Army Center of Military History]

units. Periodically there were bouts of intense combat in which the enemy suffered severely at the hands of American firepower, but the dominant pattern was one of endless groping after a skillful and elusive enemy. As 1966 drew to a close, the 1st Cavalry was conducting exactly the same kinds of operations in precisely the same places as it had been at the beginning of the year. Since no real progress had been made in pacification, it is hard to see how these operations could have yielded any real strategic benefit. Perhaps the most significant consequence of the division's activities in Binh Dinh during 1966 was the 129,000 refugees crowded around Qui Nhon and the district capitals at year's end.[52]

In February 1967 the 1st Cavalry began Operation Pershing, which encompassed all its clearing efforts in Binh Dinh until they ended in January 1968. It involved not only the division's 1st and 2nd Brigades but also the 3rd Brigade of the US 25th Infantry Division.[53] Operation Pershing was distinguished from earlier clearing operations by its emphasis on eliminating the "Vietcong Infrastructure" (VCI). This entity comprised noncombat personnel responsible for convincing villagers to support the NLF through propaganda and intimidation and for organizing them to support the armed struggle by spying on allied troops, "contributing" food and other supplies, digging fortifications, carrying supplies, manufacturing and emplacing booby traps, and joining the guerrillas. The 1st Cavalry tried to weed out the VCI by cordoning and searching hamlets in concert with South Vietnamese National Police Field Force (NPFF) units.[54] Over 900 cordon-and-search operations would be conducted by the end of January 1968 (with some hamlets being searched twenty or thirty times), and 1,700 suspects arrested.[55] Yet, although 1,300 of the detainees were initially classified as VCI members, all but 200 of them were released. American observers concluded that corrupt and fainthearted GVN officials were responsible for this suspiciously high release rate:

> According to a report on the handling of VCI prisoners, "the suspects who were released apparently were members of an organization with the means to effect reprisals or to buy the release of captured members of sufficient importance." The problem lay not in the false arrest of innocent civilians as VCI—although that undoubtedly occurred—but rather in that it was more important to the district chief that he play it safe and at the same time make some money.[56]

Despite the effort devoted to eliminating the VCI, the 1st Cavalry could not ignore enemy regular units in Binh Dinh. It continued to hunt them throughout Operation Pershing, which witnessed some of the hardest fought battles of the division's service in Vietnam. As in 1966, heliborne sweeps and encirclements sought to bring enemy regulars to battle and destroy them with overwhelming firepower. In the process, more loss of life and property damage was inflicted on the civilian population, "generating" thousands of new refugees. The division also forcibly evacuated the entire population of 93,000 from the Kim Son, Suoi Ca, and An Lao Valleys; leveled the hamlets; and defoliated the entire region with toxic Agent Orange.[57]

Despite the lack of subtlety in the 1st Cavalry's operations, their sheer magnitude slowly eroded the enemy's military strength and chipped away at his grip on the rural population. After all, in early 1967, nine US, nine Republic of Korea (ROK), and eight ARVN infantry battalions were operating continuously in Binh Dinh. If South Vietnamese Territorial Forces are factored into the equation, the ratio of allied soldiers to civilians in Binh Dinh stood at one to seven.[58] By the end of March, the bulk of the severely battered Yellow Star Division had retreated north into Quang Ngai Province. In December 1966 the division's commander, Colonel Le Truc, had warned his subordinates that heavy casualties and assaults on rear bases were causing a worrying rise in the number of "shirkers" and deserters. "Discipline had to be restored immediately, even if it became necessary to 'purge the ranks of undesirables.'"[59] Meanwhile, the portion of the population controlled or strongly influenced by the Vietcong, which had been nearly 90 percent in late 1965, declined to just over a third. Conversely, the population controlled by the government increased from less than 10 percent to over 30 percent.[60] Yet the failure to cement these gains, and the continuing presence of enemy regular units in the province, meant that a huge US military presence had to be maintained.

However, in the second half of 1967, battles raging elsewhere began to draw units of the 1st Cavalry Division out of Binh Dinh. On 1 October the 3rd Brigade began redeploying to Quang Ngai Province in I Corps so that US Marine Corps units could displace northward to confront NVA troops infiltrating across the Demilitarized Zone. Then, during November, the 1st Brigade headed west into the Central Highlands to join in the bloody Battle of Dak To. The last combat elements of the division would leave Binh Dinh for good in February 1968.

Full Circle

The 1st Cavalry's last major battle in Binh Dinh began on 6 December 1967, when the 1st Battalion, 9th Cavalry, encountered elements of the 22nd NVA Regiment in a heavily fortified seacoast village northeast of Bong Son. A bloody battle ensued that drew in the 1st Battalion, 8th Cavalry (Airmobile Infantry), and elements the 40th ARVN Regiment. In the late afternoon of 7 December, the Americans finally broke into the enemy's defenses with the aid of flamethrowing armored personnel carriers of the 1st Battalion, 50th Infantry (Mechanized), but the NVA escaped during the night. The 1st Battalion, 12th Cavalry, was hastily airlifted back from Dak To to help pursue the retreating enemy, and over the next eleven days, a series of costly engagements was fought across the northern Bong Son plains. Although some 600 NVA troops were reportedly killed, versus American losses of 58 killed and 250 wounded, there was nothing conclusive about the so-called Battle of Tam Quan. The enemy had once again been found, fixed, and subjected to the full weight of allied firepower, but the Americans suffered heavy casualties, and the NVA made its escape even though the 1st Cavalry had more than twenty-four hours to seal off the battlefield.

The division therefore ended its sojourn in Binh Dinh fighting in the very same places, using virtually the same tactics, against the same enemy units, and with the same equivocal results, as in Operation Masher almost two years before. The 1st Cavalry had come full circle by stubbornly clinging to a faulty operational methodology long after it had proved strategically profitless. Its commanders simply ignored the unpleasant facts that Binh Dinh was not being pacified and that enemy regular units in the province were not being destroyed. Instead, they continued to apply "more of the same" in the vain hope that they would eventually find the enemy's breaking point. Thus, one of the best units in the US Army spent almost two years in a futile effort to break the insurgency using traditional, firepower-intensive American war-fighting methods. When it left the scene, the Communists' domination in Binh Dinh was almost as complete as it had been before the first American troops arrived, for even as the 1st Cavalry was leaving the province, the Communists were bringing in an additional regiment of NVA regulars and going over to the offensive. In the last two months of the year, they erased most of the gains the allies had made since 1965.[61]

The ARVN troops in Binh Dinh had also come full circle, exhibiting all the deficiencies they had manifested two years before. If anything, their combat effectiveness had actually declined, as the Americans took over the bulk of the fighting while they sat out the war in static security missions.[62] In January 1968 Lieutenant Colonel William A. Donald (USMC) had an opportunity to view the results firsthand when he spent a week with the 41st ARVN Regiment in Phu My district. According to Donald, the regimental commander, Lieutenant Colonel Bui Trach Dzan, was "an astute, politically motivated commander who displays an impressive grasp of VC/NVA tactics and the military significance of terrain. He is also a supreme practitioner of caution."[63] Dzan's character was reflected in the behavior of his subordinates, who generally conducted their own operations in an extremely cautious fashion for fear of suffering casualties—always a sensitive matter in the highly politicized ARVN.

Although the regiment's primary mission was to support pacification, Donald noted that only one of its four battalions was actually doing so. An entire battalion was kept in reserve at the 41st Regiment's headquarters at Landing Zone (LZ) Crystal at all times—a needless waste of manpower, considering that the enemy had only a limited ability to mass forces in Phu My. But units throughout the regiment tended to overprotect their command posts. Indeed, their own safety seemed to be the primary concern for most of the 41st's senior officers, whom Donald characterized as a circle of favorites chosen for their political connections and "armed with an uncanny air of mediocrity" in the field of combat leadership. The regimental and battalion commanders rarely visited their troops in the field to ensure that they were carrying out their assigned tasks satisfactorily, and at night, when the mission of providing security was most important, there was no system to ensure that the regiment's many ambush patrols were staying awake (or, indeed, that any ambushes were actually being conducted). Ineffective leadership and supervision caused the regiment's troops to grow lax, and their operations were characterized by a decided lack of aggressiveness. In the autumn of 1967 the 1st Battalion failed to produce a single contact with the enemy during an entire month of mobile night patrolling. As a result, the US district senior advisor in Phu My observed, "There is damn near 80% freedom of movement for the VC at night."

The only bright spot in the 41st Regiment was its 4th Battalion, which offers an object lesson in how much of a difference good leadership can make. Its regrettably unidentified commander regularly checked the alert status of his nightly ambush patrols, often visiting them in person (something unheard of elsewhere in the regiment), and he even arranged to have Popular Forces (PF) units stage enemy activity to gauge how well, and how quickly, the ambushing units responded. Another technique he used for the same purpose was to bracket his ambushes with half a dozen unscheduled and unannounced mortar rounds. Although these practices were highly irregular, they apparently had the desired effect of improving the battalion's performance. Another unusual characteristic of this battalion commander was his concerted effort to ensure that his men did not antagonize the local population by indulging in acts of thievery and disrespect, which were endemic in many ARVN units. Donald reported:

> [The battalion commander] . . . held his company commanders strictly accountable for any disciplinary breaches of his regulations for soldierly conduct in the hamlets. He whipped and jailed troops for even minor transgressions, such as theft of coconuts and garden plants. He personally recompensed civilians for material damages inflicted by one of his soldiers, then punished the man and docked his next pay remittance. He used informants to report not only VC activity, but the misdeeds of his own troops. The closest thing to a "major incident" during the battalion's seven-month stay in the pacification AO [area of operations] was theft of a chicken.

The Tet Offensive of 1968

The 1st Cavalry Division's sympathetic biographer, Shelby Stanton, tried to put a good face on its performance in Binh Dinh, writing, "perhaps the most telling evidence supporting the 1st Cavalry Division's claim to victory was one inescapable military reality. During the major NVA/VC Tet-68 offensive . . . the former communist stronghold of Binh Dinh Province was one of the least-affected regions in Vietnam."[64] This claim is difficult to accept. When interviewed by this author, General Lu Mong Lan (ARVN II Corps commander) and General John W. Barnes (his US deputy senior advisor at the time) both insisted that Binh Dinh was the hardest-hit province in all of II Corps during Tet.[65] And this was true despite a series of miscues that hamstrung the offensive from the outset. On the night of 29 January, Nguyen Khuong, head of Binh Dinh's NLF Party Executive Committee and secretary of Qui Nhon's Party Executive Committee, was captured. Since he was overall commander for the attack on the city, it was impossible to coordinate the actions of units that had infiltrated into Qui Nhon with those that were supposed to support them from the outside. There was, moreover, confusion about which night the offensive was supposed to begin. The 2nd VC Regiment was ready to attack Phu My's district headquarters at midnight on 29 January when it received urgent orders to postpone the assault by twenty-four hours. Having detected the NVA presence, the 41st ARVN Regiment rushed in reinforcements that forced the attack to be canceled altogether.[66]

Ironically, the Tet Offensive in I and II Corps still jumped off a day earlier than in the southern half of the country, where it did not start until 31 January. In Binh Dinh, the D-10 Sapper Company and E-2B Battalion infiltrated into Qui Nhon and seized the radio station, railroad yard, Vietnamese Information Service building, and ARVN Military Security Service headquarters; they also tried, unsuccessfully, to kidnap the province chief and the provincial police chief. When these assaults failed to spark the expected popular uprising, the Vietcong units were cut off and subjected to counterattacks delivered by two CIDG companies, three ROK companies, and the 1st Battalion, 41st ARVN Regiment. By 4 February, the decimated enemy units had been ejected from Qui Nhon, leaving 225 bodies behind; however, the city was severely damaged in the process.[67]

The Tet Offensive had been planned in accordance with *Tổng Công Kích–Tổng Khởi Nghĩa*—the "general offensive–general uprising" strategy the Communist leadership had adopted in 1967. They hoped that surprise attacks on South Vietnam's cities and provincial and district capitals would spark popular uprisings, toppling the GVN at a blow and leaving the Americans no option but rapid withdrawal.[68] When no urban uprisings occurred, the attackers were left in a hopeless position, fighting on unfamiliar ground where the allies could apply the full weight of their superior firepower. Most of the attacks were repulsed within a few days, although sporadic fighting continued around Saigon until early March. Just one city was captured outright—Hue, the old imperial capital—but it was retaken after a month of bitter street fighting. Thus, although the cities suffered considerable destruction and loss of civilian life, the Tet Offensive was a military disaster for the

Communists, since more than half their assault force was killed or captured. Yet, it proved the falsity of President Lyndon Johnson's 1967 "Progress Offensive," which had wrongly claimed that enemy strength and aggressiveness were irrevocably in decline.[69] The Tet Offensive thus played a decisive role in turning the US public against the war and convincing Johnson to start looking for a way out of it.

It has often been claimed that the Vietcong insurgency was effectively destroyed by the Tet Offensive. In his memoirs, Lieutenant General Philip W. Davidson, who served as MACV's chief of staff for intelligence from 1967 to 1969, wrote: "The Viet Cong guerrillas and the VC political infrastructure, the insurgency operators, were virtually destroyed in the Tet Offensive."[70] Lieutenant General Frederick C. Weyand, MACV's last commander in 1972–1973, claimed the Vietcong were deliberately ordered to their destruction by the North Vietnamese, who wanted to eliminate them as postwar political rivals:

> Applying the test of *cui bono* (for whose benefit) it can be seen that the real losers of Tet-68 were the South Vietnamese Communists (the Vietcong or PRG) who surfaced, led the attacks, and were destroyed in the process. . . . Just as the Russians eliminated their Polish competitors [with] the Warsaw Rising, the North Vietnamese eliminated their Southern competitors with Tet-68. They thereby insured that the eventual outcome of the war would be a South Vietnam dominated and controlled, not by *South* Vietnamese Communists, but by the *North* Vietnamese.[71]

Although these claims have been echoed by other authors, they are patently absurd. First of all, the Tet Offensive focused on South Vietnam's urban centers, where the Vietcong were at their weakest and both VCI and guerrillas were relatively few. The insurgency's main strength lay in rural areas, where the VCI and guerrillas could not have been destroyed because the Tet battles occurred elsewhere. Second, if the guerrillas and VCI had, in fact, been eliminated, the allies would have won the war in short order. Despite the growing volume of supplies shipped down the Ho Chi Minh Trail or by sea through the Cambodian port of Sihanoukville, Communist regular military units operating in South Vietnam remained highly dependent on food collected by the VCI and transported by civilian porters. This was particularly true of those operating in provinces such as Binh Dinh, which were remote from sanctuaries in Laos and Cambodia. The guerrillas and VCI also supported regular military operations in other crucial ways, such as by providing intelligence and local guides, guarding infiltration routes, rallying civilian porters to carry weapons and ammunition, and constructing fortified and booby-trapped base areas for the regulars to shelter in.[72]

Since the Communist leadership was fully aware of this interdependence, claims that they deliberately sacrificed the Vietcong are just as preposterous as allegations that President Franklin Roosevelt provoked a war with Japan in December 1941 by deliberately letting the Japanese sink the fleet at Pearl Harbor (which he would need to fight any such war). This conspiracy theory also overlooks the fact that NVA units were heavily involved in the Tet Offensive and concurrent operations—such as the prolonged and costly siege of Khe Sanh—and took heavy casualties as a result. Most notably, eleven NVA battalions suffered severely in the siege of Hue. Finally, the notion that the Vietcong were destroyed during the Tet Offensive ignores the fact that they were able to launch two additional offensives within the next six months. First came the so-called Mini–Tet Offensive of May 1968, when enemy troops penetrated into Saigon, touching off a week of fighting in the capital before they were ejected, and several more weeks of heavy combat in the surrounding provinces as the allies tried to intercept the retreating foe. Elsewhere, enemy forces were generally less successful in penetrating the cities, and some attacks were completely preempted by allied military operations. Another round of city attacks began in mid-August and continued sporadically until the end of the month. Each was less intense and prolonged than its predecessor, and costly, large-scale ground assaults increasingly gave way to attacks-by-fire in which mortars and artillery rockets were used to hit cities and allied military bases from a safe distance. Even so, the fact that the Vietcong were still capable of conducting nationwide offensives proved the insurgency was far from finished.[73]

Revisionist historian Lewis Sorley believes the Vietcong insurgency was eventually defeated, but not until several years later, and certainly not because the VCI suffered a "mass extinction event" at Tet. He wrote, "It is often said that during the 1968 Tet Offensive the enemy's underground elements surfaced and were cut down, effectively eliminating the infrastructure, but that claim does not stand up under analysis. Large numbers of the enemy's forces were indeed exposed and killed during the fighting at Tet, but they were not the infrastructure, certainly not the bulk of it."[74]

Sorley's conclusions are validated by reports of the Combined Intelligence Center–Vietnam (CICV), a combined US–South Vietnamese intelligence organization whose American personnel were under the command of General Davidson. In October 1968 CICV estimated overall VCI strength at 81,700, which was just 3,000 lower than it had been on the eve of the Tet Offensive.[75] Nowhere does Davidson explain how he came to equate a 4 percent decline in manpower with the VCI being "virtually destroyed." CICV data also reveal that most of the Tet Offensive's casualties were suffered by Vietcong regular military units (Regional Forces and Main Forces), rather than guerrillas and VCI. Excluding the 2nd VC Main Force Regiment, which served as an integral part of the 3rd NVA Yellow Star Division, Binh Dinh contained 2,175 Vietcong regulars in December 1967. By the following September, Vietcong regular strength in the province was down to only 1,265—a drop of over 40 percent. But this decline hardly meant that the insurgency had been defeated—much less "destroyed"—in Binh Dinh. After all, the allies had not considered the Vietcong defeated in May 1967, when their regular military strength in the province had stood at just 1,450. It had been built up considerably in preparation for the Tet Offensive by establishing two new regular battalions—the 36th Sapper Battalion in October 1967 and the XC-11 Infantry Battalion in January 1968.[76]

Although the Tet Offensive accomplished little in the cities, it dealt a heavy blow to the GVN's position in the countryside. By March, thirty-six of the fifty-one ARVN regular battalions supporting pacification had been withdrawn and rushed to the defense of the embattled cities.[77] In their absence, the Territorial Forces succumbed to panic and abandoned entire districts. Moreover, while NLF efforts to spark popular uprisings in the cities failed, they *did* occur in many of the evacuated rural areas as villagers rushed to join the now unopposed and seemingly triumphant Communists. In Vinh Long Province, the influx of new recruits made it possible for the Vietcong to establish two new regular battalions *after* the Tet Offensive and to form a second Local Force company in two districts.[78] A captured VCI described how popular uprisings occurred in Dinh Tuong Province as well:

> Generally speaking, the atmosphere in every village was one of strong uprising, even in those villages near the [GVN-controlled] market villages and the district town, where new recruits and new guerrillas were also inducted. Before Tet there were villages without a single guerrilla, but when Tet came you could say that even the weakest villages were able to recruit ten guerrillas and send up ten new recruits [to NLF regular units]—that was in the villages that had been the very weakest all along. The liberated villages mobilized platoons of village guerrillas and sent nearly all the remaining youth off as new recruits. Apart from new recruits they were also able to mobilize civilian laborers—about thirty per village.[79]

Rural uprisings also took place in Binh Dinh, where the VCI rallied masses of civilians armed with clubs and knives, and banging on drums and tin pots, to surround GVN outposts and call on their defenders to surrender:

In cooperation with the armed forces, the provincial political forces . . . rose up and put pressure on the enemy in nearly every city and district headquarters. Nearly thirty thousand comrades in Hoai Nhon District were brought out to surround Tam Quan City, Bong Son City, and Hill 10 [the future site of LZ English?]. Thousands of mothers and sisters bearing bamboo sticks, knives and sickles chased the Popular and Regional Forces soldiers out of many posts and "strategic hamlets" in My Duc and My Loi villages, Phu My District.[80]

GVN forces abandoned large parts of the province. Twenty-two Rural Development (RD) Cadre Teams (see chapter 3) fled their assigned hamlets, and just twelve of the twenty-two Regional Forces (RF) companies that had been directly supporting pacification before Tet remained in place at the end of February. Many of the latter had been redeployed to defend the district seats, but others retreated without orders.[81] And although the enemy had already erased most of Binh Dinh's 1967 pacification gains, the Tet Offensive devastated the one area where lasting progress had been made—the four districts (Binh Khe, An Nhon, Tuy Phuoc, and Phu Cat) of the National Priority Pacification Area. This "model pacification area" had been laid waste by enemy attacks and allied counterattacks.[82] More than a thousand homes had been destroyed and hundreds more damaged, creating 15,000 new refugees who severely taxed the GVN's already overstretched relief services.[83] In late March American advisors in Binh Dinh glumly predicted: "It will probably take six months to drive the NVA from the coastal areas and return security to the RD districts so that RD groups and other GVN personnel can work undisturbed. It will take one additional year to regain political control in the countryside and return to the position achieved in September 1967."[84]

The Sky Soldiers

The desperate situation in Binh Dinh prompted General Westmoreland to order the 173rd Airborne Brigade into the province in March 1968. Like the 1st Cavalry Division, it was a relatively new formation, but its paratroop battalions all belonged to the 503rd Infantry Regiment (Airborne), the first airborne unit of that size ever formed by the US Army. The 503rd had served in the Pacific theater during World War II and made three combat jumps, including a daring daylight assault onto Corregidor—a rugged, cliff-girt island fortress guarding the entrance to Manila Bay.[85] It was deactivated in December 1945 as part of the postwar demobilization but mustered back into service during the Korean War. Since the regimental echelon of command was eliminated in the US Army during the 1950s, the 503rd was broken up, and individual battalions were sent to serve in the 25th Infantry and the 11th and 82nd Airborne Divisions. In June 1963, however, the 1st and 2nd Battalions, 503rd Infantry (Airborne), were assigned to the newly established 173rd Airborne Brigade.[86]

Upon its activation, the 173rd became a theater reserve unit for US Pacific Command and demonstrated the United States' commitment to its allies in the region by conducting combined training exercises in Korea, Thailand, and Taiwan (the Republic of China). It was during one sojourn on Taiwan that the brigade's troops received the nickname "Sky Soldiers" (or *Tien Bing*), because of their numerous parachute jumps. By 1965, the 173rd had won a deserved reputation as an elite formation and was probably as well prepared for service in Vietnam as any unit in the US Army. It would be the only American parachute unit sent there that remained fully jump-qualified throughout the war.[87]

In May 1965 the 173rd Airborne also had the distinction of being the first US Army ground combat formation to be deployed in Vietnam. It was initially assigned the mission of defending the critical air base at Bien Hoa, just north of Saigon, but within a matter of weeks, it was launching offensive operations into the surrounding countryside. The 1st Battalion, Royal Australian Regiment—Australia's contribution to the Southeast Asia Treaty Organization (SEATO) alliance's war effort in Vietnam—was attached to the brigade as its third maneuver battalion. It would be replaced in June 1966 by the newly formed 4th Battalion, 503rd Infantry; a fourth parachute battalion, the 3rd of the 503rd, would join the brigade in September 1967.[88]

Throughout 1965, 1966, and 1967, the 173rd Airborne Brigade played a leading role in nearly all the major offensives launched by General Westmoreland. These included Operation Attleboro, which targeted War Zone C in Tay Ninh Province, and Operation Cedar Falls, which sought to eliminate an infamous enemy stronghold in the "Iron Triangle" just twenty miles northwest of Saigon. The brigade's most famous exploit during this period came in February 1967 when it spearheaded Operation Junction City—another offensive against War Zone C—and made the US Army's only large-scale parachute assault of the entire Vietnam War. A total of 780 men, six 105mm howitzers, and fifteen vehicles were dropped over the village of Katum near the Cambodian border. However, all these "search and destroy" operations failed to achieve their objectives. The Communist bases in War Zone C and the Iron Triangle were only temporarily disrupted, not destroyed, and the enemy forces in them avoided contact and consequently suffered only moderate casualties.[89]

In November 1967 the 173rd Airborne Brigade fought its bloodiest battle at Dak To, in the Central Highlands of western II Corps. On 19 November the 2nd Battalion, 503rd Infantry (2/503rd), located elements of the 174th NVA Regiment atop Hill 875 and immediately moved to attack. While the battalion was attacking up the hill's northwest slope, it was suddenly struck in the rear by strong NVA forces, touching off a desperate battle for survival as the surrounded paratroops fought to avoid being overrun. The 2/503rd held out through twenty-four hours of bitter, close-quarters fighting until the 4/503rd broke through the encirclement. It would take three more days of intense combat before the last heavily fortified NVA positions on the summit of Hill 875 were captured on Thanksgiving Day. The 173rd Airborne's losses in the Battle of Hill 875 were severe, and those in the 2/503rd especially so. Particularly galling were the forty-two men killed and forty-five wounded when an errant bomb dropped by a US aircraft landed right on top of the command post and first-aid station of Company C, 2/503rd.[90]

The bulk of the 173rd Airborne Brigade moved into Binh Dinh in March 1968. The 4/503rd had already been detached to replace 1st Cavalry units conducting Operation Bolling in Phu Yen Province. The 1/503rd was assigned to Operation Walker in Binh Khe and An Tuc districts, where it was tasked with conducting search-and-destroy operations in the vicinity of Camp Radcliffe and securing Highway 19. The rest of the brigade, which then included the 1/14th Infantry, 1/50th Infantry (Mechanized), and two companies of the 1/69th Armor (all detached from the US 4th Infantry Division), launched Operation Cochise in Hoai Nhon, Hoai An, and Phu My districts. Although the new operation was intended to help breathe new life into Binh Dinh's badly disrupted 1968 pacification campaign, it would do so chiefly by seeking out and destroying Communist regular military units.[91]

The 173rd Airborne's new commander, Brigadier General Richard J. Allen, embraced this mission enthusiastically. A few weeks after assuming command in early April 1968, he launched Operation Velvet Hammer, whose modest objectives were "to capture the 3rd NVA Division Commander and eliminate the 3rd NVA Division as a threat."[92] Three US parachute battalions, elements of the 1/69th Armor, the 1st Battalion of the 41st ARVN Regiment, and CIDG troops encircled the mountains east of the Vinh Thanh Valley and closed in from all sides to fix and destroy the 2nd VC and 22nd NVA Regiments, which were known to be operating in the area.[93] Yet, as any veteran of the 1st Cavalry could have predicted, Velvet Hammer proved to be a failure:

The operation was about 10 to 12 days of very little contact, primarily because the enemy in this area don't want to fight and avoided any contact, especially with U.S. Forces; they have done so successfully since the Brigade has been in the area. Anytime the Brigade has a contact, it's of short duration. The Brigade has not even run into many mortars where there should be a lot of mortaring. In any case which should have caches, there are no caches, and where the enemy should have the capability to dig in and fight but they won't do this. The Brigade just searched out the Vinh Thanh Mountains and did a good job. However, the enemy may still be there because it would take three times as many troops as the Brigade has to really search the area out. . . . The Brigade is operating with a great deal of frustration in that everybody wants to fix and destroy Charlie, but Charlie remains elusive and it's bad for the morale of the troops and the officers.[94]

More frustrating yet was the fact that the enemy was able to strike heavy blows at times and places of his own choosing. During the Mini–Tet Offensive, Company A of the 1/50th was attacked by two battalions of the 2nd VC Regiment while it was halted for lunch on 5 May. Five out of nine M-113 armored personnel carriers were knocked out in the opening volley of B-40 rockets and 57mm recoilless rifle shells, and the stunned survivors, who formed a hasty defensive perimeter around the burning vehicles, were pinned down by heavy automatic weapons fire. Only the swift arrival of Company C, 1/50th, and the M-48 main battle tanks of Company B, 1/69th Armor, saved them from being overrun. The NVA was present in strength and fought with great stubbornness, not breaking off the battle until nearly eight hours later. American casualties were twenty-two killed and ninety-three wounded. This was the first in a series of fierce engagements that stretched over the next week as the 173rd Airborne pursued the enemy into the Crescent Mountains, suffering considerable casualties while inflicting heavier losses on the NVA.[95]

Tactical Adaptation

The 173rd Airborne's inability to engage the enemy on its own terms was emblematic of what was happening throughout South Vietnam as Communist regular units were increasingly breaking down into small groups that avoided contact with allied troops. This shift in tactics triggered a corresponding tactical adaptation on the part of American units, which gradually moved away from maneuvering in company- and battalion-size units and toward the use of small-unit patrols and ambushes to engage the increasingly elusive foe.[96] In the case of the 173rd Airborne, this tactical evolution led to the development of "Bushmaster" operations, which established small day and night ambushes along the trails used by enemy troops to access the populated lowlands. In May the 173rd reported: "The Brigade is breaking down into platoon size elements since if Charlie is going to move in small groups, the Brigade will put out small size ambushes to stop him from moving his rice or whatever he wants to do."[97] Bushmaster operations focused on finding and destroying elements of the Yellow Star Division, which was identified as "the Brigade's primary enemy." In June 1968, however, most of that division withdrew across the I Corps–II Corps boundary into Quang Ngai Province. Only the 18th NVA Regiment remained in Binh Dinh to interdict Highway 19 and maintain a threat against the pacification effort.

The Yellow Star Division's withdrawal prompted the 173rd Airborne to place greater emphasis on attacking the guerrillas and VCI. In late August it launched Operation Dan Sinh, a long-term clear-and-secure operation that was undertaken in conjunction with the 40th ARVN Regiment and was strikingly similar to the 1st Cavalry Division's Operation Pershing. The operation was conducted in three phases. Phase I consisted of a sweep through Binh Dinh's three northern districts between 22 August and 6 September. In phase II the brigade undertook "a detailed interrogation and reclassification of all civilians living in the Bong Son Plains area." Cordon-and-search operations in cooperation with NPFF personnel were the rule of the day, as American troops once again attempted to weed the Vietcong out of the villages. Considering the random methods employed, it is hardly surprising that of the 12,815 individuals singled out for detailed interrogation, a mere 122 were detained as confirmed Vietcong, and 115 as suspected Vietcong.[98] Dan Sinh's third phase, which began in late October, had the objective of preserving and expanding on the gains made in the preceding two phases. "Phase III was designed to saturate the Bong Son Plains area with allied military forces in order to prevent the return of VC/NVA forces, to develop the confidence of the civilian populace in the allied forces, and to protect the civilian populace from exploitation by VC/NVA forces so that the Rural Pacification Program, especially the continued upgrading of hamlet and village RF/PF units, might continue."[99]

The goal of saturating the province with a swarm of small patrols and ambushes accelerated the development of new small-unit tactics. Building on the Bushmaster technique, the 173rd Airborne developed the Hawk (Hunter-Killer) Team, a roving patrol ranging in size from a platoon to a fire team and operating independently for up to four days at a time. Because they were small and highly mobile, Hawk Teams could avoid detection under circumstances in which a larger unit would certainly be spotted, while also permitting a larger area to be patrolled by fewer men. However, Hawk Teams also had an offensive role. They were intended to engage any small enemy elements they might encounter, preferably from ambush, and to direct air strikes and/or artillery fire against enemy groups too large to be taken on in a firefight. If a Hawk Team was attacked or threatened with discovery by a superior enemy force, its small size and excellent mobility gave it a good chance of slipping away. Good leadership was crucial, since Hawk operations required a level of competence that could be supplied only by skilled, combat-experienced junior officers and noncommissioned officers (NCOs).[100]

Although supporting pacification was Operation Dan Sinh's top priority, the 173rd Airborne continued to launch offensive forays against enemy regular troop concentrations in the mountains. The ever-elusive 18th NVA Regiment was the favorite target of these operations, and their objectives were essentially identical to those of the 1st Cavalry Division's earlier search-and-destroy operations. The only real difference lay in the realm of tactics, since the 173rd Airborne was breaking its searching elements down into a multitude of roving Hawk Teams, as opposed to the cumbersome company-sized formations that had been standard practice in the past. The new tactics sometimes bore fruit, such as when the 1/503rd and the 41st ARVN Regiment contacted the 18th NVA Regiment's 9th Battalion in the Suoi Ca Valley on 22 September. Over the next two weeks, the American and South Vietnamese troops engaged the NVA in a series of confused engagements that killed more than 200 of the enemy.[101]

The brigade's offensive forays into the mountains continued through the end of the year and beyond. At a MACV Commanders' Conference in January 1969, the 173rd Airborne presented three offensive plans for consideration—Operations Skycourage, Skyhawk, and Skyhammer II. All three would form large-scale encirclements involving both disposable battalions of the 173rd Airborne (the 1/503rd and 2/503rd) and four battalions of the 22nd ARVN Division. Operations Skycourage and Skyhawk targeted the coastal Nui Mieu and Cay Giep mountain ranges, respectively, while Skyhammer II was to be directed against the Suoi Ca Valley.[102] Evidently, the lesson that these massive "hammer and anvil" operations invariably failed to trap the enemy had yet to be learned.

Pair Off

Another noteworthy feature of these proposed operations was that all of them were conceived as joint undertakings to be mounted in combination with ARVN units. The 1969 Combined Campaign Plan ordered that ARVN regulars be withdrawn from the area security role to which most of them had been relegated years before and used instead in mobile offensive operations against enemy regular units. However, curing ARVN units of the bad habits they had acquired in three years of virtual inactivity would be a difficult task. It was not merely a question of restoring their mobility; their inflexible logistical and fire support systems also had to be restructured, and the

lethargy of headquarters staffs that had become accustomed to the unde-
manding requirements of static defensive missions had to be overcome. One
possible means of speeding up the process was to provide on-the-job training
by conducting combined US-ARVN operations. Thus, the 1969 Combined
Campaign Plan instructed: "Combined/coordinated operations will be conducted as practicable. Plans for all major offensive operations by a FW [Free
World] force will include one or more RVNAF [Republic of Vietnam Armed
Forces] battalions when feasible. . . . When practicable, RVNAF and FW-
MAF [Free World Military Assistance Forces] commanders will collocate
command posts to facilitate coordination, cooperation, mutual assistance and
combined decision making."[103]

The 173rd Airborne Brigade was well "ahead of the curve" in this regard, since it had been mounting combined operations with the 22nd ARVN
Division almost from the day it arrived in Binh Dinh. Under the brigade's
"Pair Off" program, a battalion of the 173rd was matched up with each of the
22nd ARVN Division's infantry regiments and ordered to conduct combined
operations on a permanent basis. To facilitate smooth operational planning
and execution, the participating American and South Vietnamese units were
assigned areas of operation with identical boundaries, and their headquarters were colocated to provide on-the-job training to the ARVN regimental
staffs.[104]

The Pair Off program presaged the kind of combined US-ARVN operations that would become increasingly common in subsequent years. In the
spring of 1968, however, the idea was novel and innovative. At that time, most
American commanders were still reluctant to engage in combined operations
due to concerns about compromising operational security and their generally
low opinion of ARVN fighting quality. In the absence of specific orders to
do so, most American units preferred to avoid what was seen as an onerous
and unrewarding duty. Furthermore, even when combined operations later
became the rule of the day, few would be as large, or as prolonged, as the Pair
Off program, which ultimately involved all the American forces in II Corps
and in some cases lasted for a full year.

The driving forces behind the Pair Off program were Major General
Lu Mong Lan, ARVN II Corps commander, and his American counterpart, Lieutenant General William R. Peers, who assumed command of I
Field Force Vietnam (the headquarters for all US forces in II Corps) during
March 1968. It was also enthusiastically supported by General Cao Van Vien,
chairman of the South Vietnamese Joint General Staff. Peers considered the
"pairing" of the 173rd Airborne with the 22nd Division such a success that
he ordered the 4th Infantry Division and Task Force South (a provisional US
brigade that operated in II Corps' four southernmost provinces) to initiate

Pair Off operations of their own.[105] It proved difficult, however, to replicate the enthusiasm that existed at the highest echelons further down the chain of command. The Hawk tactics the 173rd Airborne was teaching to its paired ARVN units required that junior officers be given a great deal of latitude, as they would be operating on their own for days at a time. This was anathema to commanders in the politicized ARVN, who feared that their careers would suffer if the delegation of authority led to higher casualties. Americans were thus disappointed by "the stubborn reluctance of many Vietnamese officers to relinquish any authority to their subordinates, especially the lowly company commanders and the platoon leaders."[106] Progress was also slowed by incompetent officers, who were very difficult to replace. General Peers observed: "The assignment of officers down to the battalion level is centralized in JGS [Joint General Staff], and the Corps Commander cannot remove such commanders without their approval. It required in excess of six months on the part of General Lu Lan and myself, working through our individual channels, to replace incompetent commanders."[107]

CHAPTER TWO

Fast and Thin

The difficulty the 173rd Airborne encountered in bringing enemy forces to battle in Binh Dinh was mirrored throughout South Vietnam, since the Communists were now consciously avoiding combat in order to hold down their casualties. VC and NVA regular units were breaking down into small, highly elusive groups that reassembled only for short periods to launch an attack, then dispersed immediately afterward. Moreover, in the latter half of 1968, allied intelligence detected a major withdrawal of enemy Main Force units into cross-border sanctuaries in Laos, Cambodia, and North Vietnam. Between July and December 1968, thirty-two NVA combat and combat support battalions exited South Vietnam. Twenty-one battalion equivalents of NVA and Main Force VC left II Corps, although roughly half of them (including the bulk of the 3rd NVA Yellow Star Division) merely shifted northward across the boundary into I Corps. Another sign of enemy quiescence was that many of the regular units that remained in South Vietnam took refuge in well-fortified base areas situated in remote and inaccessible parts of the country.[1]

These developments drastically reduced the tempo of the Vietnam War and seemed to indicate a major shift in enemy strategy. In reality, the Communist leadership was reluctant to make any fundamental changes because it feared demoralizing its troops in the near term, by renouncing the goal of decisive victory, or in the long term, by creating unrealistic expectations that victory would soon be achieved.[2] In October 1968 the Central Office for South Vietnam (COSVN) of the Lao Dong (Workers) Party (North Vietnamese Communist Party) issued its Eighth Resolution, which reaffirmed the general offensive–general uprising strategy and set extremely ambitious objectives for the near future: "Annihilate and disintegrate the Puppet Army" and "Destroy the main elements of the US forces."[3] But it also emphasized the importance of protracted warfare, tempering the theme of decisive victory by explaining that this would be achieved gradually through a two–phase process wherein intensified military and political activity in the first phase set the stage for final success in the second.[4]

This effort to straddle the fence caused confusion even within COSVN's own ranks. At a COSVN cadres' conference, a senior Lao Dong official tried to finesse the contradictions in the Eighth Resolution by arguing: "There is no contradiction between the concept of a protracted struggle and that of gaining a decisive victory in the immediate future, because in both cases there always is a requirement for a quick development of the South Vietnam Revolutionary Forces in every aspect." And later: "In the First Phase [of the general offensive], many comrades had not yet learned or had not mastered the basic principles of this new phase; they thought General Offensive and General Uprising meant a 'one blow' affair."[5] Despite this equivocation, COSVN had retreated from the goal of achieving decisive victory in the near term, although it could not drop it entirely, for reasons of morale. Formally, that decision would not be made until midway through 1969. But in reality, there had already been a de facto shift in strategy simply because the inactivity and/or absence of so many regular military units meant that the Communists had no choice but to revert to lower-intensity guerrilla warfare operations.

The "One War" Strategy

US strategy was also evolving during this period under the direction of General Creighton W. Abrams, who had replaced General Westmoreland as MACV commander in July 1968. The need for a new strategy had been obvious since March 1968, when President Lyndon Johnson announced his intention to seek a negotiated end to the conflict. Yet in the nine months he remained in the White House, Johnson never gave MACV guidance as to what its new mission was, now that the strategy of attrition was dead.[6] When Abrams assumed command, he fell back on his own resources and created a Long-Range Planning Task Group to thoroughly reassess the situation and offer recommendations for a new military strategy.[7] The Task Group would not report back for several months, and in the interim, events did not stand still. In the fall, allied intelligence discovered that the Communists were creating "popularly elected" People's Liberation Committees nationwide. Abrams was concerned that these would allow the NLF to claim that it was the undisputed sovereign authority in much of South Vietnam if the Paris peace talks produced a standstill cease-fire. This was a very real danger, since large swaths of the countryside abandoned during the Tet Offensive had not yet been recovered. "Furthermore, although the so-called 'pacification assets' (i.e., RD cadres, RF/PF, and ARVN pacification battalions) were gradually moving back into the rural areas, there was a tendency on their part to assume a completely defensive attitude."[8]

Given these circumstances, General Abrams concluded that US military operations would have to contribute to pacification far more substantially than they had in the past. His operational guidance for the fourth quarter of 1968 instructed his chief subordinates that it was no longer sufficient for them to attrit Communist regular units; they would have to bring pressure to bear on the guerrillas and VCI as well.[9] What he had in mind was that US forces would conduct operations against the full spectrum of enemy forces simultaneously. There was no ban on large-scale search-and-destroy operations, and Abrams did not order his subordinates to concentrate on pacification support operations. Indeed, he specifically enjoined them not to tie their units down in such missions:

> Tactical units are to assist [pacification] primarily by a continuation of tactical operations, providing area security in the process. Tactical units may be used as necessary to seal off areas for search, but not held on static missions. Existing assets may be redeployed as necessary in order to maximize the offensive role. The actual screening of the population is to be done by those who will be living among them, i.e., the RF/PF, police forces, and any other appropriate RVN agencies.[10]

Abrams's commitment to accelerating the pace of pacification was nonetheless very real, and it was reinforced when the Long-Range Planning Task Group submitted its report on 20 November 1968. It offered a fundamental indictment of past American military strategy in Vietnam:

> All of our US combat accomplishments have made no significant, positive difference to the rural Vietnamese—for there is still no real security in the countryside. Our large-scale operations have attempted to enable the development of a protective shield by driving the NVA and the Viet Cong main force units out of South Vietnam—or at least into the remote mountain and jungle areas where they would not pose a threat to the population. In pressing this objective, however, we have tended to lose sight of *why* we were driving the enemy back and destroying his combat capability. Destruction of NVA and VC units . . . has become an end in itself—an end that at times has become self-defeating. To accomplish the most difficult task of the war—*and, really the functional reason for the US to be here*—that of providing security to the Vietnamese people—we have relied on the numerous, but only marginally effective, ill-equipped and indifferently-led Vietnamese paramilitary and police units.[11]

The Task Group advised that the creation of a secure environment was essential for the success of pacification and thus for achieving the overall US objective, which it defined as creating "a free, independent and viable nation which is not hostile to the United States, functioning in a secure environ-ment both internally and regionally."[12] However, achieving that goal could take two decades, while the state of public opinion back home was such that a policy of disengagement would continue no matter which party's candidate won the 1968 presidential race. The way out of this dilemma, the Task Group advised, was to ignore pacification per se in the near term and focus instead on the more practical goal of securing the population. It also advised that the division between the "Big War" fought mostly by Americans and the "Other War" waged by the South Vietnamese should be abolished and replaced by a fully integrated "One War" strategy in which population security replaced attrition as the objective of all allied military operations. The Task Group also hoped that designating practical, near-term objectives would enable MACV to demonstrate real progress toward victory to the American people and thereby prevent the GVN from being suddenly abandoned.

Abrams embraced these recommendations and officially launched the one-war strategy in his Strategic Objectives Plan of March 1969. It stated: "The key thrust is to provide meaningful, continuing security for the Viet-namese people in expanding areas of increasingly effective civil authority."[13] This had several important implications for the conduct of future allied mil-itary operations in Vietnam. First of all, to end the bifurcation of the allied war effort, ARVN units had to be pried out of their area security mission. The 1969 Combined Campaign Plan had already ordered that "ARVN divi-sional units will direct their primary efforts to the destruction of VC/NVA Main Force units. In order to provide maximum ARVN strength for the accomplishment of the primary mission, a gradual phase down of ARVN battalions in support of pacification will occur."[14] The missions of American regular units would also change; they would have to stop hunting the enemy in South Vietnam's remote jungles and mountains and focus their operations on the fringes of the country's populated regions. US commanders would have to end their fixation on the "body count" and instead measure the effec-tiveness of their operations by the extent and quality of the security provided to the population. Finally, since indiscriminately applied firepower could be an even greater menace to the population than enemy activity, use of artillery and tactical air support within inhabited regions would have to be strictly limited. Despite Abrams's enthusiasm for the one-war strategy, many top US commanders in Vietnam were strongly opposed to it.[15]

The Accelerated Pacification Campaign

The possibility that the United States would pull its troops out of South Vietnam prematurely had been a concern for General Abrams ever since he took command of MACV, but in the last quarter of 1968 it was heightened by fears that the enemy hoped to win a political victory by securing a cease-fire immediately after President Nixon's inauguration in January 1969:

> In September, Ambassador [Ellsworth] Bunker reported to the Secretary of State that [South Vietnamese] President [Nguyen Van] Thieu believed the enemy's strategy to be occupation of more territory, particularly rural areas. Thieu believed that Hanoi hoped to maintain a certain military pressure during the next four months, until the inauguration of President Nixon, while extending control over the countryside. This would put the enemy in a position to propose a cease-fire and then to ask for elections.[16]

Thieu argued that the proper response was to consolidate GVN control in relatively secure areas, which he claimed encompassed 80 percent of the population. MACV did not agree, since its figures showed that less than two-thirds were living in relatively secure areas, and it recommended that the allies launch a "quick fix" pacification campaign to raise that figure as rapidly as possible. MACV's own official history described it as "a campaign to plant the GVN flag" in enemy-controlled areas. Furthermore, "part of the MACV position arose from the need to counter the anti-war mood in the US. A successful, vigorous campaign could prove that the war was not endless and that the balance had swung to the GVN/US side."[17] General Abrams finally convinced President Thieu to order a special ninety-day Accelerated Pacification Campaign (APC) that would begin on 1 November 1968.

Nearly all earlier allied pacification campaigns had employed the "spreading oil spot" technique, which concentrated on communities directly adjacent to existing secure areas. These communities were supposed to be thoroughly pacified by "winning the hearts and minds" of the inhabitants so they would no longer allow the guerrillas and VCI to operate in their hamlets—and would inform on those who tried to. The chief advantage of this technique was that it obeyed the principle of economy of force: once an area was fully pacified, resources were freed for use in the next area of expansion. However, in keeping with MACV's "quick fix" concept, the APC abandoned the goal of "winning hearts and minds" and focused on securing military control of enemy-dominated communities remote from the main centers of GVN strength.[18] Specifically, it aimed to upgrade 1,000 hamlets that were rated D, E, or V under the Hamlet Evaluation System (HES) to a C rating. The HES was an automated pacification tracking system managed by the US Civil Operations and Revolutionary Development Support (CORDS) organization. CORDS had been created in May 1967 to bring the many disparate—and of-

Table 2.1 HES Rating Definitions

Rating	Definition
A	Friendly local security and law enforcement forces conduct adequate security operations in the hamlet both day and night. Armed enemy military forces are very unlikely to have entered the hamlet during the month. At most, sporadic, covert VCI activity. The enemy does not collect taxes. Many hamlet households have members participating in GVN-sponsored self-development projects. GVN hamlet chief is elected and present night and day.
B	Friendly local security and law enforcement forces conduct adequate security operations in the hamlet by day and marginal by night. Sporadic covert VCI activity; no overt activity. Enemy collects taxes sporadically. Some hamlet households have members participating in enemy activities. Largest enemy guerrilla unit regularly present in or near the village is a squad; largest main force is a platoon. GVN hamlet chief is elected and present day and night.
C	Friendly local security and law enforcement forces conduct marginal security operations. Regular covert VCI activity; sporadic overt activity. Enemy collects taxes. Up to half of hamlet households have members participating in enemy activities. Largest enemy guerrilla unit regularly present in or near the village is a squad to a platoon; largest main force is a platoon or larger. Enemy base areas are often located in or near the village. GVN hamlet chief is appointed and in the hamlet only during the day.
D	Friendly local security and law enforcement forces conduct only marginal activities. Regular covert VCI activity and overt activity day and night. Regular enemy tax collection. Many hamlet households have members taking part in enemy activities. Largest enemy guerrilla unit is a platoon; largest main force is a company. Large enemy base area is often located in or near the village.
E	When friendly security forces are present, they do not conduct security operations. Armed enemy military forces are regularly present. VCI is the primary authority in the hamlet. Regular enemy tax collection. All or nearly all hamlet households have members participating in enemy activities. Enemy guerrilla units are a platoon or larger. Major enemy base areas are often located in or near the village.
V	The enemy is in physical control of the hamlet.
N	Not evaluated.
X	Abandoned.

Source: Richard H. Schultz Jr., "The Vietnamization-Pacification Strategy of 1969–1972: A Quantitative and Qualitative Reassessment," in *Lessons from an Unconventional War: Reassessing U.S. Strategies for Future Conflicts*, ed. Richard A. Hunt Jr. (New York: Pergamon Press, 1982), 60–66.

ten divisive—American agencies supporting pacification (e.g., CIA, Agency for International Development, US Information Service) together under one roof. And to bridge the gap that had long sundered the military and civilian aspects of US strategy in Vietnam, CORDS had been grafted onto MACV as a seventh staff section coequal with the Personnel, Intelligence, Operations, Logistics, Plans, and Communications staffs (J-1 through J-6).[19]

One of the routine duties assigned to CORDS district senior advisors was to complete a monthly HES report on each hamlet in their bailiwicks, a process that required them to assign scores to eighteen separate indicators tracking friendly and enemy military activity, economic and social development, and governmental effectiveness. In Saigon, these scores were fed into a computer that generated a lettered rating for each hamlet.[20] HES ratings were grouped into categories: secure (A, B), relatively secure (C), contested (D, E), and enemy-controlled (V). Thus, by upgrading hamlets to a C rating, the APC would, in theory, shift contested and enemy-controlled hamlets into the relatively secure (and, implicitly, GVN-controlled) category.

The APC would have been impossible if Communist regular forces had remained as numerous and aggressive as they had been in years past. According to David Elliott, who spent six years in South Vietnam as a US Army advisor and civilian analyst for the Rand Corporation, Vietcong regular units' primary function was *not* to fight major battles (which they did infrequently). Instead, they were intended, first and foremost, to maintain an "umbrella of security" for the VCI and thus preserve and help expand NLF control over "liberated zones" in the countryside. Large-scale allied military operations in the liberated zones were of little concern because there could be only a few taking place in relatively small areas at any given moment, and these operations were so ponderous that the VCI had little difficulty evading them. What the Vietcong feared were allied small-unit operations that were stealthy enough to catch the VCI unawares, along with the creation of a network of allied outposts that would fragment the liberated zones. Vietcong regular units passively countered these threats by raising the "threshold of entry" into liberated zones to the point where only large allied military units dared go into them.

> What was it that raised the threshold of entry by Saigon forces into these areas? Primarily it was the threat of encountering a large (battalion or even company size) concentrated main force revolutionary unit. It was, therefore, the *possibility* of the presence of revolutionary forces, rather than the *certainty* of their presence, that was the key factor in this deterrence strategy. . . . Since it was the *threat* of an encounter with a large revolutionary unit in a given area rather than its actual presence which was the basic

deterrent to GVN operations, the effectiveness of the relatively few main force units in the province was multiplied by the number of places where they might possibly be stationed.[21]

Thus, the mere presence of a Communist regular military unit somewhere within a given region forced the allies either to refrain from dispersing their forces anywhere in it or to commit large numbers of their own regular troops to the mission of hunting that Communist unit full time. The 1968 general offensive's most important consequence was therefore the progressive decimation of enemy regular military units and their subsequent retreat into cross-border sanctuaries and remote base areas. With so many of them absent or inactive, the allies could now safely disperse their forces with little risk. Only this made it possible for the APC to scatter GVN forces in a thousand tiny new outposts that would be indefensible against large-scale attack.

The APC also benefited from a vast expansion of the Territorial Forces that had begun when President Thieu signed a general mobilization statute into law on 19 June 1968. Until that point, the Territorial Forces had generally been slighted when it came to manpower, funding, and advisory efforts. Now this policy of neglect had been reversed, and CORDS vastly enlarged programs designed to improve their training and firepower. During 1968 it started replacing the Territorial Forces' World War II–vintage M-1 rifles and Thompson submachine guns with M-16 assault rifles, which put them on an equal footing with enemy Local Force units armed with AK-47s and other modern light infantry weapons. Year-old plans to extend the CORDS pacification advisory system below the district headquarters level also came to fruition in 1968. "Most of the additional advisory spaces were used to create a total of 353 Mobile Advisory Teams (MATs), whose mission was to train RF and PF units. Each MAT was authorized 2 officers, 3 NCOs and 1 interpreter, and was tasked with training from 3 to 6 RF companies and an additional number of PF platoons."[22]

Official statistics revealed the dramatic progress achieved during the APC. By the end of January, four-fifths of the APC target hamlets had achieved a rating of C or better. Overall, "the January 1969 HES report showed that 79.2 percent of the total population lived in relatively secure areas (A, B, and C), 9.4 percent lived in contested areas (D and E), and 11.4 percent were in areas under VC control. The comparable percentages from October 1968 were 69.8, 14.9, and 15.3."[23] Furthermore, over a million People's Self-Defense Force (PSDF) militiamen had been recruited, and 7,000 VCI had been killed, captured, or induced to surrender. In many cases, the APC's quantitative objectives had not only been met but exceeded.[24]

The APC had taken the Communists by surprise because they expected the allies to continue employing the familiar "oil spot" technique and had positioned their forces to maintain an offensive threat against the cities, thus weakening their presence in the rural liberated zones. The PAVN's official history admits:

> When the United States and its puppets began to carry out their "clear and hold" strategy our battlefronts were too slow in shifting over to attacking the "pacification" program and we did not concentrate our political and military forces to deal with the enemy's new plots and schemes. Beginning in the latter half of 1968, our offensive posture began to weaken and our three types of armed forces suffered attrition. The political and military struggle in the rural areas declined and our liberated zones shrank. COSN and military region main force units were able to maintain only a portion of their forces in our scattered lowland base areas, and most of our main force troops were forced back to the border or to bases in the mountains.[25]

The APC broke up NLF liberated zones that in some cases had not been entered by GVN troops in nearly a decade, and it became far more difficult for the Communists to collect the food necessary to sustain their regular units in the populated areas. The 3rd NVA Division's official history describes the consequences in Military Region 5 (the old Vietminh *Liên-Khu* 5):

> After the devastating [allied population] relocation operations in Region 5, the mass movement forces [i.e., the Functional Liberation Associations] that controlled hamlets and villages were reduced from one and a half million to five hundred thousand persons. Because of the many difficulties they encountered, the military region's main force units had to decrease in size. . . . Beginning in late 1968 and early 1969, the revolution in the south in general, and in Region 5 in particular, had to cope with new trials. Not a few individuals and organizational elements lost their senses or suffered declines in their fighting spirit and eventually surrendered to the enemy. Many battlefields fell into conditions of protracted and serious shortages of food and ammunition.[26]

Yet, as impressive as the APC's achievements were, the battle for control of the hamlets was far from over. Historian Richard H. Schultz Jr. has persuasively challenged the logic of classifying C-rated hamlets as "secure," asking: "How can a hamlet that is experiencing regular enemy covert activity, has from a squad to a platoon-size enemy force present in the area, and also has a portion of the hamlet population taking part in enemy activities be considered secure?" He also expressed doubts about the "contested" category: "Given the description of the D-E ratings, was it appropriate to list these hamlets as contested? Weren't they really under varying degrees of VC control? . . . a more accurate classification would rank A-B hamlets as GVN secured, C hamlets as contested, and D-E-V as experiencing increasing degrees of VC control."[27] Applying this more realistic interpretation, one can see that the APC's gains generally represented the GVN contesting hamlets in which Vietcong dominance had previously been virtually unchallenged. This represented significant progress, but the hamlets were still far from being "pacified." The GVN had merely placed them under military occupation and taken the first steps toward installing an administrative presence as well. Given the degree of continuing enemy military activity indicated by the C rating, the quality of the security provided was not very great. In short, the APC's gains were paper thin and had little to do with real pacification.

There was also no doubt that many GVN officials had "massaged" APC data to prove that they were achieving their assigned goals—which was their standard operating procedure. Manipulation of data also occurred at the highest echelons in both the US and South Vietnamese governments. William E. Colby, a senior CIA official who succeeded Robert Komer as deputy for CORDS in November 1968, noted that midway through the APC, "President Thieu . . . directed that the A-B-C-D-E categories be carried as 'areas controlled by the government,' and V as 'not yet fully controlled by the government.' . . . Thieu believed he had to protect himself in the negotiations in Paris from any admission by his own Government that it conceded control of some of its communities to the enemy."[28]

Some of the APC's other accomplishments were also less impressive than they seemed at first glance. About 8,600 enemy personnel surrendered under the Chieu Hoi (open arms) amnesty program during the campaign's three-month run (see table 2.2 for Chieu Hoi numbers from 1965 to 1971).[29] This was considerably more than double the average of 3,500 enemy personnel who had turned themselves in during the first three quarters of 1968. The dramatic increase was attributable chiefly to a new feature added to the Chieu Hoi program just as the APC was beginning. This was the Third-Party Inducement program, which offered large cash awards to anyone who convinced an NVA soldier or Vietcong to surrender; the amount of the reward depended on the soldier's rank. Unfortunately, this program merely became another vehicle for official corruption:

It gradually became evident that many of the alleged ralliers were not VC at all and that the program had turned into a profitable source of monetary gain for government officials and officers who organized groups of

alleged ralliers in order to collect the inducement rewards. Far fewer ralliers now turned in weapons and most claimed to be induced by a third
party with whom they apparently split the reward. It was estimated in
early 1969 that in some areas as many as one-half of the ralliers brought
in through a third party were not true ralliers at all.[30]

It also seems that many—if not most—of the enemy personnel who surrendered during the APC were recent recruits who had joined during the rural
popular uprisings triggered by the Tet Offensive. Having opportunistically
"jumped on the bandwagon" when it seemed that the NLF was triumphant
and the end of the war imminent, many of these Johnny-come-latelies had
second thoughts once it became clear that final victory was *not* just around
the corner. Only a few hard-core Vietcong followed suit. In Vinh Long Province, just 8 of the 541 ralliers who surrendered during November and December 1968 had been in the NLF for more than a year.[31]

Senior allied commanders and policymakers were still sufficiently impressed by the APC's success that they made it the template for the 1969
pacification campaign. Indeed, from the enemy's perspective, the APC was
virtually indistinguishable from the 1969 campaign, and the Communists
used the term "accelerated pacification" to describe both. Guidelines were
issued in December 1968 that each of South Vietnam's forty-four provincial governments was instructed to follow in preparing its 1969 pacification
and development plan. The guidelines designated eight objectives for 1969
(see table 2.3) but stressed: "The overall objective of the 1969 program is to
bring security to 90 percent of the population."[32] The campaign's first phase
(1 February–30 June) would once again focus on upgrading security in D,
E, and V hamlets, while B and C hamlets would be left to languish. Only
in the second phase (1 July–31 December) would an effort be made to consolidate GVN control in relatively secure hamlets, and even then, it would
be a secondary objective. This sequencing can be likened to putting the cart
before the horse, since the rapid expansion projected for phase I was likely to
overextend the GVN, leaving insufficient resources available to achieve the
phase II objectives.

Table 2.2 Chieu Hoi Ralliers, 1965–1971

	1965	1966	1967	1968	1969	1970	1971
Quantity	11,124	20,242	27,178	18,171	47,023	32,661	20,357

Source: J. A. Koch, *The Chieu Hoi Program in South Vietnam, 1963–1971* (R-1172-ARPA)
(Santa Monica, CA: Rand Corporation, 1973), 111.

Table 2.3 Objectives of the 1969 Pacification Campaign

1.	Bring security to 90 percent of the country.
2.	Eliminate 3,000 VCI per month under the Phung Hoang campaign.
3.	Establish local government in all villages throughout the country; elect Village Administrative Committees at all secure hamlets and villages; organize a training program for village and hamlet officials.
4.	Increase the PSDF to 2 million members and arm 400,000 members.
5.	Rally 20,000 Hoi Chanhs [enemy defectors].
6.	Decrease the number of refugees to less than 1 million and resettle at least 300,000 persons.
7.	Increase the information and propaganda effort by training and making effective use of village information members and hamlet information deputies.
8.	Stimulate the rural economy by increasing the production of rice (from 5 million to 6 million tons) and other farm crops, securing farm-to-market roads, providing agricultural loans and equipment, and eliminating unnecessary restrictions placed on the movement of goods and produce.

Source: Chester L. Cooper, Judith Corson, et al., *The American Experience with Pacification in Vietnam*, 3 vols., Report R-185 (Arlington, VA: Institute for Defense Analysis, 1972), 3:287.

The APC had been highly ambitious, but the 1969 pacification campaign was absolutely reckless. In order to secure 90 percent of the population, GVN forces would have to be scattered across the full length and breadth of South Vietnam in thousands of new outposts. Just finding the funds and materiel to build them and the troops to defend them would tax GVN capabilities to the limit. It would then take years to fully pacify this multitude of newly occupied communities, and until then, the widely dispersed and largely immobile GVN forces would be extremely vulnerable. Therefore, the 1969 pacification campaign was founded on the unstated assumption that most of the enemy's regular military forces would remain absent or relatively inactive for years to come.

Even at the time, some observers worried that the 1969 pacification campaign was too ambitious. One of the doubters was John Paul Vann, a larger-than-life figure who had first come to Vietnam as a US Army advisor in 1962 and had won a well-deserved reputation as a "squeaky wheel" who was not afraid to question his superiors' decisions. Now serving as deputy for CORDS in IV Corps, he had serious doubts about the 1969 pacification plan. His main concern was that "we are involved in rapidly expanding GVN control using a 'fast and thin' technique as opposed to a 'slow and sure.'" Vann feared that in trying to expand its influence so rapidly, the GVN would overextend itself, wasting its forces in areas it could not possibly pacify anytime in the foreseeable future. He argued, "I believe we should re-examine the direction in which we are now moving for the express purpose of determining whether the GVN position in later years would not be stronger if it had firmer control over less population than the predictably modest to weak control it may have over 90% of the population if our 1969 program is successful."[33]

Operation Washington Green

In II Corps, General Lu Lan had neither emphasized the APC's importance nor held his subordinates accountable for supporting it, yet he tried to claim that all the target hamlets had been upgraded on schedule by the end of January.[34] In fact, only 257 of the 321 target hamlets in II Corps had achieved a C rating by the end of March—that is, two full months after the APC officially ended. Binh Dinh was largely to blame for this lackluster performance, since only two-thirds of its ninety target hamlets (nearly a third of II Corps' total) had been upgraded. Worse yet, the province's 1969 pacification campaign was also faltering. According to I Field Force's civilian deputy for CORDS, James Megellas: "District Advisors . . . report no significant progress on the upgrading of the 184 hamlets targeted for 1969; 114 of which are to be upgraded to a 'C' security status by 30 June 1969."[35] ARVN commanders were largely to blame, since they were unresponsive to district chiefs' requests for assistance and generally would not provide reaction forces when the Territorial Forces needed help. Yet Megellas noted that the American units in Binh Dinh had not contributed much to pacification either; their "actions (with some few exceptions) have been targeted in the mountains and base areas and have not directly contributed to the village security shield."[36]

The 1969 pacification campaign got off to a bad start because its launching coincided with the start of the enemy's nationwide Winter-Spring (or Z) Offensive, which began on 23 February and progressed through three separate high points before concluding in late April.[37] In Binh Dinh, the spring campaign's most dramatic attacks targeted the vast US logistical support infrastructure in Qui Nhon. On 23 February a mortar attack on an ordnance depot destroyed 4,411 tons of ammunition, causing critical shortages of 81mm mortar and 105mm howitzer shells throughout II Corps. The same depot was subjected to several sapper attacks in March during which tens of thousands of mines and artillery shells were destroyed, though thankfully, personnel losses were minor. On 20 March five huge tanks at a fuel storage facility were destroyed, along with over half a million gallons of gasoline and diesel and jet fuel. In the countryside, the NVA and Vietcong disrupted pacification with a mix of light ground probes, sapper assaults, and attacks-by-fire. They also used a tactic that had not been seen before: setting fire to entire communities in GVN-controlled areas. Almost 600 homes were burned in the last two weeks of March alone. Although the Communists suffered significant casualties, they succeeded in seriously harming Binh Dinh's 1969 pacification effort.[38]

Yet the Z Offensive could claim only some of the credit for stalling pacification. Megellas advised, "The primary reason for the lack of progress in Binh Dinh is the non-availability of an adequate number of territorial force units (RF/PF) to provide the village/hamlet security screen. . . . In most districts, the available RF/PF forces have been extended about as far as they can be without risking regression in relatively secure areas."[39] Meanwhile, fifteen RF companies and sixty PF platoons were tied down guarding bridges, road checkpoints, and various other installations throughout the province, instead of securing the population. The misuse of Territorial Forces in Binh Dinh even came to the attention of General Abrams when it was discovered that eight RF companies and eleven PF platoons were defending US and ARVN military bases—a role for which they were not authorized.[40] Still, even if all these units were released for duty in the target hamlets, Megellas calculated that *another* twenty-five RF companies and fifteen PF platoons would be needed to make the entire population relatively secure. Ten new RF companies would be raised in Binh Dinh during 1969, but at the end of March they

Table 2.4 HES Statistics for AO Lee, 27 March 1969

Category	Statistic	Hoai An	Hoan Nhon	Phu My	Tam Quan	Total
A+B+C	Hamlets	7	22	44	4	77
	Population	22,600	77,600	56,900	8,900	166,000
	Percentage of total population	67%	65%	59%	10%	49%
D+E	Hamlets	7	4	9	4	24
	Population	11,200	13,300	6,400	13,700	44,600
	Percentage of total population	33%	12%	7%	15%	13%
V	Hamlets	0	18	57	36	111
	Population	0	25,200	33,200	67,900	126,300
	Percentage of total population	0%	22%	34%	75%	38%

Source: APC Status Report, undated, inclosures 3–6, National Archives Records Group 472, MACV Advisory Team 42 General Records, box 12 JUSPAO Activities, 1970.

were still being recruited and trained; they would not be available in time to be of much assistance in achieving the phase I goals by 30 June. Thus, the flaws of "fast and thin" pacification were readily discernible in Binh Dinh. The 1969 pacification campaign had just begun, and the province's Territorial Forces were already badly overextended. Unless additional forces could be found, pacification would remain stuck in the doldrums.

The most pressing need was in the four northernmost districts: Hoai Nhon, Hoai An, Phu My, and Tam Quan (created in December 1968 from a portion of Hoai Nhon). They corresponded to the 173rd Airborne Brigade's Area of Operations (AO) Lee and collectively accounted for 133 of the 184 target hamlets. In three of these districts, much of the population continued to reside in V-rated hamlets that were entirely under enemy control (see table 2.4). The fourth, Hoai An, avoided this dubious distinction only because two-thirds of its hamlets were vacant, their inhabitants having fled from the fighting or been forcibly evacuated.

Megellas's solution to the Territorial Forces shortage was radical:

> Based on a rough analysis of the data . . . , it would appear that approximately 6 to 8 Free World military force battalions [including ARVN regulars] should be committed to the pacification role. The actual use of these battalions in this role (whether they are used to relieve RF/PF forces in static security, or be used in the role of an RF element) should be determined at local level. These forces must remain in the district for a considerable period of time.[41]

Despite the unprecedented nature of Megellas's proposal, it was approved almost immediately by Lieutenant General Charles A. Corcoran, who had assumed command of I Field Force in late March. It was also received enthusiastically by the 173rd Airborne's commander, Brigadier General John W. Barnes, who had served as II Corps' deputy senior advisor through most of 1968. Barnes recalled that the operation was also strongly endorsed by General Abrams himself, who saw it as a large-scale test of how well US regular troops could perform in the pacification support role: "And Abrams said, 'If this thing works we're going to do it throughout the Army.'"[42] Abrams must have had a change of heart about using American units on pacification duty, which he had expressly discouraged in his operational guidance for the fourth quarter of 1968. Still, it may be significant that no other US Army unit of equivalent size ever conducted a similar operation during Abrams's tenure, although it is not clear whether this was because he judged Washington Green a failure, had second thoughts about using American troops in that role, or found that other requirements made it impractical to commit more units in this way.

To find sufficient troops to occupy all the target hamlets, half of Binh Dinh's seventy RF companies and ten companies of ARVN regulars would have to be employed in the PF static, hamlet-security role.[43] The RF mission of securing the areas between communities and providing reaction forces for endangered hamlets would, in turn, be assumed by the 173rd Airborne and the remaining troops of the 40th and 41st ARVN Regiments. This would oblige the allied regular units to "fragment" themselves into platoon-sized outposts and saturate the plains with dozens of daytime patrols and night ambushes. General Barnes incorporated these concepts into the plan for a new operation, code-named Washington Green, that would commence on 15 April:

> Concept of Operation: The operation, in two phases, will be a long-term effort with all participating forces/agencies integrated at district level. Military efforts will be planned to support district pacification programs. To facilitate this planning and the resultant execution, a battalion Task Force will be assigned to each of the four districts in which the Brigade has operational responsibilities (AO Lee). Territorial forces, in conjunction with other GVN agencies, will actively execute the pacification program behind a security shield provided by the regular forces. The security shield will be maintained for the period of time required to insure protection of the GVN pacification effort. Primary regular force targets will be the destruction of the Viet Cong Infrastructure, the guerrilla and sapper-terrorist elements. Reaction to VC/NVA efforts to disrupt the campaign will be an essential factor of contingency planning.[44]

Washington Green would, in short, be the very antithesis of the 1st Cavalry Division's clearing operations and the 173rd Airborne Brigade's Operation Dan Sinh. Although these earlier operations had officially been conducted "in support of pacification," they were not coordinated with Binh Dinh's pacification effort, and the attrition of Communist military strength had always been their primary objective. Rather than featuring mobility and transience, Washington Green would require the Sky Soldiers to deploy in static penny packets to maintain a permanent security shield around the target hamlets. In the past, allied operations had sought to encourage or force the movement of refugees into GVN-controlled areas, whereas Washington Green aimed to resettle them in their original homes. Instead of enemy regulars, the 173rd Airborne's primary targets would be the Vietcong guerrillas and VCI. Finally, allied regulars would have to strictly limit their use of supporting fire so as not to destroy the very communities they were trying to protect. In early 1970, Operation Washington Green's restrictive rules of engagement would be described in an article published in the US Army's *Infantry* journal:

> We have a fire support problem because of our rules of engagement. The first round must be 1,000 meters from any friendly element and at least 600 meters from any known hamlet. The fire is brought to within 600 meters of the troops in 200-meter increments and below that range in 50-meter adjustments. In order to get night defensive targets registered, the troops must be off the gun-target line by at least 300 meters. The earliest illumination round I ever received during contact was 14 minutes after the initial request.[45]

General Barnes suspected that supporting pacification would be unpopular with his troops, since it was contrary to both their training and their prior combat experience in Vietnam. It also violated the principles of mass, maneuver, surprise, and the offensive as these were defined in US Army doctrine, and its overall objective was equally at odds with the traditional American aim of destroying enemy military forces. It was a bitter pill the Sky Soldiers were being asked to swallow, and the deputy brigade commander, Colonel Joseph Ross Franklin, felt obliged to urge them to adopt a positive attitude about their new mission:

> Airborne soldiers, sometimes including airborne battalion commanders, frequently turn-off and drop-out when the word "pacification" is mentioned. The principal reason for this is in oversimplified and general terms a lack of real understanding of what pacification is, plus the related notion that anything less than fighting a conventional war against main force units is undesirable and only to be endured for temporary periods until the real business of fighting can be renewed. From commander to rifleman there is a strong desire to use fire and maneuver to close with and destroy a recognizable enemy. This kind of war is easy to understand as success is easily measured, and this is what we have been trained for. . . . We can enter into pacification with reservations and simply go through the motions, or go into it with the same enthusiasm and wholehearted support that this Brigade has demonstrated in its more conventional combat operations.[46]

Colonel Franklin was right to fear that his subordinates would be unenthusiastic. Captain Jared C. Bates was still bitter sixteen years later when he was interviewed for an army oral history program. He recalled his time commanding Company D, 1/503rd, in 1969–1970 as the most disappointing experience of his long and distinguished career. Having been in the army for five years and already served in Vietnam as an advisor, he desperately wanted to lead a company in combat. Instead, Company D was scattered to the four winds throughout his tour, and for all practical purposes, Bates was again serving as an advisor. He was hardly alone in his opposition to pacification duty. "In fact, the company commanders were resistant as hell to this idea when we were going into this pacification program. We were trying to figure out ways to keep our companies together in a company formation and operate, and we were directed: 'You will not do that! You will send that platoon over there and that one over there.'"[47]

In the Hamlets

General Barnes did not intend for the Sky Soldiers to limit themselves to acting in the role of Regional Forces. He envisioned that they would become more intimately involved in pacification by deploying their outposts right on the outskirts of the target hamlets and conducting integrated operations with the Popular Forces and "demoted" RF platoons defending them.[48] This was essential because, given the Territorial Forces' ineffectiveness, only the presence of allied regulars would assure the establishment of real, meaningful security. After all, enemy forces in northern Binh Dinh had, in the past, roughly handled even battalion-sized American units. It was thus perfectly understandable if the poorly prepared Territorial Forces were intimidated and overcautious. The Sky Soldiers' presence would give their morale a shot in the arm and provide access to the wealth of indirect firepower and other support available to American troops. The same would hold true for the many other GVN personnel who had to work in the hamlets and generally had no faith in their RF and PF defenders.

Because the psychological effects of the Sky Soldiers' presence were so important, it was essential to convince both GVN troops and officials, as well as the population at large, that the Americans would not withdraw until a community had been permanently secured. Therefore, General Barnes explained: "To foster faith and confidence in long term GVN security, we planned our combined RF/PF and U.S. dispositions so that each security element, once assigned to a hamlet or group of hamlets, would remain until agreed pacification goals had been achieved."[49] This determination was echoed by Generals Abrams and Corcoran. In the event that NVA regular combat units returned to AO Lee, they would react by introducing a battalion—and, if need be, a full brigade—of the US 4th Infantry Division, rather than pull the Sky Soldiers off pacification duty.[50]

Operation Washington Green's ultimate objective was for the Sky Soldiers to "work themselves out of a job" by making the Territorial Forces capable of standing on their own. This would allow ARVN regular troops to be withdrawn from pacification duty and sent to replace American units in mobile operations against NVA and Vietcong regulars.

> When . . . PSDF, PF and RF forces are organized, equipped and trained to accomplish their mission in all the hamlets, then and only then can ARVN forces be freed from the populated areas to prevent invasion across national boundaries and to search out VC/NVA forces in mountain and jungle base areas. At this point in time U.S. and other Free World forces will no longer be required in South Vietnam. It is the current mission of the 173d Brigade to assist GVN in developing the effective PSDF, PF and RF forces needed by and in support of each target hamlet to insure its lasting security against VC attacks and intimidation.[51]

If the presence of allied regular troops was no longer required to secure Binh Dinh's rural hamlets, then the GVN could spend years—even decades, if necessary—carrying out the nation-building programs required to resolve the underlying social, economic, and political grievances that had fueled the insurgency in the first place.

General Barnes planned to enhance the performance of Binh Dinh's Territorial Forces (and the PSDF militia) by means of "learning by doing" techniques similar to those developed for the Pair Off program. Thus, colocating a US security detail with the PF or RF platoon defending each target hamlet would enable the Americans to give on-the-job training to their counterparts while conducting joint operations. All ambushes and patrols were to be conducted in a fully integrated fashion, with US and RF/PF troops each contributing half the personnel.[52] The Americans would also provide formal instruction in marksmanship, how to request and direct artillery fire, and the use and maintenance of the M-16 assault rifles, M-60 machine guns, and M-79 grenade launchers with which the Territorial Forces were being equipped. Finally, the brigade would establish Security Training Assistance Group (STAG) teams to train the PSDF militiamen recruited in the target hamlets. In short, the 173rd Airborne was going to undertake a form of "encadrement" similar to that practiced by the US Marine Corps in its Combined Action Platoon (CAP) program. Unlike the CAP program, Operation Washington Green did not lead to the creation of composite American-RF/PF units; however, the policies of colocation and fully integrated tactical operations had the similar effect of placing US combat troops in an advisory role on the front lines of pacification.

The 173rd Airborne Brigade was not without experience in this kind of endeavor. In April 1968 it had created several five-man Brigade Advisor Teams (BATs) to train and advise Territorial Forces units until CORDS Mobile Advisory Teams (MATs), which were still being formed at that time, began to arrive. Here too, the emphasis was on "learning by doing" rather than formal instruction, although the time devoted to each territorial unit was strictly limited—eleven days for an RF company, and a mere five days for a PF platoon. Nonetheless, the BAT program impressed GVN officials, and they requested that it be continued even after the arrival of the MATs.[53] In Operation Washington Green, the brigade took the BAT concept and applied it on a massive scale, so that most of its combat troops were serving in what were, in effect, small advisory units.[54]

As in the Pair Off program, US and South Vietnamese headquarters were to be colocated and assigned identical areas of operations. Since the GVN civil administration was assigned the leading role in pacification, all operational boundaries conformed with existing political boundaries. Thus, each of the 173rd Airborne's four infantry battalions was detailed to one of the four districts in AO Lee: the 1/503rd to Hoai Nhon, the 2/503rd to Hoai An, the 4/503rd to Tam Quan, and the 1/50th (Mechanized) to Phu My. Each US battalion command post was to be colocated with the district chief's headquarters. The 40th and 41st ARVN Regiments, which had separate AOs of their own covering southern Tam Quan–northeastern Hoai Nhon and southern Phu My, respectively, were to do the same and coordinate all their operations with the district chief and US battalion commander.[55]

At the next level down the chain of command, US company commanders were to colocate their headquarters with that of an RF company or RF control group (a headquarters that commanded several RF companies) and share an AO that encompassed one or more villages. All military operations were to be closely coordinated with the village chiefs. Each US platoon or detached squad would be assigned an AO corresponding to a single target hamlet, and a joint control group consisting of the American unit's leader, the RF or PF platoon commander, and the head of the RD Cadre Team assigned to the community would be formed. This group would operate under the direction of the hamlet chief, with advice from the American unit's leader.[56] In theory, American officers were supposed to defer to the district, village, or hamlet chief, who was the titular senior partner in the combined command structure. This was particularly true at the district level, where the GVN district chief and his staff, supported by their CORDS advisors, were responsible for drafting and implementing the district's pacification plan.

In addition to their security and training missions, the Sky Soldiers were supposed to assist GVN agencies in resettling refugees, holding elections, establishing schools, building infrastructure, and conducting economic development projects.[57] However, these objectives were not prioritized, and the troops were given surprisingly little guidance on how to pursue them and were allocated no additional resources for this purpose. Colonel Franklin vaguely advised, "We must assist all agencies of the GVN within our districts where we can. Good judgement and good-will will dictate this. Obviously there are some things we cannot do, but there is more we can do. The Commanding General is counting on your imagination and dedication to find these areas."[58] In fact, no true plan for civic action and nation-building activities was ever produced during Operation Washington Green. There would be a concerted effort at the brigade level to build roads and schools, but company and platoon commanders operating in the countryside were pretty much left to their own devices.

General Barnes and Colonel Franklin warned their subordinates not to succumb to the temptation to take the lead if GVN commanders did not move fast enough for their taste. Since Washington Green's success ultimately depended on the South Vietnamese becoming self-reliant, it was essential that they be allowed to do things for themselves, no matter how frustrating it might be. The Sky Soldiers were also counseled to show great patience and forbearance in all dealings with their counterparts:

> The Brigade's participation in the pacification effort must be characterized by patience and respect at all times by all members of the Brigade for the customs, traditions, attitudes, and values of the Vietnamese people. We must never forget that we are guests in their country at their request. We are allies, not conquerors. In our relations with the Vietnamese military and civilian authorities and their U.S. advisors, we must be prepared to assist, not overwhelm; to guide, not lead; to convince, not demand; to suggest, not order; to request, not command.[59]

But verbal admonitions, no matter how sincere, could not prepare the Sky Soldiers for the challenges they would encounter in their radically different new mission. None of them were trained to act as advisors, a role that demanded an understanding of Vietnamese language and culture that almost none of them possessed. These deficiencies would be manageable at the district level, since interpreters were always available, and most of the district chiefs had at least some English. Out in the hamlets, however, the GVN officials and territorial officers with whom US junior officers and NCOs would be working generally knew nothing of the English language or American culture. The likelihood of intercultural friction was accordingly very high.

The US Marines' CAP program used several different techniques to prevent friction within its combined US–South Vietnamese units. All participating Marines—at least in the early years of the program—were combat veterans who volunteered for CAP service and underwent careful screening for any evidence of racial or cultural antipathy toward the Vietnamese. Once admitted, each CAP Marine attended a two-week training session where, among other subjects, he was introduced to the Vietnamese language, learned about Vietnamese customs and culture, and was given "Personal Response" training, "which was, simply put, the Marines' attempt to make its men understand that the Vietnamese were human beings."[60] Despite its brevity, this training was of the utmost importance:

> The success of Personal Response was a matter of life and death. . . . The pettiest slights to a Vietnamese by an American could invite retribution. If a Marine propositioned a married woman, or even crossed his leg at a dinner table, the insult could translate into a booby trap placed on some commonly-patrolled trail, or a diagram of the CAP's compound given over to the local VC cadre. The need for cultural sensitivity by the Marines thus extended beyond mere civic action or even a moral imperative: it was tactically vital.[61]

Unfortunately, the Sky Soldiers were given no training in how to live, work, and fight amidst a culturally alien population. Colonel Donald F. Bletz, who succeeded Colonel Franklin as deputy brigade commander in June 1969, recalled, "As replacements came in for the brigade, it was my job to talk to them and attempt to explain what we were doing and how we were going about it. And I think that is really the extent of any formal education or instruction."[62] Needless to say, it would have been impossible to train an entire brigade's worth of troops to the same standards as the CAP program, much less screen them to ensure they were free of racial or cultural antipathy toward the Vietnamese. Still, time could have been found for at least a few days' training in Vietnamese language and culture. The language training alone would have paid great dividends in the form of reduced casualties from mines and booby traps. None of the senior officers interviewed for this study could explain why this was not done. Colonel Bletz considered it a major oversight, since some American troops "found the transition from 'Those people are our enemy and you destroy your enemy' to 'These people are not our enemies, we need to support them' difficult for them to make."[63]

Recognizing the potential for intercultural friction and other problems arising from interaction with the civilian population, General Barnes hoped to keep his troops out of the target hamlets except when joint operations obliged them to enter. Colonel Franklin instructed: "Troops should rest, feed and bivouac near the hamlets, but not in them. Troops in the hamlets are exposed to disease as well as temptations. They also become sloppy and control is most difficult when mixed with local inhabitants. Keep them apart when possible."[64] However, it was impossible to prevent routine contact between the populace and US troops, since the Americans were usually stationed right on the outskirts of the hamlets. According to Colonel Bletz, "It was exceptional that we would have a unit located right in a hamlet. Now some of these hamlets are pretty small things. Being in it, or on the edge of it . . . you're talking a hundred yards."[65]

Vietnamization

As the 173rd Airborne Brigade was preparing to launch Operation Washington Green, the fledgling administration of President Richard Nixon was developing its strategy for the Vietnam War. Even before Nixon was inaugurated, his future national security advisor, Henry Kissinger, commissioned a Rand Corporation study on the prospects for victory in Vietnam. Rand queried members of the Joint Chiefs of Staff, MACV, the US embassy in Saigon, the Defense and State Departments, and the CIA for their opinions about the likelihood of achieving victory, which was defined as follows: "The destruction or withdrawal of all NVA units in South Vietnam, the destruction, withdrawal, or dissolution of all (or most) VC forces and apparatus, the permanent cessation of infiltration, and the virtually unchallenged sovereignty of a stable, non-Communist regime."[66] The answers were so markedly bifurcated that the Rand analysts divided the respondents into two groups. Group A believed that, with the Communists decimated by the general offensive-general uprising and with accelerated pacification gaining ground, victory was still attainable. Many of those in group A favored escalating the war by extending US air and ground operations into Laos and Cambodia, unrestricted bombing and naval mining of North Vietnam, and even a limited or full-scale invasion of the north. Some argued that the mere threat of invasion or unrestricted bombing would convince the North Vietnamese to sue for peace on terms that would be tantamount to handing victory to the United States and the GVN. The respondents in group B, in contrast, believed that military victory was impossible and opposed any kind of escalation. They favored a negotiated settlement that would lead to the withdrawal of US and NVA troops and the establishment of a coalition government. Since the NLF insurgency would remain intact, the GVN could still be overthrown; however, group B judged that US credibility would not be fatally injured because the Americans would have achieved their main objective of repelling external aggression. In effect, group B was willing to accept terms that merely gave

South Vietnam reasonable odds of surviving for a "decent interval" after the last US troops were withdrawn.

Dissatisfied by this lack of consensus, Kissinger repeated the exercise, distributing a lengthy questionnaire on Vietnam to all the key national security agencies on the day after Nixon's inauguration. The results, assembled in National Security Study Memorandum 1, revealed that "there was no consensus as to facts, much less to policy."[67] Yet, as far back as the spring of 1968, Nixon had concluded that military victory was impossible and had told his chief speechwriters, "I've come to the conclusion that there's no way to win the war. But we can't say that, of course. In fact, we have to seem to say the opposite, just to keep some degree of bargaining leverage."[68] Yet he and Kissinger believed it was still possible to win a "policy victory" by using carrot-and-stick diplomacy to get the Soviet Union and North Vietnam to make concessions in the negotiations that would give the GVN reasonable odds of surviving—at least for a "decent interval," in the worst case. The "carrot" would be trade and nuclear arms control agreements dangled in front of the Soviets, while the "stick" would consist of threats of extreme military escalation (the "madman" tactic). Nixon and Kissinger would also engage in "triangular diplomacy" with China in the hope of driving a wedge between the two Communist superpowers and convincing them to reduce or terminate aid to North Vietnam. Thus, their strategy effectively "split the difference" between Rand's groups A and B.[69]

"Vietnamization" was an integral part of Nixon's strategy for ending the Vietnam War. It was a two-track policy designed to withdraw US troops from Vietnam while simultaneously expanding and modernizing South Vietnam's armed forces so they would become capable of standing on their own. It first began to take shape in April 1968, when newly appointed secretary of defense Clark W. Clifford ordered the development of a plan to improve the ARVN's firepower and mobility and shift the responsibility for fighting the war into its hands. As originally conceived, the plan would have progressed through two phases. During phase I, an expanded ARVN would be equipped with artillery, tanks, and helicopters on a vastly increased scale so that it could fight more effectively alongside American troops. Phase II called for the ARVN to be upgraded to the point where it could deal with the Vietcong on its own, after negotiations led to the withdrawal of all US and NVA troops. It was expected to take five years to complete the entire program, but in November 1968 General Abrams suggested that as much as two years could be trimmed off if phase II was begun as soon as possible. His proposal was approved the following month in the form of the Accelerated Phase II Improvement and Modernization Plan.[70]

When Nixon took office, he adopted this plan as his own but soon dispensed with the linkage to a negotiated settlement leading to the mutual withdrawal of US and NVA troops. The prime mover behind this fundamental shift in policy was Melvin R. Laird, the new secretary of defense, who coined the term "Vietnamization." Laird believed it was imperative to begin unilateral withdrawal as soon as possible in order to dampen domestic opposition to the war, and he convinced Nixon and Kissinger to adopt this view. Nixon duly announced the withdrawal of the first increment of 25,000 troops on 8 June 1969 while meeting with President Thieu on Midway Island. As a sop to Thieu, Nixon also agreed to provide funds, equipment, and training for an expansion of the South Vietnamese armed forces above and beyond that projected in the accelerated phase II plan.[71]

The policy of Vietnamization was never translated into a detailed plan that linked US withdrawals to specific enhancements in ARVN capabilities, and there was never a fixed schedule detailing the size and timing of each withdrawal increment. General Phillip Davidson insists that the failure to convert Vietnamization from a vague policy into a coherent plan happened because the unstated but paramount goal of withdrawing US troops overshadowed all other objectives. It was, he argues, a "cut and run" strategy, although Nixon tried hard to conceal that fact: "The truth is that this obscurity was intentional, since the pace of Vietnamization and the linked withdrawal of U.S. forces depended entirely on American domestic politics and not on the enhancement of the South Vietnamese armed forces."[72]

Similarly, Nixon did not publicize the fact that neither Abrams nor the Joint Chiefs of Staff in the Pentagon believed that even the enhanced ARVN force structure agreed to at Midway would ever be capable of handling *both* the Vietcong and the North Vietnamese. Even as the first withdrawals were starting in July 1969, General Earle G. Wheeler, chairman of the Joint Chiefs of Staff, stressed this about the current program:

> [It was] not designed to provide the South Vietnamese armed forces the capability to deal with both the full enemy guerrilla force in the country and cope with the North Vietnamese armed forces. [Thus, it is imperative] . . . to obtain the withdrawal of North Vietnamese formations and individuals from South Vietnam, Cambodia and Laos to North Vietnam, and the strong probability [exists] that we will have to maintain a residual support force in South Vietnam for some years to come unless and until the withdrawal of the North Vietnamese is achieved.[73]

General Abrams and his MACV staff planned for a "residual support force" that would include about 50,000 ground combat troops in two combat divisions and two combat brigades; it was modeled on the US forces main-

tained in South Korea since the end of the Korean War. This was unaccept-
able to Laird, who intended to remove all US troops.[74] Therefore, in August
1969 he directed the military leadership to develop a new plan that would
enable the South Vietnamese to cope with both the Vietcong and the NVA
on their own. Abrams responded in early September that what Laird was
asking for simply could not be done. Without the assistance of US combat
troops, the South Vietnamese could never stand up to both the Vietcong and
the NVA, and the enhancements required to give them that capability were
not feasible. According to the US Army's official historian, Jeffrey Clarke:

> Laird refused to take no for an answer. On 10 November [1969] he
> directed the Joint Chiefs of Staff to come up with a new plan, a Phase III
> plan, that would, one way or another, create a South Vietnamese military
> force that could "maintain at least current levels of security." . . . Laird's
> instructions not only ordered the services, for the third time, to come
> up with a more suitable Vietnamization plan but also put them on notice
> that a large residual support force was not in the offing.[75]

This time, seeing there was no alternative, MACV answered that a phase
III plan creating fully self-sufficient South Vietnamese armed forces was
possible if several key assumptions were made. First, pacification would
make rapid progress. This would lower desertion rates and boost recruitment
by bringing more of the population under GVN control, and it would allow
troops to be redeployed against the NVA by reducing the Vietcong guerrilla
threat. Second, US material and financial support to South Vietnam would
continue, and there would be no reduction in US support activities in neighboring countries (including offensive air operations from bases in Thailand).
Last, and most important, MACV assumed that NVA forces within South
Vietnam would decline and that those in cross-border sanctuaries would not
reenter the country. Therefore, just like "fast and thin" pacification, Vietnamization's success depended on the continuing absence or quiescence of
much of the enemy's regular military forces.

Several of these assumptions were questionable, and the notion that NVA
troop levels in South Vietnam would continue to drop was sheer nonsense—
as senior US commanders and policymakers knew full well. Clarke writes,
"Abrams and Laird both realized that the ability of the remaining allied forces
to maintain 'current levels of security' depended more on enemy inactivity
than anything else. Ignoring the North Vietnamese Army units in Cambodia, Laos, and southern North Vietnam did not make them go away."[76] Since
no phase III plan could be developed without relying on doubtful and even
ludicrous assumptions, Vietnamization was obviously incapable of achiev-

ing victory on its own. The only way the allies could win the war was by securing a negotiated settlement that led to the permanent withdrawal of all NVA troops from South Vietnam. Anything less would leave the GVN facing combined internal and external threats that neither MACV nor the Joint Chiefs believed it could survive without the direct assistance of US ground combat troops.

CHAPTER THREE

The Balance of Forces

Before tracing the course of Operation Washington Green, it is essential to understand the balance of forces that existed in Binh Dinh when it began. There are two key points that must be stressed. First, since only a handful of NVA troops remained in AO Lee, the operation would, in its initial phases, be opposed solely by the NLF insurgency. At this stage in the war, the NLF's guerrilla and regular military units were still manned almost exclusively by local recruits and native-born returnees from North Vietnam. Second, since an insurgency is fundamentally a contest for popular support, the contending parties' relative strengths were determined more by political dynamics than by military factors such as troops, supplies, and firepower. The incumbent regime generally enjoys the advantage that no matter how flawed or unpopular it might be, it already has a firm grip on the population through its political parties and organs of local government. The insurgents must therefore fight an uphill battle against social and political inertia in order to win a popular following and establish their own covert "shadow government" to compete for control of the people.

The GVN

Unfortunately for the GVN, circumstances conspired to deny it most of the advantages that usually accrue to an incumbent regime. First and foremost, the Communists had a full decade's head start in nation building, and the GVN never really caught up. The Communist-dominated government of the Democratic Republic of Vietnam was established in August 1945, four years before the French allowed the creation of the nominally independent State of Vietnam as an alternative to it. But this new regime was, in fact, merely a tool of French imperial policy; this point was underscored when it was compelled to join the French Union, where the fledgling government's powers were closely circumscribed. From 1949 onward, the titular head of state was Bao Dai, last of the Nguyen Dynasty emperors and a Westernized playboy who spent much of his time abroad. The regime's constituency was very limited, consisting primarily of those segments of the population that had benefited from French colonial rule, and most of its supporters came from Vietnam's cities. Its small rural following was drawn mostly from the wealthier classes or from staunchly anti-Communist religious minorities. Furthermore, as the First Indochinese War progressed, GVN influence in the countryside declined as more and more territory fell under Vietminh control.

By the time fighting ended in 1954, the Communists had built a pervasive shadow government throughout South Vietnam and won the loyalty of most of its population. The GVN, in contrast, had little popular support, its armed forces were inept and demoralized, it had almost no police force worthy of the name, and its bureaucrats were unaccustomed to functioning without French oversight. Worst of all, the GVN hierarchy was riddled with personal and ideological animosities that kept it in a state of turmoil as various individuals and factions constantly jockeyed for power and influence in an atmosphere of Byzantine intrigue. Cabinet ministries were operated almost like personal satrapies by the officials who headed them, making it extremely difficult to coordinate policies among the several branches of government. These weaknesses were reduced but hardly eliminated after Prime Minister Ngo Dinh Diem deposed Emperor Bao Dai in 1955 and established the Republic of Vietnam with himself as president.[1]

All these shortcomings paled, however, in comparison to the taint of illegitimacy that dogged the GVN from the instant of its conception. Although the Republic of Vietnam became truly independent in 1956, many perceived it as "little more than an attenuated French colonial regime."[2] With some notable exceptions (such as Diem himself), its leaders had served either in the colonial army or in the wartime State of Vietnam, which had been dominated by and beholden to the French. Their collaboration with French colonialism dealt a severe blow to popular perceptions of the GVN's legitimacy, particularly in the countryside, where the Vietminh were almost universally respected as patriotic heroes for expelling the hated French. Nowhere was this truer than in Binh Dinh, where Vietminh rule had been virtually unchallenged in the nine years between 1945 and 1954.

The GVN was unable to escape its association with Western imperialism because it had replaced its former reliance on the French with an all-encompassing dependency on the United States. Without American money, arms, advisors, and economic assistance, the GVN could not have survived the 1950s, and its dependency became even more pronounced in the 1960s. As the number of US advisors mushroomed, the extent of the GVN's reliance on foreigners became increasingly obvious to the generally xenophobic South Vietnamese populace. The NLF skillfully exploited the situation with a steady drumbeat of propaganda depicting the GVN and ARVN as lackeys of Western imperialism—though in reality, Americans often found it very difficult to convince their South Vietnamese clients to adopt the policies and strategies favored by the United States. Intervention by hundreds of thousands of US troops only intensified popular suspicions about foreign imperialism because many South Vietnamese could not believe that the Americans came halfway around the world to fight someone else's war purely for reasons of Cold War strategy. Awareness of its own dependency also sapped the ARVN's morale and aggressiveness. One advisor observed: "As usual, I was haranguing about the almost complete inactivity of the 2nd ARVN Division. The Province Chief replied that as long as the US provided massive support, the South would never really fight. This support sapped their pride and their will to combat their 'Brothers from the North' on equal terms. The enemy enjoys a tremendous moral and psychological advantage because he fights with relatively no outside assistance."[3]

It is true that NVA troops were not natives of South Vietnam, but they were hardly foreigners in the same sense that Americans were. They were ethnically indistinguishable from the locals, spoke the same language, and shared the same cultural and historical legacies. Moreover, many of the urban elites who dominated the GVN were themselves estranged from the traditional Vietnamese culture that survived in the countryside. During seventy years of exposure to a dominant and technologically superior foreign culture, some had even come to share Western conceits about the inferiority of other cultures.[4]

Therefore, although the GVN was superior to the NLF in funding, materiel, and firepower, it suffered from crippling political weaknesses. Its social constituency was narrow and culturally divorced from the mainstream of Vietnamese society, its legitimacy was tainted by the legacy of collaboration, and at the close of the First Indochinese War, it did not even have an effective administrative, police, or military presence in much of South Vietnam. It could be considered the "incumbent regime" only insofar as it was the titular sitting government. The GVN's chances of winning in the "second round" depended on its ability to overcome these weaknesses and mobilize a strong constituency within the rural population, but this did not happen. Diem succeeded in eliminating armed non-Communist threats to his regime by defeating an organized crime cartel and several religious sects that had been allowed to form private armies by the French. His "anti-Communist denunciation campaign" also decimated the stay-behind Communist cadres, although the arrest and "reeducation" of tens of thousands of ex-Vietminh and the execution of thousands more bore disturbing similarities to contemporaneous events in North Vietnam. But unlike Ho Chi Minh, Diem did not create a nation. Ho enjoyed a decisive advantage because only the Communists built a mass political party that spanned the entire country and both urban and rural populations. The old non-Communist *Việt Nam Quốc Dân Đảng* (Vietnamese Nationalist Party) and Dai Viet (Great Vietnam) political parties had been weakened by French and Communist oppression and had little strength outside the cities. Diem excluded them from power by means of rigged elections, press censorship, and arrests.

Revisionist historian Mark Moyar claims that these undemocratic practices were essential for the survival of a non-Communist South Vietnam and asserts that opposition to them was limited to a few self-important liberal urban elites whom he lampoons as "the tea-sipping intellectuals of Saigon."[5] This snide caricature is both highly misleading and grossly unfair to Diem's political opponents, who were numerous, diverse, and, in this respect, merely demanded the very rights and freedoms the United States professed to be defending in Southeast Asia. They included many military officers who belonged to the Vietnamese Nationalist Party and the Dai Viet, which opposed Diem's regime, and some of them played leading roles in several coups that sought to topple it.[6] Moreover, the Vietnamese Nationalist Party had once been a major force in Vietnamese politics and had impressive nationalist credentials; it had plotted against French colonial rule as far back as the 1920s and organized the abortive Yen Bai Rebellion of 1930.[7]

Moyar also gives Diem more credit than he deserves. It is true that some scholars believe authoritarian regimes offer the most efficient means of modernization and nation building in undeveloped countries. Their model is Mustafa Kemal Atatürk, the founder of modern Turkey, who won accolades for being a progressive, Westernizing modernizer who revolutionized every aspect of Turkish life and engaged the common people in the project (even to the point of briefly experimenting with a multiparty political system). Kemal was able to achieve so much thanks to his considerable charisma and the immense prestige he earned as the "father" of the Turkish nation. He led his people to victory against the invading Greeks in 1922 and then secured the nation's independence and territorial integrity by compelling the withdrawal of French and British occupation troops.

In Vietnam, however, Ho Chi Minh was generally acclaimed as the "father of the nation," and in most ways, Diem was the antithesis of Kemal. He was deeply conservative, opposed radical change, and was skeptical about the applicability of Western ideas in Vietnam. He was also an elitist who believed most of his countrymen were too ignorant and uneducated to engage in politics. He therefore made little effort to win popular support for his regime—a task for which he was, in any case, ill-suited due to his austere demeanor and lack of personal charisma. Diem's Catholicism also estranged him from many South Vietnamese who believed the government he headed favored his coreligionists. Though exaggerated, these allegations were not entirely unfounded, and there can be no doubt that Diem favored his brothers, all of whom rose to positions of great power, essentially making the GVN a family enterprise. Diem's younger brother and closest confidant, Ngo Dinh Nhu, recognized the need for a mass political movement to buttress the regime and tried to create one. However, his *Cần lao Nhân vị Cách Mạng Đảng* (Personalist Labor Revolutionary Party) and the closely associated *Phong trào Cách mạng Quốc gia* (National Revolutionary Movement) won little popular support with their esoteric "personalist" ideology that offered no real program for change, and their membership was generally limited to opportunistic bureaucrats and military officers.[8] Thus, the NLF had to overcome very little in the way of entrenched political loyalties when it began proselytizing the rural population.

Diem's efforts to assert his government's authority in the countryside were not very effective and often succeeded only in antagonizing the locals.[9] Ordinance 2 of 1955 limited rents and guaranteed tenure for tenant farmers, but it also reversed Vietminh land redistribution by obliging tenants to sign contracts acknowledging that the land they tilled still belonged to the former landlords.[10] Nothing could have been better calculated to turn the rural population against the GVN in the extensive regions controlled by the Vietminh during the First Indochinese War. Another highly unpopular reform occurred in 1956, when Diem attempted to strengthen the central government's influence by abolishing locally selected village councils and replacing them with village chiefs and councils appointed by the province chiefs—who were in turn appointed by Diem himself. This demolished the last vestiges of villages' customary political autonomy and eliminated the only marginally pluralistic governing bodies in the country. The new system also flew in the face of tradition:

> Many of the appointed officials were not from the villages or hamlets in which they served and were often appointed to their positions because of their loyalty to the Diem regime rather than for their ability. Under the previous arrangement, the chiefs and councils, though selected by consensus rather than formal elections, were nevertheless representatives of the people. Many of Diem's appointees were seen as interlopers and lackeys of the central government and as such were not given the prestige and respect previously accorded to local dignitaries.[11]

That many of these appointees would be outsiders was unavoidable, since the prerequisite for gaining any significant position within the GVN hierarchy was possession of the *tu tai*, a secondary education degree equivalent to the old French *baccalaureat* (roughly equivalent to an American high school diploma, though much more prestigious).[12] A *tu tai* was beyond the reach of most rural Vietnamese due to the expense and the scarcity of secondary schools; many rural communities even lacked primary schools. In one province with a population of 350,000, fewer than 200 people a year earned the degree.[13] Therefore, GVN posts were monopolized by the educated urban elite and members of the wealthier rural classes, and "the overwhelming majority of the rural population was simply excluded from power over the decisions affecting their own lives. Instead power was exercised by those social elements least capable of empathizing with the rural population."[14] This system also discouraged ambitious lower-class villagers from supporting the GVN because they knew their possibilities of advancement within its bureaucracy and armed forces were severely limited.[15]

Diem's overthrow in November 1963 marked the end of ARVN military professionalism because, from that point forward, the army and the GVN were synonymous. Until South Vietnam's final collapse in 1975, virtually every position of real authority in the government was occupied by a current or former military officer. Yet the military's monopoly on political power did not yield stability because the thoroughly politicized armed forces were riven by factional disputes. Factional loyalty, rather than professional competence, was the primary consideration when making military appointments and promotions, and it was usually cemented by complex webs of official corruption involving commanders and their subordinates. The wholesale embezzlement of funds and pilferage of materials provided by the United States was the largest source of illicit income,[16] but many officers also enriched themselves at the expense of the population through extortion, bribery, and outright theft. The cultural gap that yawned between South Vietnam's elites and rural villagers weakened the social sanctions that might have curbed these exploitative practices. The underpaid ARVN rank and file followed their commanders' example by stealing food and valuables from villagers and frequently committing worse abuses such as assault, rape, and murder.[17] The Confucian doctrines that pervaded traditional Vietnamese culture defined a strict code of behavior for all members of society, who were expected to respect and obey those of a higher rank while treating those below them justly.[18] "Improper" behavior offended villagers' sense of propriety and raised even more doubts about the GVN's legitimacy and fitness to rule.

But the worst consequence of the ARVN's politicization was that it created incentives for commanders to avoid engaging the enemy. Since his troops were the physical embodiment of a commander's political power, casualties among them reduced his political capital—and empowered his political rivals. The long-term threat posed by the Communists paled in comparison to the immediate risk of losing one's lucrative job to intrigue by hostile political factions. Thus, the *beau ideal* of an ARVN commander was not a successful battlefield leader against the Communists but a successful *political* warrior who triumphed over his political rivals within the ARVN hierarchy.[19] One knowledgeable American observed, "the goal is not to defeat the enemy, but to maintain their position, receive promotions, and enhance their personal fortunes. Combat at best is an extra-curricular activity to be engaged in as a last resort."[20]

The GVN Order of Battle

In April 1969 Binh Dinh's province chief was Lieutenant Colonel Phan Minh Tho, whose office combined the functions of civil administration and military command. Each of the province's nine districts was likewise headed by an appointed district chief who was an ARVN officer (usually with the rank of major) and exercised both civil and military authority within his jurisdiction. Each district, in turn, was divided into administrative villages, which were rural Vietnam's basic social and political units. But the term "village" (*Xa* or *Xom*) is misleading, since the image it conjures is one of a small town, a discrete cluster of buildings surrounded by woods or farmland. In Vietnam, however, that description best fits the *Ap*, usually translated as "hamlet," which was a subunit of a village. Thus, the closest American equivalent to the *Xa* would be a "township"—a unit of local government with clusters of dwellings dispersed over a substantial area.[21] In northern Binh Dinh, most hamlets had multiple subhamlets spread over an area of three or more square kilometers, and even the smallest villages covered at least a dozen square kilometers (and many were much larger).

The village chief and village council directed the day-to-day implementation of policies and decrees passed down from Saigon. These village-level posts had become elective offices starting in 1967, but the district and province chiefs exerted great influence in choosing the candidates who were placed on the ballots. Moreover, the elected chiefs and councils had no real power to act against the wishes of the province chief, who controlled both the purse strings and the security forces the village officials needed for their own protection. The introduction of democracy at the grassroots level therefore mattered little because the higher echelons of government were never reformed.[22]

Troops of the 22nd ARVN Division in Binh Dinh took their orders from the divisional commander, General Nguyen Van Hieu, rather than Lieutenant Colonel Tho, and this separate chain of command hindered their integration into the pacification effort. Nevertheless, while the 173rd Airborne Brigade was launching Operation Washington Green, the 40th and 41st

ARVN Regiments initiated a parallel pacification support operation called Dan Thang-69. The 40th Regiment's AO was in northeastern Hoai Nhon and southern Tam Quan, while the 41st Regiment's was in southern Phu My. The ARVN regiments were supposed to operate in the same way as the 173rd Airborne Brigade, colocating their tactical operations centers with the district chief's headquarters, "fragmenting" their battalions to guard target hamlets, and training and conducting joint operations with RF and PF units. However, Dan Thang-69 and Washington Green were not combined operations in the same sense as the Pair Off operations of 1968. US and ARVN units were no longer planning and conducting integrated operations, and the 173rd Airborne no longer had the mission of training the South Vietnamese regulars.[23]

The 40th and 41st ARVN Regiments each had four infantry battalions, but these had a "triangular" structure with three rifle companies. Thus, even at full strength, they fielded only two-thirds as many troops as a four-company US infantry battalion (638 men versus 920). In reality, both armies' battalions were usually understrength, but on average, the Americans' were still much larger. The ARVN units' strength was also significantly reduced by desertion and the practice of carrying "ghost" soldiers (men who had been killed, deserted, or never existed) on unit rosters so that commanders could pocket their pay and dependent support allowances. A typical ARVN infantry battalion therefore possessed barely half the combat manpower of its American counterpart. The average "present for operations" strength of an ARVN infantry battalion in May 1965 was only 376 men, and the aggregate average for all of 1966 was still a distressingly low 449.[24] The number of troops that could be employed in combat operations was even lower, and as General Lu Lan explained in 1991, "if you have a U.S. company, you have the size of a [ARVN] battalion."[25]

Binh Dinh also had 55 Regional Forces companies (5,553 men) and 269 Popular Forces platoons (8,032 men). Since the notional strength of an RF company was 123 men and that of a PF platoon was 35, the Territorial Forces were also understrength, though not necessarily for the same reasons as the ARVN regiments. Positions in the Territorial Forces were much sought after because they saw less action than ARVN units and allowed men to serve close to their homes; in many cases, recruits had to pay bribes to secure places in them.[26] Outright desertion was not much of a problem, but being so close to home created a powerful inducement for men to go AWOL. It was not uncommon for upward of half a territorial unit's manpower to be absent at any given moment. In many cases, territorial soldiers had to "moonlight" in civilian jobs because their meager military pay was insufficient to support their families. The fact that northern Binh Dinh was a notorious Communist stronghold also elevated absentee rates, which were among the highest in South Vietnam.[27] Only 27 RF companies and 81 PF platoons were located in the four northern districts when Washington Green began, but their numbers would soon climb as RF companies were redeployed from Tuy Phuoc and Phu Cat districts in the more secure, southern half of the province. Yet the shortfall in Territorial Forces was such that "robbing Peter to pay Paul" could not resolve the problem entirely. Eight RF companies and ten PF platoons were already in training and would start emerging from the training centers in late May, but even they would not be sufficient. Only massive new recruitment would eventually solve the problem.[28]

The Sky Soldiers, the two ARVN regiments, and the Territorial Forces would secure the target hamlets, but pacification activities within them would be conducted by Rural Development (RD) Cadre Teams. These fifty-nine-man paramilitary units comprised a Command Group; a Civil Affairs/RD Group manned by psychological warfare, intelligence, civil affairs, and medical specialists; and a thirty-four-man Security Group. They had first been developed in Binh Dinh in 1964 by Colonel Nguyen Be, a former Vietminh commander, and were later adopted nationwide. Colonel Be saw them as a means of bridging the yawning gulf between Saigon and its rural citizenry. In the past, efforts to "win the hearts and minds" of rural villagers through economic development, infrastructure improvements, and public health and education programs had been administered by remote, inefficient, and notoriously corrupt government agencies that were generally unresponsive to the needs and desires of the rural population. The RD Cadre Teams were intended to bring an effective GVN presence directly into the hamlets and to empower the inhabitants by creating elected village and hamlet governments, conducting economic development and infrastructure improvement projects chosen by the people themselves, arming them for self-defense, and eliminating the covert VCI who terrorized them.[29] RD cadres were trained to avoid alienating the villagers by consciously mimicking the techniques of the Vietcong. Thus, they wore the traditional black pajamas of the Vietnamese peasant and were trained to live and work closely with the people, treating them in every way as equals worthy of respect. However, this proved difficult to ensure in practice.

> In its period of rapid expansion, the RD Cadre program could not maintain the high quality of recruiting that had characterized . . . [the original cadres]. With the introduction of draft deferments, the program tended to become a haven for urban young men with political influence whose principal motive was avoidance of military service. Thus, many of the cadre lacked proper motivation or, because of their urban background,

were not sensitive enough to problems peculiar to the rural environment.[30]

The elites who dominated the GVN and ARVN also had a vested interest
in preserving the status quo, and they feared the consequences of mobilizing
and empowering the rural masses. Thus, while the Americans had originally named the program "Revolutionary Development," in the hope that
it would harness the ongoing revolution and steal it away from the Communists, the GVN significantly opted for the more conservative title "Rural
Development." And since the RD cadre program was specifically designed
to circumvent the cumbersome Saigon bureaucracy, it was certain to antagonize many GVN officials and discourage them from cooperating with it.
Enacting fundamental reforms at the grassroots level while the middle and
upper echelons of South Vietnam's government remained unchanged would
ultimately prove impractical.[31]

The 1969 pacification campaign directed that each RD Cadre Team be
permanently assigned to a specific village—optimally, that from which its
personnel had been recruited—in order to provide a pool of trained administrative and intelligence personnel for the village government after pacification was complete.[32] This "one team–one village" policy proved impossible
to implement in Binh Dinh (and in other provinces, no doubt), where there
were so many hamlets to be pacified that GVN officials had no choice but
to shift teams wherever they were needed at any given moment.[33] Indeed,
the 100 RD Cadre Teams present in May 1969 were completely inadequate
to meet the province-wide demand. In order to press ahead with Operation Washington Green, nine RD Cadre Teams had to be "stolen" from the
southern districts of An Tuc, Binh Khe, and Tuy Phuoc—none of which was
in a position to spare them.[34]

One of the tasks assigned to the RD Cadre Teams was to organize People's
Self-Defense Force militia in the target hamlets. The General Mobilization
Law of June 1968 made membership in the armed Combat PSDF mandatory
for all males aged sixteen to seventeen and thirty-nine to fifty, and it created a voluntary, unarmed Support PSDF for women, the elderly, and youths
under sixteen.[35] The aim was less military than political. It was hoped that
by getting rural villagers to participate in activities hostile to the Vietcong,
they could be co-opted into supporting the Saigon government. By making
participation mandatory for men of military age and encouraging the broadest possible involvement by other groups, it was hoped that social pressure
could be brought to bear on behalf of the GVN. It was, in effect, an effort
to duplicate Vietcong methods of organizing and mobilizing the rural population.[36] In April 1969 about 69,000 people were on the PSDF rolls in Binh

Dinh, but only 7,500 of them were in the Combat PSDF. The rest were in the Support PSDF, whose membership was purely nominal and signified no real commitment to the GVN. Indeed, even those in the Combat PSDF generally received only perfunctory training and lacked any real sense of dedication to the Saigon government—certainly not sufficient for them to risk their lives for it. Since most of the four northern districts remained under Vietcong domination at the outset of Operation Washington Green, the more secure southern districts accounted for the lion's share of the province's PSDF.[37]

The last and smallest armed force available to the GVN in Binh Dinh was the National Police. There were 1,176 uniformed officers on hand in January 1969—just one for every 778 civilians in the province—and most of them were concentrated in the district seats and Qui Nhon. The police shortage was a legacy of the French era, when the small rural gendarmerie focused on protecting the colonial administration and the lives and property of French expatriates. American efforts to establish a proper rural police force in the late 1950s and early 1960s failed because of Diem's desire to create a paramilitary counterweight to the ARVN.[38] It was not until 1969 that the National Police, whose structure had never extended below the district level, began to establish a permanent presence in rural villages and hamlets.[39] The weakness of Binh Dinh's police forces was a major impediment to pacification, but surprisingly, their strength rose by less than a thousand between 1969 and 1971.[40]

At the beginning of 1969, Binh Dinh also had 221 special police who worked in the Phung Hoang program, collecting intelligence on the VCI and—at least in theory—developing plans to kill, apprehend, or induce the surrender of specific members of the Communist shadow government. Execution of those plans was supposed to be the mission of the National Police Field Force (NPFF), consisting of platoon- and company-sized paramilitary units manned by police who were fully trained and equipped for combat. In Binh Dinh the NPFF was represented by 203/1 and 203/2 Companies, which had a combined strength of 314 men. However, as in most other provinces, these two companies were rarely employed in their intended role of hunting the VCI and were used instead in static defensive missions.[41]

The NLF

The National Liberation Front enjoyed a number of significant—and potentially decisive—advantages in the struggle for popular support. First of all, the NLF was the direct descendant of the Vietminh, who were generally acclaimed as patriotic heroes for throwing off the shackles of French colonial rule. Even in the late 1960s, the terms "patriotism" and "Vietminh" were interchangeable in much of South Vietnam, and peasants in the Mekong Delta region invariably referred to the Vietcong as "Vietminh" early in the decade. Since the GVN was tainted by its neocolonial origins and continuing dependence on foreigners, the NLF had grounds to argue that only it could legitimately claim the mantle of Vietnamese nationalism. In more practical terms, its Vietminh legacy meant that the NLF would not have to start its organizational work from scratch and could count on a sizable and highly experienced cadre of former Vietminh to act as the foundation for a new shadow government. Indeed, the GVN's failure to establish itself firmly in the countryside ensured that, from the beginning, the NLF had more influence in many parts of South Vietnam.

The NLF's greatest advantage was that its leadership recognized the paramount importance of political factors and shaped its structure and strategy accordingly. This stood in sharp contrast to the GVN and the United States, which persisted in viewing the war as a military contest and failed to develop a strategy that adequately integrated social and political initiatives with military operations. The NLF, for its part, did not even use the word "war," preferring the more general term *dau tranh*, or "struggle," which consisted of two distinct components: "the political struggle (*dau tranh chinh tri*) and the armed, or military, struggle (*dau tranh vu trang*)."[42] Its primary target was not the GVN's armed forces but the South Vietnamese people. By means of an unrelenting political offensive, the NLF aimed to secure a dominant political position within the rural population and, in the process, so undermine the foundations of the GVN and its armed forces that both would lack the will and the means (recruits, taxes, food, intelligence) to continue resistance. The military struggle, which embraced political violence and terrorism as well as guerrilla warfare, was designed to accelerate the progress of the political offensive. Battlefield victories encouraged existing supporters and attracted new recruits by demonstrating the NLF's strength and military prowess, while simultaneously demoralizing the ARVN. The assassination of corrupt GVN officials won favor with the population, whereas the elimination of honest and efficient ones removed a major political threat. In either case, the NLF reaped an additional benefit by terrorism's intimidating effect on surviving GVN officials. At times, the NLF also used a calculated policy of provoking the GVN into indiscriminate and excessive acts of retaliation that intensified its alienation from the rural population.[43] It honed this tactic into a fine art against the Americans, repeatedly tempting them to unleash the full weight of their firepower against rural communities.

The Vietcong Infrastructure (VCI)—or shadow government—was critical for the success of the NLF's political offensive. Renowned French political scientist and Indochina War historian Bernard B. Fall wrote: "When a country is being subverted it is not being outfought; it is being out-administered. Subversion is literally administration with a minus sign in front."[44] In February 1969 the GVN was being outadministered in the most literal sense possible, since it had just 38,000 officials at the critical village and hamlet levels, whereas the VCI numbered 70,000.[45] The RD Cadre Teams were intended to even the odds, but they often faced an uphill fight against deeply rooted popular loyalties that favored the NLF, and even their additional personnel raised the GVN's rural presence to only 63,000. Yet, what the GVN truly lacked in the villages and hamlets was not numbers but commitment. Neither GVN bureaucrats nor RD cadres were as committed—or as effective—as their NLF counterparts. Both were generally reluctant to accept the risks attendant to working on the front lines of pacification, and all too often they fled their assigned villages and hamlets when "things got too hot"—leaving the local VCI unchallenged.

Despite the GVN's huge financial, materiel, and military advantages, the VCI shadow government had a larger presence in the countryside and exerted considerably more influence over the rural population. This was arguably the single most important factor shaping the course of the Vietnam War, since it meant that in much of the country, the NLF dictated social norms and thereby determined the environment in which villagers developed their political consciousness and loyalties.

> Due to their youth and upbringing in the traditional environment . . . [NLF recruits] had . . . little knowledge of and probably few specific attitudes towards the affairs of politics beyond their village. More generalized orientations toward authority existed, but to a large extent their belief system in regard to specific political themes was ripe for indoctrination—their "political consciousness" had, literally, not been developed. In short, the internalization of much of Front indoctrination was primarily attitude formation rather than attitude change.[46]

But the political vacuum that existed in rural South Vietnam would have yielded little advantage had the NLF's presence and activities clashed with the expectations and customs of traditional Vietnamese society. Thus, unlike the GVN, which concentrated all real power in the hands of a few officials at the province level and above, the NLF consciously sought to accommodate the villages' traditional political autonomy. Douglas Pike observed, "In policy determination and execution, the principle followed [by the NLF] was great centralization in planning and policymaking—almost all of it at the national Central Committee level—and great decentralization in policy execution; great latitude was granted to provincial and even village committees in adapting general directives to local circumstances."[47] This system bore a strong resemblance to the traditional pattern of a highly centralized mandarin bureaucracy that handed down edicts from the Imperial Court but left the details of their execution in the hands of the village councils. It enabled the NLF to apply its policies flexibly and to give due consideration to circumstances unique to a particular community. Consequently, although the NLF's decision-making process was no more democratic than the GVN's, at the level of administration—where its policies had their most immediate impact on the rural population—it was generally more adaptable and responsive.

The NLF also attempted to circumvent rural Vietnamese society's habitual hostility toward outsiders by selecting its leaders from the villages or districts where they would serve. Class origins were another key criterion in selection and promotion. Determined to win the broadest possible social constituency, NLF recruitment and promotion policies consciously favored the lower classes of rural society that had the least access to power and advancement in the GVN.[48] Besides ensuring that the NLF's leadership would be well assimilated with the rural population with which it worked, this policy offered personal advancement and social mobility to individuals whose lack of education all but precluded careers in the GVN and ARVN. In the NLF's political and military hierarchies, demonstrated ability was the primary basis (after class origin) for the awarding of promotions, and capable, ambitious individuals could expect upward progress at a fairly steady rate.[49]

To avoid the corruption and abuses of power that plagued the GVN, the NLF held its cadres accountable to a strictly enforced code of proper behavior. It meted out harsh punishment for any misuse of authority or instances of corruption and enjoined all members of the NLF to avoid any show of disrespect or arrogance toward the people. But the code was much more than just a catalog of "don'ts"; it also stipulated positive steps NLF personnel should take to remain on good terms with the people. They were taught, for example, to practice the "3 Withs" (work with, live with, and eat with the people).[50] As a result, "the conduct of NLF cadres was usually exemplary—no cursing, no rudeness, no physical abuse, no lack of respect, no arrogance."[51] Even more impressive was the NLF's success in overcoming the peasantry's traditional perception of all military forces as wanton plunderers and oppressors, an achievement that was acknowledged even by the US Department of Defense.[52]

Last, but not least, the NLF offered a clear program for revolutionary social, economic, and political change that appealed to broad segments of the South Vietnamese population. French colonial policies and Vietnam's integration into the global market for commodities such as rice and rubber had widened class divisions by facilitating the concentration of landownership in the hands of European expatriates and a new class of indigenous landlords who became some of the GVN's staunchest supporters. Many peasants were reduced to tenant farming or working as agricultural laborers (many on foreign-owned rubber plantations), while others owned so little land that they too were obliged to rent fields to sustain their families. The French also intruded on villages' traditional autonomy by levying taxes and corvée labor obligations directly on individuals rather than on the community as a whole, and they reduced the village councils to advisory bodies that met only twice a year. As previously discussed, the GVN further eroded autonomy by replacing locally selected village chiefs and councils with appointed outsiders. American-backed initiatives such as the Strategic Hamlet program, which forcibly relocated entire communities, also had a disruptive effect on rural society.[53]

The NLF vowed to end foreign intrusion, restore village autonomy, replace corrupt GVN appointees with honest officials recruited in the community, and make the national government responsive to the wishes of all the people—not just GVN elites. It promised to alleviate the plight of the poor by forcing landlords to reduce rents or to stop collecting them altogether and by redistributing land (the ultimate goal of abolishing private landownership and establishing collective farms was rarely mentioned and would be pursued only after the GVN had been overthrown). The NLF also pledged to increase educational opportunities for the young, improve the rights and status of women, and boost pay and benefits for workers (of whom there were few in rural South Vietnam apart from rubber plantation employees). Significantly, the NLF not only promised to do these things but actually carried them out to the greatest extent possible in the rural communities that fell under its control.[54] In many parts of South Vietnam, older villagers recalled that the Vietminh had actually implemented a virtually identical program years earlier—although the GVN had overturned most of these reforms during the interwar period.

The GVN represented the status quo, resisted revolutionary change, and had no coherent reform agenda. Instead, it tried to win popular support with a hodgepodge of infrastructure and economic development programs that generally did not alter the existing social order, political reforms that left the real centers of power at the district level and above untouched, and ill-managed public health and education services. Most of these programs and reforms were conceived, funded, and administered largely by Americans; they were only grudgingly adopted by the GVN, but its corruption and inefficiency prevented them from having the desired effect on popular loyalties. The boldest GVN reform initiative was the Land-to-the-Tiller law of 1970, which aimed to steal the NLF's thunder by distributing land at no cost to the tenant farmers who were already working it. However, this program came much too late to cause a dramatic shift in villagers' political allegiances, and in many regions it merely legitimized land redistribution carried out long before by the NLF.[55]

Thanks to the success of its political offensive, the NLF was effectively the incumbent regime in Binh Dinh and many other parts of South Vietnam, and the GVN faced an uphill battle to win popular support. Thomas L. Ahern Jr., who wrote a multivolume official history of the CIA's role in the Vietnam War, concluded that the insurgents had already won the war politically before American combat troops arrived to (temporarily) prevent the Communists from administering the military coup de grâce. "In the light of subsequent events, it is clear that by 1965 it was already too late for the GVN to engage its own population in successful opposition to the communists. The insurgency had triumphed, and it remained only for the VC main forces and newly arrived formations from the North to finish off a dispirited ARVN and occupy the cities and towns."[56]

The NLF and NVA Order of Battle

The National Liberation Front was organized into two parallel hierarchies, one political and the other military (the Liberation Army), both of which operated under the authority of the Central Committee. In theory, the Central Committee was elected by a congress of delegates chosen at the district level by the various political parties that belonged to the NLF, but in fact, the process was undemocratic and dictated by the Communists.[57] Below the Central Committee came a hierarchy of administrative committees starting with three interzones, which were divided into zones spanning multiple provinces; then came provinces and districts. The NLF's structure did not precisely parallel the GVN's at the district and provincial levels because the Saigon regime had frequently adjusted its administrative units over the years. In some cases, entirely new provinces and districts had been created, while others were renamed or had their borders revised. This was usually done to make the situation in the countryside look better than it really was by using administrative sleight of hand either to segregate NLF-dominated areas from more secure ones or to gerrymander them out of existence.

The NLF's basic building block was at the village level, where there was another administrative committee and a series of Liberation Associations organized by the VCI. These were the most vital elements in the NLF's entire organizational structure because they allowed it to communicate with and exercise social control over the population. They formed "the village base for the entire insurgency" and included separate Liberation Associations for farmers, women, workers, youth, students, and intellectuals. In villages that were controlled or strongly influenced by the NLF, membership in a Functional Liberation Association was mandatory, although in theory, participation was voluntary. As a channel of communication, the Functional Liberation Associations permitted the NLF to tailor its ideological and social reform messages to suit the specific audience. Therefore, "for the farmer . . . the Farmers' Liberation Association meant land reform; for the village women the Women's Liberation Association meant status and more equal rights with men."[58] The Liberation Associations were also the instruments through which the NLF carried out its political offensive and supported its military units. Members participated in political demonstrations or propaganda directed at the GVN, incited ARVN personnel to desert, and collected food, money, medicines, and intelligence for the NLF's military units. They also participated more directly in the military struggle by acting as supply, weapons, and casualty bearers; constructing fortifications and planting booby traps; and serving as a reservoir of recruits. They were, in effect, a *levée en masse*.

The Liberation Army consisted of the guerrillas (or Popular Army), the Regional Forces, and the Main Forces. Typically, a handful of guerrillas could be found in each hamlet, and a small platoon at the village level. The guerrillas operated only in their own villages and were usually assigned nothing more strenuous than harassment duties (sniping, sabotage, and mine laying), although they also acted as guides and outpost guards for Regional and Main Force units. "Here was the part-time guerrilla, the type the world knew best, who would peacefully plow his field by day and dynamite bridges by night. Rural Vietnamese regarded the . . . [guerrillas] as local and civilian, not as outsider or soldier—both important distinctions in Vietnam."[59] The Regional Forces and Main Forces both consisted of full-time regular troops, but their structure and missions differed. The Regional Forces were generally organized into independent companies at the district level and independent battalions at the province level, while the Main Forces comprised a large number of independent regiments and as many as five full-strength divisions. A Regional Force unit restricted its operations to a particular district or province and received its orders from the corresponding NLF administrative committee, rather than through the military chain of command. The Main Forces could operate anywhere within South Vietnam and took their orders directly from the NLF's Central Committee.

The regular NVA units infiltrated into South Vietnam were organized and equipped exactly like the NLF's regular units. However, when Operation Washington Green began, there were almost no NVA troops in northern

South Vietnam: Communist Administrative Areas. *Source:* George L. MacGarrigle, *Combat Operations: Taking the Offensive, October 1966 to October 1977 (The United States Army in Vietnam Series)* (Washington, DC: US Army Center of Military History, 1998), CMH Pub 94-1, Map 2, 20. [Reprinted by permission of the US Army Center of Military History]

Table 3.1 Estimated Vietcong Forces in AO Lee, 15 April 1969

Force	Strength
Provincial	
X-503 Local Force Battalion	200
Tam Quan District	
D-35 Sapper Company	27
D-40 Sapper Company	80
Village and hamlet guerrillas	765
Identified VCI	44
Unidentified VCI (minimum)	44
Hoai Nhon District	
D-21 District Force Company	85
Village and hamlet guerrillas	617
Identified VCI	322
Unidentified VCI (minimum)	575
Hoai An District	
D-22 District Force Company	85
Village and hamlet guerrillas	158
Identified VCI	125
Unidentified VCI (minimum)	275
Phu My District	
Phu My District Force Battalion	190
D-23 District Force Company	95
Village and hamlet guerrillas	623
Identified VCI	964
Unidentified VCI (minimum)	90
Totals	
Regulars	762
Guerrillas	2,163
Identified VCI	1,455
Unidentified VCI (far too low)	984
Grand total	5,364

Source: 173rd Airborne Brigade, Operation Order 3-69, Washington Green, 10 April 1969, annex B, appendix 3, National Archives Records Group 472, 173rd Airborne Brigade files, S-3 Command Reports box 3.

Binh Dinh. The only NVA combat units in the province were the independent 95B Regiment and the 18th Regiment of the 3rd NVA Yellow Star Division, and they were operating farther south. The former had been tasked with interdicting allied convoy traffic on the section of Highway 19 west of An Khe since 1967.[60] On South Vietnamese and American maps, An Khe was located in Binh Dinh's westernmost district, An Tuc, which had been grafted onto the province during the Diem administration. However, the NLF continued to use the old boundaries, according to which An Tuc was part of Gia Lai (the original name for Pleiku Province). The NLF also employed the old interprovincial border as the boundary between its B-1 Front (successor to *Liên-Khu* 5) and B-3 Front, which embraced most of the Central Highlands. The 95B Regiment was subordinated to the B-3 Front and thus did not become involved in the struggle for Binh Dinh's coastal plains because that would have meant moving it into an entirely different theater of operations.[61]

The 18th NVA Regiment, in contrast, had frequently operated in northern Binh Dinh. That was where it, along with the rest of the Yellow Star Division, had contested the 1st Cavalry Division's clearing operations of 1966–1967. But in the closing months of 1968, the regiment deployed southward into Binh Khe district, where it too began interdicting Highway 19, and it remained committed to that mission throughout 1969. For the moment, the only NVA troops actually in AO Lee were the 335 men of the 500th Transportation Battalion, a logistical support unit of the 3rd NVA Division that operated in the An Lao Valley, storing and transporting rice and other supplies to the main body of the division in Quang Ngai Province to the north.[62]

In the absence of both NVA and VC Main Force units, the burden of resisting Operation Washington Green would fall primarily on the Regional Forces, which comprised Local Force units controlled by the NLF's provincial committee and District Force units subordinated to its district committees. Both consisted of highly skilled, full-time regular troops who were well armed with modern automatic weapons, mortars, and B-40 rocket launchers. The only real difference between the two was that Local Force units could be deployed anywhere in the province, while District Force units almost never left the boundaries of their home district.

In April 1969 each northern district had at least one District Force company, while Phu My also had a District Force battalion, a highly unusual situation that demonstrated the insurgency's unparalleled strength there. At the time, Binh Dinh also had five Local Force battalions, but only one of them, the X-503 (formerly XC-11) Battalion, was in AO Lee. The 50th and E210 Local Force Battalions and the 36th and 300th Sapper Battalions were all deployed in Binh Dinh's southern districts and remained there throughout

Operation Washington Green. Allied intelligence estimated that the X-503 Battalion had between 200 and 260 men organized into four companies. This strength hardly warranted the title "battalion," but compared with other Local Force units, the X-503 was well off. Both the 50th Local Force and 36th Sapper Battalions were listed as combat ineffective, with estimated strengths of 50 and 25, respectively; the E210 and 300th Sapper were believed to have approximately 150 apiece.[63]

The Regional Force units' low strengths are indicative of the price the NLF paid for its stubborn adherence to the general offensive–general uprising strategy. But the impression of impotence suggested by these numbers is misleading. First, most of them were based on data that were at least several months old. For example, the estimate for the X-503 Battalion was based on documents from November 1968.[64] Because the battalion had not been identified in combat since January, this meant it had had almost three months to recruit replacements locally or receive them by infiltration from North Vietnam, before Washington Green began. Second, although allied units had much higher ration strengths, they could not use all their manpower offensively; because of the need to protect headquarters, logistical support facilities, and lines of communication, large numbers of troops had to be kept on garrison duty. Finally, Vietcong units consisted almost entirely of combat troops, because the VCI mobilized civilians to perform the functions of specialized logistical, transportation, engineering, intelligence, maintenance, and recruiting units in the allied armies. But although the Regional Forces were not as weak as they seemed at first glance, what really mattered was that they were nowhere near strong enough to maintain the "umbrella of security" for the insurgency in northern Binh Dinh against the four American and eight ARVN battalions that were about to move into the area. The NLF's liberated zones were accordingly ripe for the picking, and US and South Vietnamese troops could safely be dispersed throughout them without fear of being overrun by superior enemy forces.

However, the true measure of the insurgency's strength in AO Lee was the unusually large number of VCI in the area. Allied intelligence estimated there were 2,439 identified and unidentified VCI present in April 1969—about 3.5 percent of the national total. Yet even that figure was certainly too low. Tam Quan was credited with just 88 VCI, even though three-quarters of its 91,000 inhabitants lived in NLF-controlled communities.[65] One is tempted to conclude that these figures were obtained simply by assuming that each of the district's forty-four hamlets had one identified and one unidentified VCI, since the totals are absurd, given the large number of guerrillas in the district. In Hoai Nhon, the ratio of VCI to guerrillas was 1.45 to 1; in Phu My, 1.7 to 1; and in Hoai An, 2.5 to 1. In Tam Quan, the ratio was supposedly only 0.11 to 1. Even if the lowest of the other ratios were applied, Tam Quan would have had more than a thousand VCI.

The US Order of Battle

The 173rd Airborne Brigade's order of battle as of April 1969 is detailed in table 3.2, but its composition would change significantly during Operation Washington Green as units were attached and detached. The 3/503rd is not listed because it had been serving with Task Force South since July 1968.[66]

In addition to those listed in the table and discussed elsewhere in this book, many other US Army units operated in direct or general support of the brigade at various times during Operation Washington Green. These included aviation companies equipped with UH-1 "Huey" utility, CH-47 "Chinook" medium, and CH-54 "Tarhe" heavy helicopters, as well as two fixed-wing aircraft companies that flew Cessna O-1G "Bird Dog" forward observer planes. The brigade would also be supported by a variety of artillery batteries armed with weaponry ranging from towed 105mm and 155mm howitzers to 175mm and 8-inch (203mm) self-propelled guns and M-42 "Duster" twin automatic 40mm self-propelled antiaircraft guns used in the antipersonnel role.[67]

The 173rd Airborne Brigade was only one element of a two-pronged American presence in Binh Dinh. The other consisted of American CORDS advisory personnel serving in Provincial Advisory Team 42. Although CORDS was a joint military-civilian organization, US military personnel filled most of the slots in Team 42—a reflection of the overall character of CORDS, which, at its peak strength in late 1969, had 6,500 military and 1,100 civilian personnel.[68] Yet civilians often occupied senior positions in the team. When Operation Washington Green began, Team 42 was headed by province senior advisor (PSA) Chalmers Wood, a civilian Foreign Service officer.[69] He had the dual mission of advising the GVN province chief and overseeing dozens of US advisory personnel who came under his command. Of these, many were found at the provincial level, working with their GVN counterparts in functional areas of pacification such as public health, agriculture, civil affairs, education, and psychological warfare. Yet it was in the security (military) aspect of the pacification effort that the advisors had their greatest influence, because it was chiefly through them that the South Vietnamese gained access to American air and artillery fire support, helicopter transport, medical evacuation, and logistics. Advisors also had to act as intermediaries between GVN authorities and the commanders and staffs of US military units operating in the area, coordinating operations, avoiding friendly fire incidents (always a problem when many small patrols and ambushes were

Table 3.2 Composition of 173rd Airborne Brigade, 30 April 1969

Unit	Comments
173rd Headquarters and Headquarters Company	
1st Battalion, 503rd Infantry (Airborne)	920 men (optimal, never achieved in practice)
2nd Battalion, 503rd Infantry (Airborne)	920 men (optimal, never achieved in practice)
4th Battalion, 503rd Infantry (Airborne)	920 men (optimal, never achieved in practice)
1st Battalion, 50th Infantry (Mechanized)	M-113 armored cavalry assault vehicles, 4 M-106 4.2-inch mortar tracks
Troop E, 17th Cavalry (Airborne)	Jeeps with 106mm recoilless rifles and .50-caliber machine guns
3rd Battalion, 319th Artillery (Airborne)	24 M-102 towed 105mm howitzers
Troop C, 7th Squadron, 17th Cavalry (Air Cavalry)	Aerorifle Platoon, 8 UH-1 utility helicopters, 9 AH-1 attack helicopters, 9 OH-6 scout helicopters
Company C, 75th Infantry (Ranger)	Ex–Company E, 20th Infantry (Long-Range Patrol)
Company N, 75th Infantry (Ranger)	Ex–74th Infantry Detachment (Long-Range Patrol)
173rd Engineer Company	
75th Infantry Detachment (Combat Tracker)	Scout Dogs
39th Infantry Platoon (Scout Dog)	
173rd Signal Company	
172nd Military Intelligence Detachment	
628th Military Intelligence Detachment	Order of Battle Intelligence
404th Radio Reconnaissance Unit	Army Security Agency
54th Ground Surveillance Radar Detachment	
51st Chemical Detachment	
24th Military History Detachment	
13th Tactical Air Control Party	US Air Force
ARVN Liaison Detachment	
173rd Support Battalion	Based outside Qui Nhon

(continued on next page)

Table 3.2 (continued)

Unit	Comments
Company A (Administration)	Based outside Qui Nhon
Company B (Medical)	Based outside Qui Nhon
Company C (Service and Support)	Based outside Qui Nhon
Company D (Maintenance)	Based outside Qui Nhon

Source: 173rd Airborne Brigade, Operational Report on Lessons Learned for the Period Ending 30 April 1969, inclosure 2, John W. Saunders Papers.

active in the same area simultaneously), securing clearance for artillery fire and tactical air missions, and generally trying to reduce the likelihood of interallied friction.[70]

Paralleling the GVN's administrative structure, CORDS's primary operational echelon was located at the district level. A small District Advisory Team worked under the direction of the district senior advisor (DSA), who was usually a US Army or Marine Corps major. In general, a District Advisory Team's missions duplicated those of the CORDS apparatus at the province level, but its role in coordinating tactical operations tended to take precedence over its other functions. Since Operation Washington Green placed large numbers of US troops in close quarters with low-ranking GVN and ARVN personnel, the DSAs and their staffs spent a great deal of their time smoothing out intercultural friction. Each district team also controlled several five-man Mobile Advisory Teams (MATs), twelve of which were operating in AO Lee when Washington Green began. Each MAT was tasked with giving on-the-job training to several RF companies and PF platoons.[71]

Among its many functions, Advisory Team 42 played a key role in efforts to eradicate the VCI. These had long been impeded by the inefficiency of South Vietnam's police and intelligence agencies and their general unwillingness to work together and share information. Therefore, in July 1967 the CIA had launched the Intelligence Coordination and Exploitation (ICEX) program to pool information on the VCI and coordinate military and police operations against it. Although the program was only moderately successful, it gained official GVN sanction in December 1967 and was renamed Phoenix. In July 1968 the South Vietnamese formally took over Phoenix, which was translated as *Phung Hoang*—a mythical bird in Vietnamese folklore. At least in theory, the American role in the program then became a purely advisory one.[72]

Phoenix was managed by a hierarchy of committees radiating outward from the Central Phung Hoang Committee in Saigon, chaired by the GVN's

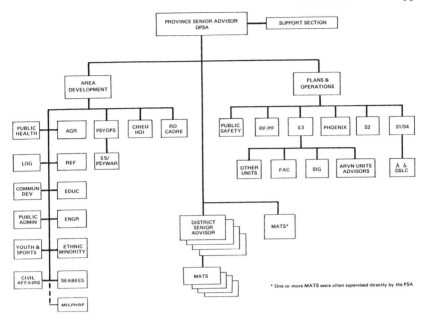

CORDS Provincial Advisory Team Organization. *Source:* Ngo Quang Truong, *RVNAF and US Operational Cooperation and Coordination* (Washington, DC: US Army Center of Military History, 1980), 154. [Reprinted by permission of the US Army Center of Military History]

minister of the interior. Similar committees existed at the military region level and in each of South Vietnam's provinces. However, the program's cutting edge consisted of the Provincial and District Intelligence and Operations Coordination Centers, which brought together officials of the National Police's Special Branch, the Military Security Service, and the Vietnamese Information Service (which had propaganda and psychological warfare missions), as well as representatives from nearly a dozen other pacification programs. Aided by their US Phoenix advisors, they were supposed to assemble and analyze intelligence on the VCI, building up dossiers that would allow specific VCI cadres to be targeted by the NPFF.[73] In reality, the NPFF's shortcomings meant that the program's most effective "action arm" was usually the Provincial Reconnaissance Unit (PRU), a platoon-sized paramilitary unit that was often manned by ex-Vietcong. PRUs first appeared in 1964 when the CIA took over and renamed the provocatively titled Counter Terror Teams created during the Diem administration.[74] The CIA covertly retained control of the US Phoenix advisory apparatus until July 1969, when full managerial authority was turned over to CORDS. It would not fully relinquish control of the PRUs until November 1972.[75]

The Phoenix program has long been one of the most hotly debated aspects of the Vietnam War, with many alleging that it was nothing but an assassination campaign. Although these claims are not entirely baseless, especially insofar as the CIA-controlled PRUs are concerned, Phoenix's dominant feature was an effort to get various South Vietnamese intelligence agencies to share data on and coordinate operations against the VCI. In Binh Dinh, the program was still in its formative phase when Washington Green began, and some of the District Intelligence and Operations Coordination Centers had yet to be established. Throughout the operation, US Phoenix advisors would struggle with uncooperative GVN agencies just to get the program's bare essentials up and running. It was therefore incapable of conducting a bloody purge of the province's VCI.

CHAPTER FOUR

Growing Dependency

There was a palpable sense of excitement in Advisory Team 42's monthly report for April 1969. Acting PSA Lieutenant Colonel Gordon Green wrote: "The 'One War' concept is in full swing. Security is now provided full time to hamlets that have been under VC control for years. Hamlet Chiefs have not only visited, but are now living in hamlets where they have not dared, in the past, to make their presence known. Refugees are asking when they can return to their ancestral homes. The overall attitude is that of confidence."[1]

The most immediate practical benefit of Operation Washington Green had been the release of twelve RF companies and fifteen PF platoons that had been guarding roads and bridges, but the psychological impact of the Sky Soldiers' commitment in direct support of pacification was even more important. The mere presence of US troops training and conducting joint operations with the Territorial Forces on a daily basis had a galvanizing effect that boosted their morale and emboldened them to become more aggressive. The province chief, Lieutenant Colonel Tho, was so encouraged that he added the partial resettlement of nine abandoned villages to Binh Dinh's already ambitious 1969 pacification campaign. Colonel Green was less enthusiastic because he feared this move could lead to overextension, but if the province was going to "secure" 90 percent of its population and resettle its unusually large refugee population by year's end, there was no choice but to push pacification at a breakneck pace. The original Washington Green plan included just eleven hamlets in phase I (15 April–30 June) and thirty-one in phase II (1 July–31 December), but the number of phase I hamlets was soon expanded to twenty-three, and in Hoai Nhon the starting date for phase II was advanced to 1 June.[2]

This rapid expansion was made possible by light opposition. Although the enemy's Z Offensive continued into the last week of April, no high point occurred during the month, enemy-initiated incidents fell sharply, and sapper attacks were conspicuously absent. The Vietcong were able to commandeer little of the April rice harvest, leading to severe food shortages; according to captured documents, the enemy had to release some Vietnamese prisoners that could no longer be fed. Binh Dinh nonetheless experienced more enemy activity in April than any other province in II Corps. Its 193 enemy-initiated

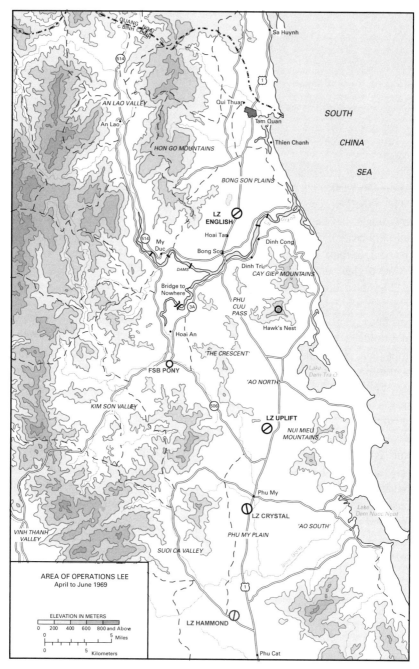

Area of Operations Lee (April–June 1969). *Source:* George L. MacGarrigle, *Combat Operations: Taking the Offensive, October 1966 to October 1977 (The United States Army in Vietnam Series)* (Washington, DC: US Army Center of Military History, 1998), CMH Pub 94-1, Map 32, p. 317. [Adapted and reprinted by permission of the US Army Center of Military History]

incidents were more than three times the next highest tally, and it also topped the list of enemy incidents in six of the seven categories tracked. Still, the 39 ground attacks and 13 attacks-by-fire accounted for just over a quarter of the total. The rest fell overwhelmingly into the "sniping and ambush" and "mines and booby traps" categories, highlighting the enemy's nonconfrontational tactics.[3]

This decline in enemy activity represented a lull between the Communists' winter-spring campaign and their upcoming summer campaign. During the intermission, the Vietcong and NVA made good their losses and were indoctrinated in a new strategy that COSVN had recently disseminated in Directives 81 and 88. Its most striking feature was that it abandoned the objective of decisive victory, which had been an article of faith in the Communist camp since 1967. Resolution 8 had anticipated this development by introducing the concept of a decisive victory achieved in two stages—a long preparatory stage, followed by a general offensive stage. But there was no mention of decisive victory whatsoever in Directives 81 and 88, which instead foresaw victory being achieved by political means.[4] The first step would be the withdrawal of all US troops from South Vietnam and the establishment of a coalition government embracing the NLF and neutralist parties opposed to the Thieu regime. Final victory would be achieved when the Communists attained a dominant position in the coalition government following national elections and the drafting of a new constitution. Accordingly, at the Paris peace talks in May, the NLF contingent introduced a ten-point peace proposal that called for the withdrawal of US troops, the formation of a provisional coalition government including NLF representatives, the holding of national elections, and ultimately the creation of a government of national reconciliation that would draft a new constitution. In June the Provisional Revolutionary Government (PRG) was established to lend substance to the NLF's claim that it was the legitimate representative of the South Vietnamese people and place it on an equal footing with the GVN in Paris. The PRG was quickly recognized by most Communist-bloc nations.

Just days after the NLF "peace offensive" began in Paris, the Communists launched the summer campaign's first high point on the night of 11–12 May. The new offensive was supposed to energize antiwar sentiment in the United States and end Nixon's "honeymoon period."[5] But COSVN knew that earlier campaigns' failure to achieve the promised decisive results had eroded its troops' morale and caused some of them to question the advisability of mounting further offensives. "[Some personnel] lost confidence in the higher echelon leadership and in the revolutionary capacity of the people. They think that our assessment of enemy capabilities is inaccurate, our strategic determination is erroneous and we will have to lower our [offen-

Table 4.1 Comparison of Enemy Offensives at the End of Their Fourth Day

Statistic	Tet 1968	May 1968	Aug. 1968	Feb. 1969	May 1969	Jun. 1969
Attacks-by-fire	268	433	95	546	539	407
Ground attacks (total)	104	52	15	125	98	60
Ground attacks (battalion or larger)	29	6	2	16	5	7
Total artillery shells fired	4,764	10,777	3,382	8,587	9,098	5,230
Enemy killed	8,417	5,120	2,610	5,361	3,806	3,543
Friendly killed	983	840	352	791	632	500

Source: Abrams MAC 7391 to Admiral McCain, General Wheeler, and Ambassador Bunker, Updated Analysis of the Enemy's So-called June "High Point," 2–3, General Creighton Abrams Messages files, Historical Records Branch, US Army Center of Military History, Fort McNair, Washington, DC.

sive] requirements and protract the war. They become doubtful of victory, pessimistic, and display a shirking attitude. Their combat determination decreases."[6]

COSVN accordingly warned against expecting too much from the peace talks and stressed that the summer campaign would be merely one step of many on the road to final victory. It also counseled caution: "Never again and under no circumstances should we risk our entire force in one attack, but instead we should preserve our combat potential for sustained action in the future."[7] Throughout the summer campaign, enemy troops therefore sought to limit their casualties by conducting standoff attacks-by-fire instead of costly ground assaults.

Communist offensive activity in Binh Dinh during May was generally limited to harassing attacks, mine and booby trap incidents, and attacks-by-fire. The only ground assaults launched in greater than company strength occurred on Highway 19, where the 18th and 95B NVA Regiments continued to attack convoys traveling to and from the Central Highlands.[8] When another high point followed in June, Binh Dinh again witnessed more Communist offensive activity than any other province in II Corps, but pacification was set back only in Phu Cat district, where the temporary absence of ROK combat units allowed the Vietcong to penetrate several GVN-controlled hamlets and burn 563 homes. On the night of 18 June they launched a mortar attack on Phu Cat air base and killed eighteen PF and PSDF soldiers at the hamlet of Thai Phu.[9] On the whole, the May and June high points had little impact in AO Lee and caused few American casualties, since the enemy was assiduously avoiding contact with US troops. Just thirty-five Sky Soldiers were killed in the first three months of Washington Green combined.[10]

Tam Quan

Since the four districts in AO Lee were all unique, the first phase of Operation Washington Green is addressed separately for each of them in the following pages. Tam Quan was by far the worst of the lot. On the January 1969 HES map, it appears as a dense cluster of Vs surrounding a solitary D representing the tenuous GVN enclave around the district seat. By the end of March, the situation had improved only slightly: the D had been replaced by a C, and a string of Es now snaked through the district from north to south, following the trace of Highway 1. This situation was nothing new. As General Barnes explained, "Except for a strip some 500 meters or so on each side of Highway 1, all of this district has been under communist control since the end of World War II."[11] Ironically, although Tam Quan had been dominated by the Communists for decades, the district itself had been created only in December 1968. Before that, its six villages had been part of Hoai Nhon. Since GVN bureaucrats resisted being posted in "Indian country," Tam Quan became a dumping ground for inept officials who frequently absented themselves from their hazardous posts. One of the worst offenders was the district chief, Captain Nguyen Huu Tai, whose all-too-frequent absences caused both US advisors and GVN commanders to recommend his replacement.[12]

Tam Quan and portions of Hoai Nhon occupied a fertile lowland region known as the Bong Son Plains (named after Hoai Nhon's district seat). It was the most densely populated part of northern Binh Dinh, with nearly 200,000 people crammed into an area barely fifteen miles long by seven miles wide. This population density would not have been remarkable in an urban setting, but this was a rural area where practically the entire population was engaged in agriculture. There were simply too many people competing for too little farmland, and there was no frontier or urban economy to act as a safety valve for the growing population. This was the cause of the grinding poverty and economic distress that Douglas Pike found in Binh Dinh, and it explains the strong appeal of the NLF's redistributive economic policies.

Responsibility for the Bong Son Plains was divided between US and ARVN units. Lieutenant Colonel Dean F. Schnoor's 4th Battalion, 503rd Infantry (Airborne), and the attached Company C (–), 1/50th Infantry (Mechanized), secured four of Tam Quan's six villages, plus bridges and checkpoints along Highway 1. The 40th ARVN Regiment was to secure the remaining two villages and an adjoining portion of Hoai Nhon, but it showed little enthusiasm for pacification duty and still had not occupied any of its target hamlets by the end of April.[13] The DSA, Major Wilmot T. Riley, explained that the ARVN troops failed "to really get involved in the pacification program because they feel it is beneath their dignity."[14] Schnoor was also unenthusiastic about certain features of his new mission. Although his headquarters was supposed to be colocated with the GVN district headquarters, Schnoor kept it separate, and the 4/503rd's high-handed behavior antagonized both the local GVN leadership and the US District Advisory Team. "Ill will between the district advisory personnel and the 503d Inf exist because of the 503d's penchant for things to be done typically American. According to all the team members, the 503d makes little effort at this time to coordinate with the district. A great deal of the DSA's time is spent smoothing over all the consternation caused by the 503d."[15] The 4/503rd feared that operational security would be compromised by collaboration with the South Vietnamese, whose ranks were riddled with enemy agents; they were also notorious for their poor radio discipline—often broadcasting critical information "in the clear."[16]

Onofre C. Espanol, a Filipino national serving as Binh Dinh's Chieu Hoi advisor, believed that cultural insensitivity was also to blame for poor interallied cooperation:

> Mr. Espanol stated that he was an Oriental. He said that he "is one of them" and "feels it when he deals with the Vietnamese people." . . . Americans should remember that the US and Asiatic approaches to a problem differ . . . westerners are not much for the social amenities when they meet Vietnamese; they get "right down to business" and go "straight to the point." On the other hand, when he deals with the Vietnamese and when Asians deal with each other, they spend a great deal of time on social amenities, "making the purpose of their visit known only at the end of the audience." Abrupt and rash treatment are not appreciated anywhere, least of all in the Orient.[17]

There were few instances of deliberate maltreatment, but the Sky Soldiers often inadvertently offended the locals due to their ignorance of the language and culture. Major Riley accordingly recommended that they not be allowed to mix with the locals, but that was impossible to prevent because the 4/503rd was constantly conducting integrated operations with the 217th and 540th RF Companies, which had been placed under its operational control. In June it assumed operational control of a third RF company, and its five-man STAGs began training the PSDF.[18] The 4/503rd also worked closely with Tam Quan's NPFF platoon, which had just doubled in size with personnel transferred from Tuy Phuoc and Binh Khe districts—leaving them without any NPFF at all. The 4/503rd used the field police officers as the search element in its cordon-and-search operations and to establish a combined resources control checkpoint on Highway 1. By June, eighteen NPFF members were permanently conducting combined operations with the battalion, rotating through the six target hamlets in a seven-day cycle. All this stood in sharp contrast to their previous habit of sitting out the war in the comparative safety of the district seat.[19]

Yet the 4/503rd's presence had no positive effect on Tam Quan's RD Cadre Teams, which had been reinforced with nine teams shifted from the southern districts. Indeed, the performance of RD cadres throughout AO Lee was almost universally abysmal during phase I. Advisory Team 42 reported, "Attrition [i.e., desertion] among the teams in Tam Quan, Hoai Nhon and Hoai An continues to be excessive. They are accomplishing little or no developmental work. In many areas the teams are doing little more than providing security for themselves. Some teams are not staying in their hamlets at night, and some are difficult to find in the day."[20]

The problem was that "fast and thin" pacification required the RD teams to be thrust into highly insecure areas where most of the local population was traditionally hostile to the Saigon regime. Such was the case in Tam Quan, where the RD Cadre Teams' efforts to conscript unwilling villagers into the PSDF militia prompted some to take to the hills to join their friends and relatives serving with the Vietcong. Thirty-two new (and still unarmed) PSDF recruits deserted on 26 May, and thirty more were abducted by the Vietcong in two separate incidents three days later.[21] Conditions were not quite as bad in the other three districts, but RD cadre morale and performance remained poor across the board. PSA Wood observed: "There continue to be many desertions, sometimes by entire teams. Attempts to punish deserters seem to be futile. At one time the threat of placing the deserters in RF/PF or ARVN was effective. Now the cadres indicate they would prefer to be in the better-equipped military units, since they are performing the same duties."[22]

Although Tam Quan held the largest concentration of Vietcong in AO Lee, enemy activity during phase I was limited to sniping, attacks-by-fire, and a few sapper raids. The 4/503rd mounted no large-scale operations either; instead, it conducted an endless cycle of static night ambushes, mobile Hawk Team patrols, and cordon-and-search missions. Opposition was minimal, as the Vietcong were rarely encountered in greater than squad strength and invariably tried to break contact. But Tam Quan remained a very dangerous place because of the mines and booby traps infesting the district. Only seven of the forty-one Sky Soldiers wounded there during phase I had gunshot wounds. Almost all the others suffered fragmentation wounds to the legs and lower body—the signature of mines and booby traps.[23] Practically all of the 4/503rd's thirteen phase I fatalities (almost as many as the rest of the brigade combined) had the same cause. On 19 April a booby-trapped 155mm artillery shell killed five men outright and fatally wounded another.[24] Thus, with every step they took, the battalion's troops had to confront the possibility of injury or sudden death. Lieutenant James R. McDonough, who served in Tam Quan during 1970, explained:

> The gruesome toll of the booby traps wore on our nerves. No matter how many we found, we knew there were others out there waiting for a misstep. The terror built. It is one thing to rush an enemy in battle and take your chances in the face of his firepower. The experience is frightening, but the momentum of the act compels you forward, sparing you the agony of considering your predicament. Thinking your way through a booby-trapped area is a completely different experience, and much more harrowing.[25]

In exchange for its own losses during phase I, the 4/503rd killed only twenty-six enemy troops and captured six more, for a disappointingly low loss ratio of just 2 to 1. Tam Quan's RF/PF fared even worse, with twenty-nine men killed, thirty-three wounded, and twenty weapons lost in April and May, while enemy losses totaled only nine killed and five weapons captured.[26] Progress was nonetheless being made in Tam Quan. The local economy benefited from a marked decline in mining and sniping along Highway 1, which began immediately after the 4/503rd assumed responsibility for securing the roadway. By the end of phase I, significant progress had also been made in establishing security in the countryside, and many refugees from the sprawling camps around Bong Son and Qui Nhon began returning to their ancestral homes.[27]

One success was Qui Thuan hamlet, whose Catholic population had fled to Qui Nhon several years before. The fact that Qui Thuan was a suburb of the district seat (just 400 yards separated the two) demonstrates just how insecure Tam Quan had been. When the parish priest learned that allied troops had occupied the hamlet and planned to stay indefinitely, he informed them that the entire population of 6,000 would move back if the church was repaired. Its reconstruction soon started with a combination of US and GVN material assistance, and within a month, most of hamlet's population had returned, with the rest close behind.[28] The population of Thien Chanh hamlet similarly grew from 42 to almost 2,000 in the first three months of Operation Washington Green. This fishing community had been abandoned in 1966 after the GVN prohibited fishing within three kilometers of the coast in order to halt seaborne smuggling from North Vietnam. The population started flooding back after the 4/503rd secured the hamlet and found a way to circumvent the fishing restrictions: a patrol boat escorted fishing craft out beyond the three-kilometer line each morning and then back in the evening. The catch was not as large as it might have been, however, since the locals' nets were designed for shallow waters close to shore. The GVN district and province chiefs both urged that the restrictions be lifted altogether, but only the Joint General Staff in Saigon could grant approval, and it moved very slowly despite a stream of entreaties from Advisory Team 42.[29]

Bureaucratic inertia also stymied progress in creating elected village governments, which played a key role in the Village Self-Development (VSD) program. VSD was intended to boost the economy, establish grassroots democracy, and foster a closer relationship between the GVN and the rural population by giving each village a budget of 1 million piasters to spend on economic development projects selected by the villagers themselves. Elections were held in all of Tam Quan's hamlets during phase I, but provincial authorities moved at a glacial pace when it came to confirming the newly elected officials. At the end of May, three village and nine hamlet governments were still awaiting recognition and could not receive their VSD budgets or even begin processing project proposals until that happened. Thus, a key component of the pacification effort was sidetracked at the very moment it was supposed to be impressing villagers with the GVN's determination to improve their lives.[30] Indeed, there seemed to be a "two steps forward, one step back" quality to most of phase I's accomplishments in Tam Quan. Nothing illustrates this better than the locals' response to the Voluntary Informant Program (VIP), which offered cash rewards for information about enemy activity and for turning in weapons and explosives. Many locals wanted the ubiquitous mines and booby traps removed, but few were willing to point them out. Instead, the devices were sometimes dragged into the middle of trails where the allied troops could easily find and disarm them, but nobody came forward to claim the reward.[31]

Hoai Nhon

Like Tam Quan, Hoai Nhon encompassed parts of the densely populated Bong Son Plains, but it also had a rugged backcountry inhabited only by enemy base camps, training facilities, hospitals, and supply caches. These were concentrated around the narrow An Lao Valley, which had been forcibly evacuated by the 1st Cavalry in 1967 and designated a free-fire zone where targets could be engaged at will. A short distance to the southwest lay Base Area 226, another extensive complex of fortified enemy cantonments and training and logistical facilities. Prior to Operation Washington Green, the 173rd Airborne Brigade and 22nd ARVN Division had operated almost constantly in these two areas, but now that all their maneuver battalions had been committed to the direct support of pacification, the task of keeping them under observation fell to the brigade's reconnaissance assets: Companies C and N, 75th Infantry (Ranger), and Troop C, 7/17th Air Cavalry. The Air Cavalry troop made low-level visual reconnaissance flights with its scout helicopters to spot enemy soldiers or draw their fire. When contact was made, the troop's aerorifle (infantry) platoon, backed up by the heavy firepower of the aeroweapons platoon's AH-1 Cobra attack helicopters, would be inserted.[32]

The two Ranger companies specialized in long-range reconnaissance patrols, sending teams of ten men or fewer to scout enemy base areas and infiltration routes for up to six days at a time. They were usually inserted by helicopter, using last-light landings, ground-hugging flight patterns, and false insertions to prevent enemy observers from fixing their positions. These teams were generally given surveillance missions and ordered not to engage enemy forces except in self-defense, but a significant number of Hawk and prisoner of war (POW) snatch missions were also conducted. Whenever possible, patrol areas were chosen on the basis of "hard" intelligence provided by informants and enemy deserters and POWs, but the paucity of such data required greater reliance on technological alternatives such as "Red Haze" aerial infrared photography and aerial personnel detector ("people-sniffer") reconnaissance flights (although the latter were largely neutralized by the enemy's tactic of placing cans of urine throughout the area). Yet, even in the absence of enemy Main Force units, the sheer volume of hostile activity in the mountains was such that the Rangers had little trouble finding the enemy. Company N spotted hostile personnel on fifty-two of fifty-six missions in April, killing eighteen enemy troops and capturing nine, while its own casualties amounted to just one wounded.[33]

The Air Cavalry and Rangers were supplemented by a series of "Red Thrust" artillery raids conducted by the 3rd Battalion, 319th Artillery (Airborne). These operations airlifted a pair of 105mm howitzers onto one of the many isolated hilltops overlooking the An Lao Valley while Rangers and "Red Raider" forward observer teams (created by the 3/319th because there were too few Rangers available) fanned out into the surrounding area. The howitzers would fire at any personnel and installations observed by the Rangers, Red Raiders, aircraft, or gun crews themselves. Only a single platoon of infantry was provided for ground defense, since the raiding force generally remained in place for only a single day—not long enough for the enemy to plan and execute a counterattack. Five Red Thrust operations took place between 19 March and 2 May and were moderately successful, sometimes catching enemy troops off guard because they believed they were beyond allied artillery range.[34] However, Red Thrust VI turned into a fiasco on 10 May when a brush fire broke out in the high grass covering the hill occupied by Battery D, 3/319th. Driven by high winds, the fire quickly swept over the position, damaging both howitzers and setting off the ready ammunition. All personnel—including three seriously wounded—were evacuated by helicopter, but the guns were not recovered until the following day due to the danger posed by exploding ammunition. The battery commander reported: "The fire that swept the howitzer position was suspected to be purposely set by VC who infiltrated the ARVN security platoon. Although 2 ARVN personnel were observed throwing ignited trip flares into the grass at the base of the hill, no conclusive evidence could be found."[35]

While enemy activity in Hoai Nhon's uplands was held in check, Lieutenant Colonel Lawrence E. Zimmerman's 2nd Battalion, 503rd Infantry (Airborne), and elements of the 40th ARVN Regiment secured the rest of the district. It was divided by the broad Lai Giang River, which marked the southern limit of the Bong Son Plains. Just to the north of where Highway 1 crossed the river on a highly strategic bridge lay Bong Son itself. Although it was not a city per se, Bong Son's half dozen hamlets merged to form a sprawling mass of buildings covering an area as much as two miles long. It was the largest population concentration in northern Binh Dinh, including 50,000 refugees.[36] Just a mile north was LZ English, headquarters and principal base of the 173rd Airborne Brigade. Most of Hoai Nhon's A, B, and C hamlets were located either in Bong Son itself or in Hoai Tan village, which lay just to the north along Highway 1. All the other hamlets north of the Lai Giang were either Vietcong controlled or uninhabited. The area south of the river was less thickly populated because the Cay Giep Mountains, which towered nearly 2,000 feet above the plains, covered almost the entire area stretching southward from the Lai Giang's right bank to Phu My and westward from the coast to Highway 1. The few hamlets in this area were either perched in narrow, level spaces between the riverbank and the northern slopes of the mountains or clustered along Highway 1 where it ran down a narrow valley to Phu Cuu Pass—which marked the boundary with Phu My.

The 2/503rd's area of operations covered the entire region south of the Lai Giang, plus Bong Son and the area immediately west of it on the northern bank. Lieutenant Colonel Zimmerman used one rifle company to defend LZ English while another, supported by the attached 2nd Platoon, C/1/50th Mechanized Infantry, relieved the RF and PF units that had been securing Highway 1. The two remaining companies moved into the three phase I target hamlets in concert with RF and PF units that had been placed under

Looking Eastward toward 2/503rd AO. *Source:* "Coming home with Bong Son bridge in the background. [Photograph]," Virtual Vietnam Archive, Item VA009588, accessed December 17, 2015, http://www.virtualarchive.vietnam.ttu.

the battalion's operational control. Company B secured Dinh Tri and Dinh Cong hamlets on the southern bank of the river east of Bong Son, while Company C moved into My Duc, a deserted hamlet that sat in the mouth of the An Lao Valley. Unlike Lieutenant Colonel Schnoor in Tam Quan, Zimmerman colocated his command post with the district headquarters at Bong Son and achieved "outstanding" cooperation with his GVN counterparts. Unfortunately, the 40th ARVN Regiment kept its headquarters elsewhere, and operational coordination suffered accordingly.[37]

Still, all was not well with US–South Vietnamese relations in Hoai Nhon. In early June John S. Figueira, a civilian field evaluator for the CORDS Pacification Studies Group, spent five days in Hoai Tan. He found that the inhabitants harbored considerable animosity toward the 173rd Airborne because of four incidents in which civilians had been killed by the undisciplined fire of its troops. The Sky Soldiers had also been accused of deliberately shooting farm animals. Figueira drew encouragement from the fact that all the shootings had occurred before Washington Green began, but he noted that animosity lingered due to the unconscionably slow pace of compensating the survivors of the shooting victims. Indemnification for private property used or damaged by American troops was also slow; some claims arising from 1st Cavalry Division operations in 1968 were still outstanding. Still, the greatest cause for animosity was the disrespectful behavior of the Sky Soldiers as they passed through the village on Highway 1:

On many occasions troops of the 173rd threw rocks from their trucks at the windshields of Lambrettas (small, three-wheeled automobiles) as they passed. Many windshields were reportedly broken in this fashion—to say nothing of the minor injuries which may have resulted from this type of action. On other occasions the troops would hit at pedestrians with long sticks in an attempt to knock off their "non las" (peasant hats). A village councilman was injured so badly in one of these attempts that it took him a week to get cured. In instances where the 173rd's vehicles forced bicycles and motorcycles off the road, the troops in the vehicles cheered and clapped their hands.[38]

On 10 July 1969 Figueira outlined these problems in a memorandum entitled "Contra-Productive Activities of the 173rd Airborne Brigade," and a copy soon found its way to the desk of General Barnes. He fired a strong protest up the chain of command, touching off a flurry of memoranda between CORDS, MACV, and the 173rd Airborne that ultimately came to the attention of General Abrams himself in August. Looking back on the incident months later, Figueira acerbically noted:

> Brigadier General Barnes was somewhat upset over the report, apparently because it contained no plaudits for his unit. . . . From my own point of view, the memo, as it was presented, was a relatively harmless work which, at most, only sought to point out areas wherein there were possibly some problems existing or developing. In this respect persons concerned with more than just statistical pats on the back would be motivated to do some gainful investigation on their own.[39]

The 2/503rd's operations in Hoai Nhon were an endless drudgery of night ambushes and daytime patrols and cordon-and-search missions, nearly all of them conducted jointly with RF and PF units. As in Tam Quan, opposition was light because the Vietcong avoided contact, and enemy activity in the district declined dramatically during phase I. The only major enemy attack came 17 June, when sappers infiltrated LZ English and, using satchel charges, grenades, and B-40 rocket launchers, destroyed one helicopter, damaged two others, and wounded sixteen Americans. B-40 (Bazooka 40mm) was the NVA's designation for the Soviet RPG-2 rocket-propelled grenade launcher, a powerful and much-feared weapon that was accurate at ranges in excess of 300 yards. The allies had no comparable weapons, since the single-shot, disposable American M-72 LAW (light antitank weapon) carried a much smaller warhead and had an effective range of less than 50 yards.

Former Refugee Rebuilds Home in My Duc. *Source:* "Refugee returns to former home village of My Duc, Binh Dinh Province to find his hut destroyed by VC [Photograph]," Virtual Vietnam Archive, Item VA053684, accessed December 17, 2015, http://www.virtualarchive.vietnam.ttu.edu/starweb/virtual/vva/servlet.

Despite the successful assault on LZ English, enemy morale in Hoai Nhon was on the wane. Just four Vietcong had availed themselves of the Chieu Hoi amnesty program in the first quarter of 1969, but the number rose dramatically once Washington Green began. Forty defected in April alone— thirty-one from a single hamlet whose GVN chief had arranged for the inhabitants to write letters urging their relatives in the Vietcong to surrender. The district's GVN Chieu Hoi chief also deserved credit, as it had been his idea to communicate with the Vietcong through their relatives.[40]

Five of Hoai Nhon's six phase I target hamlets (including in the 40th ARVN Regiment's AO) were on course to achieve a C rating by the end of June. The exception was My Duc, the deserted hamlet in the mouth of the An Lao Valley. Its refugee population refused to return a full month after the 2/503rd had secured the area, although some families daily drove their cattle out to graze in the hamlet from their refugee camp less than two miles away. At first, the problem was thought to be a deep stream that blocked the road to My Duc and would be impassable in the wet monsoon season. The Sky Soldiers constructed a bridge to replace one destroyed years ago, but although growing numbers of refugees came out to graze their cattle after it was completed on 15 May, few were building homes.[41]

It transpired that shortcomings in the GVN's Return-to-Village (RTV) refugee resettlement program were actually to blame. Under RTV, each refugee family that resettled in its native village was given a six-month rice allowance, ten sheets of tin roofing, ten bags of cement, and—after it finished constructing a new home—5,000 piasters in cash. Unfortunately, the cement supply was completely inadequate and threatened to derail both the RTV and VSD programs nationwide. In Binh Dinh, refugees were given additional cash so they could purchase cement themselves, but at the end of May the market price was more than double that on which these payments had been based—and still rising. This was a cause for concern because only a few months of dry weather remained before the onset of the wet monsoon season in October. Once the rains began, nothing could be built with concrete until the spring of 1970. A mere 36,000 bags of cement arrived in Binh Dinh during June—just enough to satisfy the requirements of Qui Nhon city.[42] However, according to Hoai Nhon's DSA, the real problem lay elsewhere: "A bottleneck is beginning to develop concerning distribution of piasters. It appears that most have overcome their doubts about security, but they are still reluctant to leave unless they receive some payment for the rice allowance promised them so they can subsist while rebuilding their homes and planting their fields. However, the current regulations state that they can receive no piasters until they return and begin to construct their homes."[43] It was a classic catch-22. The people had grown cynical after witnessing a chain of broken GVN promises that stretched all the way back to the Strategic Hamlet program of 1962, and they would not resettle until the money due them had been paid. The GVN, for its part, was understandably reluctant to pay benefits before refugees had actually resettled.[44] Advisory Team 42 ultimately concluded that the RTV program would work well only if payments were made in advance, but it is unclear whether this recommendation was ever acted upon.

Hoai Nhon's pacification effort was also impeded by a shortage of RD Cadre Teams. For unspecified reasons, half of the district's dozen teams were abruptly withdrawn in April, before they could complete their tasks in phase I hamlets occupied prior to Washington Green. Without RD cadres, the 1969 goals were unattainable because they were responsible for identifying the local VCI, holding elections, organizing the PSDF militia, and overseeing VSD projects—all of which were necessary for a hamlet to achieve the required C rating.[45] The shortage grew even worse after GVN officials and

Lieutenant Colonel Zimmerman decided to advance phase II by a full month in Hoai Nhon. The DSA, Major Elwood Sutton, protested: "By stretching out military resources somewhat, troops can be made available to secure the areas, but pacification teams are nonexistent. It would be quite impractical to pull any RD teams out of Phase I hamlets because they have only begun many of their tasks."[46] The acceleration of phase II nonetheless went ahead, against Sutton's advice. Since so little had been accomplished before mid-April, phase I had already shrunk from five months to just two and a half. Now, when phase I had been under way in earnest for only a month and a half, Hoai Nhon had to dilute its already inadequate resources even more.

All four of the 2/503rd's rifle companies were deployed in the target hamlets during phase II, and the battalion gradually occupied a chain of communities stretching along the southern bank of the Lai Giang River. Meanwhile, elements of the 173rd Engineer Company built a road to replace the footpath that was the only link to Highway 1. This was Hoai Nhon's top-priority civic action project in phase II, and ultimately, an all-weather road would stretch from the Bong Son bridges all the way to the coast.[47]

During the occupation of one of the new target hamlets, an incident occurred that illustrated just how swiftly the low-intensity war in Hoai Nhon could turn deadly. On 5 June Company A's 3rd Platoon trapped three Vietcong in a tunnel. They surrendered after literally being dug out of their hiding place, but when a bundle of clothes was hauled to the surface, a claymore mine concealed in it detonated, killing one American and two NPFF officers and wounding another thirteen Sky Soldiers. Nearly all of the battalion's phase I casualties (seven killed and seventy-six wounded) had also resulted from mines and booby traps.[48]

Phu My

Douglas Pike described Phu My as "the heartland of the communist movement in the province, as Binh Dinh is the communist heartland of South Vietnam."[49] This was reflected in the unusual size and potency of the local Vietcong, which fielded a District Force battalion in addition to the usual guerrillas and District Force company. With the richest rice fields in the province, Phu My also formed a vital link in the enemy's supply chain.[50] The district's dominant physical features were the mountains that framed and divided it. To the north, the towering Cay Giep range straddled the border between Phu My and Hoai Nhon. To the northwest, the narrow spine of the Crescent Mountains marked the boundary with Hoai An. The foothills of the main Annamite Chain covered the extreme western portion of the district, and the coastal Phu Cat range lay just across the southern border in the district of the same name. The twin masses of the Nui Mieu and Nui Nhaio mountains (usually referred to as simply the Nui Mieus) stretched inland from the coast to within a few miles of Highway 1. Coming from the opposite direction, the Crescent Mountains lapped up against Highway 1, pointing like an accusing finger at the Nui Mieus, less than two miles away. Phu My was consequently divided into two plains open to the sea on the east, but surrounded by mountains on all other sides.

This natural bipartite division of Phu My district was reflected in the 1969 pacification campaign plan. The southern plain was designated AO South and assigned to the 22nd ARVN Division's 41st Infantry Regiment. The northern plain became AO North and was assigned to Lieutenant Colonel James R. Woodall's 1st Battalion, 50th Infantry (Mechanized), which had been detached from the 2nd Armored Division at Fort Hood, Texas, in September 1967 and had served in Vietnam with both the 1st Cavalry and 4th Infantry Divisions before being attached to the 173rd Airborne. In addition to supporting pacification, the battalion assumed responsibility for securing Highways 1 and 505 in AO North and defending the Hawk's Nest—an observation post equipped with a high-power telescope that was perched atop the highest peak in the Cay Giep Mountains. Standing 2,100 feet above the coastal plain, the Hawk's Nest commanded a breathtaking view that took in all of AO North on a clear day.[51]

When the 1/50th deployed into Phu My, it detached its entire Company C and a platoon of Company A to the 173rd Airborne's other battalions, but it received Company B, 1/503rd, by way of compensation. In terms of numbers, US Army mechanized infantry battalions were slightly weaker than leg and airborne infantry battalions because they had fewer riflemen. However, the 1/50th had far greater mobility and firepower because its troops were mounted in M-113 armored cavalry assault vehicles (ACAVs), each of which was armed with one .50-caliber and two .30-caliber machine guns mounted behind armored gun shields. The ACAVs had a low ground pressure and were fully amphibious, characteristics that allowed them to traverse Vietnam's rice paddies and canals with ease. Because of their speed, cross-country mobility, and heavy firepower, ACAVs were often used in the role of light tanks, leading or supporting infantry assaults. The battalion's mortars were likewise carried on armored vehicles (M-106 variants of the M-113), and it also had a "Zippo Platoon" equipped with four M-132s (a flamethrower turret mounted on an M-113 chassis).[52] Finally, the battlion's elite Short-Range Ambush Platoon established a patrol base on Lake Dam Tra O, which separated AO North's coastline from the interior. Using airboats and inflatable rafts, it conducted amphibious operations in addition to its standard repertoire of helicopter-inserted ambush patrols.[53]

M-113 Armored Cavalry Assault Vehicle. *Source:* General Donn A. Starry, *Mounted Combat in Vietnam (Vietnam Studies)* (Washington, DC: US Army Center of Military History, 1978), CMH Pub 90-17, 74. [Reprinted by permission of the US Army Center of Military History]

In April 1969 the Vietcong controlled exactly half of Phu My's 114 hamlets (V ratings) and dominated another 8 (D and E ratings).[54] All but a few of the district's 44 A, B, and C hamlets lay in the 41st ARVN Regiment's AO South, where pacification efforts had been concentrated for two years. AO North had largely been ignored and contained practically all of the V-rated hamlets. Binh Dinh's original 1969 pacification plan had not designated any phase I target hamlets there, but when the 1/50th became available, securing that area suddenly became a top priority. Eleven new target hamlets were hastily added, and seven of Phu My's ten RF companies were concentrated in AO North.[55] By the end of May, fourteen target hamlets had been secured (three more than originally planned), ending the enemy's unchallenged control over a population of 12,000 and an area of eighteen square miles. Yet the inhabitants showed little enthusiasm for the GVN's return. DSA James A. Landberg concluded, "It will be at least several months before the people in this long VC-dominated area accept the fact that GVN forces intend to remain permanently in their hamlets."[56] He hoped popular support would rise once the villagers realized that GVN troops were not going to pull out and leave them in the lurch.

Progress was less substantial in AO South, which had been stripped of most of its RF troops on the assumption that the 41st ARVN Regiment would take their place. However, in keeping with its past record, the regiment did little to aid pacification. It not only failed to intervene when RF and PF units came under attack but also used other territorial units to defend its own base camps. In late July the regiment's senior advisor, Lieutenant Colonel Jack B. Porterfield, explained the situation to a US Army field historian:

> Of the three battalions in the regiment committed to pacification, only the 4th Battalion is doing a creditable job . . . the real reason more progress is not being made, LTC Porterfield said, is a lack of understanding of what pacification is by the ARVN. However, he said, the US is partially responsible for this because it was the US that built the ARVN up to chase VC [Main Force] units, and we have never put pressure on higher ARVN echelons to commit their maneuver units to pacification. Without clear guidance in writing from corps and above, is it any wonder that the units hesitate to support pacification?[57]

Throughout 1968 American advisors had urged that the 22nd ARVN Division be relieved of its area security mission and committed to mobile offensive operations, and the 173rd Airborne's Pair Off program had been intended to facilitate this change in mission. Yet, just when the 22nd ARVN had finally made the switch, Operation Washington Green required it to "shift gears" yet again. General Barnes attributed the division's hesitancy to embrace its new mission to the fact that its commander "General [Nguyen Van] Hieu had just been taken to task because he had stayed too close to the population, and finally had his troops operating in the hills. Then, all of a sudden we flip-flopped and said 'Okay, come back to the population.'"[58]

The impulse to hunt Vietcong rather than support pacification also afflicted the 1/50th, which had been trained and organized for rapid movement and mounted combat, not guarding hamlets. The battalion actually occupied only five target hamlets, although it escorted territorial troops when they entered the other nine and (unlike the 41st ARVN) provided effective rapid-reaction forces for RF and PF units throughout AO North. Coordination with the South Vietnamese was almost nonexistent, and Lieutenant Colonel Woodall frequently rotated his subunits between road security and pacification duties without notifying either the GVN district chief or the District Advisory Team. This practice also prevented the battalion's troops from developing close ties with particular RF and PF units, which might have alleviated their misgivings about operating with them. According to DSA Landberg, the root of the problem was that, "other than for B/503, they still want to chase the VC up and down the rice paddies."[59]

It was easy for Woodall to succumb to this temptation because the Vietcong in Phu My offered greater opposition to Operation Washington Green than anywhere else in AO Lee. In the first half of May, enemy attacks were coming at the rate of better than two a day. In one incident, five Vietcong wearing 22nd ARVN Division uniforms assassinated a GVN hamlet chief and his assistant in broad daylight. On the night of 11–12 May, the Vietcong used a catapult to hurl four satchel charges at the 41st Regiment's headquarters on LZ Crystal, injuring fourteen ARVN troops. On the following night, VC sappers penetrated the district seat and burned a refugee camp situated just 200 yards from the district headquarters. A school and eighty-seven homes were destroyed; ten civilians were killed and twenty were wounded. Another sapper attack killed five PSDF and GVN officials in the wee hours of 19 May, and a third targeting a PF bridge security detail a week later caused another six fatalities.[60] Though few in number, the sappers could bring overwhelming firepower to bear with their B-40 rocket launchers, and their attacks were executed with consummate skill. So precise was their timing that in the 19 May incident, the sappers made a clean getaway even though M-113s from the 1/50th arrived just ten minutes after the attack began.[61]

Despite poor coordination, the 1/50th did conduct integrated operations with territorial units, providing on-the-job training and instruction in the use and maintenance of the M-16 assault rifles and other modern weapons that were arriving in ever-increasing numbers. Since their RF and PF training mission had been assumed by the 1/50th, the two MATs in northern Phu My served as a channel of communication between the battalion and the two RF group headquarters in AO North. They could not have achieved much in this role because they were not kept informed of Woodall's plans.[62] Likewise, the battalion's STAGs probably accomplished little when they began training the PSDF in June, since local GVN officials proved reluctant to arm the militia. A US Army field historian reported: "Mr. Landberg wasn't sure whether the few thousand unarmed PSDF were deliberately being denied arms because of doubtful loyalty, or a shortage of weapons. If he was a hamlet chief, Mr. Landberg said, he would hesitate to arm all his PSDF until he was certain of their loyalty and faithfulness."[63]

The Vietcong nonetheless feared that the PSDF program was at least potentially threatening, since the Hoai Nhon district's NLF Party Committee ordered its village branches "to disintegrate enemy People's Self-Defense Forces" by killing the "cruel tyrants" (i.e., RD cadres) responsible for organizing the PSDF, urging the villagers not to attend military training, and convincing militiamen to desert.[64] Similar directives were almost certainly issued in the other three northern districts at about the same time.

The 1/50th's training activities also encompassed the National Police Field Force. When Operation Washington Green began, there was only a single NPFF platoon in Phu My, and it had more than enough to do in AO South. Since AO Lee had been given top priority, however, two platoons of the 203/2 NPFF Company were withdrawn from the southern districts. One went to Hoai An, and the other was sent to AO North. The NPFF was incorporated into the 1/50th's security operations along Highway 1, accompanying the Americans on patrols and road-clearing missions and screening Vietnamese civilians at checkpoints and during cordon-and-search operations.[65] But these were missions for the National Police—not the NPFF. Because there were few policemen available, the temptation to use the NPFF to fill the gap was understandable. However, it was supposed to be the "action arm" of the Phoenix program, killing or apprehending VCI identified by Phu My's District Intelligence and Operations Coordination Center. The 173rd's tendency to use the NPFF in traditional police roles was thus a source of concern for Advisory Team 42.[66] But in truth, the intelligence necessary to employ the NPFF in its intended anti-VCI role was generally not available.

Hoai An

Hoai An was the most isolated district in AO Lee. Its populated area conformed to the valley of the Kim Son River, one of the two main tributaries of the Lai Giang (the other was the An Lao River), which ran diagonally across the district from southwest to northeast. To the east, the Crescent Mountains blocked access to the coastal plains, while the peaks and foothills of the main Annamite Range blanketed the southern and western portions of Hoai An. There, the Kim Son River split into six tributary streams, each of which flowed through its own narrow valley and formed a distinctive talon-like shape on topographic maps that prompted the Americans to christen it the "Crow's Foot." Two roads linked the district to the coastal plains. Highway 3A ran down the Kim Son Valley to link up with Highway 1 south of Bong Son, while Highway 506 passed through a narrow valley (generally called the 506 Valley) between the southwestern face of the Crescent Mountains and the easternmost ridges of the main mountain range before debouching into the plains of southern Phu My.

Hoai An was statistically the best of AO Lee's four districts. In April 1969 it contained no VC-controlled hamlets, and two-thirds of its population lived in "relatively secure" areas. The impression of GVN strength was deceptive, however, since only fourteen of forty-one hamlets were inhabited, and nearly all of them were clustered in a small area along Highway 3A. Most of the district was a wasteland whose inhabitants had either fled or been forcibly evacuated years before. All seven "relatively secure" hamlets were of very recent vintage and had achieved C ratings chiefly due to successful economic development programs that skewed aggregate HES scores and obscured a still tenuous security situation.[67] Sixteen hamlets were scheduled for pacification in 1969, including three carried over from the APC, but two more were added later. Since nearly all the phase I hamlets were vacant at the start of Operation Washington Green, success would depend on the performance of the RTV program to an even greater extent than in Tam Quan and Hoai Nhon.[68] Because there was initially no population to protect, the 1st Battalion, 503rd Infantry, did not "fragment" itself into hamlet security detachments. Instead, it screened the areas being resettled by conducting sweeps, saturation patrols, and reconnaissance-in-force operations in the surrounding mountains. Meanwhile, the attached Troop E, 17th Cavalry, secured Highway 3A, releasing three PF and two RF platoons for use in the target hamlets. A platoon of Company A, 1/50th, provided light armor support.[69]

Although the 1/503rd's mission in phase I was initially more conventional than those given to the 173rd Airborne's other three battalions, it experienced considerable frustration in its new role. The Vietcong in Hoai An may have been the weakest in AO Lee, but the 1/503rd still had nearly fifty men wounded in the first three weeks of the operation, all by booby traps, while enemy losses amounted to just four killed and two weapons captured.[70] The battalion's operations nonetheless severely restricted Vietcong activity. The DSA, Major John T. Undercoffer, reported: "With U.S. and RF/PF troops deployed virtually all over the populated part of the district, VC cannot keep up with the locations [of all the allied units] and therefore their safe havens are no longer safe. These operations seem to be working very successfully."[71] As a result, there was not a single enemy-initiated incident in Hoai An from mid-April through the end of June.[72]

There were other causes for optimism in Hoai An during phase I. The district's eight RF companies, which had all been rearmed with M-16s, had become more active—particularly at night. In May the Territorial Forces engaged the enemy almost as often as the 1/503rd did and killed thirty-six Vietcong, while the Sky Soldiers accounted for only nineteen enemy fatalities. This disparity had much to do with the fact that the enemy avoided combat with Americans whenever possible, but it also seems that the Vietcong had grown complacent about the despised RF and PF and were surprised by their uncharacteristic aggressiveness.[73] Another favorable development was the appearance of an energetic district chief, Major Nguyen Van Huan, who was one of five new district chiefs appointed in Binh Dinh during March and April. Huan received high marks from his advisors, who were impressed by his interest in the morale and welfare of his troops, his routine visits to the target hamlets to ensure that GVN agencies were performing their missions and cooperating with one another, and his practice of staying in the hamlets overnight to help build public confidence in the Territorial Forces.[74]

The growing effectiveness of the district's VIP was also very encouraging. The program was of great importance to the 1/503rd because the vast majority of its casualties continued to be inflicted by mines and booby traps, and dud bombs and artillery shells were the enemy's primary source of explosives for these devices. The battalion accordingly mounted a media blitz about the VIP featuring helicopter loudspeaker missions and 90,000 hand-distributed and airdropped leaflets. The results were gratifying. During May, 203 civilians turned in 347 explosive devices ranging from 40mm grenade launcher rounds to 175mm artillery shells, plus thousands of rounds of small-arms ammunition. Largely because of the VIP's success, military and civilian casualties inflicted by mines and booby traps declined considerably.[75]

In June the battalion terminated its screening operations and began deploying security detachments into the target hamlets with colocated platoons of the 45th and 48th RF Groups. Thereafter it operated in the same fashion as the 173rd Airborne's other three battalions, securing the target hamlets and giving on-the-job training to the RF during continuous integrated operations. The 1/503rd's STAGs simultaneously began a weeklong training cycle for the PSDF militia. The change in operational methodology accelerated the positive security trends in Hoai An, since the round-the-clock American presence made it even more difficult for the VCI to conduct their usual nighttime supply-gathering and proselytizing activities.[76]

Although security had improved dramatically in Hoai An, the developmental side of pacification was not going as well. The improving security situation had convinced a growing number of refugees to resettle in the target hamlets, and some even jumped the gun by moving back into hamlets that would not be secured until phase II. However, Hoai An's RTV program was hampered by the cement shortage and the policy of delaying payments until after refugees had resettled. At the end of phase I, three target hamlets still lacked sufficient populations to qualify for HES ratings, although their exposed locations may have been a large part of the problem. Another factor that impeded resettlement on the left bank of the Kim Son—where two of these hamlets were located—was the failure to rebuild a crucial bridge across the river. A civic action project to do so had been disapproved at the provincial level. Major Undercoffer warned that this decision could prove disastrous, as there would be no other way to cross the river during the rainy season.[77]

It is possible that the cement shortage dictated the decision not to approve
the bridge project, but it is also possible that it was merely another manifes-
tation of the GVN's notoriously corrupt, inefficient, slow-moving, and unresponsive bureaucracy. All these failings were displayed in Hoai An during
phase I, and nowhere more prominently than in the Public Health Service.
According to Major Undercoffer:

> [The Public Health Service] embodies every evil cited as a damaging fac-
> tor in the GVN—corruption, laziness, inefficiency, lack of compassion,
> and lack of a feeling of urgency. The New Zealand medics are nothing
> more than laborers since the assigned workers do little or nothing. People
> in first phase hamlets receive no medical visits from the dispensary field
> worker. In fact, few hamlets do. This situation has a *definite negative
> effect on pacification.* . . . Every tactic, pressure and method have been
> exhausted by *Province* as well as District Advisors in an effort to alleviate
> the situation.[78]

Corruption and inefficiency were also endemic in the GVN logistical system, which could take months to fill routine supply requests and often would
not act on them unless bribes were paid. In the interest of fostering Vietnamization, American advisors and military units had been ordered not to yield
to the temptation (as they had done so often in the past) to act as an alternative source of supply. The idea was that, eventually, the GVN would *have* to
make its own supply system work, but in the interim, pacification suffered
from unresponsive logistical support that seriously hampered developmental
activities. In Hoai An, advisors ordered supplies for development projects
through GVN channels, knowing full well they would not arrive on time.
Meanwhile, they went ahead with the project using materials scrounged
from American sources. When the GVN supplies finally arrived, they were
used for other projects.[79]

Like the other northern districts, Hoai An lacked sufficient RD Cadre
Teams to achieve all its phase I objectives. On 30 April Major Undercoffer
had complained, "One RD team will move shortly to Tan Thanh hamlet.
One is needed there, but the hamlet it will be pulled from also needs one.
The loss of 3 RD teams, as mentioned in last month's report, proved a serious
blow to the pacification effort here. The District has no choice but to shuffle
RD teams, leaving them in a hamlet only a minimum amount of time."[80] The
situation got even worse in May when two teams went AWOL because they
had not been redeployed to a more secure district at the end of April, as they
had been promised. Although the absentees all returned to duty within a
week, this incident graphically illustrates just how poor their morale was. By

year's end, the province chief would be forced to adopt a policy of rotating RD Cadre Teams to the safer southern districts every six months to reduce the desertion rate.[81]

Despite these problems, General Barnes chose to focus on Hoai An's security gains. Every inhabited hamlet in the district was occupied by allied troops, HES statistics were improving steadily, enemy military activity was almost nonexistent, and—most important of all—the performance of Hoai An's Territorial Forces had improved dramatically. General Barnes was so encouraged that, before phase I had even concluded, he made the decision to withdraw the 1/503rd from the district at the end of July. Many Americans, especially in the 173rd Airborne, welcomed the move as a necessary test of the Territorial Forces' ability to stand on their own; others, mostly advisors, believed the withdrawal was risky and premature. Curtis D. Piper (evidently Hoai An's third DSA in as many months) told a US Army field historian in August that American troops needed to remain for at least another six months, and he bitterly denounced the decision to withdraw them:

> Declaring that the departure of the 173d Abn Bde elements from his district constitutes a breach of promise to him and to the people as well, Mr Piper accuses BG [Brigadier General] Barnes of reneging on his word. . . . The upshot of all this, in his view, is that the district is over-committed and it is a sleight of hand operation to make everyone and everything look good to justify our withdrawal. When the whole facade collapses after we withdraw, he says we can blame the Vietnamese for it by pointing out that we withdrew when the (alleged) security was at an all time high.[82]

Signs of Progress

Piper's allegations of deception were almost certainly unwarranted, since General Barnes undoubtedly believed that Operation Washington Green was succeeding at the time, and he still felt that way when interviewed by this author more than two decades later. And the operation had accomplished a great deal during phase I. Forty additional PF platoons had been recruited, and twenty-four of them were already in training. The Sky Soldiers aided the expansion by training territorial officers and NCOs at the 173rd Airborne's RF/PF Leadership School, which graduated two classes of forty each month (including students from Phu Bon and Phu Yen Provinces).[83] Substantial progress had also been made in rearming the Territorial Forces with M-16 assault rifles, M-60 machine guns, and M-79 40mm grenade launchers, whose firepower finally put them on a par with VC District and

Regional Force units. All of Binh Dinh's RF companies had been rearmed by the end of June, although 173 of its 276 PF platoons were still awaiting their new weaponry. The combination of greater firepower and on-the-job training markedly improved the Territorial Forces' combat effectiveness. RF and PF units operating with the 173rd Airborne saw their "kill ratio" against the Vietcong rise from 1.6 to 1 in April to 2.4 to 1 by the end of phase I. It would climb to 3 to 1 in the first days of phase II.[84] Rearmament of RF and PF units allowed the transfer of their old weaponry (World War II–vintage rifles, carbines, and submachine guns) to the PSDF militia. By the end of phase I, Combat PSDF strength had risen to 12,054 province-wide, and the 173rd Airborne's STAG teams had begun weapons familiarization and basic military skills training. Due to the late start, they trained only 700 PSDF militia in phase I but planned to expand the program considerably during phase II.[85]

General Barnes reported that the percentage of AO Lee's population residing in "relatively secure" A, B, and C hamlets doubled during phase I, but Advisory Team 42's reports and HES data reveal that most of the progress involved shifting "enemy-controlled" (V) hamlets into the "contested" (D and E) column. Even at the end of July, only in Hoai An and Hoai Nhon were most hamlets rated "relatively secure." Yet there was no real discrepancy: General Barnes was citing HES *security* ratings, whereas *overall* HES scores were calculated by aggregating a hamlet's security and *development* ratings. Since developmental activities (e.g., VSD, RTV programs) were lagging badly, hamlets' aggregate HES scores were generally lower than their security ratings.[86]

Enemy casualties throughout AO Lee in phase I totaled 468, more than half of which were credited to the 173rd, but since most of these losses resulted from enemy-initiated incidents, the Vietcong clearly retained the tactical initiative. Over the same period, 115 enemy personnel in AO Lee surrendered under the Chieu Hoi program, a huge increase over the mere 35 that had defected in the entire first quarter of 1969.[87] The VCI and guerrillas had been accustomed to living in their native hamlets on a more or less permanent basis, taking refuge in the mountains or in underground hiding places for brief spells when allied forces swept through but then returning immediately after they moved on. Now, however, pacification was advancing inexorably as unprecedentedly strong regular military forces penetrated and permanently occupied "liberated zones" that had remained inviolate through half a decade of intense warfare. The Vietcong now had to live a furtive existence in their hideaways, suffering from hunger and other physical hardships and from the psychological strain of prolonged isolation from their families.

The Communists themselves admitted that morale in their ranks was de-

Table 4.2 Binh Dinh HES Statistics, 1969

Month	A	B	C	D	E	V	Unrated
	Number of Hamlets by Category* (Percentage of Rural Population by Category)						
March	0 (0%)	55 (12%)	282 (55%)	72 (11%)	9 (1%)	111 (18%)	143 (2%)
June	0 (0%)	79 (19%)	285 (55%)	87 (13%)	14 (3%)	72 (9%)	117 (1%)

Source: Hamlet Evaluation System, Monthly Pacification Status Reports, 30 April and 30 June 1969, MACV Command Historian's Collection, US Army Heritage and Education Center, Carlisle, PA.

  * Some hamlets were dropped from the HES during 1969.

clining. In June the Central Committee of the People's Revolutionary Party reported: "The ideological motivation of a number of Party Chapter cadre from Committee levels was still not sufficient. They failed to launch attacks, were not vigilant, balked at difficulties and feared hardships. Therefore, the enemy has succeeded in destroying our posts and caused many difficulties to us. In some hamlets, such as northeast of Hoai Nam [*sic*]; southeast of Hoai Nhon; northeast of Phu My . . . the people were demoralized."[88] The same captured document also admitted that the Rangers were having a significant impact on Communist activity in the mountains: "In border and mountainous areas, the enemy has intensified the activities of Special Forces to search for and attack our infiltration corridors and storage facilities. He has raided our agencies, dispensaries, and production elements. He has caused a number of difficulties to our transportation and movement in areas such as: An Lao, Hoai An . . . Hoai Nhon, Phu My."[89]

The Central Committee also expressed concerns about the Phoenix program. It believed that the GVN had already placed 300 intelligence agents in hamlets still under NLF control and was forcibly indoctrinating teenagers and students to become spies. As a result, "The revolutionary movement of the masses has been wickedly oppressed. . . . Due to the overt activities and lack of vigilance of our cadre in some places, the enemy has recently discovered our underground hideouts and arrested our covert agents. This fact has caused us many difficulties and losses."[90]

Sputtering Phoenix

Vietcong fears about Phoenix were greatly exaggerated, since the program was generally ineffective in Binh Dinh during phase I. Before Operation Washington Green, most VCI lived openly in enemy-controlled hamlets, and many remained there covertly after allied troops moved in. Those whose identities were known to the GVN took refuge in tunnel complexes situated either in overgrown and densely booby-trapped lowland areas or in the nearby mountains—and in most cases, they had little difficulty infiltrating back into the hamlets by night. Others, whose identities were unknown, openly remained in the hamlets. It was Phoenix's job to hunt down both groups, but when Washington Green began, the District Intelligence and Operations Coordination Centers (DIOCCs) were still being established in Tam Quan and Hoai An, and Hoai Nhon's was rated ineffective. Only Phu My possessed a truly functional DIOCC.[91]

A DIOCC's first task was to assemble the district "blacklist"—a database containing the name, NLF position, physical description, and biographical details of every known VCI. Once the blacklist was completed, DIOCC personnel were supposed to use it to meticulously build target dossiers, which in turn would be used to plan tactical operations designed to "neutralize" (i.e., kill, capture, or convince to defect) specific VCI members. Both tasks required the collaboration of a dozen different GVN agencies represented in the DIOCCs. Unfortunately, intelligence agencies the world over are notoriously reluctant to share information, especially about their priceless covert sources in the enemy's camp. This was particularly true of South Vietnam's thoroughly politicized intelligence services; they not only distrusted each other professionally but had also been drawn into the internecine power struggles that plagued the GVN throughout its existence.[92] Phoenix was therefore afflicted by interagency feuding, and American advisors had to mediate between squabbling Vietnamese representatives as they tried to get the ball rolling. The Phoenix advisors in Tam Quan and Hoai An had a particularly hard time finding DIOCC representatives willing to serve in these dangerous, Vietcong-infested districts. Phu My's DIOCC was not fully staffed either, since there were no Census Grievance and Chieu Hoi representatives, and the aged National Police chief (and titular head of the DIOCC) was too ill to do his job.[93]

Most of the DIOCCs spent all of phase I assembling their blacklists, and operations targeting specific VCI were extremely rare except in Hoai Nhon. Thus, although General Barnes claimed that 347 VCI were neutralized *in AO Lee alone* during phase I, the vast majority were actually killed or captured during the course of routine military operations and only afterward identified as NLF cadres. Moreover, US Phoenix advisors, whose tallies did not include members of NLF Liberation Associations (which included practically the entire rural population in AO Lee), recorded just 330 neutralizations *province-wide* during phase I.[94] Binh Dinh's provincial Phoenix coordinator, Major Thomas C. Roberts, observed:

We are not operating as I thought the program would be when I heard about it in the States. I had visions of people sitting around compiling intelligence reports, and collating various intelligence reports, and finally coming up with a solution and finding out that Mr. "X" will be at point "Y" at time "Z," and going out and zapping him. This will come, it definitely will, but right now the condition is that the operations are ahead of the database.[95]

Major Roberts's confidence that targeted operations would begin once the blacklists were complete proved to be unfounded. Instead of using the database and target dossiers to plan anti-VCI operations, creating and maintaining them became an end unto itself. A set of well-organized intelligence files rarely failed to impress visitors, and building them allowed DIOCC personnel to focus on collecting and recording data instead of actually targeting VCI—which might lead to enemy reprisals. It was also well known that VCI throughout South Vietnam often paid "protection money" to corrupt GVN officials to ensure that they would be left alone. Whatever the reasons, the tendency to turn Phoenix into a "paper program" was not unique to Binh Dinh. An analysis of the program throughout Military Region 2 concluded:

Many of our Phung Hoang committees and permanent centers are still not action oriented. The mere amassing of reports in neatly kept filing systems and card indexes is of no value at all unless it is given to the action arms in a useable form. The measure of the program's efficiency must be the number of VCI neutralized, not the volume of reports, the neatness of filing systems, or the correctness and timeliness of statistical reports. Binh Dinh, Cam Ranh, Khanh Hoa, Lam Dong, Phu Bon, Phu Yen, Pleiku, Quang Duc, and Tuyen Duc are not action oriented to the degree required.[96]

Some improvements occurred as Operation Washington Green progressed. The greatest gains were made in Tam Quan, which was still in the process of setting up its DIOCC in mid-April. By the end of May, it was fully operational, and the district blacklist was nearly complete. A month later, Colonel Clayton N. Gompf—the new PSA—lauded the excellent progress made. Even more impressive results were achieved in Hoai Nhon, where forty VCI and six guerrillas were netted in April and May. Its DIOCC advisor, Lieutenant Richard C. Lutzy, estimated that 10 to 15 percent of the district's VCI had been neutralized by the end of June, but he noted that only 30 percent of captured VCI were brought to trial. The rest either bribed their way out of prison or proved to be innocent civilians. He also worried that

American involvement made the DIOCC seem more efficient than it really was.[97]

Major Roberts had no doubt that Americans were chiefly responsible for Phoenix's quantitative success in Binh Dinh. Most neutralizations were by-products of the 173rd Airborne's routine tactical operations, and the most effective and responsive intelligence networks were run either by American units such as the 525th Military Intelligence Detachment or by GVN agencies that had US advisors. Worse still, Roberts feared that the ability to draw on massive American support was causing the GVN's Phoenix capabilities to atrophy:

> Another thing that has got to happen before the [Phoenix] program can be entirely effective is all free-world force units have to move out of the area. The program is either going to have to sink or swim when we leave, and to be effective on its own feet, to stand on its own feet it must do so without the massive aid provided by helicopter assault and battalion-size CORDS searches and this type of thing. . . . NPFF is less effective than it should be. Targeting is less effective than it should be. All of these things do not work properly because there is too much damn assistance available.[98]

In the final analysis, Roberts believed most Vietnamese DIOCC representatives were little more than glorified clerks who rarely played an active part in the effort to eradicate the VCI. Phoenix advisors were therefore constantly tempted to get support from American agencies and military units, both of which were far more responsive to the program's needs. Roberts was not blind to the long-term dangers of bypassing GVN agencies, but he could see no alternative:

> If we want a PsyOps operation aimed at a certain area to induce Chieu Hoi's, it is a hell of a lot easier to go through an American PsyOps advisor, or to an American PsyOp unit, and get what you want, than go to the [GVN] Chieu Hoi man and go through Vietnamese Information Service. It is just a matter of time and timing. Once again, when we all leave, of course, this man will come into his own with practically no experience behind him. I know I am making it all sound very grim, but it is just a fact of life right now that such people as Chieu Hoi, the National Police Field Force, RD Cadre representatives, across the board, are of very little value to the DIOCC.[99]

A Growing Dependency

The dependence on American support that Major Roberts observed in the Phoenix program extended to almost every other aspect of Binh Dinh's 1969 pacification campaign. The 173rd Airborne's role in securing the target hamlets was of particular importance, since without a secure environment, the pacification effort would have made no progress whatsoever.[100] Yet its accomplishments in accelerating pacification came at the price of slowing progress toward Washington Green's primary objective—Vietnamization. Ultimate success depended on the GVN being able to maintain security without American help. Thus, if pacification progress came about primarily due to American efforts, the more important objective of making the South Vietnamese self-sufficient would not be achieved. Washington Green's planners recognized the dilemma but could find no way to escape it. The deployment of US combat troops in the target hamlets was clearly a step in the wrong direction, since it showed that the GVN was just as dependent on American assistance in the "other war" as it had long been in the "big war" against the Communist Main Forces. The 173rd Airborne hoped to minimize the damage by gradually weaning the Territorial Forces from their reliance on American support. For the moment, however, the rhetoric about joint command and integrated operations was little more than window dressing, and dependence on American resources and initiative extended well beyond the realm of security.

For example, an analysis of the province's Chieu Hoi program concluded that military activity was the decisive factor in convincing Vietcong to surrender. Since Binh Dinh had led the nation in Hoi Chanhs (Chieu Hoi defectors) in 1966–1967, despite having a notoriously corrupt and inefficient Chieu Hoi service, the flood of defectors in those years was credited to the 1st Cavalry Division. Interrogation of Hoi Chanhs who defected during phase I of Operation Washington Green confirmed that "the most basic requirement for large numbers of Hoi Chanh is military pressure. Without exception, every man put this at the top in importance."[101] Table 4.3 suggests that American units were consistently applying greater military pressure in their areas of operation than GVN and ROK forces were applying in other parts of the province.

Of the 290 Vietcong who defected in Binh Dinh in the first half of 1969, two-thirds came from areas where American combat units were operating (including An Tuc, where the 4th US Infantry Division was hunting the 18th and 95B NVA Regiments). Only Van Canh (a subdivision of Tuy Phuoc) generated a significant number of Hoi Chanhs in the absence of US combat operations. Excluding these, Binh Dinh's southern districts brought in only 8 Hoi Chanhs in the second quarter of 1969, while AO Lee's four districts pro-

Table 4.3 Binh Dinh Chieu Hoi Statistics, January–June 1969

District	Jan.	Feb.	Mar.	Apr.	May	Jun.	Total
Hoai An	2	3	12	4	4	13	38
Hoai Nhon	1	1	2	40	25	4	73
Phu My	0	7	4	4	3	5	23
Tam Quan	2	1	0	0	11	2	16
Total in AO Lee	5	12	18	48	43	24	150
An Nhon	2	1	2	0	0	0	5
An Tuc	1	0	45	2	1	0	49
Binh Khe	1	2	1	2	0	0	6
Phu Cat	6	1	1	1	0	0	9
Tuy Phuoc	2	3	0	1	3	1	10
Van Canh	1	0	0	50	0	10	61
Total in southern districts	13	7	49	56	4	11	140

Source: Vietnam Interview Tape 482-15, interview with Binh Dinh Province Chieu Hoi advisor, chart, Southeast Asia Branch, US Army Center of Military History, Fort McNair, Washington, DC.

duced 115. The 173rd Airborne's aggressive small-unit tactics were keeping intense pressure on the Vietcong, whereas the 22nd ARVN and ROK Capitol Divisions, reluctant to "fragment" their battalions, generally were not.

The improvement in RF and PF combat effectiveness was also attributable primarily to the 173rd Airborne. The Territorial Forces had been emboldened by the constant presence of large numbers of US paratroops and their lavish air, artillery, helicopter, and medical evacuation support. Binh Dinh's NPFF was no less dependent on American support. Major Roberts, the Phoenix coordinator, said, "The NPFF is very, very reluctant, of course, to operate in any area that they consider insecure, whether or not it is considered insecure officially or not. This is why I think they operate so well up north with the American firepower in combined operations and why they operate less effectively in the south where they do not operate with the ROK's, or operate completely independently."[102]

In contrast to its dominant role in enhancing territorial security, the 173rd Airborne deliberately limited its involvement in nation-building activities. It chief contributions involved building roads, bridges, and schools. The school-building program looked like a sure winner, because free public education offered the GVN its best hope of weaning rural youth away from the

Vietcong, and it was certain to be popular with villagers, whose traditional, Confucian culture placed a high value on education. Dozens of schoolhouses were built in short order, but many could not be used because the GVN's Education Ministry could not supply the personnel and equipment necessary to start holding classes. Even with RD cadres acting as instructors, there were still 215 teacher vacancies province-wide in early August,[103] and in many cases, schools still lacked basic materials such as books, paper, and pencils.[104]

Developmental activities often lagged because newly elected village and hamlet officials were overwhelmed by the "red tape" involved—particularly in the VSD program. Efforts to provide instruction in bureaucratic procedures failed because most of the new officeholders were unwilling to travel to the training center in Vung Tau, 400 miles to the south. The village and hamlet governments in Binh Dinh's southern districts, which had existed for some time, began submitting VSD project proposals in May and received approval for 113 the following month. The northern districts did not start submitting VSD proposals until June, and not a single one had been approved by the end of phase I—making a mockery of what was supposed to be a top-priority pacification program. And although 390 projects were approved province-wide in July, few were in the four northern districts, and none at all in Tam Quan and Hoai An.[105] As July drew to a close, Colonel Gompf reported, "The self-help program has been and will continue to be a miserable failure in its attempt to provide immediate assistance in most of the Phase I and Phase II hamlets in the 1969 Plan."[106]

GVN administrators at the district and provincial levels generally performed no better than the fledgling village and hamlet officials. Advisors described Binh Dinh's public health program as "a disaster" and "appallingly bad." A true crisis existed because there were only three civilian physicians available to serve a population of over 900,000, and they catered exclusively to the residents of Binh Dinh's few urban centers. The public health advisory effort in Binh Dinh was run by a New Zealand medical team, but despite its members' dedication and hard work, they lacked the means to operate outside the cities. Employees of the GVN Public Health Ministry also focused on the urban areas because the inhabitants desperately needed their help (especially in the unsanitary refugee camps), and it was much safer than working in the Vietcong-infested rural areas. Misappropriation of funds and the diversion of medical supplies to the black market were so prevalent that Eldon E. Ewing, the chief pacification and development advisor, proposed that funding be cut until the corruption was eliminated. Thus, sporadic visits by doctors and medics from the 173rd Airborne Brigade and the 22nd ARVN Division provided the only medical care available in most of AO Lee. They dealt with emergencies and addressed some of the more pressing public health needs, but the absence of a proper health system belied the GVN's efforts to show that it was willing and able to serve its rural citizens.[107]

While the 173rd Airborne could evade major involvement on the development side of pacification, Advisory Team 42 could not, since that was what CORDS had been created to do. Advisors had the ultimate objective of making the South Vietnamese self-sufficient, but their near-term objective (and the basis for judging their performance) was to achieve progress in specific pacification programs. Thus, members of Advisory Team 42 often found themselves compelled to become "doers" rather than advisors, even though they knew they were only making the South Vietnamese even more dependent. Lieutenant Colonel Frank J. Maguire, deputy senior advisor for plans and operations, admitted the dilemma:

> Now, you have the conflict of making the Vietnamese logistics system work. On the other hand, you get out on the ground and you have a bunch of kids sitting in the dirt waiting for a school to be built and you have the capability of getting the stuff and building the school. So, do you do what you should do, and sit back and make their system work, or do you look and see a bunch of kids that need help right now and you have the ability and you help them? This works in every line of endeavor we have here.[108]

Often, the problem was that Americans simply had greater resources than their Vietnamese counterparts. Thus, the GVN's VIP in Phu My languished because villagers rightly believed the Americans would pay more. Similarly, while the Vietnamese Information Service was hamstrung by the GVN's inefficient logistical system, Binh Dinh's psychological operations advisor, Major Roland L. Schmucker, was so well funded and supplied that his surpluses were passed on to advisory teams in needier provinces.[109] The inadequacy of the GVN's resources was an inevitable consequence of the "fast and thin" technique, and the worst shortfall was not funding or materiel but personnel. There were simply nowhere near enough RF and PF, RD cadres, National Police officers, trained village and hamlet officials, qualified teachers and health care providers, or competent administrators for VSD, RTV, Chieu Hoi, and a host of other programs. Prospects for future improvement were not good because the ARVN's dramatic growth since the July 1968 general mobilization was siphoning off most of the quality manpower in Binh Dinh:

> The general mobilization has seriously affected the overall quality of village and hamlet government by draining the countryside of what little qualified leadership there is left. The younger and more energetic

individuals who should be emerging to provide the leadership in this extremely important area of the government are being put in the Army. The 1969 Program puts the emphasis on the village, but the lack of leadership at this level may well doom the program to failure, or at a minimum seriously impede its success.[110]

The RD Cadre Teams were intended to compensate for the GVN's shortcomings by bringing an effective government presence directly into the hamlets undergoing pacification, substituting for a welter of ineffective agencies whose functions they largely assumed.[111] Since they failed to do so in Binh Dinh, the only way to make progress on the developmental side of pacification was for American advisors to step into the breach and provide the leadership, expertise, and material resources the South Vietnamese could not. Vietnamization would have to wait.

Taking Stock

What does Operation Washington Green's first phase tell us about the validity of the Revisionist school's claims regarding the success of pacification and Vietnamization? First of all, progress in pacification had been impressive. A semblance of security and an embryonic GVN presence had been established across broad swaths of territory that had been under Communist domination for years, if not decades. The population residing in enemy-controlled communities had been reduced by half; travel on all major thoroughfares had become much safer, greatly benefiting the local economy; and thousands of refugees had returned to their ancestral homes. These were all important achievements, and they were doubly significant because they represented the first meaningful progress made in northern Binh Dinh in many years. Yet, since "fast and thin" pacification created only the thinnest veneer of GVN control in AO Lee, it was certain to take many years to win the inhabitants' loyalty and pacify the region fully. If Washington Green succeeded in making the Territorial Forces self-sufficient, the GVN would probably have the time it needed to finish the job. But although RF and PF performance had improved substantially, it was still unclear how much progress had actually been made in Vietnamization. The answer would not be known until the 173rd Airborne withdrew from the hamlets and left the Territorial Forces to their own devices.

It was already quite clear, however, that Vietnamization was failing badly in aspects of pacification that were unrelated to territorial security—and therefore did not benefit from the influx of American troops into the target hamlets. According to the logic of "fast and thin" pacification and Operation

Washington Green, it really did not matter if political reforms, economic development programs, and public services lagged because there would be plenty of time to fix them once security was firmly and permanently established. The same could not be said of the crucial Phoenix program, since as long as the VCI survived, the insurgency could never truly be defeated. The fact that the program was so utterly dependent on American advisors and resources was a cause for major concern. If the DIOCCs did not become far more effective in subsequent phases of Washington Green, the operation's long-term prospects were dim.

The common denominator of pacification and Vietnamization in AO Lee was leadership. Phoenix would not be effective, nation-building programs would not succeed, and the RF and PF would not become capable of standing on their own unless the quality of leadership provided by ARVN and Territorial Forces commanders and GVN bureaucrats improved dramatically. Revisionist historians believe that South Vietnamese leadership got much better from 1968 onward, but apart from Major Huan in Hoai An, as of mid-1969, there was little evidence of it in Binh Dinh. Almost all the progress made had been the result of American leadership, and it had generally required constant prodding by US advisors to get the South Vietnamese to follow American initiatives. Yet, it was still early days. Only time would tell how much the GVN's civil and military leadership would improve as Washington Green continued.

CHAPTER FIVE

Overextension

A prolonged lull occurred between the last high point (5–6 June) of the NLF's summer campaign and the beginning of its autumn campaign in mid-August. July was therefore a quiet month by Binh Dinh standards and allowed phase II of both Operation Washington Green and the 1969 pacification campaign to begin under favorable circumstances. The latter had been officially retitled the 1969 Special Pacification and Development Campaign by President Thieu, who proclaimed that the new primary objective was to consolidate GVN control by upgrading half of all "relatively secure" (A, B, C) hamlets to "secure" (A, B). However, he also called for the accomplishment of the original goal of making nine-tenths of South Vietnam's population "relatively secure." Finally, the date for completing the 1969 special campaign was moved up from December to October.[1] Thieu was, in effect, demanding the simultaneous expansion and consolidation of GVN control in the countryside. This was patently impossible, since the GVN's resources had already been badly overextended by the requirements of expansion alone.

In Binh Dinh, overextension had been a problem even before Operation Washington Green began, but it mushroomed dramatically in the second half of 1969. The 2/503rd had started moving into its nine phase II hamlets a month ahead of schedule, and in July the 173rd Airborne's other three airborne battalions began occupying another twenty-five. Yet, even this ambitious program was soon eclipsed because the arrival of the 1/503rd from Hoai An made it possible to add many additional target hamlets in Phu My without thinning the security screen. Meanwhile, the ever-reluctant 40th and 41st ARVN Regiments finally began moving into their phase II hamlets as well. This was all well and good for breaking up the NLF's liberated areas, but it actually slowed the pace of Vietnamization. The ARVN regiments should have been preparing to replace the Americans in operations against Communist regulars, but a shortage of Territorial Forces made it impossible to do so without bringing Operation Washington Green to a halt. Forty new PF platoons had been recruited, and twenty-four of them had already begun training by the end of July,[2] but there would not be enough Territorial Forces available to defend all the new target hamlets until late 1970—over a year away.

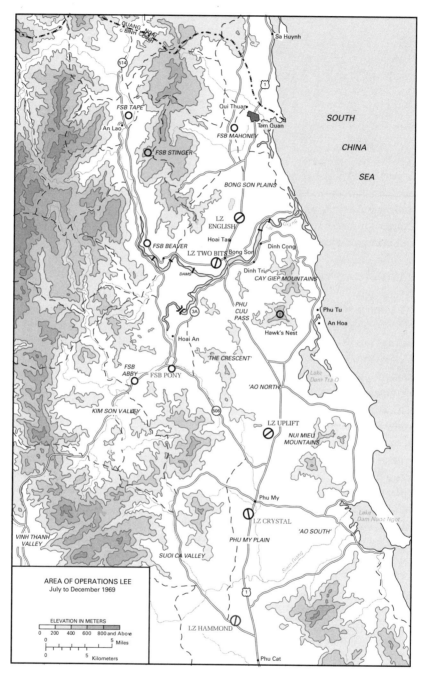

Area Of Operations Lee (July–December 1969). *Source:* George L. MacGarrigle, *Combat Operations: Taking the Offensive, October 1966 to October 1977 (The United States Army in Vietnam Series)* (Washington, DC: US Army Center of Military History, 1998), CMH Pub 94-1, Map 32, 317. [Adapted and reprinted by permission of the US Army Center of Military History]

CORDS advisors who had worried about overextension back in April, when just forty-two target hamlets in AO Lee were scheduled for pacification in 1969, expressed alarm when so many new phase II hamlets were added to the eleven that had already been added during phase I. Moreover, province-wide, forty-four uncompleted phase I hamlets and twenty-six regressed APC hamlets were simply tacked on to phase II.[3] Phu My's DSA, James Landberg, lobbied to have several remote, thinly populated coastal hamlets dropped from phase II, but he was overruled by South Vietnamese officials who were determined to bring the district's entire population under GVN control.[4] In August, Eldon E. Ewing, Advisory Team 42's chief pacification and development advisor, told a visiting field historian that "the Pacification Program for 1969 has impeded real pacification. The plan calls for too much, too soon, in areas not ready for pacification. . . . One reason the 1969 program is not responsive is the logistical and funding system in being will not support it."[5] The Public Education, Public Health, and VSD programs were all failing, he explained, due to shortfalls in funding, materiel, and competent personnel.

There were enough allied regulars on hand to occupy the vastly expanded list of phase II hamlets, but virtually every other resource required was in short supply—including RD Cadre Teams. In December 1968 the GVN had ordered that the fifty-nine-man teams be split in two because there was no other way to meet the ambitious pacification goals set for 1969. This was to be accomplished by eliminating the team's thirty-three-member security groups and reassigning their personnel in other roles. Since RD teams would no longer be responsible for their own defense, that mission was supposed to be taken on by the Territorial Forces and PSDF. This approach may have been viable in some of the safer provinces, but it was clearly impractical in those like Binh Dinh, where the insurgency remained strong and the Territorial Forces could not grow fast enough to match the pace of pacification. The provincial leadership had accordingly resisted splitting the teams until near the end of phase I.[6] The RD teams in northern Binh Dinh had been accomplishing very little even at full strength, and it was easy to predict that their performance would suffer after they were stripped of their security detachments and were forced to rely on the ineffective RF and PF and the highly suspect PSDF militia for their survival. The decision to split the teams anyway and press headlong into phase II offers further proof that "fast and thin" pacification was merely about planting the GVN flag.

Early in phase II, the 173rd Airborne was strengthened by the return of the 173rd Provisional Tank Company from Phu Yen Province, where it had been operating since 1968. This one-of-a-kind unit (which in fact possessed no tanks of any kind) had evolved from Company D, 16th Armor (Airborne

Antitank), which had come to Vietnam with the brigade in 1965. Though originally equipped with the M-56 Scorpion (a 90mm antitank gun in an open pivot mount atop an unarmored, tracked chassis), two platoons had been reequipped with M-113s just before heading to Vietnam. The third followed suit in 1967 after the Scorpions proved too difficult to maintain. The company had been so useful that it was maintained as a provisional unit for a full year after being officially deactivated in October 1968. It would finally stand down in October 1969, when its personnel and equipment were transferred to E/17th Cavalry.[7]

Despite the lull in enemy offensive activity, July proved to be the busiest and costliest month for Company N, 75th Ranger, since Washington Green began. It ran eighty-seven patrols, spotted enemy personnel eighty-nine times, and lost three men dead and fifteen wounded in exchange for twenty enemy confirmed and ten possibly killed. The fact that the enemy was being spotted on almost every mission proved that preparations for the upcoming autumn campaign were in full swing and renewed worries about the security of the coastal plains. Determined to disrupt the enemy's offensive preparations, and yet unwilling to withdraw troops from pacification duty, General Barnes secured the services of the 4th Mobile Strike Force (MSF) Battalion—a special operations unit manned by montagnard tribesmen that normally operated under command of the US 5th Special Forces Group. It launched a reconnaissance-in-force operation christened Darby Maul I in the upper An Lao Valley on 3 July. The operation continued for twenty-four days, but contact was minimal; just eight enemy troops were killed and one captured, while the 4th MSF had no losses. Yet Darby Maul I did uncover a sapper school, where captured documents revealed that infantry companies of the 3rd NVA Division were being trained in sapper tactics. In the past, sappers had been concentrated in special units at regimental level and above, but now it seemed that the NVA was trying to develop this capability in each infantry battalion.[8]

COSVN Resolution 9

The expansion of NVA sapper capabilities reflected a major shift in enemy strategy that was promulgated by COSVN Resolution 9 in mid-July. It finally abandoned the goal of decisive victory altogether, explaining that political initiatives and small-scale military operations could achieve a limited victory on their own by forcing the Americans to withdraw and agree to the formation of a coalition government. The shift was prompted by COSVN's recognition that it was facing unprecedented challenges, with its military forces severely depleted by their repeated offensive exertions and pacification making deep inroads into its "liberated zones." The logistical crisis worsened as it proved increasingly difficult to collect food from the people, and the VCI were directed to "firmly grasp that all economic and financial activities are presently centered on the production of food and food products. This is a matter which concerns the survival of the people and the revolution."[9] Personnel living outside populated areas were instructed to assume responsibility for producing some of their own food.

Given these circumstances, it is not surprising that COSVN found evidence of war weariness and defeatism in the ranks, noting, "a certain number of cadres and Party members have displayed . . . their lack of confidence in the Party's lines and strategic determination. They have shrunk from duties, turned rightist, feared violent fighting, resented sacrifices, doubted the people's revolutionary capabilities, hung back . . . and entertained peace illusions" (88). Yet, COSVN itself expressed concerns about the future in Resolution 9, noting that unless the Americans were compelled to withdraw quickly, they might prolong the war until pacification and Vietnamization had progressed sufficiently to leave the GVN in a much stronger position. Resolution 9 accordingly called for continued offensives whose principal aim would be to inflict American casualties and thus strengthen antiwar sentiment in the United States (14, 31).

Resolution 9's call for continuing offensives is hard to reconcile with the reality of Communist military weakness, but COSVN believed it knew how to attack without exposing its forces to destruction. First of all, it ordered an intensification of terrorist attacks targeting GVN officials, with repeated admonitions to "step up the destruction of tyrants" and to "kill wicked tyrants and destroy the puppet infrastructure in order to return power to the people" (64). Assassination was a "poor man's weapon" that could achieve great results at a low cost by decapitating GVN military units and organizations without having to destroy them in battle. Second, Resolution 9 called for a further refinement of the sapper and attack-by-fire techniques that had featured so prominently in recent offensives:

We must firmly grasp and more properly apply the combat method which combines small-scale attack with medium-scale and large-scale attacks, including large-scale attack conducted with small forces. We must always take the initiative in attacking the enemy; we must strive to develop the method of defeating a large enemy force with a small force composed of elite elements of the three types of arms such as sappers, light mortar units, and army engineering corps. (32)

Attacks-by-fire allowed the Communists to attack without having to engage allied forces at all, but the mortars and artillery rockets employed in such attacks were inaccurate and consequently difficult to use against well-fortified point targets.[10] Sapper attacks, though entailing greater risk, were much more precise and destructive. They had long been a staple of the Communist war effort, but under Resolution 9, sappers became the centerpiece of a new variant of revolutionary warfare. According to Mao Zedong's revolutionary warfare doctrine, guerrillas have the mission of wearing down the enemy with hit-and-run attacks in his rear areas, while revolutionary regular units engage in large-scale mobile operations intended to destroy enemy military forces and capture terrain. Now, however, the mission of harassing the allies' rear areas was increasingly taken over by small units of elite NVA and Vietcong regulars who, in effect, assumed the missions that had traditionally been performed by guerrillas.[11]

The importance of sapper tactics is hard to overstate because they allow the enemy to practice an incredible economy of force in his offensive operations. According to conventional military calculus, it would have required at least a reinforced battalion to take the 173rd Airborne Brigade's heavily fortified headquarters at LZ English. However, it could be successfully raided by as few as a dozen highly skilled sappers who would spend hours inching their way through the concentric rings of outposts, mines, barbed wire, and trip flares that surrounded the base. After entering under the cover of a mortar barrage that forced the defenders to take shelter in their bunkers, they would attack from the inside using assault rifles, B-40 rocket launchers, plastic explosives, and grenades. This was exactly what happened at LZ English in the wee hours of 17 June 1969, when sappers destroyed one helicopter, damaged another pair, and wounded sixteen Americans without suffering a single casualty. Yet the beauty of it was that even if all the sappers had been wiped out, the enemy would have lost only a handful of men.[12]

Torch Is Passed

General Barnes's tour as commander of the 173rd Airborne ended on 9 August. He left Vietnam and headed for the Pentagon, where he was slated to become director of development in the Department of the Army's Office of the Chief of Research and Development, a plum position that gave him a major role in developing all US Army equipment. On his way, Barnes stopped in Hawaii to brief Admiral John S. McCain, commander in chief of the Pacific theater (and father of the Republican senator and presidential candidate of the same name). This briefing would soon take on a life of its own and greatly impact General Barnes's future career. His part in the story of Operation Washington Green was not over just yet.[13]

The new brigade commander was Brigadier General Hubert S. Cunning-

General Barnes and General Cunningham. *Source:* The private collection of the late General Cunningham, reprinted by permission of Mr. Michael Cunningham.

ham.[14] He had barely assumed command when the Communists launched the first high point of their autumn campaign on the night of 12–13 August. The attacks succeeded in making headlines in the United States, but their military accomplishments were negligible. Pacification, though temporarily disrupted in several provinces, suffered no lasting setback, and the aim of inflicting prohibitive American casualties was not realized.[15] Binh Dinh was among the hardest hit provinces, and its Territorial Forces were the primary target. Yet they weathered the storm reasonably well, killing, on average, two enemy troops for every fatality they suffered and capturing four weapons for every one they lost. A relieved Colonel Gompf reported: "Despite the large number of attacks on 12 and 13 August, damage and casualties were light. The performance of the territorial forces was generally excellent. Reports through Vietnamese channels indicate confidence of the Vietnamese people in the ability of the territorial forces to provide security for the people."[16]

As August progressed, however, there was an upsurge in terrorism worse than anything seen since the 1968 Tet Offensive. On average, just fifteen terrorist incidents had occurred in each of the first four months of Operation Washington Green, but in August the number leaped to seventy-one, and September's tally would be even higher.[17] Most terror attacks targeted the Territorial Forces and GVN officials, but there were also a significant number of civilian casualties. Some attacks merely displayed a callous disregard

Table 5.1 Comparison of 1969 High-Point Offensives at the End of Their Second Day

Category	11–22 May	5–6 Jun.	11–12 Aug.	4–5 Sep.
Attacks-by-fire	358	214	179	125
Attacks-by-fire, 20 or more shells	89	46	22	24
Artillery shells expended	5,198	2,854	1,665	1,696
Ground attacks	68	28	44	14
Ground attacks, battalion or larger	2	4	8	3
Enemy killed	2,655	2,100	2,004	1,241
US killed	208	100	103	63
Other allied killed	235	199	249	161
Allied-to-enemy loss ratio	1:6	1:7	1:5.7	1:5.5

Source: Headquarters, Military Assistance Command–Vietnam, One War: MACV Command Overview, 1968–1972, chap. IV, 56, Southeast Asia Branch, US Army Center of Military History, Fort McNair, Washington, DC.

for civilian casualties, such as when a grenade was thrown at RF troops in a crowded Phu My marketplace on 7 August. Others, such as the 11 August grenade attack on the Bong Son medical dispensary that wounded ten, deliberately hit nonmilitary targets where civilian casualties were inevitable. This was also the case when four grenades were thrown into a town meeting in Phu Cat district on 26 August, killing twenty-six civilians and wounding another hundred. The culprits turned out to be four young boys who had carried out the attack at the direction of the local Vietcong.[18] The following months witnessed many more random terror attacks, including the bombing of a cinema in Qui Nhon that killed three and wounded thirty-four on 19 October.[19]

The random terror attacks were almost certainly prompted by fears that the NLF's grip on Binh Dinh's rural population was weakening. The unprecedented scope and intensity of the pacification effort, and the highly visible decline in Communist military strength, were eroding the NLF's political strength, and the prospects of a GVN victory looked better than they had in nearly a decade. The Communist leadership would have been particularly alarmed by developments in October, when civilian informants enabled the Territorial Forces to mount four highly successful ambushes in which nineteen Vietcong were killed and five captured, with no friendly losses.[20] Thus, although random terrorism carried the risk of alienating the people, the enemy evidently believed that it was a risk worth taking if it helped keep the "masses" in line.

While the autumn campaign waxed and waned, the 173rd Airborne was experiencing a bout of organizational turbulence as the 3rd Battalion, 503rd Infantry (Airborne), replaced the 1/50th in Phu My. For just over a year, the 3/503rd had been attached to Task Force South, a provisional brigade that operated alongside the 23rd ARVN Division in southern II Corps.[21] When the 3/503rd came home to the brigade, the 1/50th was detached to take its place in Task Force South. The relief was conducted carefully, with subunits being replaced one at a time so there would be no lapses in security.[22] The presence of the entire 3/503rd in Phu My made it possible to occupy even more phase II hamlets. The 1/50th had been unable to do so because it was weaker in personnel, and a quarter of its strength had been detached elsewhere.[23]

These redeployments were still under way when the autumn campaign's second high point began on the night of 4–5 September. It was interrupted by a unilateral three-day cease-fire proclaimed by the Communists on 6 September to commemorate the passing of Ho Chi Minh four days before. The death of "Uncle Ho," who was revered as a national hero by many South Vietnamese, revealed just how pervasive Communist influence was in northern Binh Dinh. Stephen J. Piotrowski, who was serving in Company C, 3/503rd, at the time, recalled: "Another incident that affected me deeply, and may have had other long range effects, was the death of Ho Chi Minh. . . . This happened while we were on pacification and every flag (South Vietnamese flags) in the villages were flown at half mast."[24]

The autumn campaign's intensity declined across most of South Vietnam as September dragged on, but in Binh Dinh, enemy activity remained well above average. Phu My witnessed the most attacks, with the Vietcong concentrating on high-profile targets around the district seat. The district headquarters was mortared on 9 September, but all the shots fell wide. Three days later, two enemy squads penetrated the district seat, set thirty houses ablaze, and killed and wounded eighteen people—mostly civilians. The Vietcong returned on the night of 14 September and fired five M-79 grenade launcher rounds into the district police station, without causing any casualties or significant damage. When they came back for another try the following night, the VC stumbled into an RF ambush and left behind numerous blood trails as they fled.[25] LZ Uplift, the 1/503rd's principal base camp in Phu My, had been mortared three times in August and was shelled twice more during September, though only four Americans were slightly wounded in all these attacks combined.[26] In the other three northern districts, the story was pretty much the same, as the enemy mixed attacks-by-fire on American positions with a handful of sapper raids, but without inflicting many casualties. The most successful attack of the autumn campaign occurred on 24 September in

Tam Quan, when a B-40 rocket fired at a bridge security detail of Troop E, 17th Cavalry, wounded nine Americans and three civilians.[27]

With the onset of the wet northeast monsoon season in October, enemy military activity wound down until it became indistinguishable from the usual day-to-day pattern of guerrilla warfare. The Vietcong would be unable to transport sufficient supplies to launch another offensive for several months, after the rain-soaked trails had dried out and the swollen streams had dropped back below flood stage. The enemy's terrorist campaign also waned in intensity, but Binh Dinh still experienced the second highest number of terrorist incidents (685) nationwide during 1969, resulting in 570 assassinations, 535 nonfatal injuries, and 373 kidnappings.[28] Since many of the victims were RF or PF leaders and government officials, the enemy was, in effect, conducting a "Phoenix program in reverse," which was enjoying great success at "neutralizing" the GVN's "infrastructure" in Binh Dinh.

The Communists also had their own "Chieu Hoi program in reverse," which used the threat of assassination to encourage "defections in place" by GVN civil servants and military officers. Douglas Pike described the process in some detail:

> Particularly in insecure areas and especially to low-ranking civil servants, the NLF would convey the idea that it would not harm a GVN representative providing he arranged that the programs for which he was responsible were not implemented in any effective way. This could be done by a slowdown, by snarling the program in red tape, or by outright falsification of reports to higher headquarters. . . . A military patrol leader could lead his patrol noisily down a well-travelled path and after an hour return to the hamlet, never having made a serious effort to determine whether the guerrillas were in the area, but with his superiors being none the wiser. The effect was to place a premium on mediocrity in low-level administration at a time when excellence was vital. A civil servant could imagine that he could enjoy the best of both worlds: he could perform well enough not to arouse the suspicions of his superior but not so well as to earn the hostility of the NLF.[29]

Selective terrorism was so effective at producing these "accommodations" that a high-ranking North Vietnamese official argued, "The suppression of one 'tyrant' should be regarded as tantamount to the killing of 100–200 enemy soldiers."[30]

Although terrorism was gnawing away at the GVN's vitals, there was no slackening in the pace of expansion into the phase II target hamlets. The 2/503rd had occupied the last unsecured hamlet in its area of operations on

1 September.[31] Meanwhile, the 1/503rd and 3/503rd were rapidly occupying the last unsecured hamlets in northern Phu My, and the 4/503rd was doing the same in Tam Quan. By the end of September, only five hamlets in Tam Quan remained to be occupied. All were situated in the An Do Valley, a notorious hotbed of Vietcong activity in the extreme northern portion of the district. In order to free up sufficient troops to move into them, the battalion had to drastically thin out its presence in many phase I hamlets, leaving behind its eighty-man weapons company (Company E) and half a dozen five-man STAG teams as economy-of-force hamlet security detachments. By the end of October, it had occupied a total of twenty-four hamlets, as opposed to the goal of thirteen set by the original Washington Green plan.[32]

By the end of phase II, virtually the entire inhabited region of AO Lee had been brought under allied military occupation. Thus, the primary objective of Binh Dinh's 1969 pacification and development plan had been achieved on schedule. Several formerly populated areas, such as the 506 Valley, the Crow's Foot, and the An Lao Valley, remained unsecured, but Colonel Gompf advised that only the first should be resettled because an excessive number of RF and PF units would be required to secure the others. He knew that the 1970 pacification and development plan then in preparation would require the ten ARVN and forty RF companies that had stepped into the PF's hamlet security role to return to their doctrinal missions. It was particularly important for the latter to be released, since Operation Washington Green would not succeed until the Territorial Forces had mastered not only the job of securing individual hamlets but also the RF's interhamlet security mission. The problem was that, in addition to the 40 new PF platoons already in training, 125 more would have to be found to close the resulting gaps in hamlet security.[33]

The Danger Underfoot

Mines and booby traps had always posed a major threat to allied troops in Binh Dinh—and almost anywhere else in the country, for that matter. However, the rapid expansion of the area undergoing pacification in phase II increased the risk substantially by obliging the Sky Soldiers to occupy communities that had long been densely mined and booby-trapped Vietcong strongholds. The scale of the problem is best illustrated by An Hoa, a deserted hamlet in Phu My that the 3/503rd secured in October. It did so with great trepidation because there had already been fifteen mine and booby-trap casualties in the vicinity over the preceding months. Thus, on 20 October, 62 8-inch and 339 105mm artillery shells were fired into An Hoa in the hope of touching off sympathetic detonations, after which twelve CH-47 Chinook helicopter sorties dropped a total of 120 fifty-five-gallon drums of gasoline in order to "cook off" any surviving booby traps. Finally, helicopter gunships fired volleys of 2.75-inch rockets to clear a path into the community. Only then did a platoon move in behind a herd of cattle and set up a base on the edge of the hamlet. The initial penetration went without incident, but the gasoline drops covered a surprisingly small area, and the shells and rockets had little effect. Intact booby traps were later found within five feet of impact craters. On the second day of the operation, a claymore mine killed one man and wounded four. After this setback, the troops confined themselves to the base and used bangalore torpedoes (lengths of pipe packed with explosives) to clear the surrounding hedgerows one at a time. Since it would take weeks to clear the hamlet by this means, the 3/503rd finally brought in a Rome plow (a sixty-ton bulldozer with a heavily armored cab) to strip the entire area down to the topsoil and used hundreds of gallons of gasoline to burn the foliage off an inaccessible cliff side.[34]

Mines and booby traps caused the vast majority of the Sky Soldiers' casualties during phase II. Of the ninety-six nonfatal casualties suffered by the 4/503rd in the third quarter of 1969, only twenty-one had gunshot wounds. All the rest bore the familiar hallmarks of mine and booby-trap injuries, such as "fragmentation wound right thigh," "minor fragmentation wound both legs," "amputation of both legs," and "fragmentation wound left foot."[35] Unfortunately, even under Operation Washington Green's restrictive rules of engagement, dud allied bombs and shells continued to provide the enemy with an endless supply of explosives. The Vietcong also relied heavily on allied forces for more mundane raw materials used in booby-trap construction. Empty C-ration tins were routinely used as explosives containers, stolen radio batteries powered electronic fuses, and a miscellany of cast-off objects was used to manufacture activating devices and detonators. In Phu My, the 1/50th discovered a booby trap activated by the spring-loaded striker from a used smoke grenade, so a policy had to be established to remove the strikers from all spent smoke grenades before disposal.[36]

Other factors that contributed to the Sky Soldiers' high rate of mine and booby-trap casualties were their ignorance of the Vietnamese language and inadequate training for jungle operations. One report noted that casualties could be significantly reduced by the simple expedient of teaching troops the Vietnamese word for "danger," since the Vietcong usually placed warning signs around mined areas situated near populated hamlets.[37] Elsewhere the Vietcong employed more subtle warnings such as crossed sticks, rocks, and plant leaves wrapped around tree trunks to prevent their own men from blundering into booby traps. Americans generally failed to spot the warnings because "these markings are primitive in design and are usually made from natural background materials. This makes them extremely hard to recognize to the untrained eye, but to the VC they undoubtedly stand out like a highway billboard."[38]

Assessing Progress

In quantitative terms, phase II of Operation Washington Green was a great success, despite the enemy's autumn campaign and the continuing terror offensive—whose influence on the morale and behavior of GVN officials was, to a large extent, statistically invisible. According to Binh Dinh's HES data, the population living entirely under enemy control had shrunk from 63,200 to just 1,300 in four months. And although in most cases their communities remained under enemy domination (HES ratings D and E), even that was a major achievement, considering the former state of northern Binh Dinh. An impressive number of hamlets were also upgraded into the "relatively secure" (A, B, C) category, though nearly all of them were situated in the safer southern districts. Overall, these HES statistics hardly proved that the war in Binh Dinh had been won, but GVN influence was clearly on the rise while the NLF's was waning.

Favorable portents could also be read in the improved performance of Binh Dinh's Territorial Forces during phase II. Their own fatalities had declined by more than 50 percent compared to phase I of the 1969 pacification campaign (which had begun in February), while the number of enemy personnel killed held steady. There was an even more dramatic decline in the number of weapons they lost relative to the number captured. It remained to be seen, however, if they would continue to perform as well after the Sky Soldiers were eventually withdrawn.

The Chieu Hoi program also showed dramatic statistical improvement during phase II. After the initial surge of over a hundred Hoi Chanhs in

Table 5.2 Binh Dinh HES Statistics, June–October 1969

Month	Number of Hamlets by Category* (Percentage of Rural Population by Category)						
	A	B	C	D	E	V	Unrated
June	0 (0%)	79 (19%)	285 (55%)	87 (13%)	14 (3%)	72 (9%)	117 (1%)
October	7 (2%)	150 (39%)	258 (45%)	104 (13%)	14 (1%)	11 (0%)	0 (0%)

Source: Hamlet Evaluation System, Monthly Pacification Status Reports, 30 June and 31 October 1969, MACV Command Historian's Collection, US Army Heritage and Education Center, Carlisle, PA.

    * Some hamlets were dropped from the HES during 1969.

Table 5.3 Territorial Forces' Performance in Binh Dinh during the 1969 Pacification Campaign

Statistic	Phase I (Feb.–Jun. 1969)		Phase II (Jul.–Oct. 1969)	
	Regional Forces	Popular Forces	Regional Forces	Popular Forces
KIA	124	132	63	53
Enemy KIA	244	142	235	132
Kill ratio	Combined 1.5:1		Combined 3.1:1	
Weapons lost	70	85	5	28
Weapons captured	97	76	82	64
Weapons capture ratio	Combined 1.1:1		Combined 4.1:1	

Source: MACV Advisory Team 42, Binh Dinh Province Report for the Period Ending 31 October 1969, 4–5, Province Reports II CTZ—Binh Dinh/Kontum box, Southeast Asia Branch, US Army Center of Military History, Fort McNair, Washington, DC.

April, province-wide defections averaged just forty-two over the next three months—though AO Lee continued to account for the vast majority. Defections skyrocketed once the autumn campaign began and remained abnormally high through the end of the year. The 677 Hoi Chanhs who surrendered in the last five months of 1969 greatly surpassed the number of defections in all of 1968. The autumn campaign was evidently the last straw for many enemy personnel, who shrank from the risks of yet another offensive and started surrendering as soon as the August high point began. The even higher Chieu Hoi rates in the months following the end of the autumn campaign suggest that others became demoralized after that campaign proved as barren of practical results as its predecessors.

The 259 Hoi Chanhs who defected in October was the highest monthly total recorded since May 1967, when the 1st Cavalry Division's clearing operations had been at their most intense. What is more, 102 of them surrendered as a body on 17 October, eliminating at a stroke the entire Vietcong apparatus in Phu Thu, a "hard-core" VC hamlet that had once housed the headquarters of the NLF's Phu My District Committee.[39] If morale in an enemy stronghold like Phu Thu could crack so suddenly and dramatically, perhaps there was hope for northern Binh Dinh.

General Barnes Hits the Road

Washington Green was seen from the outset as a "showcase" operation highlighting the ability of a US regular combat unit to operate in direct support of pacification. General Abrams and his deputy for CORDS, William E.

Table 5.4 Hoi Chanhs in Binh Dinh, April–December 1969

Category	Apr.	May	Jun.	Jul.	Aug.	Sep.	Oct.	Nov.	Dec.
Province-wide	110	41	34	50	102	96	259	123	97
In AO Lee	47	46	28	37	57	41	213	135	86

Sources: Pacification Studies Group, Binh Dinh Province: The Challenge—1971, annex G, John W. Saunders Papers; 173rd Airborne Brigade, Operational Report on Lessons Learned for the Period Ending 30 April 1971, inclosure C, Combat After Action Report Washington Green, chart 1, National Archives Records Group 472, 173rd Airborne Brigade files, S-3 ORLL 69–71 box.

Note: The inconsistencies in these data are likely the result of different reporting periods.

Colby (later director of the CIA), were both greatly interested in the operation and sent a constant stream of visitors to report on its progress. These included Major Stuart G. Shafer, USMC, a field evaluator with CORDS's Pacification Studies Group who visited AO Lee in early August. He was optimistic, predicting that the Territorial Forces would be able to maintain the pacification gains on their own if the 173rd Airborne remained in the target hamlets for another four to six months. Shafer recommended that other US combat units be employed in a similar fashion, yet he sounded an important cautionary note by stressing, "there is no way this technique can ensure the motivation in any Vietnamese group to use any new idea or methods."[40] Washington Green also drew the attention of US Army field historians, who conducted dozens of field interviews with personnel of the 173rd Airborne Brigade and Advisory Team 42 in the summer of 1969. The fruit of their labors, known as Project In-Depth II, was of great utility to the author of this study, but Colonel Gompf complained that the historians (and other visitors) demanded so much time and attention that his staff was finding it difficult to perform their advisory functions. Despite his protestations, the flow of visitors continued unabated, culminating with a visit by President Thieu himself on 25 October.[41]

Washington Green began to draw media attention in September, when it was the subject of feature articles penned by George W. Ashworth, correspondent for the *Christian Science Monitor*, and the influential, nationally syndicated columnist Joseph Alsop.[42] Both were impressed by the operation's novel features and optimistic about its prospects. But Ashworth wrote another article in October that sounded a cautionary note about the extent to which it depended on the 173rd Airborne. Quoting an unnamed US official, Ashworth wrote:

> You introduce money, speed, and strength in numbers. Then, when the Americans withdraw, the Vietnamese . . . cannot produce fast enough to

fill the void. Consequently, the people become disillusioned with their own [GVN] officials. You have simply provided temporary expedients to accomplish short-term goals. It is really better to leave them [i.e., the people] to the Vietcong until the South Vietnamese Government can move in to stay, rather than leave them on this disillusioning seesaw.[43]

Washington Green nonetheless did not become well known at home until mid-October, thanks to a series of public speeches made by General Barnes. Word of his briefing to Admiral McCain had spread, and on 10 October Barnes was summoned to the White House, where he repeated it to Secretary of Defense Melvin R. Laird in the morning and to the Industry Advisory Council (comprising the chief executive officers of most of the nation's leading defense contractors) in the afternoon. Laird was impressed by the presentation because, as Barnes explained, it "provided the credibility the Administration was seeking for its widely-publicized Vietnamization program."[44] Acting on Laird's instructions, Barnes gave his speech, now officially titled "Vietnamization," to the "very skeptical if not hostile" Pentagon press corps the following day. The press conference earned General Barnes a front-page story in the next day's *Washington Post* under the headline "Binh Dinh Province: General Tells of Pacification Success," as well as prominent stories in several other major newspapers.[45]

Over the next several weeks, General Barnes became an unofficial Nixon administration spokesman on Vietnamization, giving his speech to the deputy and assistant secretaries of state and defense and to the CIA. But he recalled with particular relish how, "on October 15th, which was 'Moratorium Day,' I gave my speech to one of the biggest high schools in the D.C. area, sharing equal time with an anti-war organization speaker. Although initially hostile to me, the 2,000 students at the end of our presentations were cheering me and booing my opponent."[46] Two days later, he was back in more lofty company, speaking before the President's Business Council, a biannual meeting of corporate leaders that was also attended by most of the cabinet secretaries or their chief deputies. It was, Barnes recalled, "Pretty heady stuff, hobnobbing and dining with such folks and their wives as Secretaries [George P.] Schultz, [Maurice H.] Stans, and [Paul W.] McCracken; Honorables Arthur Burns, Elliot Richardson, and William Martin; and CEO's or Chairmen [William W.] Allen of Boeing, [Frederick] Borch of General Electric, [Frederic G.] Donner of General Motors, [Neil] McElroy of Procter & Gamble, and [Thomas J.] Watson of IBM."[47]

Over the next sixteen months, General Barnes would give his Vietnamization speech more than a hundred times in forums as diverse as high schools, college campuses, television news programs, the army's Command and

General Staff College, and the House Armed Services Committee. Indeed, speechmaking took Barnes away from his Pentagon job so often that his boss refused to recommend him for promotion in his annual efficiency report for 1970. Only a glowing letter of recommendation from Secretary Laird saved his career.[48]

General Barnes's public relations blitz had a discernible impact on the national debate concerning Vietnam. It was no mere coincidence that in December 1969 President Nixon received a letter from eleven Republican congressmen urging that more US combat units in Vietnam operate in the same fashion as the 173rd Airborne.[49] It also may have influenced what members of the brigade and Advisory Team 42 said and wrote about Operation Washington Green. After all, if President Nixon himself was using the operation to trumpet the success of Vietnamization, one could hardly contradict him in public—or perhaps even in a confidential report that might find its way to the White House. Certainly, when echoes of General Barnes's speechmaking reached Binh Dinh, they did not evoke a universally favorable response. John Figueira, whose "Contra-Productive Activities of the 173rd Airborne Brigade" had earned Barnes's ire back in July, revisited AO Lee that fall. What he learned there prompted him to write a new memorandum entitled "Continuing Contra-Productive Activities of the 173rd Airborne Brigade." Figueira hesitated to discuss specific incidents of misbehavior that had been reported to him through hearsay, but he did mention the senseless shooting of a young girl in Phu Cat by a 173rd Airborne soldier. His chief sources were a group of noncommissioned officers (NCOs), all of whom had served in Advisory Team 42 for two years or more, who told him that the 173rd was "the most hated unit in the U.S. Army" by the South Vietnamese. "One of these men read a recent newspaper article about the success of the 173rd with pacification and was bitter about it in view of the unreported deeds of the brigade's off-duty troops."[50]

The Hoai An Experiment

General Barnes's Vietnamization speech highlighted Hoai An as a showcase district and depicted the 1/503rd's withdrawal from it as a critical test of Washington Green's fundamental premise that the Sky Soldiers could work themselves out of a job. At the end of June 1969, Hoai An presented an impressive picture of success. Every inhabited locality in the district had been secured by allied troops, it had the second highest VCI neutralization rate in AO Lee, Chieu Hoi figures were increasing, refugee resettlement was accelerating, and the local Territorial Forces were showing considerable improvement. The enemy had not attempted a single attack in all of Phase I, and both the guerrillas and VCI were finding it almost impossible to function because they had no intelligence networks in the recently resettled target hamlets to inform them when and where allied patrols and ambushes were likely to be encountered. They also had no arrangements in place for collecting funds and food from the villagers or mobilizing them to carry supplies, construct fortifications, build booby traps, and so forth. All this would take time to organize, and that would be almost impossible as long as the 1/503rd remained in the hamlets.

The Vietcong were no doubt relieved when word spread in late July that the battalion was about to withdraw from Hoai An, and the District Advisory Team noted an immediate decline in Chieu Hoi defectors.[51] The guerrillas and VCI must have been ecstatic when the 1/503rd actually quit the district in August. While it headed to Phu My, Troop E, 17th Cavalry, remained behind in Hoai An. Two of its platoons continued to secure Highway 3A, while the third assumed the pacification support and RF and PF training mission, but it could not possibly stand in for the full battalion that had formerly acted in that role. Hoai An's Territorial Forces were truly on their own at last.[52] The Vietcong moved quickly to exploit the situation, though offensive activity remained at a low ebb. There were just four enemy-initiated incidents during August, but that was four more than had occurred in the preceding three and a half months combined. More significantly, the Communists succeeded in reestablishing their "shadow government," and the VCI were soon routinely penetrating the target hamlets for the first time since April. DSA Curtis D. Piper reported:

It is probable that the enemy knew the 173d was about to pull out and that this gave them courage to hold out in the hills a bit longer. With the passage of time, the enemy was able to reestablish his communication system again and was able to speculate more accurately where the locations of friendly ambushes were. With the withdrawal of the 173d, a major stumbling block was removed from the path of the VCI, who have found it easier to travel from the hills to the hamlets.[53]

Enemy activity continued to increase during September. On the night of the tenth, three turncoats allowed the Vietcong to overrun a PSDF outpost, killing three militiamen and capturing thirty weapons and a radio at no cost to themselves. It was the first victory achieved by the local Vietcong in almost five months and dealt a considerable blow to public faith in the PSDF. Allied leaders could take heart from the fact that the enemy found the district's RF and PF to be more formidable opponents and scored no major successes against them during the autumn campaign. Through it all, the VCI grew steadily more active and succeeded in "taxing" a significant portion of the fall rice harvest.

While the 1/503rd was in Hoai An, intense military pressure had produced a steady stream of VCI "neutralizations" through routine tactical operations and Chieu Hoi defections. Its presence had also energized the district's NPFF,[54] but after the battalion left, the policemen reverted to type and rarely ventured out of their fortified base camps. In the first twenty-five days of December, they conducted just one poorly executed operation, and GVN forces in the district neutralized just one significant VCI.[55] Hoai An's DIOCC nonetheless continued to show improvement, with the number of operations it planned and the quantity and quality of intelligence it produced increasing markedly. However, the data being compiled mostly concerned guerrillas and Local Force units, which meant the DIOCC was neglecting its primary mission of targeting the VCI.[56] This was a province-wide problem with major consequences because counterinsurgency doctrine teaches that "if the intelligence organization is targeted on the infrastructure, you will get the order of battle as well, but if it is targeted on the order of battle, you will not get the infrastructure."[57] Unfortunately, this point was not adequately stressed in the training given to American Phoenix advisors. Colonel Gompf complained:

> The current trend in thinking seems to be that a DIOCC advisor's primary role is that of being the District Advisory Team S-2 [intelligence officer]. . . . What is questioned is the emphasis placed on the OB [order of battle] portion of his job, seemingly to the almost complete exclusion of his anti-VCI efforts. At a time when military activity is at a minimum, the emphasis must be toward increased anti-VCI operations, not away from them.[58]

This serves as a healthy reminder that it was not only South Vietnamese shortcomings that hamstrung pacification—Americans were often at fault. Certainly they were responsible for bungling Hoai An's two most important phase II civic action projects. One of them aimed to hard-surface Highway 3A all the way from Highway 1 to the heart of the Crow's Foot—a distance of 9.4 miles—and it was to be finished before the advent of the wet monsoon in October. The project was launched on 30 May by Company C, 299th Engineer Battalion (Combat), and the 15th Light Equipment Company, but it was still less than half completed at year's end. The original plan had been to employ a soil-cement stabilization process that required 70,000 bags of cement, just when the nationwide cement shortage was at its worst. In September the decision was made to use asphalt instead, but holdups in the delivery of materials delayed construction until it was too late to finish before 30 October, when torrential rains inundated much of AO Lee and made Highway 3A virtually impassable. A field historian reported, "Until the dry season comes, the entire effort on LTL-3A is solely to keep the route open to traffic. This is a full-time project and no progress can be made toward completion of the road until the end of the rainy season."[59]

Execution of Hoai An's other key civic action project—building a bridge across the Kim Son River—was even worse. The DSA, Major Arthur W. Garrett, had made the bridge a top priority because without it, the hamlets on the river's left bank would be isolated during the wet monsoon. Unfortunately, the 173rd Airborne Brigade's engineering staff did not concur:

> The 173rd Airborne Brigade did not see the importance of this bridge because their priorities were based on tactical requirements rather than pacification. They soon gave this project the nickname of "The Bridge to Nowhere," which spread to most of the American units in the area. The nickname was prompted by the fact that the selected bridge site had no approach route on either side, and no real road network on the north side of the bridge.[60]

Construction did not begin until 20 August, when 2nd Platoon, Company C, 299th Engineer Battalion, finally arrived on the scene. Given the late start, there was barely enough time to finish before the wet monsoon began—if all went well. Instead, due to an incredible oversight, the design called for a multispan bridge 304 feet long, even though preliminary reconnaissance had measured the river's width at 380 feet! When the error was discovered, the decision was made to fill the gap with a 100-foot earthen causeway, but 2nd Platoon suffered from such poor leadership and low morale that the project progressed very slowly. The pace picked up after the platoon's commander was replaced on 23 September, but the same flood that halted the Highway 3A project washed away one of bridge's completed spans and its abutment on the left bank. It also revealed a fundamental flaw in the new design: "The river came to within a few inches of the bottom of the stringers of the bridge. . . . It is estimated that if the Kim Son Bridge was completed as planned with a 100 foot causeway, the decrease in the river's width at the site would have resulted in the river rising enough to completely destroy the bridge."[61] After this latest setback, 2nd Platoon went back to the drawing board and came up with a plan to substitute two extra bridge spans for the causeway—but the projected date of completion had to be pushed back to 30 January 1970.

The flood coincided with a realignment of the 173rd Airborne's forces in Hoai An. Troop E, 17th Cavalry, left the district to take over the mission of securing the Bong Son bridges and was replaced by Company D, 2/503rd.[62] Although the paratroops were slightly more active in supporting pacification than the cavalrymen had been, they were likewise too few in number to have much impact on the district's security situation. As if to hammer the point home, the Vietcong carried out a bold assassination within days of the company's arrival, killing a GVN hamlet chief and his son just a couple hundred yards from the district headquarters on 2 November.[63]

In addition to Company D and the engineers, there was a third—much smaller—group of US troops operating in Hoai An during the fall of 1969. These were the men of the district's two Mobile Advisory Teams: MAT II-7 and MAT II-90. At full strength, each mustered only six personnel: the team leader, who was usually a first lieutenant; an assistant team leader, also a junior officer; a heavy weapons advisor; a light weapons advisor; a medic; and a Vietnamese translator. Each MAT was affiliated with an RF Group Headquarters (II-7 with the 2/48th, and II-90 with the 25th) and had the mission of training and advising the group's subordinate units.[64] This was a tall order, since each controlled four RF companies and about a dozen PF platoons. Sometimes a MAT would spend as much as a week with a single RF company, especially if it was engaged in a combined operation with American troops. However, it was more common for a MAT to work with a different RF or PF unit every day, joining in sweep and search operations during daylight hours and accompanying ambushes at night. Besides raising the question of when team members slept, this punishing schedule meant that a MAT's effectiveness was severely limited by its inability to devote much time to any particular RF or PF unit.

The MATs' weekly activity reports were an invaluable source for this study because of their unique grassroots perspective on the pacification effort generally and the Territorial Forces in particular. In conventional warfare, the "big picture" is often visible only to those at higher echelons of command, but the reverse is generally true in counterinsurgency warfare. Senior commanders have to rely on reports that distill a day's, week's, or month's worth of activity into a few easily digested facts and often employ a standardized format that encourages stereotyped or formulaic responses. And since there is usually an institutional bias in favor of demonstrating success, the discordant impressions of junior officers and NCOs are often sifted out as they are transmitted up the chain of command. The handwritten MAT reports, in contrast, followed no standardized format, allowing their authors to highlight whatever issues struck them as most important. They also came straight from the front lines, raw and undiluted. Those from Hoai An abound with accounts of shocking inefficiency and ineptitude on the part of RF and PF units, most of which were chronically undermanned because of delays in the replacement pipeline and an AWOL problem of immense proportions. Most of their daylight operations were elaborately staged "walks in the sun" in which the participating units jumped off late and understrength and lackadaisically "searched" for the enemy by moving in single file along well-traveled trails deliberately chosen to avoid known danger areas. One egregious but by no means atypical example was reported by First Lieutenant Earnest L. Ten Eyck, MAT II-90's team leader:

> We accompanied 25th Group HQ and RF [Company] 972 on an operation involving three companies. About 0900 hours, 972 made contact with an estimated VC squad. They inflicted no casualties, but forced the VC to flee, leaving some equipment behind. 972 did not develop the contact, and the Assistant Group Commander—in overall charge—made no attempts in this direction. They spent about 15 minutes "searching" the area, then quit for the day. . . . The operation was scheduled to last all day, yet no serious attempt was made to develop the contact, nor was any air or fire support either requested or utilized. Once initial contact was broken, they seemed to feel that their job was over. It is obvious that in this locale, particularly, they can have contact any time they want it. But the area is studiously avoided unless, apparently, they *do* want contact.[65]

The ubiquity of such practices within Binh Dinh's Territorial Forces had prompted Colonel Gompf to urge that "multi-company search and destroy (AVOID)" operations be discontinued entirely in favor of small-unit ambush and patrol tactics more than a month before this incident.[66]

Another source of frustration was the difficulty encountered in trying to wean the Territorial Forces from their dependence on American firepower. MAT II-90 spent much of 1969 trying to convince the 25th RF Group to use nightly harassing and interdicting (H&I) artillery missions to curtail enemy movement into the hamlets. Although this could have helped compensate for the absence of the 1/503rd, RF company commanders proved unreceptive because they feared being hit by "friendly fire" owing to the notorious inaccuracy of ARVN artillery units. They continued to drag their feet even after the RF group commander finally gave in to the MAT's urging: "In spite of the Group HQ's seeming willingness to make an effort in this area, a check with company commanders leads us to believe that they have not even taken the initial step of requesting [H&I] targets from the companies, though they claim to have."[67] One can hardly blame them, since Brigadier General C. M. Hall, I Field Force's artillery commander, noted that even ARVN regulars were reluctant to use their own artillery: "ARVN commanders would habitually call for, in order, gunships, tactical air support, and then artillery. With the time lag of up to 45 minutes to receive air support . . . much-needed artillery support was held in check and was made in consequence, less effective, timely, and responsive."[68] A vicious cycle developed in which ARVN artillery units fell out of practice for lack of use, reducing their accuracy and giving South Vietnamese commanders even greater cause not to use them.

For reasons that long remained obscure, RF company commanders were also unwilling to use their own organic 60mm mortars. Ten Eyck believed this was another case of the South Vietnamese fearing "friendly fire" due to the mortar crews' inadequate training. When the MAT devoted extra time to training them, however, these efforts did not meet with much enthusiasm. "Presence of mortar crews for training continues to be sporadic, despite the fact that one of the biggest and continuing gripes is lack of adequate and timely fire support—particularly illumination. The opportunity to have this support organically has failed to stir them. To put it bluntly, they could care less."[69] Ten Eyck also received lackadaisical responses when he raised concerns about 25th RF Group's pitiful recruiting effort, which did not yield a single recruit during November, and its dangerous practice of transmitting information "in the clear" even though the troops had been trained in proper radio security techniques.[70] Reports by MATs operating elsewhere in AO Lee reveal that Hoai An was not unusual in this respect, since many RF and PF units in other districts exhibited the same uncooperative and disinterested attitude.

The performance of Hoai An's Territorial Forces was sometimes so absurdly poor that MAT reports read like something out of a Wodehousian farce. On 4 October, for example, MAT II-7 accompanied the 980th RF Company on a blocking-force mission, but of the company's nominal strength of 130 men, only 14 troops led by a sergeant actually showed up. When asked where his commander, Captain Thangh, was, the sergeant replied that he was ill. Yet when the MAT returned to the line of departure hours later, it found Captain Thangh playfully driving the team's jeep around the area, even though the steering wheel had been secured with a chain and padlock. A virtual replay of these events occurred just two days later, except that on that occasion Captain Thangh succeeded in ditching the jeep in the Kim Son River.[71]

Yet the MAT reports also describe some operations that were very well executed. The teams were hard-pressed to account for this schizophrenic behavior, but in time they concluded that the problem was *not* that the Territorial Forces lacked the skills required to do their jobs properly. Lieutenant Ten Eyck reported in December:

We accompanied 190 RF Company on an operation involving three RF companies and elements of the 173d. We air-assaulted into a mountainous area and conducted a search operation as we moved out. Although we encountered nothing of significance, the skill demonstrated by the company and the professional manner in which the company commander and his subordinates conducted the operation belied their previous [poor] performance and recent lack of contact. It appears more and more obvious that their problems are not ones which can be corrected through training.[72]

This begged the question: if the Regional Forces were perfectly capable of performing well, why did they usually conduct their operations so poorly? Ten Eyck concluded that poor leadership was to blame. The commander of the 25th RF Group failed to supervise his subordinates adequately, did not regularly accompany operations, and simply did not care how well or poorly his units performed as long as the statistics passed on to his superiors looked good. One of the most common benchmarks used to determine a territorial unit's effectiveness was the number of operations it conducted per day, and judged by that standard, Hoai An's RF and PF were doing very well. In December there were, on average, fifty-five RF and twenty-six PF ambushes reported each day, but the MATs knew that most of them had been mounted where they were certain to encounter no Vietcong, while many others never actually happened at all. When Ten Eyck approached the 25th RF Group's commander with proof of faked ambushes, he refused to admit that such a thing could happen.[73]

There is an old military axiom that the only things that get done right are those things the commander makes sure get done. The absence of commanders who were willing to take personal and professional risks to ensure that things were done properly was the greatest problem afflicting Hoai An's Territorial Forces. Why should the average RF or PF soldier take risks when he could play it safe without censure from his superiors, most of whom were doing the same thing? Ten Eyck bluntly summarized the root of the problem: "They get the feeling that nobody else much gives a damn, so why should they?"[74] This simple statement calls into question the whole logic of Operation Washington Green. If the Territorial Forces could not stand on their own because of inadequate firepower and tactical skills, the 173rd Airborne Brigade could resolve those deficiencies. If, however, the problem was one of motivation, how could the Sky Soldiers change the behavior of troops drawn from a very alien culture, especially when they were recruited from a population that was traditionally hostile to the GVN? And if motivation was indeed the crux of the matter, did it even make sense to keep the MATs in place, fruitlessly training and advising RF and PF units that needed neither to do their jobs well when they were so inclined?

This was not simply a rhetorical question, since it was clear that Hoai An's Territorial Forces were becoming increasingly dependent on the MATs. We have already seen how reliant they were on US supporting fires. But as the district's RF and PF rapidly expanded, they also became ever more dependent on the MATs for equipment and supplies that their own corrupt, inefficient, and badly overstretched logistical system could not or would not deliver. It turned out, for example, that the RF companies' reluctance to use their 60mm mortars was a result of supply problems rather than poor training.[75] If they fired off the few shells they had, it could take weeks or even months to get resupplied. Not surprisingly, RF commanders chose to save their ammunition to defend against enemy attacks and would not use it for routine fire missions. Since the MATs had access to a vast cornucopia of material resources, the Vietnamese naturally looked to them as an alternative. Ten Eyck reported that the 25th RF Group's supply officer "does not trust his supply system, and prefers to ask his advisors to 'give' him materials than to request them through proper channels. He has the idea that we have helicopters on call for his use only and gets quite upset when we can't supply him with that support at his request. He has picked up the idea that we are here to give him whatever he desires, including personal needs."[76]

The evidence of the Territorial Forces' dependence and ineptitude presented in the MAT reports stands in sharp contrast to the optimistic gloss put on RF and PF performance by Revisionist historians such as Mark Moyar, who claims that their leadership improved dramatically nationwide during this period. No such improvement had occurred in Hoai An, where appallingly poor leadership continued to undermine both pacification and Vietnamization. General Barnes's Hoai An experiment had undeniably failed, raising serious doubts about how AO Lee's other three districts would fare when the Sky Soldiers eventually withdrew from them as well. In early 1970 the Vietnam Special Studies Group (VSSG) reported, "The importance of U.S. presence is highlighted by recent developments in Hoai An District. After the removal of one battalion of the 173rd Airborne Brigade, GVN control dropped from 53 percent in October 1969 to only 30 percent in December 1969. This drop, stepped-up terrorism, and pre-Tet jitters caused by the entry of additional NVA units into the highland areas explain the drop in GVN control during the past few months."[77]

The Yellow Star Division Returns

The NVA troops that had appeared in Hoai An belonged to the 3rd NVA Division, which had recently returned to Binh Dinh from Quang Ngai Province. The division's official history explains that this was done to counter

Operation Washington Green's unprecedented challenge to the Communists' decades-long grip on the population. "The situation caused the province innumerable difficulties and losses. The enemy retook nearly all the areas that were liberated in 1967 and 1968. They had encroached deeper into the areas bordering the coastal lowlands, occupied the high mountain peaks, conducted sweeps, persistently destroyed the rear base areas, and cut the transportation routes linking the base areas with the coastal lowlands."[78]

When the Yellow Star Division's headquarters was detected in AO Lee during September 1969, General Abrams fulfilled a pledge he had made to General Barnes that if NVA units reappeared in northern Binh Dinh, he would "commit, first of all, a battalion from the 4th Division, and then a brigade from the 4th Division before they had my [173rd] people come off the pacification program."[79] The 1st Battalion, 12th Infantry, was accordingly detached from the 4th Infantry Division (whose 1st and 2nd Brigades were operating in Binh Dinh against the 18th and 95B NVA Regiments[80]) and attached to the 173rd Airborne. On 30 September it established LZ Tape in the upper An Lao Valley. A task force comprising the 3/503rd's Companies A and B and Company C of the 2/503rd was simultaneously withdrawn from pacification duty and reestablished Fire Support Base (FSB) Lisa in the valley's northernmost extremity. Together, the two units conducted Operation Darby Trail III between 1 and 5 October.[81]

Darby Trail III was the 173rd Airborne's portion of a much larger operation conceived by General Abrams to trap and destroy the Yellow Star Division along the I Corps–II Corps border. While the 1/12th, the task force, and a regiment of the 22nd ARVN Division operating farther east blocked enemy retreat routes to the south, the 11th Brigade of the US Army's 23rd "Americal" Division and the 4th Regiment of the 2nd ARVN Division operating in Quang Ngai closed in from the north. As was always the case with pincer-type operations, the NVA slipped away through the cordon. Just fifty-five enemy troops were killed and twenty-three weapons captured, and since the Yellow Star Division's combat elements had not yet begun moving into Binh Dinh, the American units operating in the An Lao Valley had practically no contact at all. On 5 October all elements of the 173rd Airborne returned to pacification duty except Company A, 3/503rd, which joined the 1/12th to conduct several days of bomb damage assessment missions in B-52 target zones in the upper An Lao.[82]

The 2nd VC Regiment crossed into Binh Dinh between 25 and 30 October and took position in the An Lao Valley and the Hon Go Mountains that separated it from the Bong Son Plains.[83] The regiment's reappearance after an absence of more than a year added an entirely new dimension to the war in northern Binh Dinh and greatly increased the magnitude of the enemy

B-52 Bombers. *Source:* George L. MacGarrigle, *Combat Operations: Taking the Offensive, October 1966 to October 1977 (The United States Army in Vietnam Series)* (Washington, DC: US Army Center of Military History, 1998), CMH Pub 94-1, 54. [Reprinted by permission of the US Army Center of Military History]

challenge to Operation Washington Green. The regiment was soon joined by other NVA units, including the 400th Sapper Battalion, which opened the Yellow Star Division's new campaign in Binh Dinh on 2 November with attacks on two American fire support bases. At FSB Mahoney in Tam Quan, the sappers were decimated by alert defenders who detected them before they had finished breaching the barbed wire, and the survivors were hotly pursued by elements of Company A, 4/503rd. All told, twenty-one NVA troops were killed, while the Americans lost one man killed and six wounded. FSB Stinger, a lonely outpost atop a mountain on the eastern flank of the An Lao Valley, was defended solely by a battery of the 3/319th Artillery, in accordance with the 173rd Airborne's policy of having its artillery units guard their own perimeters so that the maximum number of riflemen could be deployed in the target hamlets. Even though they were not trained as infantrymen, the "Redlegs" proved more than a match for the sappers, killing nine of them while suffering only two wounded themselves.[84]

The Yellow Star Division's next blow fell on Veterans Day, when its 300th Artillery Battalion subjected LZ English to an intense attack-by-fire with 82mm mortars and 75mm recoilless rifles, killing two Americans, wounding fifteen, and damaging three helicopters. The 300th also mortared LZ Two Bits that same night.[85] The last major attack on the 173rd Airborne that month occurred on 19 November, when the 400th Sapper Battalion raided the headquarters of Company A, 4/503rd, about half a mile southwest of Tam Quan's district seat. The attackers were again detected while breaching the barbed wire and lost ten killed. This third fiasco in less than three weeks rendered the 400th Sapper hors de combat for over a month. A dramatic tactical success was also achieved in Phu My on 5 November after scout helicopters of Troop C, 7/17th Air Cavalry, spotted five people running into a cave on the eastern slope of the Nui Mieu Mountains. The troop's aerorifle platoon was inserted and cordoned off the area until troops of the 3/503rd arrived. They flushed and killed one Vietcong and discovered the underground hiding places of twenty-eight more, who wisely chose to surrender rather than perish. This eliminated at a stroke an entire platoon of the Phu My Local Force Battalion's C-1 Company.[86]

These victories were a boon for the brigade's morale but did not halt the ominous enemy buildup. It was therefore unfortunate that the temporarily attached Company C, 75th Ranger, had departed the 173rd Airborne early in the fall of 1969. That left only the 61 men of Company N, 75th Ranger, available to scout the enemy's mountain trails and base camps, until General Cunningham decided in November to double its strength to 128 men.[87] Surprisingly, most of the new Rangers were found by sifting through infantry replacements that had just arrived in Vietnam, rather than by taking combat veterans from the ranks of the 173rd Airborne. Battalion commanders would have been unwilling to part with their best men, and "past experience has shown that personnel who have been recruited from the infantry battalions have, in varying degrees, adjusted to the peculiarities of those units and are not necessarily apt students of Ranger tactics and techniques. Often, the habits which are considered good in a battalion would not be apropos to a ranger operation."[88]

Meanwhile, General Abrams was putting the second phase of his contingency plan into effect by deploying the 2nd Brigade, 4th Infantry Division, into AO Lee. While the 1/12th Infantry continued to operate out of LZ Tape, the 1st Battalion, 22nd Infantry, established FSB Beaver near the An Lao Valley's mouth on 1 November. The two battalions would spend two and a half months scouring the valley in Operation Putnam Wildcat, but the 2nd VC Regiment left the area in late November. To avoid the Americans operating up in the mountains, the regiment made bold night marches through the Bong Son Plains. On 23 November the 93rd Battalion passed just 1.25 miles west of LZ English on its way south, and the regiment's 120th Signal Company and other units took the same route three nights later. By early December, the entire VC regiment was installed in the mountains south of the Crow's Foot, well placed to strike into either Phu My or Hoai An.[89] This

presented General Cunningham with a quandary. The 2nd Brigade, 4th Infantry Division, could not follow the 2nd VC Regiment south, since sizable
command, combat support, and logistical support elements of the Yellow
Star Division remained near the An Lao Valley, and there were strong indications that the 22nd NVA Regiment was moving into the area from Quang
Ngai as well. And, as fate would have it, the 4th Division's 1st Brigade was no
longer available. On 11 November it had left Binh Dinh to counter an enemy
buildup around Ban Me Thuot in the Central Highlands. The 4th Infantry
Division was left with only two battalions to secure Highway 19 and Camp
Radcliffe. A rash of cratering incidents along the highway and a highly successful 15 November sapper attack on Camp Radcliffe that destroyed nineteen aircraft confirmed that no help could be expected from that quarter.[90]

As December progressed, rumors and prisoner and Chieu Hoi interrogations began to suggest that the enemy was preparing a major offensive in
northern Binh Dinh. As in 1968 and 1969, the blow would probably come
during the Tet holiday and feature large-scale conventional ground assaults
that the tiny hamlet security detachments could not resist. The enemy had
the means to launch such attacks, since allied intelligence had confirmed
the presence of over 3,000 Yellow Star Division combat troops in AO Lee
or adjoining portions of Phu Cat and Binh Khe districts. The 22nd NVA
Regiment, the reconstituting 400th Sapper Battalion, and elements of the
200th Antiaircraft and 300th Artillery Battalions were located in and around
the An Lao Valley, where the 4th Infantry Division's 2nd Brigade would hold
them in check. However, the 2nd VC Regiment and remaining NVA units
were poised in the mountains surrounding Hoai An, opposed only by the
173rd Airborne's weak reconnaissance forces. General Cunningham therefore made the difficult decision to remove the 3/503rd from pacification in
Phu My, and on 13 December it began hunting the 2nd VC Regiment.[91] It
would be joined, two days before Christmas, by the 3rd Battalion, 506th
Infantry (Airborne), which formally belonged to the 101st Airborne Division but transferred from Task Force South. The new battalion colocated
its headquarters with the 3/503rd's at FSB Abby in the heart of the Crow's
Foot.[92]

The 3/503rd's departure forced the 1/503rd to spread its troops so thinly
that it was hard-pressed to maintain security in northern Phu My—particularly since it had the better part of a company tied down guarding bridges
on Highway 1. Necessity being the mother of invention, the battalion soon
developed a novel means of securing the bridges that allowed it to dispense
with static guard detachments. Acoustic sensors suspended underneath the
stringers of the bridges proved sensitive enough to detect anyone moving
or talking in the vicinity. When one of the sensors activated, a mechanized

Table 5.5 NVA in AO Lee, January 1970

Unit	Strength
2nd VC Regiment	980
22nd NVA Regiment	975
200th NVA Antiaircraft Battalion	250
300th NVA Artillery Battalion	245
400th NVA Sapper Battalion	250
90th NVA Engineer Battalion	325

Source: I Field Force Vietnam, Operational Report on Lessons Learned for the Period Ending 31 January 1970, 1, National Archives Records Group 472, HQ-USARV files, ORLL box 3, I FFV file.

infantry platoon mounted on M-113s would dash to the scene and chase the Vietcong off before they could finish preparing the bridge for demolition. In this way, the force required to secure the bridges was trimmed from seventy-two troops to just eighteen men and four M-113s.[93]

Still, the removal of an entire American battalion from Phu My significantly undermined security. From the outset, General Barnes had intended for the Sky Soldiers to remain in the target hamlets until the Territorial Forces were capable of securing them without any assistance. By its mere presence, the Yellow Star Division had obliged General Cunningham to abandon that policy, scoring a bloodless victory against the pacification effort. The unwelcome reappearance of the Yellow Star Division therefore marked a turning point in Operation Washington Green. The dispersion of allied regular combat units in direct support of pacification had been possible only because the weakness of the Communists' regular forces in AO Lee had greatly lowered the threshold for entry into enemy "liberated zones." With the return of the Yellow Star Division, the enemy had suddenly restored the "umbrella of security" for the guerrillas and VCI. To prevent the vulnerable outposts in the plains from being overrun, General Cunningham had no choice but to compromise Washington Green's primary objective by withdrawing his troops prematurely.

The same problem was arising in other parts of South Vietnam as well, since twenty-eight of the thirty-two NVA battalions that retreated into cross-border sanctuaries during the latter half of 1968 had returned. Thus, even while the plan for phase III of Vietnamization (which was supposed to make the ARVN capable of dealing with both the Vietcong and the NVA) was still in development, its key assumption that NVA strength inside South Vietnam would not rise was being invalidated. This was not clear to American policymakers at the time, since allied intelligence was slow to detect the NVA battalions' return. Thus, while a recapitulation of the enemy order of battle produced by CICV in February 1972 would conclude that there had been 188 NVA combat and combat support battalions in South Vietnam at the end of March 1969, at the time, it reported that only 163 were on hand. CICV would continue to underestimate NVA strength in-country by ten battalions through the summer of 1969 and would still be five battalions short at year's end.[94]

Allied intelligence was slow to detect the rise in NVA strength in part because, in keeping with COSVN Resolution 9, the returning battalions launched few large-scale attacks. Instead, they generally limited themselves to ambushes, sapper attacks, and attacks-by-fire, which made them difficult to distinguish from the Vietcong. Some of the reinfiltrated NVA units found it difficult to adapt to their new and unfamiliar mission. In the spring of 1969 five NVA regiments were sent into the Mekong Delta, a region that had hitherto been the exclusive province of the Vietcong. The NVA troops were initially bewildered by the flat, exposed, densely populated delta, which in many places completely lacked the jungle and mountain bases where they were accustomed to sheltering from allied attacks. They consequently suffered high casualties.[95]

The New Optimism

Despite the ominous massing of NVA regulars, General Cunningham and the new PSA, Colonel William J. Mendheim, could take heart from the fact that December's HES report showed 89.6 percent of the province's rural inhabitants living in A, B, and C hamlets, while the enemy totally controlled barely a thousand people—just one-tenth of 1 percent. The allies had achieved their primary objective of "securing" 90 percent of the population and had all but eradicated the NLF's "liberated zones," which had contained almost a fifth of the rural population as recently as April.[96] Dramatic quantitative gains had also been made in other aspects of pacification where progress had been sluggish earlier in the year. In December alone, 8,000 new PSDF militia were organized, bringing the total to 120,976, and nearly 18,000 weapons had been issued to them. In the area of development, 1,339 VSD projects had been approved province-wide, of which 771 had already been completed; about half of the rest were in the final stages of completion. Finally, about 73,000 refugees had been resettled in their native hamlets, causing the number of hectares under cultivation to climb to 70,000—the highest figure since 1965.[97] A visiting journalist was struck that, "Instead of talking about battles, assaults, and dead enemy soldiers, General Cunningham dwells at length on village reconstruction, red tile roofs, rice fields that are once again under cultivation, and new roads. 'Look there, another tile roof,' he said yesterday on a tour of one village. 'That means the people are putting money into permanent houses, and that takes confidence.' There are many new red tiled roofs in this area."[98]

Washington Green's accomplishments were also attested to by the most unimpeachable source of all—the enemy. In November 1969 the NLF held a "political reorientation congress" in the mountains of Binh Dinh at which a high-ranking cadre addressed the situation throughout Military Region 5. He reported that although 350,000 people had been brought under the NLF's control during the spring campaign, only 30,000 to 40,000 were added in the summer campaign, and virtually none over the course of the autumn campaign. He added, "In northern Binh Dinh Province, the enemy pacification elements scored many successes due to local Party officials' loose leadership and inadequate planning."[99]

What he did not say was that the NLF's problems in Binh Dinh were also caused by the Sky Soldiers' continuing refinement of their small-unit tactics. In southern Hoai Nhon, Company B of the 2/503rd was now conducting all its tactical operations at night and had dispensed with static ambushes in favor of roving patrols of four or five men that used grenades as their primary weapon (so their positions could not be detected). They not only ambushed the enemy's nocturnal movements but also pursued the fleeing guerrillas and VCI all night if necessary. To deal with elusive Vietcong spotted at long range, the company's reconnaissance platoon enlarged its Hawk Teams to seven men, including a .50-caliber heavy machine gun crew. The machine gun was used as a semiautomatic sniper weapon, accurate up to 2,000 yards. An enemy document captured in the area lamented:

Presence of US and RF troops in the hamlet areas are making it difficult to procure rice and supporters will not rally. Sympathizers are dwindling and popular support is at an all-time low. The mountains are no longer a sanctuary. The US and RF troops are penetrating and locating base camps in the Tiger Mts. [the northern portion of the Cay Giep range] by use of squad and platoon reconnaissance in force. US troops choose to fight under all circumstances, and will insanely pursue us into the mountains.[100]

And it was not only in Binh Dinh that the insurgency was in trouble. It was also facing unprecedented difficulties throughout Military Region 5. The PAVN official history admits: "By the end of 1969 the population of our liberated areas [in Military Region 5] had shrunk to 840,000 people and the enemy had gained control over an additional 460,000 people. The strength of our guerrilla forces in the entire region dropped by 4,600 soldiers and our local forces declined by 2,000 soldiers as compared with their 1968 year-end strengths."[101]

Indeed, the 1969 pacification campaign was a great success nationwide. According to HES, the objectives of securing 90 percent of the national population and of upgrading half of all "relatively secure" hamlets to A or B ratings were exceeded. In like fashion, the Chieu Hoi program generated 47,000 defections as opposed to the target of 29,600 set for the 1969 special pacification campaign (the original target had been just 20,000). In addition, a quarter of a million new PSDF militia had been recruited, elections had been held in all but a handful of South Vietnam's rural communities, and 488,000 refugees had either returned to their native villages or been permanently resettled elsewhere. Impressive gains had also been made in reviving the rural economy, which benefited greatly from improvements in security on all major highways and the large-scale introduction of IR-8 "miracle rice," a hybrid that produced yields up to double those of indigenous strains. The only major disappointment was the poor showing by the Phoenix program; still plagued by the halfhearted and poorly coordinated efforts of the participating GVN agencies, it failed to meet even the revised goal of "neutralizing" 21,600 VCI (33,000 neutralizations had been called for in the original 1969 plan).[102] James Megellas, II Corps' deputy for CORDS, observed, "Although statistically impressive in 1969, no positive evidence existed that the Phung Hoang program had, in any significant way, damaged the VCI organization in II CTZ. An estimated VCI strength of over 12,000 remained in active operation at the close of 1969."[103]

Despite Phoenix's disappointing performance, it seemed that "fast and thin" pacification was working. Very inefficiently to be sure, the allies finally seemed to be winning the war in the villages. Several influential journalists began to spread the word about the "new optimism" in the final months of 1969, including Pulitzer Prize winner Alfred Friendly of the *Washington Post* and nationally syndicated columnist Joseph Alsop. Both highlighted the "conversion" of Sir Robert Thompson, a renowned counterinsurgency theorist who had been one of the architects of Britain's victory over Communist guerrillas in Malaya during the 1950s. Thompson, who had published a decidedly pessimistic book about the Vietnam War earlier in the year, became far more optimistic after a November 1969 visit to the country undertaken at the request of President Nixon. If current trends continued, he now suggested, it was possible that the Vietcong might be defeated and relative normality restored in the countryside by the end of 1972.[104]

Robert G. Kaiser, another correspondent for the *Washington Post*, was one of the first to report on the "new optimism," but he did not overlook the many fundamental problems obscured by all the auspicious statistics. Therefore, his articles also addressed the GVN's endemic corruption and inefficiency, the Territorial Forces' uneven performance, the manipulation of Chieu Hoi and PSDF statistics, the lack of true grassroots democracy, and the fact that the restored GVN presence in the countryside was only a thin veneer. Ultimately, however, he dismissed these as causes for pessimism. He wrote, "Officials acknowledge that the situation today would be much less favorable for the government if rural security and prosperity depended on the complete success of pacification programs. But the new optimists obviously think they have a successful formula for progress based on a combination of partially effective government programs and feeble resistance from the Vietcong."[105]

Partially effective programs would suffice, Kaiser explained, because the new optimists believed victory could be achieved without winning the population's active support for the GVN:

> The basic assumption of the current pacification program is that active allegiance to the government is less important than a security that would allow people to live normal lives and have reasonably good public services. Whether the government can prevail without winning the active allegiance of the masses will probably depend largely on the resilience of the Vietcong. Many of the new optimists now believe that it is too late for a Vietcong political revival in the foreseeable future.[106]

This, in a nutshell, was the fundamental premise of "fast and thin" pacification. If the Vietcong had, in fact, been irrevocably crippled by their own reckless offensives of 1968–1969, then it might be enough to offer the rural population security and basic public services. And if this were sufficient for the insurgency to wither away, then fundamental reforms to remedy the GVN's manifold shortcoming were not a precondition for victory.

Although the "new optimism" won many adherents and played a decisive role in fostering Vietnam War revisionism in later generations of historians, many doubters remained. President Nixon himself was reluctant to accept the rosy statistics at face value. In this case, his distrustful nature was no doubt intensified by an awareness of the misfortunes that had befallen Lyndon Johnson due to his uncritical acceptance of statistics emanating from Saigon. Therefore, in September 1969 Nixon established the Vietnam Special Studies Group (VSSG) to produce analyses of the situation in Vietnam that would not be filtered through MACV before reaching the Oval Office. The VSSG was chaired by then national security advisor Henry Kissinger and also included the undersecretary of state, the deputy secretary of defense, the director of central intelligence, and the chairman of the Joint Chiefs of Staff.[107] At its first meeting, the VSSG commissioned an interagency task force to prepare a study on the situation in the countryside. Accepting the premise that insurgencies are best studied from the bottom up, the task force chose to write case studies on key provinces—one of which was Binh Dinh—instead of producing a macrocosmic analysis of the situation throughout South Vietnam. Because it lacked a reporting system of its own, the VSSG had to use HES data, even though it was dissatisfied with how that system assessed GVN influence. The task force therefore developed the VSSG control indicator, which used an alternative method of evaluating HES data to determine the quality of GVN control. The VSSG took great pains to distinguish "security"—which it took to mean the occupation of a hamlet by friendly forces—from "control," which required more. "The immediate objective of the war for both sides is to be able to exercise control over people and resources and to deny them to the other side. . . . The establishment of durable control involves effective anti-subversive mechanisms, a government that is sensitive to popular attitudes, and adequate government performance in economic, political, and social matters as well as military and administrative matters."[108]

In other words, "control" involved not just the military occupation of a hamlet but the military, political, and psychological mobilization of its population in support of the GVN and against the Communists. The VSSG control indicator also ruled out GVN control of a hamlet if any one of a series of "vetoing factors" applied (e.g., the VCI remained intact and active in the community or the GVN hamlet chief was not present at night).[109] The VSSG's findings were consequently much less encouraging than the raw HES data. In September 1969, for example, the HES showed 85 percent of Binh Dinh's rural population living in "relatively secure" (A, B, C) hamlets and, by implication, under GVN control. The VSSG analysts, in contrast, calculated GVN control that month at just 44 percent (though this was still twice as high as at the start of Operation Washington Green). They also noted that the population under enemy control had fallen from 20 percent to just 5 percent over the same period. Overall, while the situation in Binh Dinh was not as favorable as MACV claimed, the VSSG agreed that for the first time in years, the allies held the upper hand in the struggle for control of its population. Similar circumstances existed in most of the provinces the VSSG examined.[110]

Nevertheless, there was a fly in the ointment that raised troubling questions about GVN dependency. The VSSG found that throughout South Vietnam there existed an intimate relationship between the efficacy of US

regular military operations and gains in GVN control. "The principal proximate cause of the improved control situation in the past year was the great
shift in the relative strength and effectiveness of GVN and VC local security
forces. In most cases, however, GVN local security forces were able to extend GVN control only in the context of a much more favorable Allied posture in the main force war than had existed before 1969." In Binh Dinh, the
spectacular progress made since April 1969 was credited solely to the 173rd
Airborne. The VSSG could find no causal link between the operations of
40th and 41st ARVN Regiments and the improving control situation in the
province: "Information concerning the effectiveness of the eight ARVN battalions normally stationed in Binh Dinh is limited. Even the Province Senior
Advisor's reports contain little information on ARVN activities. Such statistics as KIA [killed in action] ratios and the limited operational information
which is available, however, indicate clearly that they have been less aggressive than U.S. and Korean forces. The role of ARVN in providing security
in the lowlands is not clear."[111] Perhaps the most telling statistics about the
22nd ARVN Division was that in June, July, and August of 1969 it conducted
approximately 1,800 ambushes in which it suffered a total of just ten fatalities
and killed only six enemy troops.[112]

Similar circumstances were found in most of the provinces analyzed; the
role of ARVN regular units in shifting the balance of the Main Force war
in the allies' favor and facilitating gains in the war for population control
was minimal. Furthermore, while US regular combat units such as the 173rd
Airborne Brigade had developed novel tactics and operational methodolo-
gies that accelerated the positive trend in the war for population control,
the VSSG found no evidence of similar innovations by ARVN units. It was
therefore obliged to reach the unsettling conclusion that, "at least in these
provinces . . . ARVN prospects for success in taking over the burden of the
main force war appear questionable if the enemy is able to rebuild his large
units."[113] Unfortunately, the Communists *were* rebuilding NLF regular units
with North Vietnamese replacements and simultaneously sending NVA battalions that had withdrawn into cross-border sanctuaries back into South
Vietnam. The future of pacification in the key provinces examined by the
VSSG (and undoubtedly others as well) was thus very much in doubt, and
the revelation that gains in GVN population control were dependent on the
presence and aggressive action of large numbers of US and ROK regular
troops did not bode well for Vietnamization.

CHAPTER SIX

Slowdown

As 1970 began, it was widely expected that the Yellow Star Division would launch a major offensive during the ill-omened Tet holiday season. I Field Force headquarters predicted:

> In Binh Dinh Province the buildup of enemy forces is similar to the one which took place prior to Tet 1968. Reports indicate that the enemy intends, by employing the 3d Division, to conduct major offensive activities in the province in an attempt to disrupt or destroy the GVN Pacification Program. This offensive will probably be most intensive in the northern four districts and may consist of relatively large scale ground attacks and attacks-by-fire against RF/PF units, district headquarters and Allied installations in conjunction with wide-spread LOC [line of communications] interdiction and terrorist activity directed against GVN officials.[1]

Enemy propaganda and actions strengthened this suspicion. After the 400th Sapper Battalion had been mauled at FSBs Stinger and Mahoney in early November, the VCI in Tam Quan had warned locals that the district was going to be "trashed" at Tet. Indeed, the enemy began attacking high-profile targets in Tam Quan several weeks before the holiday. The district headquarters compound and LZ English were both subjected to intense attacks-by-fire, the Tam Quan village office was blown up by sappers, and Truong Xuan hamlet was struck by a heavy ground assault. The 9 January attack on LZ English dropped twenty to thirty mortar shells on troops who were playing volleyball and assembling to watch a movie, killing four Americans and wounding eighty-six.[2] If the 173rd Airborne's main base camp could be mauled in this fashion, one could hardly blame the Territorial Forces for being intimidated. As January progressed, many of them went AWOL; in Tam Quan, checkpoints had to be set up on Highway 1 to intercept deserters. The entire 222nd PF Platoon simply disappeared on 19 January. Attempts to locate its commander by radio and visits in the field proved completely unavailing.[3] Many GVN civil servants also joined the exodus. In Hoai Nhon, one hamlet's chief and assistant chief and the com-

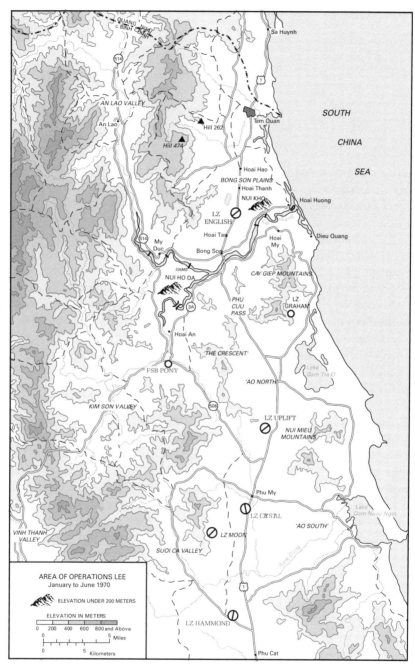

Area of Operations Lee (January–June 1970). *Source:* George L. MacGarrigle, *Combat Operations: Taking the Offensive, October 1966 to October 1977 (The United States Army in Vietnam Series)* (Washington, DC: US Army Center of Military History, 1998), CMH Pub 94-1, Map 32, 317. [Adapted and reprinted by permission of the US Army Center of Military History]

US Troops Search Rock Formation in An Lao Valley. *Source:* "Operation Thayer II [Photograh]," Virtual Vietnam Archive, Item VA029867, accessed December 17, 2015, http://www.virtualarchive.vietnam.ttu.edu/starweb/virtual/vva/servlet .starweb. [Reprinted by permission of the Vietnam Center and Archive, Texas Tech University, Lubbock, TX]

mander and deputy commander of the local PF platoon all made themselves scarce on the eve of Tet.[4]

General Cunningham was so concerned by the looming menace that on 22 January he initiated phase IIA of Operation Washington Green, which was specifically intended to counter the anticipated Tet Offensive. The three battalions on pacification duty adjusted their deployments so reaction forces could be concentrated at central locations, and they prepared contingency plans to deal with assaults on the enemy's most likely targets in their respective AOs.[5] Meanwhile, the 3/503rd and 3/506th continued to hunt the

2nd VC Regiment in the mountains around the Crow's Foot, but with little success, as the enemy was moving in small groups and avoiding contact. Nevertheless, there could be no doubt that large numbers of NVA regulars were in the area after the 3/503rd discovered several hastily vacated base camps capable of housing a multibattalion force. Captured documents revealed that it was a training facility where the 2nd VC Regiment had been receiving instruction in sapper tactics.[6]

Meanwhile, the 2nd Brigade, 4th Infantry Division, was scouring the mountains around the An Lao Valley for the 22nd NVA Regiment, but with no better success. At midmonth, the brigade began a new operation in the heart of Base Area 226. Since this redeployment uncovered Tam Quan, the 3/503rd and 3/506th were shifted to the eastern flank of the An Lao Valley on 17 January. The removal of these two battalions from the Crow's Foot in turn left Hoai An and Phu My dangerously exposed. The gap was closed by the 1st Brigade, 4th Infantry Division, which was rushed into the area on the eve of Tet. In total, there were eight US infantry battalions operating in Binh Dinh's highlands at the end of January, and they would be joined in February by an entire regiment of the ROK Capital Division and a battalion of the 47th ARVN Regiment temporarily deployed from Phu Yen Province. All told, the allies had committed more than a division's worth of regular troops to safeguarding Binh Dinh's pacification gains.[7]

By the time the calendar was approaching the last days of January, the 3/503rd and 3/506th had made their way thirty miles westward into the mountains from Tam Quan without any significant contact. Concluding the NVA had to be closer in, General Cunningham pulled the two battalions back to the lowlands and began a new sweep outward, starting at the first ridge of high ground overlooking the Bong Son Plains. On 3 February the 3/506th poked under the right rock and was met with a hail of fire from Hill 474.[8] What it had found was the 22nd NVA Regiment's headquarters, its 8th Battalion, and its 41st Reconnaissance, 43rd Antiaircraft, 44th Mortar, and 49th Sapper Companies. They were housed in caves and a heap of massive boulders that covered the hill's northeastern face. The latter formed an intricate, three-dimensional maze with myriad openings that provided access to small rock chambers.[9] The 3/506th reported that the "naturally-formed rock caves consisted of such an undefinable number of openings and crevices from which to engage friendly troops, that it was found impossible to concentrate friendly fire on any one suspected location. Should any friendly penetration of the enemy's fortification be accomplished, the connected nature of the caves easily allowed the enemy to bring fire in areas thought to be cleared in the friendly advance."[10] Since a direct assault on this natural fortress was sure to yield long casualty lists, General Cunningham decided instead to besiege it. After a cordon was thrown around the hill, it would be pummeled day and night with as much firepower as could be brought to bear. In the intervals between bombardments, troops in platoon strength or less would cautiously advance into the encirclement and destroy enemy strongpoints one at a time.

The cordon was formed by two battalions of the 40th ARVN Regiment on the plains east of the hill and by the 3/506th and elements of the 3/503rd on the west; it was thickened by fields of acoustic and seismic sensors. An observation post was established on Hill 262, which offered an excellent view of Hill 474 across the half-mile-wide valley that separated the two peaks. To prevent the NVA from escaping at night, searchlights kept the hill constantly illuminated, and a helicopter gunship equipped with a searchlight and an infrared vision device often orbited overhead.[11] Each day, troops of the 3/506th gingerly swept downhill, marking cave and bunker entrances with paint for the benefit of pilots and artillery observers, and contaminating the interiors with CS tear gas crystals. More than 23,000 pounds of CS-2 was used for this purpose, and nonlethal chemicals were also employed to suppress the enemy's defenses before air strikes and ground assaults. If a particularly heavy concentration was needed, CH-47 Chinook medium helicopters dropped sling loads of up to seventy E-158 CS canisters at a time.[12]

Although every allied aircraft in II Corps was invited to dump unused ordnance on the hill, and it was kept under almost constant artillery bombardment, neither proved very effective. It was nearly impossible to score direct hits on the entrances to the caves and crevices where the enemy was ensconced, and nothing else did much harm to the occupants. In some cases, even that was not enough, as an NVA soldier captured during the first days of the siege revealed that his company was sheltered in a cave that wound its way into the hill for hundreds of yards and had multiple entrances.[13] A 155mm howitzer emplaced on Hill 262 had some success firing into bunker and cave entrances over open sights, but flame weapons proved most effective because liquid or jellied gasoline (i.e., napalm) could seep through the cracks between boulders and suffocate enemy troops sheltering in shallow caves. Chinooks were used to drop sling loads of eighteen fifty-five-gallon drums of gasoline, which splattered over a wide area and was then ignited with tracer ammunition.[14]

Surprisingly, the enemy troops on Hill 474 made no concerted effort to escape, although it would have been easy to do so early in the siege. The Yellow Star Division's official history asserts that only the 22nd Regiment's headquarters was present in the "Ong Huong rock formation" and that by remaining there, it pinned down allied forces and thus eased the way for the 2nd VC Regiment to attack in Phu My.[15] These claims are impossible to reconcile with American accounts. In any event, the enemy clearly had sufficient ammunition to hold the hill for a long time, as proved by the tremendous volume of fire directed against allied aircraft throughout the siege. However, the NVA was reportedly short on food almost from the first day. Some was acquired from local civilians who left food packets near the base of Hill 474 while working their fields during the day. After nightfall, these would be recovered by NVA troops slipping through the cordon, which was manned by ARVN troops on that side. But as the siege progressed, the flow of food from this source was considerably reduced. Even so, NVA morale remained good, and efforts to induce defections with leaflet drops and loudspeaker broadcasts proved fruitless. Despite mounting casualties and dwindling supplies, a mere eleven NVA troops surrendered during the entire siege, and most of them had been wounded. One admitted that morale in the 3rd Company, 8th Battalion, was low because it had lost all but fourteen of its forty-five men, but he did not expect many of his comrades to surrender because their officers and NCOs provided strong leadership and were highly respected by the rank and file.[16]

After forty-three days, the siege ground to an inconclusive halt on 18 March when the surviving enemy troops slipped out through the cordon. Allied troops had captured forty-seven weapons, including five machine guns, four B-40s, two 57mm recoilless rifles, and a pair of 82mm mortars. A total of 101 enemy troops were confirmed dead, but there were, of course, more corpses that were never found because they were either entombed in collapsed bunkers or hidden in the farthest recesses of the deeper caves. A prisoner revealed that a chasm in one cave had been used by the NVA to dispose of its dead, but efforts to substantiate this claim were abandoned after a paratrooper was lowered 200 feet into it without finding the bottom.[17]

The siege of Hill 474 forestalled the 22nd NVA Regiment's planned offensive against Tam Quan, which suffered only one significant attack during February. The target was the 27th PF Platoon in Hoai Hao village, which was assaulted before dawn on 4 February. At that point, the battle of Hill 474 was less than twenty-four hours old, and the cordon around the hill had yet to be established. The 1st Company, 8th Battalion, 22nd Regiment, carried out the attack with assistance from guerrillas, who guided it over the three-mile approach march from the hill. Two platoons deployed on opposite sides of the PF perimeter had been instructed to lay down suppressive fire, while a third performed the actual assault. This plan went awry when the assault platoon, charging forward after the covering fire began, unexpectedly found itself confronted by an unbreached fifth barbed wire fence (preliminary reconnaissance had reported only four). The delay allowed the defenders to mow down the easy targets piled up between the fourth and fifth fences. Five NVA soldiers were killed, and three AK-47 assault rifles and a B-40 were taken as trophies by the jubilant PF troopers, whose own losses amounted to one man killed and two wounded.[18]

It was only fitting that the one major attack attempted in Tam Quan proved abortive, since the much-heralded Tet Offensive failed to material-ize anywhere in Binh Dinh. There were several big attacks-by-fire during the Tet holiday, including a fifteen-round mortar attack on LZ English on 1 February. A salvo of eleven 122mm rockets slammed into Phu Cat air base on the following night, killing one American and wounding nineteen, but almost none of the expected large-scale ground assaults took place.[19] Enemy activity in Hoai An actually declined. Phu My, which had been expecting a wave of assaults by the 2nd VC Regiment—and, in particular, an assault on LZ Moon, the base camp of the 3rd Battalion, 41st ARVN Regiment—witnessed nothing more than a modest increase in the routine tempo of VC guerrilla attacks. The story was much the same in Hoai Nhon, where Tet was marred only by a solitary terrorist incident in which five civilians were killed; NVA activity remained conspicuously absent.[20]

The Communists' failure to launch another Tet Offensive suggests that they never intended to do so in the first place and that allied intelligence had either fallen for a ruse or become fixated on the notion that the enemy would not allow the holiday to pass without incident. Still, there was plen-tiful evidence that another offensive had been planned in Binh Dinh. If so, why did it not occur? One possibility is that it had to be postponed due to logistical difficulties, since enemy personnel in Military Region 5 had been short of food since mid-1969. The PAVN official history reports, "In Mil-itary Region 5 our troops lived by the slogan 'food production is the same as fighting the enemy.' Each unit devoted 10 to 15 percent of its strength to food production."[21] Food was certainly a concern in Binh Dinh. A Hoi Chanh who deserted from the 400th NVA Sapper Battalion in early March said: "The A-20 campaign was to begin prior to Tet 1970. However, a se-vere shortage of supplies and food delayed the offensive. Due to a shortage of rice, his battalion had been forced to retrieve potatoes from a plantation operated by the 3d NVA Div. As far as he knew, the lack of supplies was division-wide."[22] The battalion's planned assault on LZ Moon had there-fore been pushed back a month until late February. Captured documents produced by the Finance and Purchasing Section of Hoai Nhon's NLF District Committee revealed:

The enemy has faced a lot of difficulty in collecting and buying supplies, as well as transporting supplies . . . the people don't pay the VC tax and their cadres are not willing to do their missions, especially from April 1969, which was the time the GVN launched the pacification program.

The result was that 70 tons of rice that the VC had hid in Hoai Huong and Hoai My [villages] became rotten because the VC could not get the rice out.[23]

The incessant series of operations conducted in Base Area 226 by the 4th Infantry Division and the ROK Capital Division in late 1969 also contributed to the enemy's logistical woes by destroying food caches and interrupting the flow of rice. In November 1969 the 2nd VC Regiment reportedly was unable to accept 200 replacements from North Vietnam due to food shortages.[24] Finally, the dozen US, ROK, and ARVN battalions that were combing through Binh Dinh's mountains in January and February must have interfered with the enemy's offensive preparations. The defector from the 400th Sapper Battalion also told his interrogators that the delayed attack on LZ Moon had to be postponed yet again in late February when the sappers' planned route was found to be teeming with ROK troops.[25]

Yet, even if the allies had indeed forestalled an enemy offensive in Binh Dinh, the respite was only temporary, since the Yellow Star Division was perfectly capable of trying again later. Moreover, the scale of the allied countermeasures and the leading roles played by US and South Korean troops raised troublesome questions about their sustainability. One could foresee a day in the not-too-distant future when there would be no US or South Korean troops left in Binh Dinh. How likely was it that the 22nd ARVN Division could hold the Communist forces in the mountains at bay all on its own? And that was only half the problem: even while a dozen allied regular battalions were out beating the bush, another fourteen (the three remaining battalions of the 173rd Airborne, eight belonging to the 40th and 41st ARVN Regiments, and three ROK battalions) were securing the coastal plains. The 22nd ARVN Division might eventually become capable of handling either the NVA in the mountains or the Vietcong in the plains, but it seemed inconceivable that it could ever do both simultaneously.

The 1970 Pacification Campaign

At least in theory, the 1970 pacification campaign departed from the "fast and thin" technique, since its prime objective was to upgrade existing C hamlets. The next order of business was to prevent D and E hamlets from slipping back under enemy control. Expanding into D, E, and V hamlets was relegated to third place in the order of priorities.[26] The 1970 campaign also featured a shift back toward the "spreading ink blot" pacification technique in the form of the "area security concept." Devised by MACV headquarters, it divided South Vietnam's territory into four different zones—each of which

Table 6.1 **Area Security Zones**

Category	Description	Responsibility
Secure area	A and B hamlets	PF, PSDF, National Police
Consolidation zone	C hamlets	RF/PF, PSDF, National Police (supported when necessary by regular military forces)
Clearing zone	D, E, V, and X hamlets and unpopulated areas adjacent to consolidation zones	Regular military forces
Border interdiction zone	Unpopulated border areas	ARVN Ranger units

Source: Headquarters, Military Assistance Command–Vietnam, One War: MACV Command Overview, 1968–1972, Southeast Asia Branch, US Army Center of Military History, Fort McNair, Washington, DC.

would be the responsibility of different types of military and paramilitary forces.

Operation Washington Green was at odds with the area security concept because it placed allied regular troops in the consolidation zone. Instead, they were supposed to be operating in the clearing zone and initiating a ripple effect of expanding security:

> When a target [pacification area] was selected, the RVNAF/Free World Military Assistance Forces would conduct clearing operations in the area to eliminate enemy main force units. The area could then be considered temporarily secured. But since holding Allied units in static defense would be an uneconomical use of force and a damper to aggressive execution of the war, the [allied regular] units next moved to the periphery of the area and conducted preemptive operations against the enemy. The original area then became a "consolidation zone" with the new, expanded area forming a shield around it.[27]

The secure areas and consolidation zones were to spread across the countryside, linking up until South Vietnam's entire national territory had been brought under GVN control.[28] Their expansion would also facilitate Vietnamization: as the RF, PF, PSDF, and National Police assumed sole responsibility for securing ever-larger areas, growing numbers of ARVN regular troops would become available to replace American troops in the clearing zone. It was hoped that a similar ripple effect would occur by establishing

PSDF Key Inter-Teams (KITs)—that is, thirty-five-man platoons selected from among the most physically fit and militarily talented members of the Combat PSDF and given five weeks of instruction at Popular Forces training facilities. The KITs were supposed to assume much of the PF's static hamlet defense. The PF units would then be able to adopt a more mobile posture, which in turn would permit the Regional Forces to replace allied regulars acting as mobile reserves for the populated regions. A total of 14,000 KITs were to be organized—enough to deploy at least one in each of South Vietnam's 11,709 inhabited hamlets.[29]

Major changes were also afoot for the Phoenix program, on account of its less than sterling performance in 1969. Two of the most common complaints had been that DIOCCs "padded" their neutralization statistics by counting guerrillas and NLF civilian supporters as VCI, and that the criminal justice system moved at a glacial pace, often taking more than a year to bring an accused VCI to trial. To resolve these problems, the 1970 Combined Campaign Plan established three alphabetically ranked categories for classifying Vietcong suspects:

> Class A elements included full or probationary members of the People's Revolutionary Party and all who had command and operational functions. Class B included all those elements who did not have any command function or significant position in the communist ranks, but were VCI cadre at any echelon from central [committee] to hamlet level. . . . Class C included all other elements engaged, voluntarily or involuntarily, in activities beneficial to the enemy.[30]

Only Class A and B suspects would be counted as VCI. This policy, it was hoped, would encourage the DIOCCs to invest more time and energy in targeting specific, high-ranking NLF cadres. To streamline the judicial process, automatic minimum sentences were decreed for each of the three classes—two years' imprisonment for Class A defendants, at least one and no more than two years for Class B, and a maximum of one year for Class C (though leniency was officially encouraged and immediate parole was often granted). Finally, as a spur to the slow-moving justice system, no captured VCI could be counted as "neutralized" until after he or she had been tried and sentenced. This also ensured that the many suspects who bribed their way out of prison before coming to trial would not be included in neutralization statistics.

The 1970 pacification campaign's most revolutionary feature was the Land-to-the-Tiller (LTTT) program, which redistributed farmland to those working it at no cost. This program had great potential for weaning rural peasants away from the Communists, but the law authorizing it was not passed by the Vietnamese National Assembly until 16 March 1970. The inevitable delays involved in setting up such a large and complex program ensured that it would accomplish little before 1971.[31] Otherwise, the 1970 pacification campaign was not much different from its predecessors. Like them, it focused on "securing" and "controlling" the population rather than convincing people to actively support the GVN. And it too required the pursuit of two contradictory objectives—the simultaneous expansion and consolidation of GVN control. This made even less sense in 1970 than it had the year before: by expanding the area it was obliged to defend, the ARVN's dependence on American troops actually increased just when they were departing the country in droves. It would have been wiser to slow the pace of pacification or, better still, adopt a policy of retrenchment. The GVN would have lost little had it withdrawn from the many marginal communities where it had only a nominal presence and concentrated on fully pacifying the country's most populated and economically vital regions.

Binh Dinh's 1970 pacification and development plan closely followed the guidelines established at the national level. Its primary goals were to "insure security (A, B, and C hamlets) to every citizen of the province, and security (A and B hamlets) to at least 75% of the population."[32] Other phase I objectives included neutralizing 630 Class A and B VCI, resettling 40,000 more refugees, "rallying" 700 Chieu Hoi defectors, boosting PSDF strength to 144,000 (with 41,000 combat members), and redistributing 136 hectares (336 acres) of farmland (the target was so low because the LTTT program did not begin until halfway through the phase). Finally, in keeping with the area security concept, six of the 40th and 41st ARVN Regiments' eight infantry battalions were to be redeployed into the clearing zone. As we have seen, Americans had spent most of 1968 trying to pry the 22nd ARVN Division out of pacification duty—only to reverse course when Operation Washington Green began. Now they flip-flopped yet again. The ARVN withdrawals were supposed to begin in late February but had to be postponed because there were not enough territorial troops available to replace them. The six RF companies and ninety-seven PF platoons established in Binh Dinh during 1970 would eventually suffice to close the gap, but only twenty-five of the platoons—and none of the companies—would become available before the end of phase I.[33]

American troops were also being withdrawn from pacification duty. The 2/503rd began pulling out of Hoai Nhon in February, although its heavy weapons company remained behind to guard the stretch of Highway 1 between the Bong Son bridges and Phu Cuu Pass.[34] Unlike in Phu My, there were enough Territorial Forces on hand to replace the 2/503rd without leaving any gaps in security. It soon became clear, however, that the district's RF and PF units were no more capable of standing on their own after ten months of training and combined operations with the 2/503rd than Hoai An's had been after their three-month-long tutelage by the 1/503rd. GVN officials in Hoai My village were petrified by the American withdrawal. One hamlet chief advised a visiting MAT that security would collapse, even though the American platoon leaving his community would be replaced by two RF platoons.[35] His apprehension was understandable, given that the Vietcong had brazenly entered his hamlet and kidnapped two Hoi Chanhs the day before the Americans left; the following night the Vietcong returned to burn down the schoolhouse. When the district authorities—acting with commendable speed—began to rebuild the school almost immediately, the Vietcong simply torched the building for the second time in a week. The MAT leader did the best he could by temporarily basing his team in the hamlet, but it could prop up only one community at a time. Thus, just two weeks after the 2/503rd left Dieu Quang, one of the most isolated hamlets in Hoai My village, it was suddenly abandoned by its entire population.[36]

In most communities, however, it was not the population that fled but RF and PF leaders and GVN civil servants. A growing number of them could never be found at their posts, although their subordinates always had a ready explanation for their absence. Like the incompetent Major Major in *Catch-22*, these elusive individuals were always absent from their posts when someone came calling but were supposedly present at all other times. In one particularly egregious case, a hamlet chief had taken up permanent residence in Bong Son and visited the community he was supposedly governing three days a month at best. The GVN district authorities were informed of this situation several times but took no action to remedy it.[37]

Although the 173rd Airborne's after-action report tried to claim that security in Hoai Nhon had improved sufficiently to allow the 2/503rd to be withdrawn without prejudicing the pacification effort, it made no effort to conceal the fact that the redeployment was motivated by concerns about the looming threat posed by the Yellow Star Division:

A post-Tet analysis of conditions in AO Lee revealed sufficient progress in Hoai Nhon and Hoai An to permit the release of the 2d and 3d Battalions of the 503d Infantry from a purely advisory and pacification support role. The shift by these battalions into a more conventional combat role marked the beginning of Phase III of Operation Washington Green and was triggered by an enemy buildup along the western periphery of AO Lee.[38]

The Yellow Star Division therefore won another bloodless victory by forcing the premature removal of a second US battalion from pacification duty. Less than four months after the division had reappeared in northern Binh Dinh, the 173rd Airborne was obliged to use half its organic maneuver battalions to guard the highlands of AO Lee, whereas an air cavalry troop and a small Ranger company had previously been deemed sufficient. Colonel Mendheim warned that the security screen was already so thin that no additional allied regulars should be withdrawn from the hamlets at least until the end of the year, but his warning would be ignored.[39]

The 3/503rd, 3/506th, and newly released 2/503rd went after the NVA regulars with a will but enjoyed almost no success in bringing them to battle. The NVA was always encountered in tiny groups that invariably tried to break contact as quickly as possible—and usually succeeded. Aside from the siege of Hill 474, the only significant contact during the first quarter of the year came on St. Patrick's Day, when Company A, 3/503rd, fought a six-hour battle against the 400th Sapper Battalion's 2nd and 5th Companies in the Crescent Mountains. This solitary success was the result of an intelligence windfall the week before when the enemy unit's political officer had been captured in the vicinity by PF troops. The 2/503rd and 3/503rd together claimed just 75 confirmed enemy fatalities and 70 prisoners captured in the first quarter of 1970, while their own losses totaled 14 killed and 123 wounded—though many of the latter were the result of accidents rather than combat.[40] In early March the 3/503rd complained that it would be more effective at engaging the elusive enemy if it had a sniper capability, yet it currently had neither trained snipers nor sniper rifles. This evidently prompted action on the part of General Cunningham. By the end of the month, the battalion had finally received an M-21 sniper rifle and its first fully qualified sniper.[41]

The 4th Infantry Division was having no more success hunting the 18th NVA Regiment in and around Base Area 226. There too, the enemy's standard response to a major allied operation was to fragment into small groups and exfiltrate the area. Like the 173rd Airborne, the 4th Infantry had generally ceased operating in cumbersome, company-size formations during 1969, breaking its battalions down into platoons and even smaller and stealthier patrol or ambush teams. However, the division's commander, Major General Glenn D. Walker, was so frustrated by the paltry results of recent operations that he decided to experiment with other means of cornering and destroying the NVA. What he had in mind bore a strong resemblance to the large-scale search-and-destroy operations that had failed on so many occasions in years past. Walker hoped that things would be different this time because the cordons would be so unprecedentedly dense that it would be impossible for the enemy to slip through them.

This hypothesis was put to the test in Base Area 226 during Operations Earhart White (11–19 March) and Eichelberger Black (24 March–7 April). The first of these deployed five battalions of the 4th Division's 1st and 2nd Brigades in a circular cordon that advanced steadily inward. The second involved a linear sweep by three battalions of the 1st Brigade, with Ranger patrols ambushing likely enemy escape routes ahead of the advance. Both proved to be bitter disappointments. Companies were assigned frontages of 650 yards in Earhart White because, with an average strength of 100 men, that would maintain a density of one man to every 6.5 yards. Yet the planners had not allowed for the fact that the entire operational area was covered by steep, jungled slopes that stretched what appeared to be 650 yards of horizontal distance on the map to half again as much on the ground. Company frontages were accordingly cut to 330 yards in Eichelberger Black, but even that proved too long to create a sufficiently dense cordon. All told, just nineteen enemy personnel were killed and one captured in both operations, and most of them were credited to the Rangers because the enemy found it so easy to avoid the ponderous yet porous cordons advancing slowly in lockstep.[42]

Since neither old-fashioned search-and-destroy operations nor "new model" operations featuring saturation ambushes and Hawk patrols proved capable of destroying the Communist regular units in northern Binh Dinh, the best possible outcome would be to temporarily disrupt their offensive plans. Operation Washington Green was not intended to destroy the Yellow Star Division, but no matter how much progress was made in pacification, the GVN's position in the province would never be secure as long as it remained on hand.

Mirror Imaging

Instead of trying to overthrow pacification in Binh Dinh by means of another Tet Offensive, the Communists "fragmented" their regular units and sent their personnel to augment the Vietcong guerrillas. This development had been foreshadowed in COSVN Resolution 9:

> The provincial troops, sub-region troops and elements of the main force
> must properly apply the principle of troop concentrating and dispersing.
> When concentrated, they will wipe out enemy units and fight battles
> of a definite spectacular nature; when dispersed, they will support the
> [revolutionary] movement, motivate the people to rise up to eradicate
> cruel tyrants [and] pacification agents, wipe out spies, disband the

civilian self-defense personnel, defeat the enemy's pacification scheme, seize control of the population at the grass-roots level, and expand the liberated area.[43]

VC Local Force units in Binh Dinh had been instructed to disperse half their manpower to the guerrillas back in August 1969, but the Yellow Star Division did not follow suit until 1970.[44] In February the 22nd NVA Regiment was broken up and its battalions converted into Local Force units: the 7th Battalion would go north to Quang Ngai, the 8th would remain in Binh Dinh, and the 9th would go south to Phu Yen Province.[45] Although they retained their separate identities, most of the Yellow Star Division's other units were also integrated with the Vietcong. Battalions were broken down into companies that separately infiltrated the coastal plains and sometimes even dispersed into three-man cells to support the VCI.[46] The fact that the Communists had to resort to such extremes revealed just how much the Vietcong had been weakened. A captured document produced by the NLF's Binh Dinh Province Committee reported:

> The number of friends of guerrillas in mountainous and lowland areas and province capitals since the beginning of 1969 to Jun 70 seriously decreased. On the average, it decreased by 42%, but decreased 60% or 70% in some areas, and from only 10 to 40% in mountainous districts. The decrease in guerrilla strength is still going on. . . . At present, the number of guerrillas in many villages is very small. In some places, especially in the southern area, there are no guerrillas. Regarding the secret guerrillas [in allied occupied hamlets], they have been developed but not on a regular basis. In many villages no secret guerrilla forces were activated. The gains only made up for the losses. Only 20% of secret guerrillas were operative. The rest dared not to engage in combat activities because they were afraid of being discovered by the enemy or driven out of their areas of operations.[47]

The policy of reinforcing the Vietcong with NVA units was implemented nationwide, and according to the PAVN official history, by the end of 1970, "most of the cadre and soldiers of the [VC] regiments and armed operations teams in the lowlands were natives of North Vietnam."[48] Revisionist historians have seized on this as proof that the Vietcong had been defeated, but the insurgents' growing dependence merely meant that the Communist war effort now reflected the situation that had long existed in the allied camp. If NLF regulars were now dependent on the North Vietnamese, ARVN regulars had been dependent on Americans since 1965. And if the guerrillas had also become dependent on NVA personnel, the Territorial Forces had always been reliant on their US advisors and allied regular troops. Allowing for units held in reserve to fight larger battles, the Yellow Star Division sent perhaps three battalions to serve with the guerrillas in AO Lee—where there were already a dozen allied regular battalions operating in the role of Territorial Forces. Advisory Team 42 described the enemy's new stratagem as the "mirror-image" of Operation Washington Green: "There are strong indications that the enemy has embarked upon a pacification program patterned after the program of the GVN. Both enemy local forces and some main force units are being broken down and moved into the populated areas."[49]

The Communists also mirrored allied tactics by intensifying their "Phoenix program in reverse." Terrorism mushroomed dramatically nationwide in the first half of 1970, with terrorist incidents rising by two-thirds and casualties by 89 percent. But Binh Dinh was in a category of its own, since its terror casualties skyrocketed by 274 percent and accounted for nearly 8 percent of the nationwide total. Worse yet, while the province was home to just 5 percent of South Vietnam's population, about 20 percent of all casualties involving GVN village and hamlet officials occurred within its borders. During March, Tam Quan alone lost three hamlet chiefs, two deputy hamlet chiefs, a deputy village chief, and a Vietnamese Information Service (VIS) cadre assassinated; another deputy hamlet chief was seriously wounded.[50] The Yellow Star Division's official history describes the carnage with great gusto: "The drive to kill tyrants and break the GVN control over the people in the countryside increased to unprecedented levels. Villages established 'tyrant killer' units. Guerrillas killed tyrants, elderly people killed tyrants, even children participated in killing tyrants. In Hoai Thanh and Hoai Nhon villages, they formed tyrant killer units composed of children. These units were called 'swallow' units."[51]

Table 6.2 Terrorism Casualties, 1970

Area	Jan.	Feb.	Mar.	Apr.	May	Jun.	Total	Village/ Hamlet Officials
Binh Dinh	87	114	134	373	239	325	1,272	112
II Corps	360	857	962	1,751	1,417	1,084	6,341	275
Nationwide	1,632	1,626	2,291	3,765	3,679	3,079	16,072	535

Source: MACJ01R, Fact Sheet: Terrorism in Binh Dinh Province, 28 July 1970, 1–3, Province Reports II CTZ—Binh Dinh/Kontum box, Southeast Asia Branch, US Army Center of Military History, Fort McNair, Washington, DC.

At the end of 1970, Binh Dinh would rank first among South Vietnam's provinces in assassinations (649) and woundings (1,098), third in kidnappings (428), and second in total terrorist incidents (855).[52] The NLF's Province Committee claimed even higher numbers, reporting that it had "annihilated 507 tyrants and spies, suppressed 360 local administrative personnel and spies, and sent 670 others for thought reform."[53] The bulk of the kidnappings and thought-reform incidents targeted PSDF militiamen. COSVN had ordered that they should not be treated as enemies except in combat situations, but many were marched off at gunpoint for lengthy spells of "reeducation." Random terror attacks targeting civilians also occurred, particularly in communities where the Communists had been unable to maintain their Functional Liberation Associations. In Phu My, a captured document instructed, "If in some places we cannot organize the people we have to spread the word to kill the cruel, eliminate the spies, and force the people to participate in revolutionary actions."[54] But, on the whole, the terror offensive focused on the GVN's grassroots leadership, which was literally being massacred. The consequences went far beyond the loss of experienced personnel, because surviving GVN leaders increasingly made survival their top priority, even if it meant neglecting their jobs or negotiating "accommodations" with the VCI. The 3rd NVA Division's official history explains: "Many tyrants had to request transfer to a different area, or resign from their positions. In many locations, the local masses [i.e., the VCI] used these situations to bargain with the enemy, to demand freedom of movement, to resist military conscription, and oppose tyranny. The enemy's grip on the hamlets and villages in the northern part of the province gradually loosened."[55]

Terrorism offered the perfect counter to the massive commitment of allied regular troops in direct support of pacification. Terror attacks required few personnel—or even just a lone assassin—and were often carried out by "legal" VCI whose identities were unknown and who could therefore travel around the populated regions with impunity using GVN-issued identity papers. Allied regulars could neither defend against terror attacks nor hunt down their perpetrators. That, of course, was the mission of the Phoenix program, but it had failed to make much of a dent in VCI strength in Binh Dinh. Until it did, the enemy's bloody and highly successful "Phoenix program in reverse" could not be stopped.

The K-8 Campaign

Even while they were energetically killing "tyrants," Communist forces across South Vietnam had been preparing for the K-8 spring-summer campaign, which began on April Fool's Day. In Binh Dinh, it targeted most of the objectives that allied intelligence had expected to be hit at Tet, but the attacking forces were generally smaller than expected. Tam Quan's district seat was attacked, though only a single twenty-man platoon made the actual assault. The defending 267th RF Company nearly wiped out the attackers, who left eighteen bodies on the barbed wire. The enemy had better luck in Phu My, where they penetrated the district seat and set many buildings ablaze, just as they had done nearly a year before.[56] The extent to which security continued to depend on the Sky Soldiers was revealed in Hoai Nhon, where many locals had no faith in the Territorial Forces' ability to protect them now that the 2/503rd had been withdrawn. Four-fifths of one hamlet's population decamped to Bong Son every night during the April high point, and when two VC platoons entered it on 8 April, the local PF platoon refused to leave its fortified compound to push them back out. Only after a lengthy delay and intervention by the district chief was an RF platoon finally sent to do the job. The RF Group Headquarters initially refused to send troops into the hamlet because it was judged "too dangerous."[57]

The K-8 Offensive's "main event" was the long-deferred attack on LZ Moon, base camp of the 3rd Battalion, 41st ARVN Regiment, which was situated atop an isolated, 450-foot-high hill in southern Phu My. The 400th Sapper Battalion and elements of the 2nd VC Regiment assaulted it on the night of 31 March. In typically hyperbolic style, the Yellow Star Division's official history claims that the entire 3/41st was wiped out, but the reality was bad enough. The NVA overran the battalion headquarters, killing six ARVN troops and wounding twenty-three. Artillery and helicopter gunships eventually drove off the attackers, who left behind twenty-two bodies.[58] The assault on LZ Moon was the first major battle the Communists had fought in northern Binh Dinh since 1968, but it would not be the last. On 5 April the 1st Company, 3/41st, was assailed by three NVA companies while moving along the base of the mountains just 1.25 miles northwest of LZ Moon. Allied firepower once again saved the day, though casualties were heavy on both sides—twenty-five NVA troops were killed, while friendly losses amounted to nine dead, nine wounded, and four M-113s and a helicopter gunship destroyed. Just after dawn the following day, an ARVN task force comprising three battalions of the 41st Regiment, the 3/14th Armored Cavalry, and the 3rd Battalion, 40th Regiment, encountered several enemy battalions in the same general area. This time, the butcher's bill was more lopsided: the South Vietnamese had only three killed and fifteen wounded, compared with eighty confirmed NVA fatalities. However, thirteen helicopters were damaged or shot down during the two-day battle.[59]

The 3/40th ARVN was present because it had been hastily pulled off pacification duty in Tam Quan. Its sister unit, the 2nd Battalion, 40th ARVN

Regiment, had been hurriedly withdrawn from Hoai Nhon at the same time. These precipitous withdrawals gravely undermined territorial security and were greeted with alarm by the GVN district chiefs and their American advisors. In Hoai Nhon, eight hamlets and subhamlets in Hoai Huong village were now defended by a mere five PF platoons and the 181st RF Company, even while the 2/503rd was clamoring for Territorial Forces to relieve its Company E in the mission of securing Highway 1.[60] Thus, although the 2nd VC Regiment's battles in Phu My did not achieve their stated goal of destroying the 41st ARVN Regiment, they caused a marked decline in security throughout AO Lee.

The Yellow Star Division's official history also claims that the 2nd VC Regiment "penetrated deep into eastern Phu My District and in one surge attacked 'strategic hamlets' in the villages of My Duc, My Chanh, My Tho . . . killing and capturing hundreds of regional and popular force troops and 'pacification' cadre."[61] Though American records do not confirm this breathless account of NVA triumphs, they confirm that the district's Territorial Forces were being severely tested. Many attacks were directed at the PSDF as the enemy tried to break the morale of the poorly trained militiamen, who lost forty-eight weapons in four separate incidents during April— chiefly because of traitors in their ranks. Recruits' identities were supposed to be checked against the VCI blacklist before they were accepted as Combat PSDF, but evidently that had not been done. The DSA, Major Anthony C. Robnett, concluded that the K-8 campaign had significantly impacted Phu My's pacification effort:

> On two occasions the 3d Bn, 41st ARVN withdrew hamlet security forces from southern My Tai village in order to provide additional security for LZ MOON, the battalion headquarters. On each occasion . . . the four hamlets in the area had no security forces other than PSDF. Since one of the major objectives of the present offensive being conducted by the enemy is to force friendly forces out of the hamlets and back into secure base areas, it would seem that some part of the objective has been accomplished.[62]

The 173rd Airborne Brigade tried to relieve the pressure on Phu My by shifting the 2/503rd to attack the 2nd VC Regiment's bases in the Suoi Ca Valley on 10 April. Two days into the operation, Hawk Team 220 encountered platoon-sized NVA units on two separate occasions. The results—eleven NVA soldiers killed and two machine guns, one rocket launcher, one grenade launcher, and a radio captured—stand in mute testimony to the effectiveness of the Hawk technique. Aside from these skirmishes, however, the 2/503rd had no contact with the enemy. On 20 April it shifted its attention to the valley's northern reaches and was reinforced by E/17th Cavalry and Company B, 3/503rd. More contact occurred in the new operational area, but American casualties mounted alarmingly. One paratrooper was killed and four wounded on 21 April by a booby-trapped 2.75-inch rocket. On the following day, 1st Platoon, E/17th, was almost wiped out when eighteen men were wounded by a command-detonated 155mm artillery shell. Elsewhere that day, fifteen more men were wounded by a mortar attack on the command post of B/3/503rd.[63]

When the Suoi Ca operation ended on 25 April, all the 2/503rd had to show for its own numerous casualties were twenty-nine enemy bodies, two prisoners of war, and eleven captured weapons. It had demonstrated yet again the sheer futility of allied efforts to clear enemy regular units from Binh Dinh's rugged uplands, for although there was no doubt that much of the 2nd VC Regiment was present in the area, the enemy been able to avoid contact on all but a handful of occasions. The 173rd Airborne estimated that the 2nd VC Regiment and its attachments suffered 250 fatal casualties in April, while the South Vietnamese claimed 1,200 Vietcong and NVA killed province-wide during the month.[64] However, the latter tally is probably inflated, and in any case, nearly all those casualties resulted from battles of the enemy's own choosing. When they chose not to fight, the allies could not force them to.

Though this lesson seems obvious in retrospect, at the time, it was apparently ignored. How else can one explain Operation Darby Sweep, which was launched in response to the discovery that the 2nd VC Regiment's 95th Battalion had installed itself in the Nui Mieu Mountains? The operation began with Companies B and C of the 1/503rd, E/17th Cavalry, local RF and PF units, and four battalions of the 40th and 41st Regiments throwing a cordon around the mountains. After a twenty-four-hour preliminary artillery bombardment, the 2/503rd and 3/503rd began a meticulous sweep of the entire massif on 28 April. Like nearly all operations of this type conducted in Binh Dinh, Darby Sweep was a "bust." The 2/503rd killed one Vietcong and captured ten more, but the 3/503rd did not lay eyes on a single enemy and made no significant material finds.[65] The operation's failure could be attributed in part to the gratuitous daylong bombardment, which merely ensured that most of the enemy troops in the Nui Mieus had slipped away before the first Sky Soldier set foot in them. Yet there is no reason to believe that Darby Sweep would have been more successful even if the bombardment had been dispensed with. An operation of this scale, and particularly one involving so many ARVN and RF and PF troops, could not possibly be planned without enemy spies becoming aware of it.

The Unfavorable Psychological Climate

Despite the drawdown in troops on pacification duty, there were still twenty-four allied regular battalions in Binh Dinh at the start of April, but nearly half of them were gone by month's end.[66] The 3/506th left the 173rd Airborne for good, while the 40th ARVN Regiment and the entire 1st and 2nd Brigades of the 4th Infantry Division headed west to participate in the Cambodian incursion. The 4th Division's 3rd Brigade left Vietnam and returned to its home base in Colorado. Only the 3/12th Infantry and divisional reconnaissance units remained behind to defend Camp Radcliffe and secure Highway 19. But the political furor the Cambodian incursion ignited back in the United States was so intense that all American troops left that country by 16 May. However, the 40th ARVN Regiment would continue to operate across the border until the end of June.[67]

When the regiment pulled out of Tam Quan between 26 April and 4 May, it left behind a yawning void in Hoai Thanh and Hoai Hao—the district's two southernmost villages. This necessitated a painful thinning out of security forces elsewhere so that the two RF companies could be deployed into the regiment's now almost defenseless former AO. And since Tam Quan's Territorial Forces were still incapable of standing on their own, the 4/503rd had to realign its deployments as well so that Companies A and B could be inserted into Hoai Hao and Hoai Thanh alongside the RF companies. The manpower available to maintain territorial security had thus been reduced by better than half in three of Tam Quan's most densely populated villages.[68]

Meanwhile, the second phase of the 41st ARVN Regiment's planned relief was under way in Phu My. There too, district authorities had to "rob Peter to pay Paul" in order to find sufficient Territorial Forces to replace the departing regulars. However, the district's RF and PF were already stretched so thin that it proved impossible to withdraw the entire 3/41st by the end of May as planned. Instead, only half the battalion was pulled out of the hamlets, but even that required shifting an RF company from AO North, which inevitably opened gaps there.[69] Advisory Team 42 did not try to hide its displeasure at the withdrawal of so many ARVN regulars from pacification duty right in the middle of the K-8 Offensive. "The shifting of FWMAF and ARVN troops has completely negated the original plan to replace these units with territorial forces. Province is hard-pressed at present to provide minimum security to some of the populated areas that have been left uncovered by the main force units."[70]

Even if more territorial units had been available, security probably would have declined anyway. In Hoai Nhon, four of the six PF platoon commanders in one village went missing on 7 May—just hours before the Communists launched the K-8 campaign's next high point.[71] No large-scale ground attacks took place, though there were several dramatic sapper raids. The most spectacular occurred on 9 May, when sappers succeeded in damaging the Highway 1 bridge at Bong Son—and, in the process, thoroughly embarrassing the troops of the 2/503rd who were tasked with its defense.[72] Although a temporary repair was quickly made, this represented a major psychological triumph for the enemy because it proved that even the most important and closely guarded installations were not secure against their depredations.

The night of 9 May also witnessed a sapper attack on LZ Graham, a compound housing the 1/503rd's 4.2-inch heavy mortar platoon situated on a southeastern foothill of the Cay Giep Mountains. Sappers from the 400th Sapper Battalion's C-1 Company managed to enter the position, despite being fired on by a sentry while breaching the barbed wire. The sentry was driven from his post by a hail of small-arms fire and grenades while B-40 rockets slammed into LZ Graham from positions on opposite sides of the perimeter. The hill's terraced sides protected the sappers from the defenders' fire and allowed them to move laterally around the perimeter in almost perfect safety. The Americans held the enemy off until their supply of hand-launched illumination flares was exhausted. During the interval of darkness that ensued while one of the mortars was being prepared to fire illumination rounds, the sappers drove the defenders from half the perimeter, set a bunker on fire, and threw grenades into the Fire Direction Center (FDC). The defenders held out in the other half of the perimeter until they were reinforced by troops from Company D, 1/503rd. The enemy departed before dawn, leaving behind a B-40 and two bodies. The defenders lost just one wounded, but their casualties would have been higher had the enemy's grenades worked properly. Of the two that had been thrown into the crowded FDC, one failed to detonate, and the other exploded with an unusual noise and an odd red glow—but little blast effect or shrapnel. One cannot help but be impressed by the sappers' skill and suicidal bravery, particularly since perhaps as few as three of them actually entered the perimeter.[73]

The attack on LZ Graham was but one incident among many demonstrating that NVA regulars were now present on the southern slopes of the Cay Gieps. During the first two weeks of May, elements of the 1/503rd repeatedly encountered NVA troops in the area. On 13 May a fierce battle broke out after Company D's 3rd Platoon spotted fourteen North Vietnamese washing clothes in a stream. Reinforced by the rest of Company D and two RF companies, they killed sixteen enemy troops while their own losses amounted to six wounded. The NVA withdrew from the area after this setback and shifted into the Crescent Mountains.[74]

The 2nd VC Regiment had meanwhile returned to the Suoi Ca Valley and was thought to be preparing for a return performance in southern Phu My. The allies responded by pounding the Suoi Ca with B-52 air strikes. After the bombing was done, two companies of the 3/503rd entered the valley on 20 May, while troops drawn from the 1/503rd, E/17th Cavalry, and Territorial Forces formed a cordon in southwestern Phu My; Company N, 75th Rangers, placed a screen of ambushes to the north; and the 203rd Reconnaissance Aircraft Company (O-1 "Bird Dog" spotter planes) kept the southern end of the valley under observation. Yet, forewarned by the preliminary bombing, the 2nd VC Regiment was nowhere to be found. The operation was terminated after three days passed without any contact, but as soon as the Sky Soldiers were gone, the NVA began moving back into the valley. By the end of the month, allied intelligence reported that the 2nd VC Regiment's 95th Battalion was once again present in the area.[75]

As the K-8 campaign continued into June, it was Tam Quan, not Phu My, that witnessed the most enemy activity. Its district seat was subjected to an incessant series of small harassing ground attacks between 27 May and 15 June. The almost routine cycle of attacks-by-fire on allied military installations also continued, including a pair of dramatic attacks on LZs Crystal and Uplift by the 300th NVA Artillery Battalion using 122mm and 140mm rockets. The K-8 campaign finally ran out of steam by the end of the month, and although there were hints that a third high point was scheduled for late July or August, for the moment, enemy activity remained at a low level.[76] According to Binh Dinh's HES statistics, the offensive had done little to hinder pacification. There were about 10,000 fewer people living in A-rated hamlets at midyear than in February, but the loss was minor compared with the increase of 90,000 people living in B-rated hamlets. There had also been some slippage in C-rated hamlets, but the populations involved were small.

Although HES statistics showed Binh Dinh's rural A+B population con-

Table 6.3 Binh Dinh HES Statistics, 1970

Month	Number of Hamlets by Category (Percentage of Rural Population by Category)						
	A	B	C	D	E	V	Unrated
February	4 (2.5%)	183 (48.7%)	263 (38.7%)	95 (9.9%)	0 (0%)	7 (0.2%)	12 (0.9%)
June	9 (1.4%)	215 (58.2%)	221 (29.0%)	105 (10.7%)	0 (0%)	10 (0.1%)	8 (0.6%)

Source: Hamlet Evaluation System, Summary Reports, 28 February and 30 June 1970, MACV Command Historian's Collection, US Army Heritage and Education Center, Carlisle, PA.

Table 6.4 VSSG Control Indicator, Binh Dinh, August 1969–April 1970

	Aug. 1969	Sep. 1969	Oct. 1969	Nov. 1969	Dec. 1969	Jan. 1970	Feb. 1970	Mar. 1970	Apr. 1970
GVN control	28%	29%	35%	30%	32%	24%	23%	22%	18%

Source: Vietnam Special Studies Group, Binh Dinh Province: Control Assessment, 28 October 1970, 6, John W. Saunders Papers.

sistently above 50 percent and rising in the first half of 1970, according to the VSSG control indicator, the GVN-controlled population had been falling since November 1969 and stood at just 18 percent in April.[77] The VSSG's five "vetoing factors," which negated GVN control of a hamlet regardless of other considerations, made all the difference. The most important one in AO Lee was the unwillingness of GVN officials and RF and PF leaders to stay in a hamlet overnight. The problem had grown to epidemic proportions in northern Binh Dinh by the second quarter of 1970, and a growing number of civil servants and territorial commanders refused to visit rural communities even in broad daylight. PSA Colonel Mendheim explained that their timidity was caused primarily by the enemy's brutal but highly effective terror campaign:

> The cumulative impact of the continuing communist campaign of political terrorism in the last three months has slowed, and in certain areas apparently has reversed, the progress in the pacification program. . . . The declining Chieu Hoi return rate (34 returnees in June—the lowest since July 1969) and the recently-reported reluctance of An Nhon District PSDF to act are symptomatic of the unfavorable psychological climate in several rural areas. The GVN forces and leadership in the province have not yet adjusted their tactics to the terror campaign.[78]

In his classic *War Comes to Long An*, Jeffrey Race argues that popular attitudes per se are not truly decisive in counterinsurgency warfare because "the potential represented by a diffuse low-level feeling of goodwill among a segment of the population will go unexploited without a highly-motivated minority who will risk death to realize that potential."[79] Race found that the NLF's grassroots leadership in Long An Province was generally willing to accept that risk, while the GVN's was not. The same was true in Binh Dinh, although Operation Washington Green had altered the equation by essentially giving GVN officials and RF and PF commanders American bodyguards. However, the psychological climate began to deteriorate in late 1969, when the Yellow Star Division returned and the first US battalion was removed from pacification duty. Things went from bad to worse in 1970, when another American battalion and almost all the ARVN regulars pulled out of the hamlets, even while the terror campaign escalated and NVA troops were farmed out to the Vietcong. Most of the GVN's junior leadership responded to this dramatic shift in the local balance of power by reverting to past habits of passivity, absenteeism, and dereliction of duty. Not surprisingly, rank-and-file troops and civil servants followed suit. Why should they do any different when their leaders set such a poor example?

The VCI, in contrast, had generally "stuck to their guns," even when things were most desperate for them in late 1969. Many cadres had either been eliminated by intense allied military pressure or lost heart and defected under the Chieu Hoi program, but most had doggedly hung on through thick and thin—thereby ensuring that the insurgency did not lose its grip on the people. Most hamlets remained accessible after dark to the "illegal" NLF cadres who hid nearby during the day, and practically all had at least a few "legal" VCI living clandestinely among their populations. In October 1970 the VSSG reported:

> The efforts of both legal and illegal cadres have been successful in maintaining Communist political influence and undermining GVN political support in Binh Dinh, despite the failure of VC/NVA military programs. Further, the nearly pervasive presence of these cadres gives the Viet Cong the potential of making large control gains—particularly among the contested population—after favorable military developments or in the disorganization which might follow a coup, a cease-fire, or US withdrawals.[80]

The VSSG was decidedly pessimistic about what would happen when the Sky Soldiers left the hamlets for good: "In these northern areas, GVN control gains are extremely sensitive to continued US presence. US withdrawal from the northern districts would turn most of the rural areas back to the Viet Cong."[81]

Back to Square One

This reversion was already happening in Hoai An, where, by mid-1970, the Territorial Forces had been virtually on their own for ten months. From August through October 1969, only a single platoon of E/17th Cavalry was on pacification duty, although the troop's other two platoons were also in the district securing Highway 3A. The reconnaissance troop was replaced by two platoons of Company D, 2/503rd, but they too devoted most of their energies to securing the highway. It was not until January that they became more directly involved in pacification by forming several five-man STAG teams to train the PF and PSDF. Even this marginal US regular military presence ended in the third week of February when the 2/503rd was pulled off pacification duty.[82]

Aside from the District Advisory Team, the only Americans who remained in Hoai An belonged to the district's three MATs (II-7, II-44, and II-90). Starting in January, they began focusing their efforts on training and advising Hoai An's PF and PSDF—a significant change from their earlier policy of working almost exclusively with the Regional Forces. They quickly learned that whereas most RF units were reasonably proficient in small-unit tactics, many PF units were shockingly deficient in even the most fundamental combat skills. MAT II-90's leader, Lieutenant Earnest L. Ten Eyck, reported that the entire complement of one platoon seemed to be afraid of their weapons and flinched when firing them. Night ambushes were "completely fruitless," Ten Eyck reported, and they were conducted so poorly that he considered it unsafe for his team to accompany them.[83] In one case, the MAT members and some STAG personnel had to move away and set up a separate defensive perimeter for their own safety. First Lieutenant Melvin Metzer, leader of the recently formed MAT II-44, found the situation so discouraging that on 18 January he unsuccessfully lobbied for his team to be reassigned to another district.[84]

The MATs were frustrated not only by the Popular Forces' abysmal performance but also by the chronic absenteeism and inaction of GVN village and hamlet officials. One hamlet chief was absent for almost the entire month of February, and his disinterest in working with the Americans filtered down to his subordinates. As a result, efforts to finish weapons training for the hamlet's PSDF militia were repeatedly foiled by poor attendance.[85] However, the chief was merely following the example set by his superiors, who were almost always absent from their posts and had not inspected the PSDF in six months.[86] Lieutenant Ten Eyck observed, "If the PSDF is ever to be an effective force and 'hamlet security' more than a joke, someone besides American advisors is going to have to take an interest."[87]

This lax attitude was typical of many GVN officials and RF and PF commanders who failed to keep tabs on their subordinates. Their lack of oversight enabled territorial units to shirk their duties and report themselves at or close to full strength when they were in fact experiencing extremely high AWOL rates. MAT II-7 reported in late February that some PF platoons were actually not present in the locations where the district headquarters thought they were, and the platoon commanders could not account for the majority of their men. In one case, only seven troops from a platoon with a nominal strength of over thirty could be located.[88] Lieutenant Ten Eyck reported,

"Visits . . . by the Province I.G. [inspector general] to 2 of our RF units revealed some rather startling discrepancies. Surprise visits of this sort should occur more frequently and without advisor urging. Just the knowledge that one could occur anytime would be incentive enough for commanders to keep their 'house' pretty much in order."[89] Unannounced field inspections were, unfortunately, few and far between.

The enemy exploited the situation by infiltrating a VC regular company into the Nui Ho Da, a steep ridge that dominated the lowlands lying west of the confluence of the An Lao and Kim Son Rivers. It was discovered there on 26 March by the 945th and 972nd RF Companies, which, liberally supported by artillery and airpower, killed twenty-three enemy troops while suffering only one fatality themselves. Yet, the fact that an enemy unit of that size could establish itself right in the heart of Hoai An's densely populated lowlands stood as dramatic proof of the ineffectiveness of territorial security. When the first high point of the K-8 campaign began a week later, enemy forces had little difficulty penetrating the hamlets.[90] The Vietcong launched no major ground attacks, so the nearest thing to a proper battle occurred on 14 April, when the 981st RF Company encountered a VC platoon lying in ambush. A firefight ensued during which MAT II-7 rendered invaluable assistance by directing artillery, helicopter gunships, and air strikes against the enemy. The honors of the day were evenly split, as both sides lost eight killed.[91]

When American advisors and fire support were not available, however, most of Hoai An's territorial units engaged the enemy only when directly attacked themselves. Night ambushes, which were essential to deny the enemy access to the hamlets, were poorly conducted when they happened at all. MAT II-7 reported, "It is felt that night ambushes are only effective if accompanied by MAT, and then only if prior notice was given that the MAT will accompany the ambush." When no Americans were present, the Territorial Forces were far more concerned about ensuring their own safety than engaging the enemy. Most ambushes were actually night defensive positions, and their locations were selected with an eye to maximizing defensibility rather than impeding enemy movement. They were often deployed in the same places every night, precisely so the Vietcong could more easily avoid them.

As always, poor and/or absentee leadership was at the root of most of the Territorial Forces' shortcomings. MAT II-90's new leader, First Lieutenant David L. Winship, made a blistering report about the commander of the 25th RF Group in Hoai An:

> We received three to four 60mm mortar rounds in and around our perimeter which killed one RF and wounded three, whom we medevaced.

After the attack, when we were finding out exactly what had happened, the Group Commander was nowhere to be found. It is our opinion his absence at this time and previous incidents indicate the man is either totally afraid, or incompetent as a field commander. He evidently had no idea about requesting a medevac; at least, we had to find him to ask if he wanted one. . . . Since he has been the Group Commander, he has accompanied his troops on only two occasions. All other operations he has directed companies from the Group HQ.[92]

Poor motivation and leadership at all levels allowed the Vietcong to score a victory in Hoai An during the April high point, although the district's RF and PF outnumbered them many times over. The victory was not won cheaply, since it cost the enemy fifty confirmed dead, but its real value could not be calculated in terms of casualties inflicted or territory captured. According to those traditional benchmarks for measuring military success, the April high point had been a failure. Instead, the Vietcong had won a psychological victory whose effects were visible in the population's growingly willingness to support the NLF. The District Advisory Team reported, "Following the period 1–10 April, the VC capitalized on their costly but successful 'high point' by collecting rice and taxes from the people. They have enjoyed success in this endeavor although the District Chief has aggressively attempted to deny the VC this success."[93]

The deteriorating situation in Hoai An was being replicated wherever allied regulars had been withdrawn from pacification duty. As soon as they were gone, the Territorial Forces and GVN officials reverted to their habitual passivity and avoidance of risks, and the Vietcong—now "beefed up" with NVA troops—became more aggressive. Villagers, sensing which way the wind was blowing, became more willing to pay NLF taxes, participate in NLF Functional Liberation Associations, and spy on the allies. One sure sign was the growing frequency with which ambushes were being "blown" by the locals, who used fires, lanterns, flags, and gongs to warn the Vietcong when allied troops were nearby. In parts of Hoai Nhon, families with relatives in the Vietcong sometimes had to be forced to spend the night in RF and PF compounds to prevent them from signaling. The downside was that they were able to acquire intelligence on the territorial units' nighttime security procedures.[94]

The Territorial Forces' inability (or unwillingness) to stand on their own was the principal cause of the deteriorating situation, but ARVN regulars also bore some of the blame. When a third battalion of the 41st Regiment left Phu My's AO South in late June, it was replaced by a task force comprising a company each from the 1/503rd and 3/503rd, and Troop E, 17th Cavalry.

On the very first day in its new operational area, one of Troop E's platoons and an accompanying RF platoon stumbled upon an enemy base camp in the southern foothills of the Nui Mieus that was defended by C-4 Company, 95th Battalion, 2nd VC Regiment. By the skillful application of supporting fires, the allies managed to kill twenty-one enemy troops and capture thirteen weapons without taking any casualties themselves.[95] However, ARVN troops had supposedly swept through the same area the previous day without finding the long-established base camp. It seems certain that they were fully aware of the camp's location and had simply chosen to avoid it. Such a choice would have been fully in accordance with the 41st Regiment's recent behavior. According to the DSA, Major Anthony C. Robnett:

> Since the withdrawal of the majority of their troops from direct pacification support, the 41st ARVN Regiment has not discharged its responsibility for clearing NVA/VC base areas adjacent to the populated areas of the district. This is due, in part, to a reluctance to engage large enemy forces even when the opportunity is presented and, in part, by their lack of honest effort when they do operate in enemy base areas. In the latter part of May an ARVN battalion contacted a large NVA force in western My Hiep Village. Rather than closing with the enemy, the ARVN battalion called in artillery, gunships and air strikes and used this cover to withdraw to LZ Crystal.[96]

The long-term implications of the 41st Regiment's lackluster performance were alarming. The South Vietnamese would soon have to prevent NVA incursions into the coastal plains without American assistance, but instead of preparing for that day, the 41st ARVN had lapsed into a pattern of inactivity that was reminiscent of its behavior in the years between 1965 and 1968, when it had mostly sat out the war. The regiment was once again neither supporting pacification nor conducting effective mobile operations. It was, in fact, doing little more than defending its own base camps. Major Robnett caustically observed: "The 41st ARVN continues to fail in coordinating their efforts, or rather their lack of effort. They have two battalions which have done an outstanding job of securing LZ Crystal."[97]

The deteriorating situation forced General Cunningham to go back to square one in phase IV of Operation Washington Green, which commenced on 10 May. Since the miscellany of different training schemes developed by units of the 173rd Airborne had failed to improve the Territorial Forces' performance, they would all be replaced by the Accelerated RF/PF Training Program—a standardized training regimen that provided intensive instruction in the fundamentals of marksmanship, weapons care, patrolling,

General Cunningham with I Field Force Commander General Arthur S. Collins
(second and third from left). *Source:* The private collection of the late General
Cunningham, reprinted by permission of Mr. Michael Cunningham.

ambushing, artillery fire direction, mine warfare, and other basic military
skills. The highly structured twelve-week schedules detailed a 192-hour RF
platoon training curriculum and a 120-hour PF platoon curriculum; a quarter of each would consist of on-the-job training at night. Each of the brigade's
four maneuver battalions would oversee the Accelerated RF/PF Training
Program in a different district: the 1/503rd in Phu My, the 2/503rd in Hoai
Nhon, the 3/503rd in Hoai An, and 4/503rd in Tam Quan.[98]

The Accelerated RF/PF Training Program represented a long-overdue ra-
tionalization of the 173rd Airborne's training efforts, but its underlying logic
was flawed. First, how could the Territorial Forces acquire basic military skills
in just twelve *weeks* when they had failed to do so during a full twelve *months*
of American tutelage? Second, what the RF and PF lacked was not training
but leadership and motivation—and there was nothing the Sky Soldiers could
do to remedy these shortcomings. If General Cunningham recognized this
stark reality, he gave no hint of it in his official reports and public pronounce-
ments, which were uniformly optimistic. But then, how could he admit that
Washington Green was failing when the Nixon administration had made the
operation a centerpiece of its public relations effort to show that Vietnamization was a success? Under the circumstances, the only real option was to try
another round of training in the hope that it might make a difference.

Phase IV of Operation Washington Green also went back to square one by reinserting US troops in direct support of pacification in Hoai Nhon and Hoai An. While this was essential to halt the alarming deterioration in those two districts, it revealed the extent to which the GVN's very survival in northern Binh Dinh continued to depend on American troops. It also required General Cunningham to accept the risks involved in removing troops of the 2/503rd and 3/503rd from clearing operations directed against the Yellow Star Division. The two battalions accordingly kept the forces committed to propping up the Territorial Forces as small as possible.

In Hoai Nhon, the need for an American military presence was greatest in the extreme northeastern portion of the district, where Hoai Huong village had been left dangerously exposed by the exit of the 1st Battalion, 40th ARVN Regiment, in early April. Company D, 2/503rd, was inserted into the village in the second week of May, but only a single platoon of American troops was actually employed in the hamlet security role. The rest of the company concentrated on searching for enemy hideouts on the nearby Nui Kho ridge. Although the Americans were unable to bring the enemy to battle and suffered a disturbing number of booby-trap casualties, both security and the performance of Hoai Huong's RF, PF, and PSDF improved dramatically.[99] During June, enemy activity throughout the district fell off considerably as the K-8 campaign ran its course. The 2/503rd was able to reduce its presence in the hamlets to a pair of five-man STAG teams, but its Company D continued to comb through the Nui Kho, while the battalion's reconnaissance platoon began combined operations in the Cay Giep Mountains with an RF recon platoon. The two recon units were joined near the end of May by two reinforced rifle companies from the 3/503rd and saturated the area with a swarm of Hawk patrols that produced many contacts with small groups of Vietcong and NVA.[100]

The situation in Hoai An was so tenuous that the entire 3/503rd had to be sent into the district. In concert with local RF units, the battalion began intensive screening operations in the Crescent Mountains and along the fringes of the lowlands west of the Kim Son River. Like its sister battalion in Hoai Nhon, the 3/503rd tried to keep the number of troops deployed in the hamlets as small as possible and rotated them at two-week intervals. At any given moment, only the two US platoons engaged in the Accelerated RF/PF Training Program would actually be involved in direct support of pacification. Each simultaneously trained three PF platoons during its rotation through the training mission. "US platoons present two weeks training to each PF platoon, replaced at a later time by another US platoon that will conduct an additional two weeks training. This program continues over a given time period resulting in all PF platoons receiving 12 weeks of training without stagnating any US platoon from the primary role of conducting combat operations."[101]

Security improved dramatically within days of the 3/503rd's arrival. Even the 20 May departure of two of the battalion's companies for several weeks of operations in the Suoi Ca Valley and Cay Giep Mountains did not slow the rebound. Enemy activity of all kinds declined precipitously as the Vietcong and NVA were forced to disperse into small groups in order to avoid incessant allied patrols and sweep operations. The downward trend in enemy military activity became even more pronounced during June, when the 3/503rd and the local RF and PF shifted from platoon- and company-size operations to patrols mounted by individual squads and even fire teams (5,100 night ambushes and 35 company-size and 512 small-unit daylight operations were conducted during the month).[102] But while enemy offensive activity almost ceased, terrorist attacks continued. On 2 June the 3/503rd lost its commander, Lieutenant Colonel John J. Clark, who was killed by small-arms fire while riding in a helicopter. Although it is unclear whether Clark was deliberately assassinated, the 3/503rd went after the VCI with a vengeance, devoting its elite reconnaissance platoon to the task of hunting them down. By reacting instantly to intelligence produced by the battalion's intelligence staff and Hoai An's DIOCC, the reconnaissance platoon racked up an impressive tally of "neutralized" VCI during July.

The situation in Hoai An at the end of the month was almost identical to that in mid-1969. The decimated Vietcong were on the run, struggling to avoid starvation and experiencing many defections due to low morale.[103] And once again, instead of remedying the many shortcomings of the district's Territorial Forces, the American presence merely enabled them to become even more lax. Some RF and PF units even got into the habit of having all but one or two of the men participating in an "ambush" bed down for the night. On one occasion, a MAT went out at night with a PF platoon and the American squad training it and reported:

> The entire ambush was terrible. Not only did the PF's sleep, but they brought *hammocks* to sleep in—the first time we have seen this particular stunt. The platoon leader was the epitome of incompetence—shouting in the middle of the night, leading his ambush in front of every home in the hamlet; it seemed as though he was trying to impress the locals with the number of Americans he had with him, as a warning not to fool with his ambush.[104]

Despite the growing number of "hammock ambushes" being reported in Hoai An, this provoked no action on the part of senior RF and PF commanders, demonstrating that the 3/503rd's presence had done nothing to improve the quality of GVN leadership. For a few brief days in late May, MAT II-90's leader, Lieutenant Winship, had dared to hope that things would improve, given that the appallingly bad 25th RF Group Headquarters had been replaced by the 24th RF Group Headquarters transferred from Hoai Nhon. By the end of the week, however, it had become clear that although the new commander was more competent than his predecessor, things were not going to change for the better. The 24th Group's subordinate units were putting out as few ambushes as possible and invariably positioned them in the same locations night after night. Worse yet, the entire group was openly hostile and antagonistic toward the MAT; its advice was ignored as a matter of course, and it was never informed in advance about upcoming operations. This was the last straw for Lieutenant Winship, who wrote: "I would suggest that the MAT be removed from this location and not replaced. The 24th Group has received all the possible training, all the possible advice, and the only benefit the MAT holds for them is in the area of supplying them with items they cannot get immediately through supply channels and the equipment they can steal from us."[105] The Accelerated RF/PF Training Program was equally futile, Winship argued:

> The platoon from the 173rd working with our PF's doesn't seem to understand just what their function is supposed to be. They have been here a week and I see no progress whatsoever. The only change I see is the PF's are much richer from the cameras, watches, and food they have stolen from the Americans. The [American] squad we ambushed with asked us if they could ambush *without* the PF's. If these people are to be used in training, it seems to me they should have been briefed as to just what they were supposed to do.[106]

Clearly, the 3/503rd's policy of rotating new platoons into the training mission every two weeks was severely detracting from the program's effectiveness, and the participating Sky Soldiers undoubtedly viewed the whole affair as nothing more than a brief vacation from their "real job" of hunting the VC and NVA. Their enthusiasm for the training mission was not increased by the theft of supplies, equipment, and personal property by the territorial units with which they were colocated. On a few occasions, tempers flared to the point where Americans and South Vietnamese came to blows and almost opened fire on each other.

The notoriously corrupt and inefficient South Vietnamese logistical system was largely to blame for this wave of larceny; it was also an underappreciated cause of the Territorial Forces' reluctance to engage the enemy. One of Hoai

Nhon's MATs spent the entire first half of 1970 unsuccessfully trying get its RF and PF units resupplied with M-79 grenade launcher ammunition.[107] Requesting supplies through GVN channels was so futile that some Territorial Forces had given up on submitting requisitions and were wholly dependent on scrounging, theft, and American largesse. Incredible as it seems, the RD Cadre Teams were even worse off because their ammunition requisitions had to be sent all the way to the Ministry of Rural Development in Saigon for approval.[108] MAT II-90 had an opportunity to experience the GVN logistical support system firsthand when its jeep broke down in mid-January. As part of the effort to wean the Vietnamese from their dependence on American logistical support, MATs had been instructed to rely on the GVN for supplies and maintenance whenever possible. So in January the team sent its jeep to a GVN automotive maintenance facility to have the clutch replaced. Four months later, it was still waiting to get the vehicle back, and queries always elicited the same response: the mechanics were "waiting for parts."[109] Phu My's District Advisory Team had an even worse horror story to tell:

On February 20, advisory vehicle 122308 was turned in to the Province A&DSL [Administrative and Direct Support Logistical] Company for repair of the differential and headlight wiring. When the vehicle was picked up on 21 April, the two new batteries in the vehicle had been replaced with two old ones with cracked cells, four new tires had been removed and four dry-rotted tires installed, the fan had been removed and replaced with one which had a blade missing, the fan belt had been replaced with an old one, the wiring on the distributor was loose, the carburetor connections were broken, the oil was low, the electric gas pump had cracked and gasoline had leaked all over the inside of the vehicle, and over 300 miles had been registered on the speedometer over the mileage which showed when the vehicle was turned in.[110]

Running in Place

Operation Washington Green was still faltering in mid-1970, despite the innovations introduced in phase IV. Statistical indicators were taking a favorable turn since the K-8 campaign had ended and US troops had returned to Hoai An and Hoai Nhon. But the ARVN regulars, RF, PF, PSDF, RD cadres, and GVN bureaucrats continued to exhibit all the same deficiencies they had fourteen months previously, when Washington Green began. And these deficiencies were not limited to the security sphere; they extended across the board to embrace every facet of the pacification effort. In a virtual replay of 1969, the entire first phase of the 1970 pacification campaign passed without a single new Village Self-Development project being completed in AO Lee. In fact, the 1970 VSD program was not even launched until March because no project proposals could be selected until village council elections had been held. Instead, the first quarter of the year was spent wrapping up 452 incomplete projects left over from 1969.[111] Little was accomplished in the next two months either, since village officials were overwhelmed by paperwork, and provincial authorities had approved just one new proposal by the end of May.[112] The situation improved only slightly in June, as the program continued to be held up by a shortage of forms and squabbles among village, district, and provincial authorities over how much money, manpower, and materiel each would contribute to the projects' "self-development" component. Since the 1970 VSD program failed to make any progress until July, the centerpiece of Binh Dinh's civic action effort achieved virtually nothing in the first half of the year—for the second year in a row.[113]

The Phoenix program was also plagued by the same shortcomings that had crippled it in 1969, although Binh Dinh's impressive "neutralization" statistics disguised that fact. The province had a phase I neutralization goal of 630 VCI, and by the end of June, GVN statistics showed that 1,421 had been neutralized (415 killed, 739 captured, and 267 defected).[114] But the vast majority of them had occurred during routine combat activity or random cordon-and-search operations. DIOCC participation in the planning and execution of those operations had been marginal at best, and in most cases nonexistent. The Pacification Studies Group reported: "In early 1970, Regional [i.e., II Corps] Phung Hoang inspection teams rated the Phung Hoang Program in Binh Dinh Province in the highest category, but only based on their high number of neutralizations. The effectiveness of individual District Phung Hoang Centers [DIOCCs] and the Province Center [PIOCC] was poor, marked by incomplete dossiers and a complete lack of any specific targeting of VCI."[115]

An inadequate VCI database and a lack of specific targeting were, of course, the very problems that US Phoenix advisors had been harping about since the program's inception. They had focused on getting the database built, reasoning that it was the essential prerequisite for specific targeting. By late summer 1969, all the DIOCCs had made significant progress in assembling district "blacklists" and were taking the first steps toward producing target dossiers. However, at that point, the program simply ran out of steam. The various DIOCC agencies lost interest as soon as the blacklists were complete, and in those few places where target dossiers were prepared, the agencies showed little inclination to act on them. And because the files were not kept up-to-date as new intelligence on the VCI became available, their value steadily declined.[116]

The consequences were greater than one might suspect, since incomplete and out-of-date DIOCC files greatly complicated the task of prosecuting captured VCI. The Phoenix inspection teams reported, "A continuing indication of the lack of proper dossier preparation has been the repeated failure of the Province Security Committee to sentence detainees to appropriate imprisonment. This has been attributed, time and again, to the failure of Phung Hoang Centers to furnish sufficient evidence to convict those detainees forwarded to the Province Security Committee for trial."[117] Since Binh Dinh accounted for the majority of suspects apprehended in II Corps, it is not surprising that the average sentence handed down to convicted VCI in the region in early 1970 was just nine months. However, time spent in prison awaiting trial was not deducted from a sentence, and Binh Dinh's Province Security Committee (PSC) processed cases at an agonizingly slow pace. Not a single suspect captured in 1970 was sentenced until April, and at the end of May there were still 779 awaiting trial (out of a total of 1,009 in all of II Corps).[118]

The PSC was supposed to meet weekly, but in fact it assembled only once a month. The same was true throughout II Corps, since the region's dozen PSCs met a total of just seventy-six times in the first half of 1970.[119] It is hard to escape the conclusion that they were just going through the motions, and their obvious lack of interest was replicated throughout the GVN chain of command. Phoenix inspection teams visiting Binh Dinh in 1970 always found the same lack of command emphasis by provincial and district authorities, as well as a crippling reluctance to share intelligence. Phu My's DIOCC accomplished almost nothing in early 1970 because the Police Special Branch (PSB) refused to supply intelligence to the NPFF and other Phoenix "action arms." Things went from bad to worse in May, when the PSB essentially opted out of the program by replacing its two full-time DIOCC representatives with one who divided his time between police duties and running a private business.[120] Many other agencies likewise provided only part-time PIOCC and DIOCC representatives and often assigned inexperienced, low-ranking personnel who sometimes did not even understand their mission.

> District and Deputy District Chiefs have not had the time to devote to the supervision of Phung Hoang Centers. This duty has been left to young Sub-Sector S-2's [district intelligence officers], usually first or second lieutenants. These officers have been militarily and "Order of Battle" oriented, and their equally young and inexperienced [US] Phung Hoang Advisors soon became so oriented and more interested in tactical operations than the dull, by comparison, [anti-VCI] operations of the Phung Hoang Center.[121]

In terms of results achieved by the DIOCCs, the anti-VCI effort in northern Binh Dinh was almost as futile in mid-1970 as it had been when Washington Green began. This is not to say that there were no targeted operations. In Hoai An, nineteen suspects were apprehended in February after captured documents revealed the identities of the "legal" VCI in two hamlets. A similar purge occurred five months later, after the district's NLF propaganda chief defected and gave up the names of the entire covert NLF apparatus in An Huu village. Yet these successes resulted from intelligence windfalls rather than patient detective work.[122] There would never be enough lucky breaks to cripple Binh Dinh's VCI, which possessed a hydra-like ability to replace its losses. According to a captured document, the NLF postal transportation and communication network in Hoai Nhon had been placed under great strain by allied military activity during the first half of 1970. The combination of identity card checks and ambushes in the lowlands and Hawk and Ranger patrols in the mountains severely restricted its activities and ultimately cut the "illegal" postal route between Hoai Nhon district and the NLF Province Committee. In addition, eleven village- and four district-level communications-liaison personnel had been killed, captured, or defected out of a total of fewer than fifty. During the same period, however, twenty-six new communications-liaison personnel were recruited, and a "legal" postal link to the Province Committee was established as a replacement for the blocked "illegal" route.[123]

Most Revisionist historians assert that the allies won the Vietnam War at some unspecified point before the Paris Peace Accords were signed, but Lewis Sorley dates the victory to 1970. At the year's midpoint, however, victory remained as elusive as ever in Binh Dinh. Despite fourteen months of intensive effort, Operation Washington Green had made almost no progress toward its ultimate objective of Vietnamization. The RF and PF still showed no hint of developing the ability to maintain territorial security without the assistance of regular troops, the ARVN regulars remained incapable of facing the Yellow Star Division on their own, the Phoenix program was almost dead in the water, and GVN leadership showed no sign of improvement. For the moment, the 173rd Airborne was "keeping the lid on" and preserving much of northern Binh Dinh's hard-won pacification gains. But the clock was starting to run down on Operation Washington Green, and when the Sky Soldiers eventually pulled out of the hamlets for good, the whole edifice of pacification seemed certain to come crashing down. At least in Binh Dinh, there was still no sign of the Revisionists' "lost victory," and the window of opportunity for achieving it was shrinking by the day.

CHAPTER SEVEN

The Red Queen's Race

It was not only in Binh Dinh that the 1970 pacification campaign was falter-ing. MACV's command history admitted that it "fell far short of the momen-tum generated during 1969."[1] In the first half of the year VCI neutralizations and Chieu Hoi defections both came up short of their targets, and April was the first month since Tet 1968 that HES showed a nationwide regression in security. One reason for the decline was that many allied units operating in key provinces had been withdrawn to participate in the Cambodian incur-sion. Another was the introduction of HES-70, which reduced subjectivity by having CORDS advisors answer objective questions instead of assign-ing scores, as in the original HES. Hamlets rated A, B, and C immediately declined by about 5 percent.[2] The 1970 pacification campaign also suffered from a lack of emphasis by President Thieu, who was distracted by the Cam-bodian incursion and civil disturbances in Saigon involving students and dis-gruntled war veterans.

HES ratings would start rising again in the latter half of 1970, but it is unclear how significant the upward trend really was. Since the "fast and thin" 1969 campaign had placed most of South Vietnam's rural communities under military occupation and established elected governments in all but a small fraction of them, opportunities to make further easy *quantitative* gains were starting to become scarce. Instead, the allies now had to turn to the far more difficult task of making *qualitative* gains across the board. HES was ill suited for tracking qualitative progress in leadership, morale, aggressive-ness, tactical competence, psychological climate, and so on. Quantitative data were much easier to "capture" and often involved measuring inputs (e.g., elections held, PSDF recruited, RF and PF units established, VSD projects completed) rather than results. It was therefore possible for HES to show that progress was being made even if the governments were ineffective, the PSDF useless, the RF and PF avoiding contact, and VSD projects failing to alter popular loyalties. This situation could persist as long as the enemy adhered to the low-intensity, protracted war strategy adopted in COSVN Resolution 9 and remained content to undermine pacification gradually rather than trying to overthrow it by main force.

HES data were also subject to manipulation. In early 1969 the GVN had

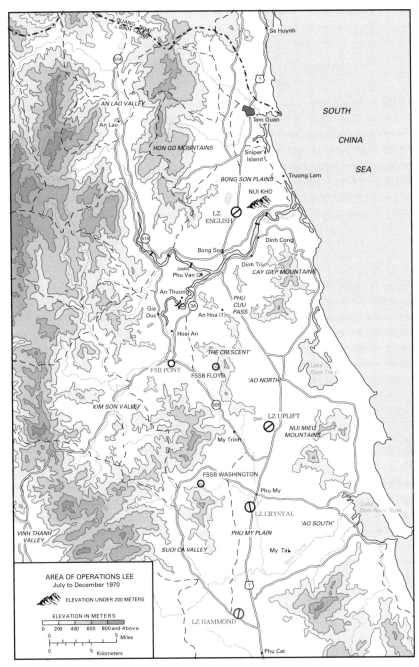

Area of Operations Lee (July–December 1970). *Source:* George L. MacGarrigle, *Combat Operations: Taking the Offensive, October 1966 to October 1977 (The United States Army in Vietnam Series)* (Washington, DC: US Army Center of Military History Pub 94-1, 1998), Map 32, 317. [Adapted and reprinted by permission of the US Army Center of Military History]

decreed that "villages and hamlets that are underpopulated can be merged with adjacent ones,"[3] thus making it possible to gerrymander Vietcong-dominated communities out of existence. In Dinh Tuong Province, the number of villages fell from 93 to 78 and the number of hamlets declined from 629 to 462—in one case, six V-rated hamlets were consolidated into just two.[4] A similar process took place in Binh Dinh, where the number of rural hamlets dropped from 672 in March 1969 to just 568 by June 1970.[5] Not all of them were eliminated by consolidation, however. Some were dropped from HES because they were unpopulated and situated in indefensible regions such as the An Lao Valley, which the GVN had no intention of resettling. Yet, even this less objectionable practice was subject to falsification. Aerial reconnaissance conducted in early 1970 revealed that 178 "abandoned" hamlets in Pleiku Province that had been dropped from HES a year earlier actually had a combined population of at least 17,500. It is hard to see how such a gross error could have gone undiscovered for so long unless there was a concerted effort to keep this mass of enemy-dominated D, E, and V hamlets out of HES.[6]

Therefore, even HES-70 substantially overstated pacification gains and obscured the fact that the NLF's political influence in the countryside still eclipsed the GVN's. In the summer of 1970 VSSG produced a study that analyzed four different cease-fire scenarios: an in-place cease-fire that would permit NVA units to remain wherever they were in South Vietnam; an agreement stipulating that they would be "regrouped" into a handful of border provinces; a cross-border withdrawal into Laos and Cambodia; and a complete withdrawal back to North Vietnam. If an in-place cease-fire brought a lasting cessation of hostilities, VSSG predicted that just nineteen provinces would remain firmly under GVN control, while seventeen would revert to Vietcong control and eight would be "toss-ups."[7] The predicted outcome in Binh Dinh was the same in all four cases—the Communists would secure control of the rural population in short order:

> Gains in government control disguise the continuing power and vitality of the VCI—it has almost unrestricted night-time access to nearly all hamlets in the province. In the northern districts of Binh Dinh in particular, communist sympathies are strong and deep-rooted—it is estimated in any cease-fire situation they would revert to NLF control. The size of the VCI and the lack of [a] comparable GVN [grassroots political] structure lead to the conclusion that, politically a ceasefire in Binh Dinh would be to the NLF's advantage.[8]

Indeed, the authors of the cease-fire study believed that this was the GVN's Achilles' heel everywhere and would fatally undermine its prospects in a post–cease-fire environment. Poor as their performance often was, South Vietnam's million-strong armed forces were far more effective than the organs of the civil government when it came to extending and preserving control in the countryside. Since it lacked both a mass political following in the rural areas and the effective grassroots political organization necessary to create one, it was only on military terms that the GVN could hope to compete for control of the population. If the military pressure was suddenly relieved due to a lasting cease-fire, the absence of opposition would give the VCI an opportunity to make extensive political and psychological gains. In the event of an in-place cease-fire, VSSG predicted a rapid decline in Saigon's influence because the mere presence of NVA regulars would pose a threat the VCI could use to cow the populace, whose faith in a GVN victory would have been seriously undermined by the unilateral American withdrawal.

The 1970 Special Pacification and Development Plan

In June President Thieu sought to breathe new life into the faltering 1970 pacification campaign by announcing that its second phase, due to begin on 1 July, was being superseded by the 1970 special pacification and development campaign. To a large extent, this was simply a matter of semantics, since the special campaign neither modified any existing objectives nor dictated any real changes in methodology—although, as in 1969, it advanced the end date from 31 December to 31 October. Its three main components—the Special Self-Defense, Special Self-Development, and People's Information programs—merely placed a new emphasis on major elements of the existing pacification effort rather than constituting entirely new programs.[9]

- The Special Self-Defense program decreed that RF companies were to be used in mobile, offensive operations instead of static, defensive duties and had to employ half their manpower in ambushes and patrols every day. PF platoons were to mount ambushes with two of their three squads seven nights a week. Expansion of the National Police below the district level was to be accelerated, as were ongoing efforts to boost the effectiveness of Phoenix.
- The Special Self-Development program was intended to build a partnership between the GVN and the rural population by giving villagers greater input in the planning of civic action and nation-building activities.
- The People's Information program sought to rally support behind pacification by publicizing the goals and methodology of the various GVN programs and highlighting the benefits that would flow to the rural population through them.

Prospects that the new campaign would achieve its goals were slim. High-level decrees that the RF and PF operate more aggressively and that the GVN's grassroots bureaucracy become more responsive to popular wishes meant nothing unless the GVN hierarchy's intermediate echelons ensured that the directives were actually put into effect. Otherwise, many Territorial Forces units would continue to avoid contact with the enemy, and civic action programs would continue to fail due to bureaucratic indifference and the wholesale misappropriation of funds and materiel. Thus, the 1970 special pacification campaign's fundamental flaw was that the upper ranks of the hierarchy responsible for implementing it were generally unwilling to insist that their subordinates act aggressively, honestly, and efficiently. After all, their own standing would suffer if units under their command suffered heavy casualties as a result of accepting tactical risks, and they themselves were the chief beneficiaries of the institutionalized system of corruption that undermined civic action programs.

Developments in Binh Dinh revealed just how difficult it would be to remedy fundamental shortcomings at the grassroots level by means of diktats issued from on high. In August 1970 provincial authorities launched the Village and Hamlet Defense Plan program, which required all rural communities to prepare formal plans for defense in the event of enemy attack. Specific defensive sectors and fields of fire were to be allocated to each military or paramilitary unit present in a community, and detailed orders were to be drawn up stipulating how they would respond in various tactical scenarios. Defensive and final protective fire missions were to be designated for organic and supporting mortar and artillery units (with firing data computed and targets preregistered), and arrangements were to be made for the dispatch of reinforcements by neighboring units. Without such plans, defensive countermeasures had to be extemporized on the spot—inevitably resulting in confusion, delay, and inefficiency. US advisors were instructed that helping GVN officials prepare defense plans was their top priority. In Hoai An, such great importance was attached to this task that the MATs were ordered to suspend participation in RF and PF operations until the plans had been completed.[10]

At first glance, the job looked deceptively simple: all the MATs had to do was sit down with village or hamlet officials and the local RF, PF, and PSDF commanders to hammer out a basic defensive scheme, assign targets to supporting artillery, and arrange for superior headquarters to designate reinforcements that would be sent if the community came under attack. But it proved extremely difficult to accomplish in reality. For one thing, just getting all the necessary South Vietnamese personnel together under the same roof at the same time was difficult because so many of them rarely ventured into their assigned villages and hamlets. In Phu My, neither the My Tai village chief nor any of his hamlet chiefs lived in the village, and they visited it only sporadically during daylight hours. Since their active participation was essential, no progress had been made in producing the village's defense plan by the last week of October.[11] In many cases, South Vietnamese officials not only were routinely absent from their posts but also repeatedly failed to keep appointments arranged by MATs for the express purpose of preparing defense plans. In Hoai An, MAT II-90 was finally able to corral one elusive hamlet chief by inviting him to attend a working lunch, complete with steak and beer.[12]

Such halfhearted participation was typical and by no means limited to those on the bottom rungs of the GVN hierarchy. In Phu My, advisors discovered that all the plans were virtually identical because district authorities had distributed a standardized form on which village and hamlet officials merely filled in the blanks with specific unit designations and artillery target data.[13] It goes without saying that these generic plans gave little consideration to the many factors that made each community unique and were therefore of little value. The fact that GVN officials were willing to settle for sketchy, assembly-line defense plans suggests that they viewed this task as just one more onerous bit of red tape that had to be completed and then filed away and forgotten. The same attitude of polite disinterest was apparent in their response to American efforts to rehearse the defense plans so that troops and commanders could become familiar with their assigned roles and any deficiencies could be identified and set right. Because they were of little value unless they had been rehearsed, the village and hamlet defense plans could not be judged complete until they had been practiced at least once. In AO Lee, only Tam Quan could report any completed plans at the end of October 1970—and even there, rehearsals had been conducted in just two of forty-four hamlets. It was one of only three districts in the province that had put the finishing touches on even a fraction of their defense plans by that time, and some districts did not expect to finish until 1971.[14]

GVN officials were uninterested in preparing defense plans because they were generally not worth the paper they were printed on. Any serious attack was almost certain to come after dark, and they knew full well that Territorial Forces units rarely came to one another's aid even in broad daylight. In most cases, an RF or PF unit could not be relied on to reinforce friendly troops in contact unless a MAT was on hand to push it forward and ensure access to fire support. The latter point was crucial because territorial units invariably tended to pull back as soon as contact was made with the enemy and call in artillery and helicopter gunships.[15] This failing could not be laid at the doorstep of the South Vietnamese alone, since they were merely following the example set by their American mentors. In 1969 the US 4th Infantry Division had reported:

OBSERVATION: On too many occasions, contact with the enemy follows a format of:

(1) Contact established.
(2) Artillery and/or gunships called.
(3) Area swept w/ negative results.

EVALUATION: While the decision of the best way to engage the enemy must be left to the commander on the ground, when combat is the result of a meeting engagement and the enemy is not dug in—aggressive fire and maneuver to close with and kill or capture the enemy . . . would produce more meaningful results and battlefield intelligence.[16]

Village and hamlet officials also had good reason to be dubious about the indirect fire support detailed in their defense plans. As already noted, neighboring units rarely supported each other with mortar fire due to shortages in ammunition. Thus, no matter how urgent the need, most RF and PF units prudently chose to husband what little mortar ammunition they had against the day they came under direct attack themselves—knowing full well that their own pleas for fire support would elicit no better response. There was also an almost universal reluctance to call on ARVN artillery units for fire support because they were notoriously slow and inaccurate. MAT II-94 wrestled with this problem in Hoai Nhon for months and finally gave up altogether after a particularly dispiriting incident at midyear:

On 23 June the 733 RF Company made contact with the enemy. The enemy began to withdraw and the RF unit called for artillery blocking fire. . . . They received it 25 minutes later, 700 meters off target. Approximately 15 minutes later a smoke round finally hit the target and "fire for effect" was given whereupon 4 HE [high explosive] rounds came in 400 meters off target. We received an "end of mission" after which we went and had a beer, resigning ourselves to use mortars next time.[17]

When one considers these facts, it is no surprise that the South Vietnamese did not take the village and hamlet defense plans seriously. Most GVN officials and RF and PF commanders obviously saw them as yet another exercise in bureaucratic futility—as another worthless program that would not contribute one iota to the defense of their communities. The only ones who took the whole business seriously were the American advisors, although it seems that even some of them doubted the plans' utility.

Another well-intentioned but fruitless attempt to decree better performance came in November when the new I Field Force commander, Major

General Charles Brown, ordered American advisors (including MATs) to cease planning training programs for Territorial Forces. Henceforth, the Americans would participate in training activities only if they were planned by the South Vietnamese themselves. Conceptually, it was a worthwhile effort to advance Vietnamization by weaning the Territorial Forces from their dependence on American initiative. The flaw in General Brown's logic was his assumption that RF and PF units would conduct training on their own if the Americans were no longer prodding them. Instead, many happily ceased training altogether. Three weeks after the order was issued, MAT II-7's leader reported on his meeting with the 48th RF Group's operations officer:

> They have never conducted practice training exercises. I told him I want to assist if they ever would train. . . . We cannot find out what priorities the RF and PF have. They appear to have none. 48th Group does not have one claymore [mine] on the perimeter, they have not put out the air flares they have (we showed them how to set them up), and they do not conduct any training. Plus, operations and ambushes are at a minimum.[18]

Although the rhetoric of Vietnamization dictated that their mission was to provide "advice," Advisory Team 42's personnel had, in fact, played a leading role in Binh Dinh's 1969 and 1970 pacification campaigns. Without their constant prodding and cajolery, without their taking the initiative in training and operations, and without the moral and material support they provided to the South Vietnamese, little or nothing would have been accomplished. No simple directive from General Brown was going to break this cycle of dependency, just as no stroke of President Thieu's pen could remedy the ingrained, counterproductive habits that had characterized the GVN since its creation. One looks in vain for any sign that the 1970 special pacification campaign led to improvement in the performance of either the South Vietnamese armed forces or the civil administration in the province. Instead, all the familiar pathologies of institutional failure—weak motivation, poor tactical execution, fragile morale, execrable leadership, and accommodation with the enemy—continued to manifest themselves with undiminished frequency in the second half of 1970.

The Red Queen's Race

Alice looked round her in great surprise. "Why, I do believe we've been under this tree the whole time! Everything's just as it was!" "Of course it is," said the Queen, "what would you have it?" "Well, in OUR country," said Alice, still panting a little, "you'd generally get to somewhere else—if you ran very fast for a long time, as we've been doing." "A slow sort of country!" said the Queen. "Now, HERE, you see, it takes all the running *you* can do, to keep in the same place."

—Lewis Carroll, *Through the Looking Glass*

On 20 August 1970 Colonel Mendheim took the unusual step of personally writing the after-action report on an ambush in Hoai An the day before. A platoon of the 181st RF Company had gone to purchase rice in An Thuong hamlet about 2.5 miles east. As it was returning along the same trail, the unit inexplicably broke up into two groups separated by about 500 yards. The leading group of eighteen passed through a notorious ambush site where the trail ran between two low hills without incident, but the trailing group—which included the platoon leader—was not so lucky. Moving bunched up and with no point or flank security deployed, this group was devastated when the Vietcong detonated three claymore mines at point-blank range. Four men died instantaneously, and the three survivors were all seriously wounded. The enemy made off with four M-16 rifles, an M-79 grenade launcher, and ten 60mm mortar rounds.[19]

What Colonel Mendheim found so unsettling was that a virtually identical ambush had occurred at precisely the same spot on 21 March. On that occasion, a squad of the 943rd RF Company—also returning from a rice-purchasing trip—had been ambushed between the two hills. It too had been moving with no point or flank security when it was annihilated by claymore mines and automatic weapons fire. Five men died and a sixth went missing, along with five M-16s and an M-79 grenade launcher.[20] It seems impossible that the same scenario could have played out again so precisely, since the 181st was certainly aware of what had happened to the 943rd. Moreover, as the thoroughly bewildered Colonel Mendheim pointed out, the 943rd itself had been given fair warning when it lost two men in the same area just ten days before the massacre of 21 March. This was the aspect of South Vietnamese behavior that Americans found most incomprehensible. Why did RF and PF units not perform better when lax tactical execution was obviously putting their own lives at risk? One MAT leader threw his hands up in despair: "If a man does not respond to my advice when I make it clear his life is in danger, as well the assistant platoon leader of [PF Platoon] 266's life was endangered, I am at a loss for a method of helping these people. I hope someone finds one."[21]

The sense of déjà vu prompted by Colonel Mendheim's two after-action reports is by no means unique. There is a monotonous, repetitive quality to many advisory reports written in Binh Dinh during 1970. Time and again, one reads the same complaints about the same shortcomings. Often it is the same DSA or MAT leader raising the same issue about the same GVN official or ARVN, RF, or PF unit cited in many earlier reports. Yet, just as often, one sees almost identical complaints made by different authors about different officials and units in different places at different times. Although they make for tedious reading, they prove beyond a shadow of a doubt that Washington Green had not broken the cycle of South Vietnamese dependency.

Indeed, the entire war in Binh Dinh was dominated by a series of deeply rooted cycles that defied every American effort to alter them. First of all, there was a daily cycle that seemed as timeless and unvarying as the patient labor of the peasants toiling in the rice paddies. At dawn, allied units would begin stirring in their defensive perimeters, sending out the day's first patrol and clearing the roads of the mines that had invariably been planted overnight. As the morning progressed, they would launch that day's sweep or cordon-and-search operation, covering the same ground that had already been swept and searched on innumerable occasions extending back over years and decades. Many ARVN and RF and PF operations would be performed like ritualistic dances, with troops moving along the same paths, avoiding the same dangerous areas, performing the same perfunctory search, and generally producing the same negative results. As the afternoon wore on, GVN officials would start scurrying to reach the safety of Bong Son or the district seats before dark, while everywhere allied troops began folding back into their defensive perimeters. As night fell, the Vietcong would come to life and make their way down into the hamlets. Meanwhile, allied artillery units would start firing their nightly harassment and interdiction artillery programs while ambush patrols moved into position—in many cases in the exact same places where they set up every night. After collecting supplies and intelligence in the hamlets and proselytizing the inhabitants, the Communists would race back to their hideouts before sunrise.

There was also a cyclical pattern to both sides' major operations in Binh Dinh. Communist offensive campaigns consisted of several high-point offensives spaced out at the rate of one a month so that NLF and NVA units could move up supplies, absorb replacements, and carry out preliminary reconnaissance of their targets. After three or four months, the campaign would peter out, but the Communists would immediately begin collecting supplies and absorbing replacements in preparation for its successor. Allied operations were just as predictable. For weeks and months on end, allied troops would chase the same VC and NVA regular units back and forth through the same mountain base areas. Every once in a while, several battalions would come together for a big operation that tried to seal off one of the base areas, but they never succeeded in trapping a significant number of enemy troops. When allied troops left the area after destroying whatever supply caches they could find, the Communist troops soon oozed back in. In time, their presence would be discovered, prompting yet another big roundup that would simply be the latest installment in a cycle of such operations that stretched back nearly a decade.

The interplay of these cycles lent the war in Binh Dinh an endless, repetitive quality that Americans, with their "can-do" mentality and determination to achieve quick results, found maddening. Day after day, month after month, year after year, the war dragged on, waxing and waning in intensity as the contenders' relative strengths and strategies shifted, but the war's fundamental characteristics never seemed to change. The most frustrating cycle of all was the enemy's phoenix-like ability to rise from the ashes of seemingly irreversible defeats time after time. The same units would be "destroyed" or "rendered incapable of offensive action" again and again, but they always reappeared a few months later, seemingly as potent as ever.

Facelift

The United States had often sought to use its vast material resources and technological prowess to break the Vietnam War's immutable cycles. In late 1970 the 173rd Airborne Brigade would try again with a series of major land-clearing operations. These were usually referred to as "Rome plow" operations, since they employed Caterpillar D-7E bulldozers equipped with armored cabs and special tree-cutting blades manufactured by the Rome Plow Company of Rome, Georgia. These lumbering, sixty-ton behemoths were almost unstoppable. They could split trees up to three feet in diameter with ease, crush lesser timber into matchsticks, and shrug off an explosion equal to that of a 155mm artillery shell with little or no damage.[22]

What prompted General Cunningham to call in the Rome plows was the unacceptably high rate of mine, booby-trap, and sniper casualties his troops were suffering. These losses were being inflicted by Vietcong guerrillas and District Force units that operated from unpopulated and overgrown portions of the lowland hamlets. Although mountains were the enemy's preferred refuge, they were located too far from many communities in the Bong Son Plains to allow the Vietcong to make the round-trip under cover of darkness. Instead, they lived in tunnels and bunkers constructed in the overgrown lowland areas and surrounded by dense belts of mines and booby traps. These strongholds were treated as "no go" areas by the Territorial Forces, and American troops who ventured into them had a much better chance of taking booby-trap casualties than of locating the cunningly hidden bunkers.

The presence of these enemy bases right in the midst of ostensibly GVN-controlled communities demonstrates the extent of the enemy's psychological hold on the population. Many villagers knew where the bunkers and booby traps were located because they had helped construct them in the first place, and they were now keeping the VCI and guerrillas hiding there supplied with food and intelligence on allied operations. If these people had turned informer, the Vietcong would have been doomed—but few ever did. Fear of terrorism was certainly a factor, but the province's decades-long association with the Communist cause and the residents' extensive family ties to the insurgents were more important considerations. Since the 173rd Airborne could not locate these enemy hideouts, it resorted to the brute-force solution of simply leveling all the areas where they might be. If the Americans could not alter the psychological landscape of AO Lee, they could at least change its physical landscape.

The first small-scale land-clearing operation aimed to eliminate a particularly troublesome enemy stronghold known as Sniper's Island, situated in the tidal lagoon that separated the "mainland" of northern Tam Quan from the long, curving sand spit that formed the district's northern coastline. The island's western shore came to within a few hundred yards of Highway 1, giving the Vietcong with an excellent position from which to snipe at passing traffic. Between 15 and 19 August the problem was eliminated by a platoon of Rome plows that stripped the island of all natural cover and destroyed a large number of bunkers. No complaints would be heard about Sniper's Island for some time.[23]

This success was noted by the 173rd Airborne's new commander, Brigadier General Elmer R. "Roy" Ochs, who had succeeded General Cunningham on 10 August. General Ochs was well acquainted with the peculiarities of Operation Washington Green and northern Binh Dinh because he had been serving as the brigade's deputy commander since December 1969. Impressed by the results of the Sniper's Island operation, he decided to launch a far more ambitious land-clearing campaign that was code-named Operation Facelift. The target of its first phase, which began on 6 September, was the plains surrounding Nui Kho Mountain in Hoai Nhon. Close-in security was provided by M-113s and dismounted cavalrymen of Troop E, 17th Cavalry, while Companies B and D of the 2/503rd and elements of the 40th ARVN Regiment—which had returned from its Cambodian sojourn in July—threw a cordon of blocking forces around the entire area. At first the enemy offered little opposition, but after a few days, the Vietcong began to plant booby traps in the areas being cleared. Although these were practically worthless against the Rome plows themselves, they presented a serious danger to the foot soldiers and lightly armored M-113s. The solution was to have the plows cut a swath around the area to be cleared before the M-113s moved in and unloaded their troops. After this was done, eliminating any booby traps in the

Rome Plows at Work. *Source:* George L. MacGarrigle, *Combat Operations: Taking the Offensive, October 1966 to October 1977 (The United States Army in Vietnam Series)* (Washington, DC: US Army Center of Military History Pub 94-1, 1998), 389. [Reprinted by permission of the US Army Center of Military History]

process, the cavalrymen would deploy at regular intervals within the cleared band and not stray out of it until the day's work was done. Once this practice was adopted, no further booby-trap casualties occurred.[24]

By 15 September, the Rome plows had completed their mission in Hoai Nhon and began heading north to initiate Operation Facelift's second phase. Between 16 September and 10 October, they cleared a total of 3,500 acres in Tam Quan's three northernmost villages (an average of almost 150 acres a day) and destroyed 763 tunnels and bunkers.[25] Immediately thereafter, the plows headed to Phu My's AO North, where they flattened enemy strongholds in My Trinh village and along the flanks of Phu Cuu Pass. Another 3,400 acres were cleared in the new operational area, and 250 bunkers destroyed.[26]

Operation Facelift was judged to be a great success. Tam Quan's District Advisory Team reported that Rome plow operations and the return of the 40th ARVN Regiment had given "a tremendous shot in the arm" to local GVN officials' morale. The VCI, guerrillas, and District Force units had no choice but to flee to the mountains as their lowland hideouts and supply caches were literally wiped off the map. The same results were achieved in

Hoai Nhon, where two VC District Force companies were forced to leave the now-inhospitable plains and take refuge in the Cay Giep Mountains. In both districts, the few Vietcong that remained lived a furtive existence, scuttling back and forth between the few remaining pieces of cover in tiny groups that experienced great difficulty finding food and communicating with one another. Hoai Nhon's DSA credited the Rome plow operations with causing a sharp decline in enemy offensive activity during October. Only seven enemy-initiated incidents occurred district-wide, and just one in the area cleared by Facelift.[27]

Operation Facelift also had another effect, similar to turning over a non-descript rock to reveal a whole hidden world of insects living under it. In Tam Quan, the magnitude of covert Vietcong activity unearthed by the Rome plows was so great that HES ratings had to be drastically reduced. A shocked Colonel Mendheim reported, "Evidence which has accumulated in the wake of Rome Plow operations in Tam Quan indicates that enemy activity in the area was far more extensive than we had imagined."[28] A large tunnel complex housing a Vietcong secret police headquarters was discovered in Truong Lam hamlet. Most of the inhabitants must have known about the tunnels, since many of the underground facilities were sited directly under their houses. The GVN district authorities decided to raze the entire community and relocate the inhabitants to new homes that would be constructed in another portion of the hamlet directly adjacent to a PF outpost.

Though weakened, the local Vietcong refused to accept this verdict. In the predawn hours of 5, 9, and 11 October, the Vietcong burned 243 of the new homes. The second night of arson coincided with an attack on 2nd Platoon, Company B, 4/503rd, which was guarding one of Truong Lam's three subhamlets. It was commanded by First Lieutenant James R. McDonough, whose memoir *Platoon Leader* details his experiences in Binh Dinh during the second half of 1970. On that night his platoon was, as usual, understrength, with only twenty men available for duty. A sixth sense caused McDonough to call back an ambush shortly after midnight to thicken his undermanned defenses. No sooner had it returned than the perimeter was hit by a rapid-fire barrage from half a dozen M-79s. All but one of the defenders reached the safety of the trenches unscathed, and McDonough radioed for artillery illumination and air support. His troops repulsed two enemy charges and held on until helicopter gunships arrived and tipped the scales decisively in their favor. Shortly afterward a platoon of armored personnel carriers and M-551 Sheridan light tanks from E/17th Cavalry arrived and joined one of McDonough's squads in launching a counterattack that inflicted further losses on the fleeing enemy. The light tanks had been acquired from US 4th Infantry Division units that were departing Vietnam.[29]

The local Vietcong had not given up, however, and launched a sapper attack on 2nd Platoon just a few weeks later. Lieutenant McDonough's luck held, as the platoon's Kit Carson scout (a VC defector serving as a scout and translator) sensed that one of the members of a recently arrived RD Cadre Team was a Vietcong agent. Sure enough, within a matter of days the man was caught trying to rig the ammunition bunker for demolition. Clearly, the enemy had planned to rush the position after the defenders were killed or disabled by the explosion of their own ammunition. Once the enemy's "inside man" was unmasked, McDonough quietly alerted his troops. They wiped out a five-man sapper team that had been detected cutting its way through the barbed wire and then fought an inconclusive firefight with the rest of the enemy force until the approach of dawn forced the Communists to break off the botched attack.[30]

The events in Truong Lam show that although Operation Facelift seriously inconvenienced the Vietcong, it did not take them long to bounce back from the setback. The same was true in most of the other communities in Tam Quan that had been visited by the Rome plows. On 28 October six people, including Tam Quan's village chief, were assassinated in broad daylight by half a dozen Vietcong who were disguised as PF soldiers and armed with M-16s.[31] At best, Operation Facelift had been a qualified and temporary success.

Fire Support Surveillance Bases

The 173rd Airborne also sought a technological solution to the problem of interdicting enemy movement from the mountains into the populated lowlands. The task was nigh impossible because the maze of interlocking ridgelines looming above the plains was several times longer than AO Lee's thirty-mile, straight-line western boundary. The brigade had long been augmenting its Ranger patrols and aerial reconnaissance flights with a system of remote seismic, acoustic, and magnetic sensors known by the code name Dufflebag. Fields of air-dropped and ground-emplaced sensors had been established at a number of points along the fringes of the mountains to identify the routes the Communists took when moving down into the lowlands. The Dufflebag data were used primarily as a source of operational intelligence. By identifying the areas where enemy traffic was heaviest, the sensors helped the brigade staff determine where to concentrate its Ranger, Hawk, and clearing operations.

It was difficult to use Dufflebag as a source of tactical intelligence (i.e., for targeting) because the battery-powered sensors could transmit data only over relatively short distances and along a direct line of sight. Because the frontage that had to be covered was so great and the lines of sight were restricted by steep mountain ridges, it proved impossible to achieve blanket coverage of AO Lee. Consequently, in mid-1970 the brigade began to develop an alternative method of employing Dufflebag that involved concentrating sensor fields in a few crucial areas, together with firepower assets that could engage enemy troops immediately upon detection. Thus was born the Fire Support Surveillance Base (FSSB), an installation that married Dufflebag and other surveillance and target acquisition systems to an impressive array of direct- and indirect-fire weaponry sited atop a prominent height that allowed line-of-sight observation of a major axis of enemy movement.[32]

The first FSSB was constructed in Hoai An's 506 Valley, an area that saw a great deal of enemy traffic because it offered the shortest route from the main, western mountain chain to the Crescent Mountains and thence onward to the Cay Giep Mountains, which were separated from the Crescents only by the narrow Phu Cuu Pass. By mid-August, allied intelligence confirmed that most of the reinforced 2nd VC Regiment and several Vietcong District and Local Force units were based in the mountains surrounding the valley. Much of this order-of-battle information was secured by patrols from Company N, 75th Ranger, and the reconnaissance platoon of Company E, 3/503rd, both of which spent the latter part of the summer tracing the enemy's trail network and identifying which ones were most heavily traveled. To corroborate their findings, a temporary sensor field was established covering all of these "hot" areas. After a few weeks, denser, permanent grids were installed in those places where sensor data had confirmed that movement was occurring on a regular basis. The three types of sensors (seismic, acoustic, and magnetic) were used in mixed groups to increase the likelihood of detection, and they were emplaced in strings so that an enemy column's length and direction of travel could be ascertained.[33]

On 3 August Company E, 3/503rd, began constructing FSSB Floyd at the end of a 600-foot-high ridge finger thrusting out from the northern side of the 506 Valley. Besides the Dufflebag data-processing gear, it was equipped with two 81mm and two 4.2-inch mortars, a quadruple .50-caliber antiaircraft machine gun (highly effective against personnel targets), a PPS-5 ground surveillance radar, a light-intensifying night sight, and a pair of 20-power naval binoculars. The first twenty-six days of Floyd's existence passed without major incident. Although several missions were fired in response to Dufflebag sensor activations, no large-scale enemy movement was detected until a major redeployment occurred in the last days of the month as the Communists finalized preparations for their fall campaign.[34] Several hours before dawn on the morning of 29 August, the sensor grid detected a column of enemy troops entering the 506 Valley's southern reaches. A radar sweep confirmed that at least 120 individuals were marching northward up the valley. Then, as an article in *Infantry* magazine later explained:

> The decision was made to engage the rear of the column in hopes of getting a second try at the head of the column. The rear was hit with mortar fire and, as expected, the remainder of the column marched on. The radar continued to track the enemy, and additional sensors began activating. By this time the night observation device had picked up the activity. As the head of the column activated a predetermined sensor, it was halted in its movement by 105mm howitzer, 4.2-inch mortar, and 81mm mortar fire. After this concentration, the PPS-5 and night observation device confirmed that the enemy was fleeing to the west. Quad .50 fire pursued the fleeing enemy and mortar fires blocked his escape to the west.[35]

When the valley floor was swept at first light, the American troops found six corpses, numerous blood trails, and one seriously wounded NVA soldier who was taken prisoner. Interrogation of POWs and Hoi Chanhs over the coming months would reveal that the 3rd Battalion, 2nd VC Regiment, had suffered substantially heavier casualties, including one of its company's executive officers. The 173rd Airborne's psychological warfare staff tried to exploit this success by saturating the area with air-dropped leaflets depicting a mythical, all-seeing Vietnamese demon living in the 506 Valley. Readers were warned to "Chieu Hoi or be killed by the demon of death," and this theme was repeated in loudspeaker broadcasts:

> They were told that the demon was watching, and to convince the enemy of this fact, their movements were described in detail. As mortar rounds slid down the tubes, they were told the demon was going to strike. After the initial impact, the enemy was told there was no hope of escape. If he attempted to flee, the mortar fired. Maximum effort was made to capitalize on traditional Vietnamese fears and superstitions.[36]

What impact this crude propaganda campaign had on enemy morale in the 506 Valley is unclear, but only two Hoi Chanhs were induced to defect as a result. Nonetheless, General Ochs was sufficiently impressed by FSSB Floyd's success that in early September he ordered the construction of FSSB Washington to interdict the routes used by the enemy to move rice from the plains of Phu My into the Suoi Ca Valley.

The FSSBs' effectiveness soon declined, however, as the VC and NVA learned to avoid the areas where the sensor grids were emplaced. Just twelve enemy killed, two POWs, and one Hoi Chanh were credited to the FSSBs in the third quarter of 1970, and the Dufflebag grids had become almost completely inactive by the end of September. Things picked up slightly in the last months of the year, when FSSB Floyd conducted thirty-two fire missions, but FSSB Washington fired only nineteen because the enemy had greatly reduced his movement from Phu My into the Suoi Ca Valley. This was still a victory, since any restriction imposed on enemy movement was a definite gain.[37]

Ferret

As long as the Communists adhered to their low-intensity, protracted war strategy, the chief threat to Operation Washington Green was not the enemy regulars in the mountains but the ubiquitous VCI in the lowlands. General Ochs explained: "While great success had been achieved in reducing the effectiveness of VC/NVA main force units, local forces, and even village and hamlet guerrillas, the VCI in northern Binh Dinh remained intact. Progress in pacification reached a plateau and further progress was hampered by the inherent capability of the VCI to maintain a level of resistance through terrorism and insurgency type operations."[38]

When General Ochs took command of the 173rd Airborne, he immediately focused the brigade's energies on the VCI and gave the mission top priority in phase V of Operation Washington Green, which began on 1 September 1970.[39] This reinforced a trend toward greater American involvement in anti-VCI activities that had started in late July, when the 173rd Airborne had launched its own anti-VCI program dubbed Operation Ferret. The Phoenix program was still stuck in low gear, unable to finish even the basic task of creating and maintaining VCI databases and target files. As the sands were clearly running out on Washington Green, this state of affairs had become intolerable to General Cunningham. He had therefore launched Operation Ferret, "with the specific aim of acquiring and compiling intelligence information for use in targeting VCI personalities. It aimed to create an English-language database that would be used to upgrade the DIOCC files while at the same time providing units of the brigade with targeting intelligence." In other words, the Americans had decided to dispense with the notion of letting the South Vietnamese take the lead in the anti-VCI effort. As General Ochs explained, "The task of eliminating the VCI was primarily a GVN responsibility; however, GVN agencies in some areas appeared reluctant to aggressively pursue VCI elimination operations."[40]

Operation Ferret's "cutting edge" consisted of POW interrogation (IPW) teams supplied by the 173rd Airborne—and, later, the 4th Infantry Division—which were doled out at the rate of one per district. However, no teams became available for Hoai Nhon and Hoai An until October and November, respectively.[41] The teams' first task was to build up detailed, up-to-date village and district "wanted lists" by carefully reviewing all existing and incoming VCI intelligence. Since enemy POWs and Hoi Chanhs were the best sources of information, and since interrogations conducted by GVN agencies were often cursory and inadequately documented, the IPW teams subjected all captured or surrendered enemy personnel to a second round of questioning. Once the data-collection phase had been completed in a particular district, the IPW team would begin transferring the information contained in its English-language database into new target dossiers that were simultaneously being prepared by DIOCC personnel. The IPW teams were also supposed to assist the DIOCCs in preparing and distributing wanted posters publicizing the monetary rewards being offered for information that led to the death, capture, or defection of important VCI. The teams' efforts were aided by the assignment of US Army counterintelligence NCOs as assistant DIOCC advisors in the early autumn; the presence of a second advisor greatly boosted the effectiveness of American input to the DIOCCs by cutting down on the district Phoenix advisors' workload.[42]

Ferret got off to a rapid start because its initial data-collection phase was an all-American enterprise. By the end of September, Ferret databases had been completed in Phu My, An Nhon, and Tam Quan; a month later, they were finished in all the districts except Tuy Phuoc and Hoai An—where IPW teams had yet to be deployed. However, printing wanted posters and publishing the wanted lists on which they were based was held up considerably because they had to be screened and approved by the Province Security Committee. Tam Quan, which became the first district to submit its wanted lists on 26 October, did not get the go-ahead to print its posters until 21 November; elsewhere, progress was even slower. At year's end, four districts (all located outside AO Lee) were still waiting for approval of their lists; three others (including Phu My and Hoai Nhon) received their first posters from the printer on Christmas Eve. Hoai An, which did not get an IPW team until 23 November, had not yet drawn up its wanted lists.[43]

Still, Operation Ferret's greatest weakness was that the intelligence it had compiled and injected into the Vietnamese-language DIOCC databases and target dossiers had to be continuously updated by GVN agencies if it was to be of any lasting value. Predictably, this did not happen. In Phu My, for instance, the Police Special Branch had worked up 110 new target dossiers by the end of December, but they included very little intelligence from other agencies; almost all the information contained in the dossiers had been acquired from Ferret or the PSB's own sources.[44] The same circumstances were reported in Hoai Nhon, where the PSB had a hard time extracting VCI intelligence from the other agencies in the DIOCC.[45] There is evidence that these were not isolated cases, suggesting that the degree of cooperation necessary to maintain the Ferret databases would not be forthcoming. Worse yet were province-wide indications that the DIOCCs were turning the whole program into nothing more than a paper-shuffling exercise. In November, Colonel Mendheim reported:

> The Phung Hoang Program in the province has made a significant improvement in the last month due to the infusion of data from the English-language Ferret data base. Comparison of these two repositories of information about VCI have made vivid the lack of a valid, up-to-date VCI listing by the DIOCCs. . . . The new VCI Target Folders (dossiers) were inspected at the same time and were noticeably deficient. The major problem is that the name, DPOB [date and place of birth], and communist position is recorded in the folder and then it is refiled and forgotten. Phung Hoang personnel have not learned to levy information requirements on representative agencies. The PIOCC Deputy Center Chief stressed this point during his inspections. In many cases the only information recorded in the target folder is that taken from the Ferret files.[46]

The DIOCCs' lackluster follow-up to Operation Ferret was offset, to a certain extent, by the 173rd Airborne's greater investment in anti-VCI operations during the fall of 1970. As before, most of those "neutralized" during this period were netted by tactical operations rather than those designed to kill or capture specific VCI. However, since the 173rd began collecting and responding more swiftly to "perishable" intelligence concerning Vietcong activities, its contribution to the third- and fourth-quarter neutralization figures increased substantially. My Tai village in southern Phu My offers a striking example of American troops' effectiveness at achieving "untargeted" VCI neutralizations. Before the village was occupied by the Sky Soldiers in late June, it had been secured by elements of the 41st ARVN Regiment. The local VCI—who had grown accustomed to ARVN troops' less aggressive habits—lost fifty personnel in August alone to relentless US ambushes, small-unit sweeps, and "hard seal" cordon-and-search operations. During that same month, three joint operations conducted in northern Phu My by the 1/503rd and 117th RF Company on the basis of locally produced intelligence accounted for the neutralization of six village- and two district-level VCI.[47] Indeed, August was one of Phu My's best months ever for VCI neutralizations. On the first day of the month, a tunnel housing the provincial Supply

Section and T.20 Agent Section was destroyed during a three-company RF operation mounted along the border with Phu Cat district. A province-level NLF counterintelligence cadre and two other Vietcong were killed. Later in the month, another RF operation planned on the basis of DIOCC information captured six members of a ten-man sapper agent cell. Yet even these were not targeted operations that aimed to kill or apprehend specific VCI.[48]

Evidence of specifically targeted anti-VCI operations occurring elsewhere in AO Lee during the latter half of 1970 is equally skimpy. Hoai Nhon's DIOCC finally began selective targeting in August, but it came to a screeching halt the following month after the Central Phung Hoang Office in Saigon introduced a new, standardized target form. So much time was consumed transferring data from the existing target dossiers to the new forms that the DIOCC accomplished almost nothing else during September.[49] Hoai An's DIOCC was completely ineffective in planning targeted anti-VCI operations because five of its members were absent for training, and its head, Captain Nguyen, focused on generating tactical intelligence. Moreover, even at the end of November, the DIOCC's files and dossiers were found to be practically worthless because they were outdated and did not list sources for the data they did contain.[50] Nonetheless, the district's neutralization figures for the months of September and October remained high due to intense pressure being applied by the 3/503rd and particularly the battalion's reconnaissance platoon, which was held in a constant state of readiness to act on hot leads. On 12 November, for example, an ambush yielded documents that led to the capture of several important enemy agents, one of whom was a GVN deputy hamlet chief![51]

There was one *very* selectively targeted anti-VCI operation in Hoai An that autumn, but the backstory made it absolutely unique. The 3/503rd's commander, Lieutenant Colonel John J. Clark, had been killed back on 2 June, and ever since, the battalion had been itching to exact revenge on those responsible for his death—one of whom was known to be an NLF province executive. After months of painstaking work, it learned that the culprits would visit the hamlet of An Hoa (1) on 10 October. On the appointed day, Recon Team 3 accompanied an intelligence agent to an ambush site nearby and, after a lengthy wait, saw a Vietcong platoon descending the slope of the nearby Crescent Mountains. The main body halted some 200 yards away, but five individuals continued walking until they were right in the middle of the kill zone. Four Vietcong died instantly when the recon team's claymores were detonated. A citation was found on one of the bodies, lauding his part in the killing of Lieutenant Colonel Clark. This gave the 3/503rd the satisfaction of knowing for certain that it had gotten its man.[52]

Yet the fact remained that Phoenix was demonstrably failing both in Binh

Dinh and throughout South Vietnam. This caused British counterinsurgency expert Sir Robert Thompson to shift ground yet again. Late in 1969, he had become one of the "new optimists," advising President Nixon that it might be possible to defeat the Vietcong conclusively by 1972. However, the failure to eliminate the VCI caused Thompson to adopt a far more pessimistic tone when he paid another visit to the White House in October 1970:

> The main theme of Sir Robert's findings was that despite some successes in pacification, . . . there has been a general failure in police and intelligence efforts aimed at eliminating Vietcong apparatus in the country. The Thompson report was said to have emphasized that success in other aspects of pacification cannot solve the basic political problem in Vietnam after the withdrawal of the bulk of American forces so long as the Vietcong apparatus remains virtually intact.[53]

Another Swing of the Pendulum

For all the 173rd Airborne's experimentation with Rome plows, FSSBs, and the Ferret program, the cyclical patterns of the war in northern Binh Dinh were as immutable as ever in the second half of 1970. For one thing, the seemingly endless cycle of enemy regular units being driven out of the coastal mountains only to return within a matter of days or weeks continued, although one might have expected the allies to tire of the game by this point. In July they launched Operation Wayne Span II, which attempted yet again to encircle and destroy the 2nd VC Regiment's 95th Battalion in the Nui Mieu Mountains. In a virtual replay of April's Operation Darby Sweep, two battalions of the 1st Brigade, 4th Infantry Division, and two more from the 40th ARVN Regiment began scouring the mountains on 28 July while elements of the 1/503rd, 2/503rd, 3/503rd, and E/17th Cavalry, plus two battalions of the 41st ARVN Regiment and Phu My Territorial Forces units, deployed blocking forces around the entire range. Wayne Span II was, predictably, an utter failure, since none of the units involved had any significant contacts or material finds by the time the operation had run its course on 6 August. By early September, the 95th Battalion would be back in the Nui Mieus, launching attacks into the surrounding plains as if nothing had ever happened.[54]

The 95th Battalion's temporary withdrawal fit into a larger pattern of enemy regular units pulling back from the coastal plains to rest their personnel and absorb and train replacements. This phenomenon—which had first been first detected in June, when the 400th Sapper Battalion and other NVA units withdrew to the Crescent Mountains from the Cay Gieps—became more general in July as the rest of the 2nd VC Regiment pulled out of Phu

My and took up residence in Base Area 226. These redeployments hinted that a lengthy interlude could be expected before the enemy's autumn campaign began. As it turned out, the Communists would rest for more than seven weeks before launching another wave of attacks. During July, all four northern districts reported a major reduction in enemy-initiated incidents, although, significantly, terrorist incidents did not decline as rapidly. Yet even terror attacks started to drop off in August and continued to do so for the next two months (falling to less than half the average of seventy incidents a month reported in February–July).[55]

The decline in enemy activity, and the reintroduction of US troops in support of pacification in Hoai Nhon and Hoai An, caused GVN control in Binh Dinh to rebound dramatically. By the end of August, GVN control as measured by the VSSG control indicator had climbed back above 40 percent, while VC control stood at just about 2 percent.[56] The rise allowed the Nixon administration to continue to tout Washington Green as proof that Vietnamization was succeeding, and the 173rd Airborne was obliged to host a parade of VIPs coming to see for themselves how much this showcase operation had accomplished. During the summer lull, the brigade hosted two of its most distinguished guests yet. On the Fourth of July the secretary of the army, Stanley R. Resor, paid a visit; after a briefing at LZ English, he was flown out into the field to get a firsthand look. Former MACV commander and then US Army chief of staff General William C. Westmoreland followed suit on 15 July.[57] Unfortunately, there is no record of their impressions, so it is impossible to say whether they grasped that the relative tranquility they witnessed was only temporary.

The summer lull also witnessed a major shake-up in the enemy's command structure, which allied intelligence initially interpreted to mean that the Yellow Star Division was disbanding. According to the division's official history:

> In July 1970, due to difficulties regarding levels of personnel, provisions, weapons, and ammunition, the Regional Party Committee and the Military Region 5 Party Committee decided to realign their regular army units and strengthen local units to cope with the enemy's new schemes in a timely fashion. As a result of this decision the Yellow Star Division shrunk, after disbanding the 22nd Regiment once more [?], with the intention that when conditions permitted it would quickly regroup. The division command element retained only a few key cadre and became the forward element of the military region headquarters, headed by division commander Huynh Huu Anh, who at that time also was the Military Region Assistant Chief of Staff.[58]

Since the 22nd NVA Regiment had disbanded earlier in the year and the 18th NVA Regiment continued to operate independently, divisional headquarters was left with only the 2nd VC Regiment and the 200th Antiaircraft, 300th Artillery, 400th Sapper, and 500th Transport Battalions under its direct command. During July the 2nd VC Regiment's existing 93rd, 95th, and 97th Infantry Battalions were renumbered the 1st, 2nd, and 3rd, and the 200th, 300th, and 400th became its new 6th, 5th, and 4th Battalions.[59] The 173rd Airborne's intelligence staff believed this had been done because a divisional headquarters was no longer needed to control such a relatively small force. But the brigade's intelligence officers also suspected there might be an altogether different explanation for the restructuring:

> Perhaps the most significant factor of the 3d Div's disbandment is the political implication. As the allied role in the Vietnam War is ending and US forces are concentrating on strengthening the Vietnamese fighting forces while simultaneously accelerating troop withdrawal, the North Vietnamese have been forced to develop an adequate counter strategy. COSVN Resolution 10 . . . revealed COSVN's De–North Vietnamization Program. An analysis of the Resolution revealed that all NVA forces in South Vietnam will eventually be resubordinated under the various VC military HQ's in each province. All new personnel arriving from the infiltration trails would be assigned to various VC South Vietnamese units. This strategy would . . . legalize NVA forces in South Vietnam, thus providing them with a convincing argument for world opinion support while they continued the war on both the military and political fronts.[60]

Here it is important to recall that although by late 1970 most of its troops were North Vietnamese, the 2nd Regiment was a *Vietcong* Main Force unit raised in Binh Dinh during 1962. The Communists may have hoped to claim that the 2nd Regiment was a "native" South Vietnamese unit if a future cease-fire accord demanded the withdrawal of all foreign troops.

In any event, this reshuffling did not interfere with preparations for the enemy's next offensive. The NVA units that had pulled back from the fringes of AO Lee during June and July started returning in the final weeks of August and were back in their old haunts before the fall campaign started on the night of 29 August. Yet, apart from the 2nd Battalion, 2nd VC Regiment, which launched three attacks from its familiar bases in the Nui Mieus, enemy regular units were almost completely inactive during the August high point. FSSB Floyd deserves much of the credit for this because its ambush of the 3rd Battalion, 2nd VC Regiment, on the night of 29 August certainly forestalled other planned attacks. However, the most dramatic allied success of the month occurred in Binh Khe district on 22 August, when the 100th PF Platoon killed forty troops of the 90th NVA Engineer Battalion and captured three more in a masterfully executed ambush laid at an enemy crossing point on Highway 19.[61]

Enemy offensive activity picked up in the first two weeks of September, including fifty-one ground assaults, though none of them involved enemy forces in greater than platoon strength. The most spectacular occurred on 4 September, when the 5th Company, 300th VC Sapper Battalion, took advantage of lax security in Qui Nhon to launch an attack on the provincial PSDF training center that killed seventeen and wounded twenty-two. On 26 September this same unit wounded fifteen Americans in a mortar attack on the US Army's Qui Nhon Support Command Headquarters, proving yet again that even the most secure areas were not immune to attack. Terrorist incidents also continued to exact a heavy toll.[62] One of the worst killed and wounded twenty-eight civilians when a claymore mine was detonated during a 28 August election meeting in Tam Quan.[63] Few attacks were as spectacular as these, but collectively they conveyed the intended message: the Communists were still a force to be reckoned with. Colonel Mendheim wrote that the enemy was "like an evil but ignored genie which periodically emerges from its bottle just to remind all that he is still around."[64]

Communist offensive activity declined as September wore on, and enemy troops were increasingly diverted to the crucial task of collecting rice during the eighth-month (August–September) and tenth-month (October–November) harvests. As in years past, enemy regular units broke down into small detachments that guarded the guerrillas and VCI while they "taxed" the harvests and helped carry the rice into mountain caches. The allies countered by mounting a large-scale rice-denial effort that mirrored the enemy's tactics by dispersing US and ARVN regulars to keep an eye on the harvesters and bolster the Territorial Forces. Other troops thickened up the security screen along the fringes of the plains. In Tam Quan and Phu My, where the 4/503rd, 1/503rd, and elements of the 40th and 41st ARVN Regiments remained on pacification duty, the rice-denial program necessitated little more than a temporary redirection of effort. In Hoai Nhon and Hoai An, however, the absence of regular troops in the hamlets obligated the 173rd Airborne and 22nd ARVN Division to reallocate forces from other tasks.[65]

In Hoai An, the task fell to the 3/503rd, which still had three rifle companies operating in the district's mountains (C Company was in southern Phu My).[66] But the 1st Battalion, 2nd VC Regiment, was already present in the lowlands, operating in ten-man squads under the orders of NLF village and hamlet committees, and security suffered accordingly. The situation improved dramatically, however, when twelve PF platoons were each augmented by a US squad. At the end of September, Hoai An's DSA enthused: "The economy is buoyant, spirits are high, and VC influence is declining. There is an air of optimism even though the NVA have deployed to augment the local forces. The 3/503rd's presence is countering the NVA augmentation."[67] The Vietcong were so thoroughly straitjacketed that they failed to collect much rice, and security in the district remained firm during the fall campaign's second high point, which began on 4 October. The Communists again attempted no large-scale ground assaults, although Camp Radcliffe and the 539th General Support Group's command headquarters in Qui Nhon were both subjected to intense attacks-by-fire. The 4th Battalion, 2nd VC Regiment (ex–400th Sapper Battalion), had planned to attack a fire support base in Phu My, but the company ordered to make the assault was decimated by the 3/503rd's Recon Team 3 on 1 October.[68]

Recon Team 3 was an elite eight-man unit including two snipers armed with highly accurate M-14/XM-21 rifles (one mounting a Starlite Scope night-vision device). The team had been deployed into northern Phu My on a three-day operation mounted in response to reports that personnel of Company E, 3/503rd who were constructing FSSB Washington had observed flashlights moving in the lowlands to the east night after night, accompanied by the incessant barking of dogs. Since enemy troops were spotted moving on a trail at the foot of the mountains below FSSB Washington on several occasions in the first two days of the operation, Recon Team 3 set up an ambush along the trail featuring a "daisy chain" of a dozen claymore mines linked by detonation cord. The team's standard operating procedure stipulated that, to prevent their positions from being detected, only the snipers would fire, except in self-defense. Other team members would join in the ambush solely by throwing grenades. At 2300 hours on 30 September, NVA troops failed to penetrate the barbed wire around FSSB Washington only half a mile away. At 0515 the next morning, the retreating NVA marched right into the ambush and were devastated by the simultaneous detonation of the claymores, a volley of grenades, and the rapid fire of the team's snipers. Supported by illumination and high-explosive mortar fire from FSSB Washington, Recon Team 3 drove the surviving NVA from the field and found twenty-seven dead and dying bodies littering the trail. A dozen small arms, two B-40 rocket launchers, five pounds of documents, 131 grenades, three bangalore torpedoes, and various other accoutrements of the sapper's trade were captured. This was unquestionably the single most impressive tactical success achieved by any element of the 173rd Airborne Brigade in all of Operation Washington Green.[69]

In mid-October all troops of the 3/503rd on rice-denial duty were withdrawn, and the bulk of the battalion moved into Phu My.[70] No sooner had it left Hoai An than the Communists again began penetrating the hamlets on a regular basis. The problem was that the two RF groups that assumed the mission of screening the mountains around Hoai An's lowlands did a terrible job. The 48th RF Group's night ambushes and daytime sweep operations were poorly executed at best, while the 24th RF Group was almost completely inactive—as it had been since replacing the much-maligned 25th Group back in May. It faked practically all its night ambushes and ran a mere eight tactical operations in the four months from July to October, accounting for precisely one Vietcong killed in action. In the absence of American troops, the local Vietcong were able to act with impunity.[71]

The pendulum had now swung three times in Hoai An. On each occasion, the deployment of US troops into the hamlets had driven the district's guerrillas and VCI seemingly to the verge of extinction. Yet each time the Americans pulled out, the enemy immediately bounced back and reasserted his psychological dominance over the district's population. Through it all, the only thing that remained constant in Hoai An was the almost uniformly poor performance of the district's Territorial Forces and PSDF.

A Paddy-Level Fifth Column

The fall campaign ended abruptly when Tropical Storm Louise roared into Binh Dinh on 28 October. It brought several days of torrential rain that put most of the coastal plains underwater—roof high in some places—forcing everyone to seek refuge on isolated pieces of high ground. Normally placid rivers, streams, and canals suddenly converted into raging torrents that drowned man and beast alike and washed away any structures that chanced to be in their way. In Phu My, two joint US–RF/PF defensive perimeters were destroyed, and a first lieutenant from the 1/503rd drowned.[72] In Hoai An, several spans of the infamous "Bridge to Nowhere" were carried away, cutting off access to the left bank of the river. A US engineer unit rushed in to make repairs but learned, to its dismay, that the 231st PF Platoon, which had been detailed to secure the bridge site, had instead devoted itself to charging tolls on a makeshift footbridge thrown up across the river. The PF troopers also tried to steal the lumber that had been delivered to repair the bridge but were foiled by American sentries.[73]

Tropical Storm Louise forced the Communists to delay the start of their winter campaign, since they urgently needed to collect rice to replace caches destroyed by the flood. Thus, NVA and Vietcong military activity was unusually light during the first three weeks of November. Enemy forces in Hoai An continued to refrain from offensive military activity even after the new campaign began in the last ten days of the month. Instead, they concentrated on proselytizing the civilian population and assailing the weakest link in territorial security—the PSDF militia. Exploiting the 24th RF Group's inactivity, a squad of Vietcong entered Gia Duc hamlet on the night of 14 November and abducted thirteen PSDF who had failed to post any sentries and were surprised in their sleep. The militiamen were led away at gunpoint, but by all accounts, about half of them went willingly. Some were still carrying their weapons as they marched off.[74] When Colonel Mendheim investigated the incident, he found damning evidence of collusion with the enemy:

> The District Deputy for Security reported that both Village and Hamlet Chiefs were aware that the VC would come into Gia Duc Hamlet on the night of 14 November 1970 and that they had this intelligence prior to 1400 hours on the same day. The information was not passed to district. The only reaction to this intelligence was that some weapons were evacuated out of Gia Duc Hamlet to Duc Long Hamlet, also in An Duc Village. This was done at the direction of the Hamlet Chief of Gia Duc.[75]

The Communists were similarly unopposed when they kidnapped five youths and collected food and cash in Phu Van (2) on the night of 18 November. The same scene was played out yet again four nights later, when at least thirty Vietcong entered An Thuong hamlet and abducted three teenagers and three PSDF, some of whom went willingly with their "captors."[76]

Yet the most extreme cases of collusion involved several Caucasians who accompanied the Vietcong during these abductions. A deserter from the 173rd Airborne was allegedly present in Gia Duc, and four Americans were reportedly active participants in the kidnappings at Phu Van (2). Nothing else was heard of them until 1 December, when PF troops spotted Americans moving with Vietcong a mile or two west of Bong Son. Finally, on 14 December, enemy propaganda leaflets were found in northern Phu My that listed the names of three American deserters who were supposedly fighting with the Vietcong. Regrettably, the available documentation offers no additional clues about the identities and possible motives of these men, and it does not address the possibility that they were acting under duress as part of a Communist psychological warfare gambit. Still, it is clear that senior US commanders took this matter seriously. On 22 December a high-ranking officer flew up from Saigon to investigate and was escorted out to Phu Van (2) by MAT II-90.[77]

The discovery that renegade Americans might be fighting with the enemy was certainly unsettling, but Colonel Mendheim was far more worried about the reliability of the PSDF. Seven of the thirteen PSDF abducted at Gia

Duc were released on 24 November, and all of those kidnapped had returned home by mid-December. Mendheim took the enemy's leniency as a bad sign:

> The specter of a paddy-level fifth column loomed in three locations; Hoai An, Phu Cat, and Tam Quan. The remainder of the November-abducted PSDF in Hoai An returned. GVN authorities promptly incarcerated and interrogated them. An estimated 50% of the returnees are alleged to be VC agents/informers or sympathizers. District authorities believed the purpose of abduction was to gather the VC elements "abducted" for additional training in preparation for future attacks on the PSDF and pacification. In Phu Cat, three of five recent abductees "escaped" after 2 weeks of captivity. The feeling prevails that these three returned to act as VC informants. The fox was apparently in the hen house in Tam Quan. On 23 December, NVA sappers entered the perimeter through the PSDF sector right past several disconnected claymores.[78]

This problem was hardly a new one. Back in May, Tam Quan's District Advisory Team had observed: "The greatest problem with PSDF development in Tam Quan is the fact that members and prospective members are not trusted by the GVN hamlet, village and district officials. Due to the many years of VC control within the district, there are very few families which are not linked with the VC through family ties."[79] One cannot blame GVN officials for adopting this attitude or for their obstructionist policy when it came to arming the militiamen. Binh Dinh was 3,749 weapons short of its target for PSDF weapons distribution when the 1970 special pacification and development campaign ended on 31 October. About 2,700 weapons were already on hand, gathering dust in warehouses, because the II Corps Logistics Command had been waiting four months for Saigon to authorize their distribution.[80] The VSSG concluded: "The PSDF are virtually worthless in Binh Dinh. Although their number is impressive enough, they are woefully underarmed and badly led."[81]

The creation of PSDF Key Inter-Teams, which was one of the 1970 pacification campaign's primary objectives, also progressed slowly in Binh Dinh. The chief impediment was that prospective KIT leaders avoided attending the six-week training session because most could not afford such a prolonged absence from their farms and jobs—particularly since the GVN failed to pay family support allowances on time, and the trainees' daily stipend was so small that they had to pay for most of their own food.[82] Things went from bad to worse after the provincial PSDF training center was wrecked in September. Training ground to a halt until the center was repaired, but since night classes were now prohibited, it was unable to process as many train-

Table 7.1 PSDF in Binh Dinh, December 1970

Category	1970 Goal	Organized	Trained	Distributed
Key Inter-Teams	515	537	425	—
Combat PSDF	51,270	55,292	47,359	—
Support PSDF	120,350	140,754	44,710	—
Weapons	23,436	—	—	25,228

Source: Republic of Vietnam, Ministry of Interior, Office of Undersecretary of State, Field Trip Report 207-BNV/VPTT Binh Dinh Province, 30 December 1970, 4, Province Reports II CTZ—Binh Dinh/Kontum box, Southeast Asia Branch, US Army Center of Military History, Fort McNair, Washington, DC.

ees as it had before the attack. In November it was finally decided that only PSDF militia from Qui Nhon proper would be sent there; all others would be trained in their own hamlets by sixty-one Mobile Training Teams created at the district level. However, no training could occur while the Mobile Training Teams themselves were being organized and trained.[83]

By year end, Binh Dinh's PSDF program had exceeded its goals for distributing weapons and organizing KITs, but training still lagged badly. But it hardly mattered because, whether armed and trained or not, the PSDF contributed almost nothing to the allied war effort in Binh Dinh. Worse yet, as information generated by Operation Ferret was fed into DIOCC databases, more and more PSDF members were showing up on the blacklists. The province chief became so alarmed that he threw the program into reverse. Underscoring just how empty its quantitative accomplishments were, he began purging the ranks and withdrawing weapons. In mid-December he ordered that 1,792 weapons be turned in by the end of February 1971.[84]

Anti-Americanism

This study necessarily dwells on the topic of South Vietnamese shortcomings because they were the chief obstacle to achieving Operation Washington Green's objectives. However, the performance of US troops in Binh Dinh was far from spotless—particularly insofar as relations with the civilian population were concerned. Indeed, they were so poor that violent anti-American demonstrations erupted in Qui Nhon on 7 December 1970. Their proximate cause was the killing of a twelve-year-old boy by an American soldier:

The soldier, a few minutes earlier, had given chase to another young boy who had stolen a fire extinguisher from the rear of the truck while the driver (another US soldier) had stopped to readjust his load. The soldier said he put a round in the chamber of his M-16 rifle to frighten the boy, which it apparently did, as the child dropped the fire extinguisher and fled. The soldier then returned the extinguisher to the truck and climbed aboard the truck bed to help the driver adjust the load. He forgot, however, to remove the bullet from the chamber of the weapon. As he was rearranging the boxes on the truck, the weapon discharged, with the round instantaneously killing the schoolboy, who was sitting on a fence perhaps twenty yards away. The two US soldiers, possibly unaware of the killing, but probably panic-stricken, drove away from the scene. Their vehicle was eventually halted a few miles away at a checkpoint by military police who had been alerted by ARVN soldiers. The soldier who shot the boy was arrested by military police.[85]

The soldier would be sentenced to six months' imprisonment after a court-martial in early 1971, but the consequences in Qui Nhon were immediate. Two hundred students carried their dead classmate through the streets, along with the student bodies of several other schools that had come out in support. The marchers proceeded to the provincial headquarters and demanded to speak with the province chief, who was castigated for allegedly covering up earlier incidents in which Americans had killed or injured civilians. He reasoned with the crowd and eventually had the corpse taken to the morgue at the provincial hospital, but some of the leaders removed it and again paraded it through the streets. Violence broke out as mobs vandalized US military vehicles and businesses catering to Americans late into the night, and the rioting resumed the next morning. The 173rd Airborne was forced to place the city off-limits to all its personnel.[86]

The outburst of 7 December was not merely a response to the fatal shooting earlier that day. It was, in fact, the result of pent-up frustrations generated by a long-standing pattern of misconduct by the 173rd Airborne and the 16,000 other American soldiers and civilians present in and around the city. A CORDS Pacification Studies Group (PSG) field evaluation team reported:

> Basic to a background study of the Qui Nhon anti-American demonstrations . . . is the recognition of a long-existing, latent vein of virulent hostility toward Americans, an anti-American sentiment stimulated by an American record of several years of overt disrespect shown to all strata of Vietnamese society. . . . The US presence in Binh Dinh, both civilian and military . . . has filled the Binh Dinh Province Public Safety Advisor's incident files with four years of dramatic misconduct against the Vietnamese populace.[87]

Indeed, Advisory Team 42's records reveal that cases of American misconduct were disturbingly common. Complaints about the 173rd Airborne included allegations of theft during cordon-and-search operations in Phu My, armed holdups of motorcyclists on Highway 1, and drunken assaults and break-ins in Hoai Nhon.[88] Sky Soldiers manning checkpoints on Highway 1 also illegally seized goods that they believed had been stolen from the US Army, simply removing all American commodities and military supplies from passing trucks without even inquiring about their origins. An incident in Hoai An ended with troops from the 980th RF Company firing on a detachment of US Army engineers (fortunately, there were no casualties). The RF company commander had come to the aid of a civilian whom the engineers believed had stolen a transistor radio from them; his troops started shooting after an American NCO almost struck him in the head with a broom handle during the ensuing altercation.[89]

There were also three other cases in which Americans had allegedly murdered Vietnamese civilians in 1970. The first occurred in Qui Nhon on 15 February, when two American employees of the Dynalectron Corporation allegedly killed a fourteen-year-old boy they believed to be a Vietcong. The second incident involved an unidentified American—possibly a deserter—who shot and killed a PSDF militiaman who tried to stop him at a Qui Nhon checkpoint after he had run through an earlier checkpoint without halting.[90] The third occurred in Phu My, where two members of Company C, 1/503rd, claimed they entered a hamlet after midnight on 24 February and, upon hearing a suspicious noise, apprehended a civilian who had no identification card and killed him when he tried to escape.[91] The hamlet's residents claimed the two Americans had forced the deceased from his home, bound his hands with a fishnet, and led him away to be shot. No documents could be found recording the ultimate fate of the accused, but Sergeant Ron Baker Jr. recalled some twenty years later that the scuttlebutt in Company C was that the killing had resulted from a drug deal gone bad.[92]

Yet by far the most common—and gratuitous—form of mistreatment involved American convoys passing on Highway 1. The PSG report ran through a whole litany of offenses:

> Reckless driving; the running of Vietnamese motorists, cyclists and pedestrians off roads; local Vietnamese being hit by sticks, thrown cans and rocks, Vietnamese women being slapped by GI's in passing trucks; convoys indiscriminately reconning by fire in populated areas; cases where innocent civilians were killed because of gun trucks firing into hamlets without cause . . . ; the joy-killing of water buffalo and cattle; Vietnamese pedestrians and motorists being killed by US vehicles; . . .

a recent case of GI's driving the road with a fire-extinguisher and spraying cyclists and pedestrians; . . . cases of gun trucks intimidating both Vietnamese and US motorists by leveling 50 caliber machine guns on them as they try to pass.[93]

The PSG field evaluators traced the causes of US misconduct in Binh Dinh to a lack of command emphasis on community relations and a general relaxation of discipline that was exacerbated by racial animosity between black and white soldiers, skyrocketing drug abuse, and poor leadership. These problems were burgeoning throughout the US armed forces in the later years of the Vietnam War, and even the elite 173rd Airborne was not immune to these pathologies as its ranks were increasingly filled with unmotivated draftees and its officer billets with hastily trained and often poor-quality ROTC graduates.[94] Normally, the brigade's senior NCOs could be counted on to maintain discipline, but after five years of constant warfare, those who had not been killed or incapacitated were retiring in droves. To close the gap, the army was forced to create what were derisively referred to as "shake and bake" NCOs—taking men straight out of basic training and promoting them to the rank of sergeant after little more than a year of additional training. They were not adequate substitutes for the professional, long-service NCOs they replaced.[95]

Colonel John D. Waghelstein, who served as the 173rd Airborne's S-1 (personnel officer) in late 1969 and early 1970, confirmed that these symptoms of indiscipline were shockingly common. Having come to Vietnam from the elite, all-professional 8th Special Forces Group in Latin America, then-Major Waghelstein was appalled by the drug abuse, poor leadership, racial tension, and AWOLs he witnessed in the 173rd Airborne. There were even cases of officers and NCOs of the 173rd Airborne being attacked by their own troops—a practice so common in Vietnam that the term "fragging" was coined to describe it (attacks were generally carried out with fragmentation grenades because, unlike firearms, they could not be used to identify the assailant). Waghelstein recalled, "We had fragging incidents even right at LZ English. As I remember there were at least two court-martials . . . [involving] fragging incidents . . . during my tenure, and the incidents occurred at English."[96]

The Whole Ball of Wax Could Melt Away
The Sky Soldiers' behavior so antagonized the South Vietnamese that it was probably just as well they would soon be leaving the hamlets. Yet it was hard to see how territorial security could be maintained without them.

In the last week of November, Company B, 2/503rd, was sent into Hoai An and provided one final, dramatic illustration of the difference even a few American troops could make. The 24th RF Group "came alive" as soon as the Americans were dispersed among its subunits, one squad to each of its four companies and another to each of the five PF platoons in the most endangered villages in its area of operations. As on so many prior occasions, the Sky Soldiers' presence encouraged the territorial troops to be far more active than when operating on their own. Yet the galvanizing effect was more transitory than ever, since Company B was withdrawn for good on 5 December.[97]

Company B's exit was not an isolated event but part of a much larger realignment of forces prompted by the withdrawal of the 4th Infantry Division's last combat elements at the start of December.[98] Their departure from Vietnam ushered in the sixth and final phase of Operation Washington Green. The entire 2/503rd was taken from the brigade and sent to Camp Radcliffe to guard the many support units that remained there. It would be joined later in the month by the 3/503rd, while the 1/503rd and 4/503rd would be pulled off pacification duty and sent inland to conduct clearing operations in the mountains. During the final weeks of the operation, these units were primarily concerned with turning their compounds over to ARVN and RF and PF units and demolishing those that were now superfluous. Enemy forces rushed to exploit the gap in the coastal plains, and the demoralized Territorial Forces proved incapable of stopping them. By the time Washington Green formally ended on 31 December, the enemy had already made deep inroads into AO Lee's hard-won pacification gains.[99]

The deterioration was worst in the Bong Son Plains, where Communist influence had historically been strongest, but deputy PSA Francis B. Corry stressed, "The problems stem as much from what the GVN is not doing as from what the enemy is doing."[100] One village's GVN officials ran their offices out of a tent in a military compound on Highway 1, and even there they were present only from nine until noon. They spent the rest of their time in the safety of Bong Son, but no one could blame them, since their predecessors had been wiped out by a sapper attack in June. Elsewhere, paralyzed RF and PF units were coming under attack almost every night, and the VCI were collecting and burning identification cards by the thousands to make it easier for their covert agents to move about without detection. In short, the enemy was running amok in the Bong Son Plains, and the Territorial Forces were doing little to hinder him.

Enemy forces in Binh Dinh were only marginally weaker than they had been a year before. In December 1969 their total strength had been estimated at 11,438, and although allied forces claimed 10,890 Vietcong and NVA killed or captured during the year, they still totaled about 9,800 in December

Table 7.2 Estimated Vietcong Military Strength in AO Lee, 15 April 1969 and 31 December 1970

Force	15 Apr. 1969	31 Dec. 1970
Provincial		
X-503 Local Force Battalion	200	—
8th (X-503) Local Force Battalion	—	293
Tam Quan District		
D-35 Sapper Company	27	—
D-40 Sapper Company	80	—
DH-15 District Force Company	—	23
DH-13 (D-40) District Force Company	—	36
Village and hamlet guerrillas	765	Included in Hoai Nhon figure below
Hoai Nhon District		
D-21 District Force Company	85	—
DH-10 District Headquarters Unit	—	45
DH-11 District Force Company	—	45
DH-12 District Force Company	—	38
DH-14 District Force (82mm mortar) Company	—	31
Village and hamlet guerrillas	617	922
Hoai An District		
D-22 District Force Company	85	—
DH-16 District Headquarters Unit	—	32
DH-17 District Force Company	—	28
DH-18 District Force (82mm mortar) Company	—	22
Village and hamlet guerrillas	158	104
Phu My District		
Phu My District Force Battalion	190	204
D-23 District Force Company	95	—
Village and hamlet guerrillas	623	523
Totals		
Regulars	762	797
Guerrillas	2,163	1,549
Grand total	2,925	2,346

Sources: 173rd Airborne Brigade, Operation Order 3-69, Washington Green, 10 April 1969, annex B, appendix 3, National Archives Records Group 472, 173rd Airborne Brigade files, S-3 Command Reports box 3; 173rd Airborne Brigade, Operational Report on Lessons Learned for the Period Ending 30 April 1971, inclosure 1, Strength and Enemy Forces in Binh Dinh Province as of 31 Dec 70, National Archives Records Group 472, 173rd Airborne Brigade files, S-3 ORLL 69–71 box.

1970.[101] Province-wide, VCI strength had declined by just 7 percent (from 4,718 in May 1969 to 4,399 in January 1971).[102] Separate figures are not available for the northern districts, but even if all 319 of the unreplaced losses had been concentrated there, it would not have made much of a dent in the area's total VCI strength, which had been estimated at 2,439 in April 1969.

Yet Advisory Team 42 reported in December that the GVN had enough troops to deal with enemy forces in Binh Dinh, no matter how strong they still were:

> There was no shortage of friendly forces, either line formations or Territorial Forces. Yet, the overall degree of security and/or denial of enemy freedom of movement did not measure up to the potential inherent among these total forces. Two critical deficiencies continued to plague pacification or Vietnamization. Both must be corrected by the Vietnamese, stress Vietnamese, if we are to ever complete our purposes here with any modicum of success. These deficiencies are the lack of self-reliance and the lack of supervision [i.e., leadership]. The logistical umbilical needs to be severed; strand by strand it is true, but nonetheless severed. As to the lack of supervision, this is so endemic that all of our effort put forth to date, all of our human resources expended to date, all of our material input provided to date, the whole ball of wax could melt away if some good, hard, personal, continuous, honest-to-God supervision and on-the-spot corrective action isn't soon applied by responsible Vietnamese officials at all levels.[103]

The same note of frustration—and fatalism—had been struck by Colonel Mendheim at the end of November. He argued that Advisory Team 42 had long since reached the saturation point when it came to providing advice and material support. As he saw it, the South Vietnamese neither wanted nor needed advice; all they desired from their advisors was better access to American financial, logistical, and fire support. As long as this parasitic relationship was allowed to continue, the South Vietnamese would never learn to stand on their own. Therefore, he had already taken steps to reduce the advisory "footprint" in Binh Dinh. He planned to eliminate six MATs by February 1971; merge Hoai An's and Hoai Nhon's District Advisory Teams, and look into doing the same in Binh Khe and An Tuc; trim all remaining District Advisory Teams to just three men; and reduce the size of the provincial advisory staff. Mendheim closed with this provocative statement:

> In Binh Dinh there are sufficient ARVN, Territorial Forces, and Free World Military Forces to provide the security umbrella for the forward

movement of pacification and development. It's now up to the Province Chief, in conjunction with the Vietnamese and Allied agencies, both military and civilian, to pull the Vietnamese toward success—we can't push them there. There may be those who argue for continued heavy American presence and involvement. Such arguments should be ignored. If the Vietnamese aren't ready to carry the ball by now, another 8 or 10 months or years of advising at the present level won't make them any more capable. It will, in fact, only make it that much more unlikely that they will want to break away from their dependence on us.[104]

CHAPTER EIGHT

Aftershocks

The 173rd Airborne soldiered on in Binh Dinh for much of 1971, getting a new commander in January when General Ochs was replaced by Brigadier General Jack MacFarlane. While the 2/503rd continued to guard Camp Radcliffe, the other three paratroop battalions scoured the mountains surrounding AO Lee and southwest of An Khe in Operations Greene Storm and Greene Lightning. In mid-March the 2/503rd was relieved from its defensive mission to join in Operation Greene Sure, which targeted the Cay Giep Mountains. But the brigade's offensive strength did not increase for long, since by the end of April, the 1/503rd had been reduced to zero strength and its colors flown home. The Sky Soldiers' last major combat operation in Vietnam was Greene Gun, a combat interdiction operation in the Crescent Mountains and Base Area 226 that commenced on 21 April. After it was completed, the brigade's remaining units began standing down for redeployment back to the United States. The 2/503rd left at the end of July, and the 173rd's headquarters and the last two paratroop battalions were deactivated in August.[1]

This final phase of the brigade's six years of distinguished combat service in Vietnam was marred by a series of events that threatened to tarnish its illustrious reputation. The first occurred on 24 January 1971, when NBC television correspondent Phil Brady broadcast an exposé about a major heroin operation located within LZ English at a building known as the "White House." Brady reported that US Military Police could not raid the "White House" because it was Vietnamese property, and the GVN's National Police refused to take action. He alleged that ARVN troops based at LZ English also sold drugs to American soldiers. Secretary of Defense Melvin R. Laird was so incensed that he fired off an angry telegram to Admiral Thomas H. Moorer, chairman of the Joint Chiefs of Staff, demanding an immediate investigation into Brady's allegations. Moorer passed the request on to General Abrams, who responded with a report indicating that Brady's story had been correct in most of its particulars. The "White House" was demolished within a matter of days.[2]

Just a few weeks after the "White House" broadcast, another wave of anti-American demonstrations broke out in Qui Nhon on 12 February—only this time, they were incited by the chairman and other members of the Province Council. Rioters threw rocks at American installations, vandalized places of business that catered to Americans, and burned a US Army jeep and roughed up its three occupants.[3] As in December 1970, the demonstrations were provoked by incidents in which Vietnamese civilians had been killed by Americans. The first had occurred on 18 January, when a sixteen-year-old fisherman was shot and killed while trying to recover food containers that were being dumped overboard from a barge. The American soldiers were shooting at the containers to make them sink and continued to do so even though several fishing boats had swooped in to gather them up. Three days later, a Vietnamese schoolteacher was killed by rifle fire from a passing 173rd Airborne Brigade truck, which failed to stop. On 2 February came the death of a five-year-old boy who had been struck three days earlier by a stone allegedly thrown by an American. Finally, on 9 February, an American sentry mistakenly fired an explosive shell from his M-79 grenade launcher instead of an illumination round. It landed in the nearby home of an ARVN soldier, killing a seven-year-old boy and wounding four other civilians. Pacification Studies Group field evaluators concluded that deadly incidents continued to occur with such alarming frequency because "there had existed an ostrich-in-the-sand attitude toward these offenders which bespeaks a certain mushiness in both [US] military justice and discipline. In the past, justice has been neither swift nor certain, and transgressors have been comparatively free to repeat their acts with impunity."[4]

Ironically, the field evaluators also identified "the announced withdrawal of American troops" as one of the causes for both sets of anti-American demonstrations. Fears of abandonment and betrayal were rife after the 4th Infantry Division left South Vietnam and the 173rd Airborne Brigade was pulled off pacification duty. Though they deeply resented the Americans' high-handed and sometimes life-threatening behavior, local civilians had little confidence that either ARVN regulars or the Territorial Forces would be able to protect them once the Sky Soldiers were gone. Their feelings toward US troops were therefore complex and contradictory. Michael Hopson, a 173rd Airborne veteran, recalled that the people "hated and feared us, but didn't want us to leave."[5] Pacification Attitude Analysis System surveys conducted after the February demonstrations revealed that a high percentage of Binh Dinh's population believed that US troop withdrawals were unwise, whereas most of the respondents nationwide thought they were wise.[6]

Unsettling though the anti-American demonstrations were, they made little impression on public opinion back in the United States. But in March 1971 came the shocking news that General John W. Barnes and Colonel Joseph R. Franklin, the 173rd Airborne's former commander and deputy commander, had both been accused of covering up war crimes. These allegations were made by Lieutenant Colonel Anthony B. Herbert, who had been the brigade's inspector general from August 1968 until February 1969, when he assumed command of the 2/503rd. He was relieved of command in early April 1969, just before Operation Washington Green began. General Barnes explained his reasons for taking this highly unusual action as follows:

> Herbert turned out to be a ruthless, unfeeling, combat-happy com-
> mander who would not change his ways despite frequent counseling by
> both myself and my deputy commander. . . . When I assigned Herbert's
> battalion a mission, he would land and personally accompany the assault
> platoon on its mission. This was fine for that platoon, but it left the rest
> of his battalion bereft of his leadership and the battalion suffered for
> it. Also, it got to the point where I could never believe his after action
> reports; what he reported one day would be completely inconsistent with
> what he had reported the day before. Eventually, I lost trust and confi-
> dence in him, and when we were assigned the pacification mission [in
> Operation Washington Green], I knew that Herbert could never adapt to
> the role we would have of helping the Vietnamese take over the responsi-
> bility of fighting for their own survival and rebuilding their nation.[7]

There is no doubt that Herbert, a highly decorated Korean War hero who had risen from the ranks, was an unusually aggressive battalion commander who liked to lead his troops personally in combat. His memoir *Soldier*, published in 1973, describes several such incidents in detail and proudly records that, during the two months it was under his command, the 2/503rd killed at least twice as many enemy troops as any other battalion in the brigade. Colonel Franklin suspected that some of the dead were innocent civilians, and on one occasion he verbally accused Herbert of massacring women and children, though no formal report was made and no charges were brought.[8]

Charges were brought against Sergeant Roy E. Bumgarner, a veteran of multiple tours in Vietnam who was the top NCO in the 2/503rd's elite reconnaissance platoon. Bumgarner was a larger-than-life figure renowned for his tactical skill, enthusiasm for combat, and personal body count, which was rumored to be in the hundreds. On 25 February 1969 he led a recon patrol that killed three unarmed Vietnamese civilians, planted grenades and mortar shells on their bodies, and then reported them as killed in action. There were also allegations that the corpses had been mutilated by castration. Bumgarner was court-martialed for premeditated murder but was convicted on the lesser charge of manslaughter and sentenced to reduction in rank to private and a six-month reduction in pay. He was allowed to remain in Vietnam and reenlisted for another combat tour. Herbert had nothing but praise for Bumgarner in his memoirs and was dismissive about the charges against him.[9]

Herbert claimed that his removal from command had nothing to do with either his battalion's body count or his "up front" leadership style. After all, he noted, just days before being relieved, he had received letters of commendation from both General Barnes and Lieutenant General William R. Peers, the former commander of I Field Force. Instead, Herbert insisted that he was relieved because he had pressed for the investigation of eight separate war crimes. These included the execution of a Vietnamese prisoner and the murder of an American lieutenant by troops of the 173rd Airborne, and the killing of five detainees by South Vietnamese police on 14 February 1969 (which he called "The Saint Valentine's Day Massacre"). Herbert also claimed that he had witnessed three incidents of torture, two of which were committed by South Vietnamese police in the presence of their American advisors, and another wherein US troops had used water torture. General Barnes and Colonel Franklin were determined to cover up these crimes, Herbert alleged, and removed him because he did not belong to the "West Point Protective Association," whose members could be trusted to protect one another's careers.[10]

Herbert's removal was followed by a career-wrecking officer efficiency report that rated him "in the lowest category on cooperation, moral courage, integrity and understanding, and recommended that he never again be allowed to command a unit."[11] Herbert appealed his relief, but a military tribunal held in Saigon ruled against him. He then sought to have the damning efficiency report expunged from his record, but that appeal was denied in December 1969. After being passed over for promotion in May 1970, Herbert made another attempt to have the efficiency report expunged in September, but this time, he also asked that Barnes and Franklin be investigated for covering up war crimes. After six months had passed and the investigation had yielded no results, Herbert became suspicious that the army was trying to drag out the process until the statute of limitations had expired. In March 1971 he formally accused Barnes and Franklin of dereliction of duty, failure to obey lawful regulations, and concealing a felony—and went public with his allegations.[12]

Herbert's talk of war crime cover-ups, which came while the My Lai Massacre trial of Lieutenant William Calley was under way, drew immense media attention. The fact that he implicated General Barnes, who had become an unofficial Nixon administration spokesman on Vietnamization, made the story irresistible to print and television journalists. Barnes, who had just been promoted to the post of army director of plans and programs, found himself intercepted by reporters as he and his wife were heading to a square dancing competition in full costume. Herbert himself became an instant celebrity; his story was carried on the front pages of all the major newspapers, and he soon made the first of three appearances on the influential *Dick Cavett Show*. Meanwhile, the US Army's investigation went ahead behind the scenes, exonerating Franklin in July and Barnes in October 1971. The keystone of their successful defense was that the army could find no record of Herbert reporting the war crimes prior to September 1970. Herbert insisted that he had informed Barnes and Franklin about the incidents in 1969 but had not brought them up during his earlier appeals because he feared the members of the military tribunal might close ranks against him.

When the details of the army's investigation were released to the public, some of Herbert's former supporters in the media began to doubt his veracity, including Barry Lando, an associate producer for CBS's *60 Minutes*. As Lando and others dug deeper into the story, they found many errors and inconsistencies in Herbert's story, particularly concerning dates. He claimed, for instance, that Colonel Franklin had radioed him on 14 February 1969 to turn over prisoners to the South Vietnamese police, who then killed them. However, it seems that Franklin was actually on leave in Hawaii on that date. Moreover, many witnesses named by Herbert failed to corroborate his accounts of various events in the saga, although he suggested that the army had coerced them to lie. By the end of 1971, Herbert was starting to be attacked in the press, with the *National Observer* publishing a piece entitled "Colonel Herbert: A Hero or a Liar?" Herbert retired from the army in February 1972 but continued to try to vindicate himself. In February 1973 he was invited to appear on *60 Minutes* but found himself ambushed by Mike Wallace, who challenged his credibility and suggested that he himself was guilty of war crimes.

Herbert believed the White House had pressured CBS into discrediting him, and he sued the network for libel. Given what the Watergate investigations were revealing about how the Nixon administration dealt with perceived enemies, these suspicions could not be dismissed as mere paranoia. The case of *Herbert v. Lando* would become one of the longest-lasting legacies of the Vietnam War as it dragged on for three decades. In 1979 it yielded a landmark US Supreme Court ruling that the defendants could not seek dismissal of the suit on the basis of First Amendment protections. However, the suit was ultimately dismissed by the US Court of Appeals in New York in 2005 on the grounds that the CBS story was accurate in most of its particulars, and the federal courts should not be tied up resolving minor points of contention.[13]

Herbert nonetheless won vindication of a sort just a year later when the *Los Angeles Times* published an article revealing that while the army was trying to discredit Herbert, it had also kept 127 cases of detainee abuse committed by troops of the 173rd Airborne under wraps. The archived documentary records of the army's Vietnam War Crimes Working Group and the Criminal Investigation Division proved that soldiers of the brigade's 172nd Military Intelligence Detachment had frequently administered beatings, electrical shocks, and water torture during interrogations. Twenty-nine members of the unit were identified as taking part in these incidents, and fifteen of them admitted to doing so, with some claiming that "this was de facto command policy." Nevertheless, only three were ever convicted, and they received fines or reductions in rank rather than prison sentences.[14]

A Failing Grade

While the 173rd Airborne was fighting its battle against negative publicity, the GVN was facing the ultimate test of whether it had overcome its dependency on American support in Binh Dinh. It was a dependency that went far beyond reliance on the Sky Soldiers to maintain territorial security. In his first monthly report of 1971, Colonel Mendheim stated that so many GVN agencies and military units in Phu My were "pirating" electricity from the District Advisory Team that its backup generator could not be used without first disconnecting as many as thirty wires. The South Vietnamese had grown so accustomed to getting power this way that they believed they had a right to it and got upset whenever their wires were detached. Mendheim argued that the only way to get the locals to stand on their own was to rapidly draw down the advisory effort. He suggested, "Let's 'unhook our generators' and give these people a chance to run on their own steam. We might be pleasantly surprised. Their ability to survive may exceed our often-voiced opinions to the contrary in this matter."[15]

Mendheim soon had to admit, however, that the naysayers had been right all along. In February the pattern of long lulls punctuated by brief offensive high points that had characterized the war in Binh Dinh during Washington Green came to an end. The Communists, having resolved to "attack continuously and unwaveringly," never let a night go by without assaulting an outpost or a day to pass without trying to eliminate more "tyrants." They also revived a tactic last seen at Tet 1968: organizing "uprisings" in which crowds of civilians armed with improvised weapons and drums surrounded GVN outposts and noisily called on the defenders to surrender. In many cases, they either fled or gave themselves up.[16] At the end of February Mendheim reported, "In Tam Quan, he [the enemy] has a solid hold on the population and terrain, and bitterly resents any attempts to infringe on his holdings. . . . In Phu My, he operates with impunity and relative freedom."[17] In fact, across northern Binh Dinh, the thin veneer of GVN control created by Operation

Washington Green was being stripped away to reveal the naked truth that the Communist grip on the region had never been broken at all. With the Sky Soldiers out of the hamlets for good, enemy troops were having a field day against the dispirited Territorial Forces. By the end of March, they could do pretty much as they pleased in Tam Quan and Phu My at any hour of the day.[18] In Tam Quan they collected ID cards from civilians in the district seat in broad daylight. The insurgents were able to act so boldly because the plentiful and well-armed Territorial Forces did almost nothing to stop them.

Matters only got worse in April, when thirty-three GVN officials were assassinated and the Phoenix program remained stuck in neutral. Colonel Mendheim observed that although there were still 3,273 category A and B VCI in Binh Dinh, "Specific targeting is still not effective as a neutralization tool. The DIOCCs, for the most part, have beautiful records and dossiers in their files but that is the extent of their operations."[19] The PAVN official history claims that it "liberated" more than 100,000 people in Binh Dinh during this period and rebuilt many of its former bases in the coastal plains.[20] This is generally confirmed by Advisory Team 42, which reported at the end of May that the Communists had attained a position of ascendancy in all four northern districts, controlled most of their populations, and had re-established liberated zones stretching all the way from the mountains to the sea.[21] Yet the new PSA, Daniel L. Leaty, hastened to add that this situation had not arisen due to an insufficiency of friendly forces:

> The enemy has the capability to do almost anything he chooses at any time. Conversely, friendly forces also have the ability and capability to do anything they want at any time they choose, but *they do not appear to want to do anything anytime*. At the present time there are adequate Vietnamese forces in the Province to handle the situation, but until they receive the necessary command guidance, direction and leadership, the enemy will continue to gain support from the people. The enemy's administrative, political and military organizations are more actively effective than the same GVN organizations which exist in name only and, although not dead, are in a full state of dormancy.[22]

Thus, despite everything that had happened since 1969, the GVN was still—as Bernard Fall put it—being "out-administered" in Binh Dinh. The Pacification Studies Group observed, "The GVN in Binh Dinh is fighting a war with two fronts: one against the VC/NVA, the second against itself. Neither war is going well."[23]

HES was slow to depict the full extent of Communist domination, but in July the DSAs received new guidance that changed the picture dramatically.

Table 8.1 Binh Dinh HES Statistics, June 1970–August 1971

	Number of Hamlets by Category (Percentage of Rural Population by Category)						
Month	A	B	C	D	E	V	Unrated
June 1970	9 (1.4%)	215 (58.2%)	221 (29.0%)	105 (10.7%)	0 (0%)	10 (0.1%)	8 (0.6%)
September 1970	6 (0.9%)	266 (64.5%)	198 (22.6%)	88 (10.7%)	1 (0.1%)	13 (0.8%)	7 (0.4%)
December 1970	5 (0.8%)	321 (68.9%)	185 (22.5%)	65 (7.3%)	0 (0%)	0 (0%)	6 (0.4%)
April 1971	2 (0.3%)	191 (47.1%)	260 (35.5%)	134 (16.7%)	5 (0.4%)	2 (0.1%)	0 (0%)
August 1971	3 (0.2%)	161 (28.3%)	275 (45.3%)	123 (18.0%)	2 (0.1%)	61 (7.6%)	0 (0.1%)

Source: Hamlet Evaluation System, Summary Reports, 30 June, 30 September, and 31 December 1970, 30 April and 31 August 1971, MACV Command Historian's Collection, US Army Heritage and Education Center, Carlisle, PA.

In the past, they had always answered "no" to the HES indicator question "Do enemy forces physically control this hamlet?" as long as RF and PF units were present during the day. Now, however, they were directed to answer "yes" if the Territorial Forces merely hunkered down in their defensive perimeters after nightfall or retreated to safer ground along Highway 1.[24] The result was an "HES bombshell" whose echoes reverberated all the way up the chain of command when V-rated hamlets in Binh Dinh spiked from just four in June to sixty-one in August. Leaty stressed that GVN control had *not* declined during those months—it had actually withered away much earlier:

> Binh Dinh really has not changed. The July HES readout showed an increase of thirty-five (35) VC controlled hamlets. Actually the hamlets were always VC controlled. . . . What caused the severe drop in July ratings was the guidance provided to the DSAs. They were told that just because an RF/PF unit was assigned to a hamlet it did not mean the hamlet was controlled by the GVN. If the RF/PF unit withdraws to [Highway] QL-1 at night or secures itself in its outposts, the hamlets should be classified as VC controlled. As an example, during the month a platoon responsible for guarding two bridges on QL-1 received a report from district officials that the enemy would attack both bridges that

night. The action taken by the PF platoon was to completely withdraw from the bridge sites.[25]

The Red Queen's race had therefore already run its course in Binh Dinh by Operation Washington Green's second anniversary in April 1971. For all intents and purposes, the situation was right back where it had been two years earlier—and indeed, before the first American troops ever set foot in the province in 1965. Washington Green had not altered any of the fundamental realities of the war in northern Binh Dinh. The VCI were still omnipresent; Communist troops were still numerous and potent; the population was still more supportive of the NLF than the GVN; and, most important of all, the South Vietnamese were still utterly dependent on American support. With the advantage of hindsight, Leaty now believed that the operation had been ill conceived from the outset:

> It is felt that one of the major contributing factors to the sad shape Binh Dinh is in today is that of the past mission of the 173d Abn Bde by being broken down into squads and platoons in almost every village and hamlet in the northern sector, and doing just about everything for the RF, PF and District Chiefs, it appears those leaders and their troops are still waiting for the Americans to do everything. However, the Americans are gone from the villages and hamlets, and the enemy, not the GVN, is filling the gap.[26]

Operation Washington Green had backfired. Instead of making the South Vietnamese self-reliant, it had left them more addicted to American support than ever. Indeed, the massive infusion of US troops and resources had compensated for the shortcomings of the Territorial Forces and the GVN bureaucracy to such an extent that improving their performance actually became *less* imperative. But if the 173rd Airborne had not been committed in direct support of pacification, it is quite certain that no progress at all would have been made. This was the real-life catch-22 that had always vexed Americans in Binh Dinh—and many other provinces as well. If they did not take the initiative, nothing got done; if they did take the initiative, it became less likely that the South Vietnamese would ever stand on their own.

The Whole Ball of Wax Melts Away

Although the failure of Operation Washington Green was unmistakable by mid-1971, the full extent of the GVN's weakness in Binh Dinh was not revealed until the following year, when the Communists launched their in-

The Easter Offensive. *Source:* Richard W. Stewart, ed., *American Military History*, Volume 2: *The United States Army in a Global Era, 1917-2003* (Washington, DC: US Army Center of Military History Pub 30-22, 2005), Map 20. [Reprinted by permission of the US Army Center of Military History]

famous Easter Offensive. Known to them as the Nguyen Hue Offensive—named after the Tay Son rebel from Binh Dinh—it began on 30 March with a massive assault across the Demilitarized Zone that overran the 3rd ARVN Division and went on to conquer all of Quang Tri Province within four weeks. In the Central Highlands of western II Corps, troops of the NVA's B-3 Front were already besieging ARVN firebases on "Rocket Ridge," northwest of Kontum. By the end of April, the last of these had been captured, and powerful enemy forces supported by large numbers of T-54/55 tanks laid siege to the city. A similar situation developed in northwestern III Corps, where the 5th, 7th, and 9th VC Divisions (which were in fact manned predominantly by North Vietnamese) invaded South Vietnam from their Cambodian sanctuaries in the first week of April, captured the city of Loc Ninh within a matter of days, and drove south down Highway 13 toward Saigon until they were halted at An Loc, the capital of Binh Long Province. The Communists continued to attack on all three fronts throughout May, and the fighting resolved itself into a pair of epic sieges at Kontum and An Loc and an NVA effort to push south into Thua Thien Province toward Hue, the old imperial capital. However, since the enemy's Main Force units were now fighting large-scale, conventional battles, they presented lucrative targets for US airpower, which proceeded to savage them with a torrent of high explosives and napalm. "Arc-light" B-52 air strikes proved to be particularly effective against the massed Communist forces.[27]

The fourth area where the Communists mounted a major thrust during the Nguyen Hue Offensive was in Binh Dinh, where the intent was evidently to link up with the attackers in the Central Highlands and cut South Vietnam in half. On 9 April the Yellow Star Division, heavily reinforced by the 2nd NVA Division's 21st Regiment and the 403rd, 406th, and 450th Sapper Battalions, came boiling up out of Base Area 226 and assailed LZ Pony in Hoai An. The compound's RF defenders succumbed to the assault within two days, prompting the CORDS senior advisor in II Corps, the legendary John Paul Vann, to insist on a counterattack by two battalions of the 40th ARVN Regiment. Vann's biographer, Neil Sheehan, paints a vivid portrait of the ensuing ARVN debacle in Hoai An. Colonel Tran Hieu Duc, commander of the 40th ARVN Regiment, was so unnerved by the situation that he refused to either attack or mount a credible defense of the rest of the district. "Duc would not fight. He made no attempt to regain Pony or to hold any of the high ground farther down the [Kim Son] Valley. Instead, he let his battalions keep falling back toward the district center. His advisor, Lt. Col. David Schorr, could put no spine into him. . . . There were twenty-nine PF platoons in the district. They were deserting."[28] Finally, on 18 April, Duc decided to abandon Hoai An and pull back to Bong Son, but his precipitate flight the following day turned the retreat into a rout, with many of the fleeing ARVN troops throwing away both their weapons and their uniforms as they ran.

GVN forces elsewhere in the province had stood up reasonably well to the Nguyen Hue Offensive's first blows. In Tam Quan, they had bloodily repulsed ground assaults on the district seat and LZ English (now headquarters of the 40th ARVN Regiment)—inflicting at least 150 fatalities on the 403rd and 406th Sapper Battalions. However, the rout in Hoai An dealt a crippling blow to the morale of GVN troops in neighboring Hoai Nhon; they quickly gave way before the pursuing NVA and fell back in disarray. Many of the retreating troops took advantage of the chaotic situation by deserting and blending into the columns of civilian refugees. These events, in turn, demoralized the defenders of Tam Quan and Phu My, who also began to show signs of panic and disintegration. Elsewhere in the province, the 18th NVA Regiment succeeded in seizing a portion of Highway 19 in the vicinity of An Khe Pass and kept the road closed for two weeks starting on 14 April. Lieutenant Colonel Willard B. Esplin, the deputy PSA, delivered a stinging indictment of South Vietnamese military performance during this period:

> Two of the northern districts have been lost and a third will be evacuated due to enemy pressure on friendly forces who failed to realize their mission was to fight. The loss was not due to an active enemy. It was due to inaction on the part of the friendly forces. There were only occasional bright spots in RF/PF performance, and ARVN and VNAF [Vietnamese Air Force] generally were less than adequate.[29]

South Vietnamese troops had also abandoned the Vinh Thanh Valley in Binh Khe district, accompanied by 6,000 refugees. Thus, the entire GVN position in Binh Dinh seemed to be on the verge of collapse in early May. Tam Quan had to be abandoned because the remaining 40th ARVN and RF and PF troops were too demoralized to defend it. While they were being evacuated by sea, the Yellow Star Division was already raising havoc in northern Phu My, seeming to set the stage for an almost unopposed NVA march southward to Qui Nhon. On every side, Territorial Forces and PSDF militiamen were deserting in droves (by the end of May, ninety-two PF platoons and a dozen RF companies had simply vanished into thin air), the 41st ARVN Regiment was beginning to show signs of panic, and a "brigade" composed of 2,700 students, teachers, war veterans, and civil servants was being hastily organized for the last-ditch defense of Qui Nhon. It was therefore nothing short of a miracle when the Yellow Star Division halted its drive southward at midmonth. According to PSA Leaty:

Morale appeared to be at its lowest ebb and Binh Dinh apparently was ripe for picking with only token resistance to be offered by ARVN and TF [Territorial Forces]. The enemy drive abruptly halted as he had possibly over-extended himself. Significant [enemy] gains had been made at the expense of heavy losses resulting from the two-day stand at LZ English and supporting naval and artillery gunfire and numerous air strikes. During the latter half of the month enemy activity was characterized by VC elements moving throughout the remaining six districts. . . . NVA elements have not elected to maintain the initiative but appear content to consolidate the areas taken in the first two months of the current offensive.[30]

In Binh Dinh, as on its other three main battlefronts, the Nguyen Hue Offensive was halted by growing logistical difficulties, incremental casualties (including those incurred during failed attacks on Phu My's district seat and another fortified base in Phu Cat district), and massive US firepower. Of the three, the last was clearly the most decisive. In late June Advisory Team 42 reported: "NVA elements have not been able to mass significant forces to conduct major attacks as they have been kept off-balance by a heavy volume of air strikes, gunships, direct support artillery fire, and occasional B-52 strikes."[31] Yet South Vietnamese troops proved reluctant to seize the initiative even when supported by this American firepower. A 22 May counterattack designed to recover northern Phu My faltered because troops of the 41st ARVN Regiment refused to venture away from their defensive compounds along Highway 1. Even the dispirited and understrength RF and PF did better—reoccupying two firebases the NVA had chosen not to defend.[32]

The relaxation of enemy pressure in the second half of May gave GVN forces the time they desperately needed to regain their equilibrium, refit, and reorganize, but they remained incapable of offensive action for another seven weeks. Most of their casualties had resulted from desertion rather than combat. From the beginning of the Nguyen Hue Offensive through the end of June, ARVN units in Binh Dinh lost 198 killed, 311 wounded, and 669 missing, while the province's Territorial Forces reported 155 killed, 223 wounded, and an astounding 3,457 missing.[33] Colonel Esplin suggested that "unaccounted for" would be "a more accurate term [than missing] since the majority appear to have fled the battle and not been overrun."[34] The hiatus in Communist offensive activity allowed the South Vietnamese commanders to track down many of these deserters, force them back into the ranks, and begin restoring discipline.

The stalemate in Binh Dinh persisted throughout June. Elsewhere, the sieges of Kontum and An Loc were broken, and an ARVN counterattack was launched toward Quang Tri City.[35] Although it was now obvious that the Nguyen Hue Offensive had failed, the Communists hoped to retain their new "liberated zone" in Binh Dinh and expand it into Quang Ngai Province. Therefore, on 15 July the bulk of the Yellow Star Division began heading north, leaving behind only the 4th Battalion, 18th NVA Regiment, the 14th NVA Engineer Battalion, and two Local Force VC battalions to defend the "liberated zone." The departing units were urgently recalled just two days later when preparations for a massive ARVN counteroffensive were detected, but it was too late; for once, the South Vietnamese had surprise on their side.[36] On 19 July the 22nd ARVN Division attacked up Highway 1 with its refitted 40th, 41st, and 42nd Infantry Regiments, supported by the 2nd and 6th Ranger Groups, the 19th Armored Cavalry Squadron, and the 215th RF Battalion. This juggernaut simply rolled over the weak enemy units that had been given the unfamiliar and uncongenial mission of holding a fixed defensive line based on Phu Cuu Pass. Bong Son was retaken on 22 July; Tam Quan's district seat was liberated the following day, and Hoai An's on 26 July. Advisory Team 42's report for July nonetheless ended on a somber note: "In summary—for those South Vietnamese who died in the initial onslaught of the NVA invasion or were murdered by them later—the battle is over. For those who survived—the battle to rebuild their shattered homes and lives is just beginning."[37]

The GVN's ability to stand on its own in Binh Dinh was tested during the Nguyen Hue Offensive and found to be no better than before the first American troops arrived in the province. The events of April and May 1972 were virtually a replay of what had happened in the Tet Offensive of 1965 (see chapter 1). And, as in 1965, this had been accomplished by Communist forces that possessed no advantage in numbers and nothing remotely close to the firepower and logistical support enjoyed by their opponents (unlike the other main battlefronts of the Nguyen Hue Offensive, the enemy employed no tanks or heavy artillery in Binh Dinh). What the ARVN regular and Territorial Forces troops in the province lacked was not numbers, firepower, supplies, or advisors but the will to fight. Without it, they were effectively defeated as soon as it became clear that the enemy was launching a major offensive. In its postmortem, Advisory Team 42 noted with dismay that the enemy with "relative ease rolled back psychologically defeated ARVN/TF. Even more alarming was the ineptness of friendly forces in establishing any reasonable semblance of a second line of defense and their strong propensity to withdraw at the first sign of enemy forces."[38]

As always, the root of the problem was poor leadership. Revisionist historians suggest that South Vietnamese leadership had improved dramatically in the years between 1968 and 1971,[39] but the Nguyen Hue Offensive proves otherwise. According to Dale Andrade, who authored the standard account of the offensive: "At the root of Saigon's predicament was a failure to improve its officer corps. Tied firmly to the politics of patronage practiced by President Thieu, South Vietnamese generals were generally corrupt or incompetent—often both."[40] Colonel Gerald Turley (USMC), who served as an advisor in Quang Tri, described incompetent, defeatist, and perhaps even treasonous behavior by ARVN commanders.[41] Indeed, on all the major battlefronts, ARVN leadership collapsed under the first onslaught, with senior officers fleeing, surrendering, and—in one notable case—defecting to the enemy. Many others, fatalistically convinced that defeat was inevitable, lapsed into apathy and sat passively in their command bunkers waiting for the end to come. In these desperate circumstances, US advisors often had to step into the breach and provide the leadership their counterparts would not. The most famous example was John Vann, who, despite being a civilian, took control of II Corps from the incompetent Lieutenant General Ngo Dzu.[42] Even when they did not effectively assume command of faltering ARVN units, American advisors played a decisive role by coordinating the massive US supporting fires that ultimately saved the day. In general, ARVN commanders still lacked the skills—and the qualified staffs—necessary to perform these tasks. The leadership crisis was so dire that President Thieu conducted a wholesale purge of his senior commanders. In Binh Dinh, the province chief and four district chiefs were replaced, and two sets of commanders in the 40th and 41st ARVN Regiments were sacked between April and July 1972.[43]

In Binh Dinh, as elsewhere, the Nguyen Hue Offensive was defeated only because enemy troops and supply lines were relentlessly pummeled by American aircraft and US Navy ships lying offshore. Former ARVN lieutenant general Ngo Quang Truong candidly admitted: "Quang Tri City could not have been retaken, nor could ARVN forces have held at Kontum and An Loc, had it not been for the support provided by the United States Air Force."[44] Although US firepower was applied on a lesser scale in Binh Dinh, it still played a decisive role in halting the Yellow Star Division's advance; the entire province probably would have been overrun if it had not been available. The same can safely be said for the entire country, since the GVN clearly would have been doomed without the massive intervention of US airpower in both North and South Vietnam.

Finis

The ARVN reconquest of northern Binh Dinh in July 1972 did not mean that it was solidly under GVN control. The district capitals and main roads

had been reoccupied, but most of the surrounding countryside remained under enemy domination. Furthermore, the Communists were determined to
retain control of Hoai An, which was their only remaining "liberated zone"
in the coastal plains of central Vietnam.[45] Elements of the Yellow Star Division stubbornly clung to the bulk of the district throughout the remainder of
1972, preventing the return of the Territorial Forces and GVN officials.[46] In
any event, many of Hoai An's hamlets (particularly in the Kim Son/Crow's
Foot Valley) were unpopulated, having been abandoned by their inhabitants
either back in April or more recently due to the continuous fighting in the
area. Thus, while there had been no unrated hamlets in Binh Dinh prior to
the Nguyen Hue Offensive, in November 1972 there were ninety-three.

The Communists were anxious to maintain their grip on Hoai An because, after years of deadlock, secret negotiations between Henry Kissinger
and North Vietnamese diplomat Le Duc Tho finally seemed ready to bear
fruit. Since 1969, President Nixon had been insisting on a mutual withdrawal
of US and NVA forces from South Vietnam. Yet neither "triangular diplomacy" with China and the Soviet Union nor military escalation (bombing
Cambodia in 1969, invading it in 1970, invading Laos in 1971, and bombing
North Vietnam and mining its ports in 1972) had convinced Tho to yield an
inch on this issue. By the fall of 1972, unilateral withdrawals had reduced
the number of US troops in the country to just a few thousand—leaving the
Americans nothing to bargain with. Anxious to secure an agreement before
the November general election, Nixon and Kissinger finally dropped the demand, and the North Vietnamese abandoned their long-standing demand for
President Thieu's removal.[47]

After this breakthrough, Kissinger proclaimed on 26 October, "We believe
that peace is at hand"—though ironically, this statement was immediately
followed by rival "Land-Grab Offensives" designed to stake out territorial
claims before the in-place cease-fire took effect. Enemy forces gained ground
in many parts of the country, but they were largely driven out of the newly
conquered territory, with heavy casualties, when the expected cease-fire did
not occur.[48] Although enemy activity in Binh Dinh during this period was
limited to small-scale ground attacks and attacks-by-fire, the "secure" (HES
categories A and B) population fell to just 16 percent in October, and the
November HES map showed almost the entire northern half of the province
under NLF control (V-rated hamlets).[49]

No cease-fire took place at the end of October 1972 because Thieu was
bitterly opposed to the Kissinger-Tho agreement, about which he had largely
been kept in the dark. Revisionist historians may assert that the cease-fire
agreement was the capstone to a victory already won, but Thieu clearly saw
it as a betrayal. Unlike the Revisionists, he had no illusions that his armed

forces were capable of standing on their own against both the NLF and the NVA, and one of his principal objections to the agreement was that it would allow more than 100,000 North Vietnamese troops to remain in South Vietnam. Thieu insisted on dozens of amendments, which were passed along by Kissinger; this caused the North Vietnamese to demand changes of their own. Negotiations continued, but they came to an impasse and recessed on 13 December. Within five days, US aircraft were pummeling Hanoi and Haiphong in the "Christmas Bombing" of 18–29 December 1972. Nixon's chief objective was apparently to reassure Thieu that massive US air support would always be available to preserve the GVN, but he also hoped this final attempt at "madman diplomacy" might extract concessions from the North Vietnamese and make them fear that bombing would resume if they violated the cease-fire and openly invaded South Vietnam. As it turned out, the North Vietnamese made no substantial new concessions after negotiations resumed on 1 January, and the final cease-fire agreement that was hammered out over the following weeks still did not reflect Thieu's demands. He accordingly denounced it as a "surrender agreement" and refused to sign. Only after President Nixon threatened to conclude a unilateral cease-fire did Thieu bow to the inevitable and agree to accept the terms of the Paris Accords, which were finally signed on 27 January.[50]

The Communists launched another Land-Grab Offensive in the final days before the cease-fire. In Binh Dinh, the 18th NVA Regiment pushed into Tam Quan from its bases in the An Lao Valley, while the rest of the Yellow Star Division overran GVN outposts in Hoai An and cut Highway 1 just south of Phu Cuu Pass.[51] Heavy fighting also erupted in Hoai Nhon, Phu My, Phu Cat, and Binh Khe districts.[52] The NLF's objective was to win overt control of hamlets—including those it had long dominated psychologically—so it could raise its flag over them and peg out territorial claims that would be recognized by the International Commission of Control and Supervision after the cease-fire took effect. This objective was largely achieved in Binh Dinh, where overt Communist liberated zones grew to encompass almost all the territory in the four northern districts. The January 1973 HES map therefore looked remarkably like that of January 1969. The region once again appeared to be a forest of Vs surrounding a few forlorn-looking Es and an even smaller number of Ds.

Despite its success, the second Land-Grab Offensive left Communist forces throughout South Vietnam in a highly vulnerable state. Having attacked nationwide, they were dangerously dispersed and badly weakened by their losses (including those suffered in the first round of land-grab attacks). They had also lost their "invisibility," since they were committed to openly defending the hamlets where the NLF flag now flew. Initially, the Com-

Table 8.2 Binh Dinh HES Statistics, August 1972–January 1973

Month	Number of Hamlets by Category (Percentage of Rural Population by Category)						
	A	B	C	D	E	V	Unrated
August 1972	0	117	165	95	39	218	3
	(0%)	(26.1%)	(23.8%)	(11.2%)	(4.9%)	(23.3%)	(10.7%)
October 1972	0	92	168	91	76	208	3
	(0%)	(16.1%)	(30.8%)	(14.1%)	(8.7%)	(16.1%)	(14.1%)
November 1972	6	112	168	78	77	194	93
	(2.6%)	(20.4%)	(27.6%)	(11.5%)	(9.4%)	(14.4%)	(14.1%)
January 1973	6	207	154	94	73	193	44
	(0.8%)	(33.7%)	(23.3%)	(16.6%)	(8.4%)	(14.8%)	(3.4%)

Source: Hamlet Evaluation System, Summary Reports, 31 August, 31 October, and 30 November 1972, 31 January 1973, MACV Command Historian's Collection, US Army Heritage and Education Center, Carlisle, PA.

munists were not worried because they apparently believed the cease-fire would bring at least a temporary cessation of hostilities, and they expected the struggle to become an increasingly political contest. The PAVN official history states, "On our side, we were, to some extent at least, deluded by illusions of peace and thought we could passively wait to see what happened."[53] However, President Thieu had no intention of allowing the enemy to retain his eleventh-hour gains. Able for once to use their superior firepower against static and readily identifiable targets, ARVN and territorial troops launched a counteroffensive that eliminated many of the enemy's new liberated zones in the first few months of 1973.

The PAVN official history admits that the liberated areas in Hoai Nhon and Phu My were lost, but it claims that those in Hoai An and Tam Quan survived. It also asserts that, after the NLF and NVA abandoned the futile tactic of openly defending liberated hamlets, they were able to reconstitute their forces and regain the initiative in the second half of 1973. Using more familiar guerrilla tactics, they managed to reestablish many of the former liberated zones, including in Phu My.[54] These claims are generally in accordance with the facts in Binh Dinh, but precisely how the situation looked to the allies is hard to determine because, per the terms of the Paris Accords, all American advisors were withdrawn in February 1973. Thus, January 1973 is the last month for which HES data are available in US archives; from then on, provincial-level reporting by representatives of the Defense

Attaché's Office at the US embassy in Saigon was sketchy and focused on tracking pacification program performance rather than describing the military situation.

In any event, Binh Dinh remained a secondary battlefront in the continuing Vietnam War until early 1975. Throughout this period, the 22nd ARVN Division was constantly engaged in trying to prevent the Yellow Star Division from interdicting Highways 1 and 19 and penetrating into the coastal plains.[55] Operations in Binh Dinh assumed greater strategic significance in March 1975, when the Communists launched their Campaign 275, which aimed to conquer the Central Highlands. Before the main offensive began with an assault on Ban Me Thuot, the capital of Darlac Province, enemy forces launched supporting attacks designed to sever the roads linking the Central Highlands to the coast. On 4 March the 3rd NVA Division cut Highway 19 at An Khe Pass, while the 95B NVA Regiment blocked it again at Mang Yang Pass west of An Khe. These attacks also had a deceptive purpose, since they helped convince Major General Pham Van Phu, commander of II Corps, that the enemy's main effort would be directed against Pleiku rather than Ban Me Thout.[56]

While General Phan Dinh Niem, commander the 22nd ARVN Division, vainly tried to clear An Khe Pass, three enemy divisions fell upon the single ARVN regiment defending Ban Me Thuot on 10 March and overran the city in two days. The defeat prompted President Thieu to make the fateful decision to abandon Pleiku and Kontum to free the troops necessary to retake Ban Me Thuot. Since Highway 19 was still blocked in multiple places, General Phu decided to use Highway 7B for the retreat to the coast, even though it was a disused, overgrown track on which a key bridge was missing. Hoping to achieve surprise, he also neglected to prepare detailed plans for the massive withdrawal that would include one tank, three artillery, three engineer, and nineteen infantry battalions (all but one of them ARVN Ranger units); plus numerous logistical support and RF and PF units; and tens of thousands of civilians. The operation devolved into a rout almost as soon as it began on 16 March. Traffic control broke down, splintering most of the combat units into a leaderless mob of stragglers who became hopelessly intermixed with hordes of panic-stricken civilians. Only a few gravely weakened units made it to the port of Tuy Hoa as cohesive combat formations, and most of the fugitives were swept up by the 320th NVA Division, which laid a gauntlet along Highway 7B. Within a few weeks, South Vietnam had lost the Central Highlands and a large fraction of the ARVN's total force structure—and the Communists had fulfilled their decade-old ambition of cutting the country in two. Meanwhile, an attempt to pull the overstretched ARVN forces in I Corps back into coastal enclaves around Hue, Da Nang, and Chu Lai had

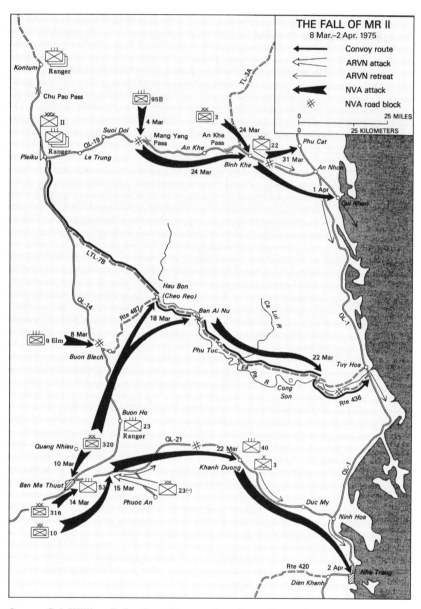

Source: Col. William E. Le Gro, *Vietnam from Cease-Fire to Capitulation*
(Washington, DC: US Army Center of Military History Pub 90-29, 1985), Map 19,
148. [Reprinted by permission of the US Army Center of Military History]

likewise degenerated into a rout that ended in the loss of the entire region and most of the troops defending it.[57]

Units of the 22nd ARVN Division had generally fought well in the vain effort to clear Highway 19 and inflicted heavy casualties on the Yellow Star Division. However, the evacuation of Pleiku made reopening the road pointless, and the disasters occurring on Highway 7B to the south and in I Corps to the north made it obvious that the GVN forces in Binh Dinh could not hold out much longer. The 22nd Division's 47th Infantry Regiment was driven out of Tam Quan on 28 March by Communist reinforcements streaming south from Quang Ngai Province. It tried to make a stand at Phu Cat air base but was effectively destroyed there, and its commander, Colonel Le Cau, committed suicide. Meanwhile, elements of the Yellow Star Division had infiltrated into Qui Nhon, aided by an uprising in the city, and cut off the 41st and 42nd Regiments at Binh Khe. They were ordered to fall back to Qui Nhon on 30 March but were unable to dislodge the enemy troops already in the city. Instead, they cut their way to an open beach four miles south of the harbor where, supported by naval gunfire, they were picked up by ships of the Vietnamese navy. About 7,000 ARVN and territorial troops were evacuated in the first two days of April, although Colonel Nguyen Huu Thong, commander of the 42nd Regiment, refused to leave and took his own life. As the last landing craft pulled away from the beach, South Vietnam had just five weeks to live.[58]

Triumph Mistaken

Revisionist historians claim that the United States won a lost victory in Vietnam due to the success of pacification and Vietnamization in the years after Tet 1968. By now it should be clear that neither succeeded in Binh Dinh, despite the unique commitment of an entire US combat brigade in direct support of pacification for eighteen months. There were many causes for Operation Washington Green's failure, but the most important was that its twin objectives of pacification and Vietnamization were at odds with each other. General Barnes assumed that both could be pursued simultaneously, but experience proved that every advance the 173rd Airborne made in pacification only broadened and deepened the GVN's dependence on American support—and leadership. In Binh Dinh, as elsewhere, "fast and thin" pacification's achievements were largely the result of "gathering up the slack" in regions where the insurgency had gone unchallenged for years. NLF liberated areas were broken up, dozens of enemy-controlled hamlets were shifted into the "contested" category, and many less committed VCI and guerrillas were convinced to defect. But after the Sky Soldiers took up the slack, only the South Vietnamese could do the "heavy hauling" needed to finish off the weakened insurgency.

Washington Green became hopelessly bogged down at this point because little or no progress was ever made in Vietnamization. This was particularly true of the all-important Territorial Forces, which had become more reliant than ever on American support. A 1972 study by the Institute for Defense Analysis suggested that "brigading" US and RF and PF troops together, as they were in northern Binh Dinh, was actually counterproductive:

> On balance, the use of the buddy system with ARVN units was a most effective training technique, since ARVN units had the [same] general level of supporting arms and services as US units. However, in the case of brigading US units with the territorials . . . it may well be that the combat performance of Territorial Forces which have become accustomed to a high level of US support (particularly helicopters), may be degraded when forced to operate with the more limited Vietnamese external support resources.[1]

Operation Washington Green also undermined efforts to boost the 40th and 41st ARVN Regiments' performance by overextending the Territorial Forces to the point where gaps in population security could be closed only by using ARVN regulars in the role of RF troops. This was expedient as long as there were few Communist regulars on hand, but it impeded Vietnamization by making it impossible for the ARVN troops to replace American units in mobile offensive operations. The 1970 campaign plan set the pendulum swinging back in the opposite direction by requiring ARVN units to be employed offensively in the clearing zones, but it proved very difficult for the 40th and 41st Regiments to make the adjustment (particularly as the continuing shortage of Territorial Forces greatly slowed their redeployment). The yearly oscillation back and forth between the two very different missions of supporting pacification and combating Communist regulars left the regiments ill prepared to perform either one effectively. ARVN commanders in Binh Dinh accordingly tended to act with excessive circumspection in both roles—reinforcing their habitual inertia and defensive mentality.

The fundamental weakness that plagued both the ARVN regulars and the RF and PF—and the GVN's civil administration—in Binh Dinh was, of course, poor leadership. It hamstrung Operation Washington Green at every turn, preventing the Territorial Forces from achieving self-sufficiency, slowing refugee resettlement, undermining civic action initiatives, and ensuring that Phoenix remained only a "paper" program. Sheer incompetence was frequently to blame, although the theft of materials and the embezzlement of funds by GVN officials were often the principal reasons why public service and economic development programs failed to meet their objectives. However, the greatest shortcoming in leadership was excessive caution. Most ARVN and RF and PF officers in Binh Dinh neither aggressively pursued the enemy nor ensured that their subordinates did. In many cases, their inactivity was the result of tacit "accommodations" negotiated with the local Vietcong— and the scale of the problem was huge. In April 1971 the Pacification Studies Group estimated that between 60 and 80 percent of all GVN officials in Phu My had made accommodations with the enemy.[2] This was the GVN's greatest weakness—the regime's inability to motivate even its own leaders to risk their lives on its behalf—and no amount of US training, equipment, funding, or material support was ever going to overcome it. American advisors tried without success to improve South Vietnamese leadership in Binh Dinh using every means at their disposal, employing flattery and cajolery, pressing for the replacement of incompetent and cowardly commanders, and even threatening to cut off financial and material support. But at the end of the day, there was simply nothing they could do to alter their counterparts' behavior unless their South Vietnamese superiors also made it a priority.

The dismal performance of South Vietnamese commanders in Binh Dinh is at odds with Revisionist claims that the GVN had generally resolved its leadership problems by the early 1970s. Mark Moyar specifically asserts that this was accomplished even in Binh Dinh and the other Communist stronghold provinces of the old Vietminh *Liên-Khu 5*. "When the GVN installed good leaders, it succeeded in forming village governments and effective territorial forces from the hamlet populations of every single province, including the coastal provinces from Phu Yen to Quang Nam where many villagers were still poor and landless and had relatives in the VC."[3] Curiously, the only source cited in support of this sweeping statement is my own dissertation, whose pessimistic findings about the GVN's leadership and Territorial Forces in Binh Dinh are identical to those presented here, and it has little to say and reaches no conclusions about any other province.

It would be wrong, however, to attribute Operation Washington Green's failure solely to the GVN's shortcomings. The Communists, recognizing that the deployment of allied regular troops in the hamlets challenged their hold on Binh Dinh's population as never before, took robust countermeasures that ultimately succeeded in negating the threat. Most importantly, they countered the allies' dozen regular infantry battalions with six of their own by sending the 3rd NVA Division back into the province. This was a seminal event in Washington Green's history because it revolutionized the military situation in AO Lee and robbed the operation of much of its early momentum. It also demonstrated the interdependence between the insurgency and Communist regular military units. If the VCI had been incapable of collecting large quantities of food, it would have been impossible for the Yellow Star Division to sustain itself in northern Binh Dinh. Conversely, the arrival of nearly 5,000 additional NVA and Vietcong regulars (including in support units) greatly reduced allied military pressure on the guerrillas and VCI. Although the Yellow Star Division would not launch a major offensive for another two and a half years, by restoring the "umbrella of security," it obliged General Cunningham to prematurely pull half of his brigade off pacification duty. Its presence also cast a pall over Binh Dinh that deflated GVN morale and made South Vietnamese commanders even more risk-averse. This phenomenon was most discernible at Tet 1970, when the looming threat posed by the NVA and the ill omens associated with the season paralyzed pacification throughout the first quarter of the year, but its effects were more or less permanent thereafter.

The Yellow Star Division also played a more direct role in frustrating Operation Washington Green after it began sending detachments of troops to serve as fillers in local Vietcong units in February 1970. They made a vital contribution to the enemy's war effort because the relentless and unprecedented military pressure being applied by the 173rd Airborne had made it exceedingly difficult for the insurgents to find new recruits. In December 1970 Advisory Team 42 reported: "There does not appear to be much local recruiting. Enemy recruiting data is scarce and the quality is poor, but an educated guess would be that well under 500 (perhaps 250–300) persons have been recruited into the enemy armed ranks from the province in 1970 and most of these from enemy influenced villages in the northern districts."[4] Without NVA troops detached from the Yellow Star Division or infiltrated directly from North Vietnam, the Vietcong military forces in Binh Dinh would have been significantly less potent.

Yet the Yellow Star Division could not claim the lion's share of the credit for defeating Operation Washington Green. That honor belonged to the VCI, which played the decisive role by preserving the insurgency's hold on the rural population. The war in the villages was decided by the relative efficacy of the GVN's and NLF's grassroots leadership—the "active minorities" that mobilized the people in support of their respective causes. Despite the unprecedented risks and hardships caused by Operation Washington Green, the Communists always managed to maintain a hard core of VCI cadres in Binh Dinh who were willing to make the sacrifices necessary to keep the insurgency alive. They were able to do so because the Phoenix program never really got off the ground in northern Binh Dinh. This left the VCI intact to attack the GVN's poorly motivated "active minority" through its highly effective "Phoenix in reverse," which also yielded innumerable "defections in place" by GVN officials who sought safety through chronic absenteeism, dereliction of duty, and collaboration with the Communists.

In terrorism, the Communists found an asymmetric means of combating the massive commitment of allied regulars in direct support of pacification. The Sky Soldiers generally managed to prevent enemy troops from entering hamlets in northern Binh Dinh, but they could do little to protect local officials against "legal" VCI assassins who were already living in those communities in the guise of innocent civilians, complete with GVN-issued identity papers. Even if all the VCI had been forced out of a given hamlet, they could usually dragoon one of their many civilian supporters into throwing a grenade or carrying out an assassination. In Tam Quan, one hamlet chief was shot in broad daylight by a nine-year-old boy acting on the orders of a relative in the VCI (though struck by two small-caliber pistol bullets, the victim survived).[5] Binh Dinh was consistently at or near the top of the list of provinces that suffered the most terrorist incidents of all kinds.

Finally, the 173rd Airborne was also partly responsible for Washington Green's failure, but not because it was unable to adapt to the novel tactical requirements of operating in direct support of pacification. Since they

Table 9.1 Terrorism in Binh Dinh, 1969–1971

Year	Terror Incidents	Assassinations	Abductions	Woundings
1969	685 (2nd)	570 (2nd)	313 (6th)	883 (3rd)
1970	855 (2nd)	649 (1st)	428 (3rd)	1,098 (1st)
1971 (as of 30 April)	365 (1st)	172 (2nd)	449 (1st)	161 (4th)

Source: Pacification Studies Group, Binh Dinh Province: The Challenge—1971, annex H, John W. Saunders Papers.

Note: Figures in parentheses show the rank order out of South Vietnam's 44 provinces.

had already spent most of 1968 and early 1969 perfecting small-unit ambush and patrol tactics, the Sky Soldiers made the transition with relatively little difficulty and succeeded in their primary mission of establishing rural security. Whenever even relatively small numbers of American troops were deployed in the hamlets, enemy activity fell sharply, friendly casualties declined, refugees returned home, GVN officials remained around the clock, and the RF and PF became more aggressive. The brigade accomplished all this without suffering heavy casualties, although its troops were dangerously dispersed and fought without the full benefit of their superior firepower due to Washington Green's stringent rules of engagement. In the operation's first six months, the brigade suffered 67 killed and 725 wounded. These casualties were not inconsequential, but an average of a dozen combat fatalities a month was hardly severe. The number of wounded was more worrisome, but most of the injuries were inflicted by mines and booby traps. When it came to actual combat, the Sky Soldiers consistently outfought their adversaries, even when battling the NVA.[6]

Where the Sky Soldiers fell short was in their behavior toward the ci-

Table 9.2 173rd Airborne's Cumulative Losses during Washington Green

Date	US Killed	US Wounded	Enemy Killed
31 July 1969	35	377	208
31 October 1969	67	725	438
31 January 1970	104	1,085	692
31 December 1970	227	2,236	1,961

Source: 173rd Airborne Brigade, Operational Reports on Lessons Learned for the Periods Ending 31 July 1969, 68; 31 October 1969, 2; 31 January 1970, 3; and 30 April 1971, inclosure C, Combat After Action Report Washington Green, 19, National Archives Records Group 472, 173rd Airborne Brigade files, S-3 ORLL 69–71 box.

vilian population, which was all too often disrespectful, abusive, and even life-threatening. These abuses not only undermined the 173rd Airborne's desultory efforts to "win hearts and minds" in the countryside but also antagonized the pro-GVN urban population—particularly since the US military justice system proved slow to pursue malefactors and generally imposed trifling sentences on those who were tried and convicted. Colonel Waghelstein concluded that committing a regular US combat unit in direct support of pacification had been wrongheaded to begin with: "The very idea that a US conventional combat force was somehow going to be capable of dealing with this kind of war, I think was just a terrible, terrible oversight on our part" because "it's counterproductive, it usually pisses off the population and screws up the ecology."[7] When he commanded the US advisory mission in El Salvador during the early 1980s, Waghelstein sometimes found the congressionally mandated fifty-five-man limit on the size of his command annoying. But on the whole, he believed it was a good thing because it kept the disruptive American presence small.

Disruptive though it was, the Sky Soldiers' behavior did not decisively impact the outcome of Operation Washington Green—especially considering the ambivalent feelings many locals had about the US military presence. Instead, the 173rd Airborne Brigade's effort to pacify northern Binh Dinh foundered on the twin shoals of the enemy's great strength and effectiveness and the GVN's all-encompassing weakness and ineffectiveness. US Army official historian Richard Hunt penned the epitaph for Operation Washington Green:

> Examined over the long term, Washington Green offered little reason for optimism. The finding is significant, for Washington Green was a model operation, lasting far longer than most and using conventional forces in a sophisticated counterinsurgency role. The Viet Cong, however, was as determined and resourceful as ever and was able to rebuild. The performance of government forces and officials during the operation raised doubts in the minds of advisors about whether the regime by itself could cope with a resurgent Viet Cong movement.[8]

Pacification and Vietnamization both failed in Binh Dinh, but was that outcome an aberration? If the province was the "Communist heartland" of South Vietnam, was what happened there representative of what occurred elsewhere in the country? This is not an easy question to answer, since there was, in fact, no such thing as a truly representative province. In keeping with the premise that insurgencies are best studied from the bottom up, one would optimally answer this question by consulting in-depth analyses of provinces throughout South Vietnam. Unfortunately, only a handful have been written,[9] but significantly, their authors all reach conclusions that are remarkably similar to those presented in this book—that is, the insurgency survived, the GVN failed to win the active support of the rural population, and Vietnamization did not succeed. Yet, since these studies cover only a tithe of South Vietnam's forty-four provinces, the question of Binh Dinh's representativeness still stands.

The Territorial Forces were the key to making pacification and Vietnamization work. In April 1971 Colonel Neil W. Wheeler, director of Territorial Forces in II Corps, warned his superiors about the dismal performance of RF and PF units throughout the region: "It's not a happy task to outline what I believe is the situation in MR [Military Region] 2, but I think it's time for a note of realism in all the euphoria of Vietnamization and withdrawal. In other words, I'm telling you at the outset that I'm not optimistic about the future; in fact I'm probably the resident pessimist in MR 2. And the situation is not at all good."[10] Although the RF and PF units in II Corps were reporting, on average, almost 3,000 small-unit operations every day, only about 32 of every 1,000 made contact with the enemy. And this was not, Wheeler added, due to a lack of enemy activity; rather, he attributed it to an inverse relationship between the intensity of enemy activity and Territorial Forces' aggressiveness. He concluded that most territorial units had adopted a "live and let live" policy toward the enemy. They were able to do so because of a lack of oversight by senior commanders, who almost never visited RF companies and PF platoons in the field, preferring instead "to listen to bullshit briefings at sector and subsector and consume leisurely lunches."[11] They also refused to stay overnight in rural districts in most of II Corps' provinces, and US advisors were the only ones who accompanied night ambushes. Since there was nothing Americans could do to alter the situation, Wheeler's prognosis for the future was pessimistic in the extreme:

> The Territorial Forces in MR 2—as they stand now—are not going to hack it. They do not have the will to do the job because they are not motivated. They are not motivated because their leadership—by and large—is interested only in itself, not in finding and killing the enemy. In my opinion, the leadership is not going to improve until we stop doing things for them; in short, until we get out and force them to fight for what they have or want. My only fear is that we might well see the VC flag flying over some provincial capitals if we do get out. Nevertheless, it must be done. These people don't need advisors; or, if they do, then we have already failed. Charlie doesn't need advisors when he conducts a sapper attack. He doesn't need Tac air or gunships or artillery. He's hun-

gry and he's got a cause and he's motivated. Therein lies the difference. On our side nobody is hungry and few are motivated because leadership is lacking.[12]

Colonel Wheeler's gloomy conclusions about II Corps pose a fundamental challenge to the Revisionist hypothesis that the war had effectively been won by 1971. The abysmal performance of Binh Dinh's Territorial Forces—and the poor leadership that allowed it—was no anomaly. The exact same problems afflicted the Territorial Forces throughout a dozen provinces embracing nearly half of South Vietnam's territory. Yet, since few senior officers were as outspoken and as brutally honest as Wheeler, to find out what happened in the rest of the country, one must fall back on quantitative data, even though they overlook vital qualitative factors and their reliability is still a matter of debate. Despite these flaws, historians have no choice but to use such data, and the Revisionists rely on it heavily, even though statistics from the war's later years are not truly in accord with their "lost victory" hypothesis.

The most important quantitative data concern the strength of the VCI, since as Dale Andrade, Mark Moyar, and others have demonstrated, it was the *primum mobile* of the insurgency. If it were destroyed, the NLF would be finished. Conversely, as long as it survived, the insurgency could never be conclusively defeated. It is surprisingly difficult, however, to find VCI strength data in published accounts of the Vietnam War, which usually provide nothing more than "snapshot" estimates on a handful of dates. Even Moyar's *Phoenix and the Birds of Prey* does not present serial data in support of its contention that the VCI had been decisively weakened by the early 1970s.[13]

Research conducted for this book failed to unearth VCI strength data for the entire war, but a CICV assessment provides retroactive monthly estimates from August 1967 to August 1972—covering nearly the entire period in which the Revisionists' "lost victory" was purportedly won. The data reveal that after dropping just 23 percent in the four years between Tet 1968 and December 1971, VCI strength supposedly shrank by *another* 20 percent in just eight months after the South Vietnamese assumed sole responsibility for producing the estimates in January 1972. This is highly unlikely, since the last US combat units (which were responsible for a disproportionate share of "neutralizations") withdrew in 1972, and based on the precedent of the rural uprisings that occurred at Tet 1968, VCI strength probably rose as "fence-sitting" villagers threw in with the seemingly triumphant Communists during the Nguyen Hue Offensive. In August 1972 a Pacification Attitude Analysis System (PAAS) survey of 3,400 villagers in thirty-eight provinces found that 21 percent of the respondents thought the VCI was more effective

Table 9.3 **Retroactive VCI Strength Estimate (Thousands), 1967–1972**

Year	Jan.	Feb.	Mar.	Apr.	May	Jun.	Jul.	Aug.	Sep.	Oct.	Nov.	Dec.
1967	—	—	—	—	—	—	—	85.2	86	84.4	83.8	84
1968	84.7	83.1	83	86	86.2	79.9	79.7	81.8	81.8	81.7	81.9	82.7
1969	81.2	79.3	78.9	78.9	78.8	83.6	85.4	84.9	76.8	75.6	75.2	74
1970	76.4	78.4	73	74.1	71.6	67.4	65.5	65	63.8	63.4	75.6	72.3
1971	68.7	68	63.8	66.9	62.3	62.1	63.9	69.7	68.9	65.6	65.3	65.2
1972	59.3*	55.1*	53.1*	53.1*	48.1*	52.6*	47.5*	48.1*	—	—	—	—

Source: "CICV Order of Battle Summary, 30 September 1972, Volume II," III-1 to III-8, Vietnam Virtual Archive, item F015900180206, http://www
.virtualarchive.vietnam.ttu.edu/starweb/virtual/vva/servlet.starweb (accessed 11 July 2015).

* Estimate produced solely by South Vietnamese.

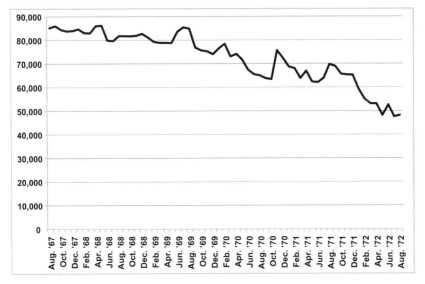

Retroactive VCI Strength Estimate. *Source:* Kevin M. Boylan (based on data from "CICV Order of Battle Summary, 30 September 1972, Volume II," III-1 to III-8, Virtual Vietnam Archive, item F015900180206, accessed July 11, 2015, http://www .virtualarchive.vietnam.ttu.edu /starweb/virtual/vva/servlet.starweb)

in their village than it had been a year before, and only 13 percent said there was no VCI presence at all.[14]

It must be stressed that while the ranks of NLF military units were increasingly filled by NVA replacements, the vast majority of VCI were always native-born southerners. The CICV data therefore dispute Revisionist claims that the VCI was emasculated in the years after Tet 1968. What emerges is a picture of an organization under considerable pressure, but hardly one that had been incapacitated, much less destroyed. In October 1970 Sir Robert Thompson advised President Nixon that the VCI remained virtually intact, at a time when its total strength stood at 63,400.[15] So it seems reasonable to conclude that it was just as intact a full year later, when its estimated strength had actually risen by several thousand.

In Binh Dinh and throughout South Vietnam, the VCI survived because the Phoenix program had failed. Many VCI were killed, captured, or convinced to defect, but the vast majority came from the lowest echelons in the NLF hierarchy and were swept up in the course of routine allied military operations. The true instigators and organizers found at higher echelons were both less exposed and better guarded, but only their "neutralization" would break the insurgency's back once and for all. However, that required patient detective work and precisely targeted operations that very rarely happened. In April 1971 the US Defense Department's Office of Systems Analysis (OSA) reported: "The real problems in the attack on the infrastructure begin to appear when we examine the *quality* of those neutralized. The purpose of the program is to neutralize the driving force behind the enemy; it is critical that we deprive him of his leadership. In 1970 and 1971, less than 3% of those neutralized were full or probationary party members [who monopolized all positions of true power] above the district level."[16] The OSA also noted that of the 10,443 VCI killed over the preceding fifteen months, a mere 616 had been specifically targeted by Phoenix.[17] In September 1971 it explained that the failure to cripple the VCI made for an uncertain future:

> The VCI continue to number about 60,000, and at current neutralization rates, will still pose a serious threat in 1972–73. It is showing considerable staying power, and has previously shown its ability to resurge strongly. This could lead to an intensified, protracted struggle which the GVN might well lose; only the introduction of US forces saved the GVN in the last such struggle. Success this time will depend on the good leadership and staying power by the GVN.[18]

Most PSAs and deputy PSAs also considered Phoenix a failure. In their completion-of-tour reports, they were asked to identify the three most and three least successful pacification programs in their provinces. In a sample of forty-seven reports written between 1969 and 1973, Phoenix appeared on the "least successful" list twenty-one times (more than any another program) and on the "most successful" list only twice. Even advisors who did not put Phoenix in the "least successful" category generally gave the program only mixed reviews. Over three-quarters of the sample identified at least some of the same problems that crippled Phoenix in Binh Dinh: a lack of South Vietnamese command emphasis, GVN agencies' unwillingness to share intelligence, no specific targeting, failure to keep DIOCC files up-to-date, suspiciously brief sentences handed down to captured cadres, VCI paying bribes to be left alone, and so on.[19]

Revisionist historians either do not address this abundance of contrary evidence or deny its relevance. Moyar, who wrote most extensively on the subject, rejects the PAAS surveys because "both the methods of collection and the questions that the studies try to answer contain too many flaws."[20] He likewise discounts the OSA's conclusions because the statistics it employed were "the product of faulty data collection methods."[21] The PSAs' negative opinions about Phoenix must also be considered "faulty evidence," according to Moyar, because "they knew little about the CIA's attack on the VCI and said that the attack on the VCI—as they knew it—was ineffective, whereas pacification or regular military activities were effective [at incidentally neutralizing VCI]."[22] This peremptory dismissal of several entire species of data seems like special pleading, particularly as Moyar does not elaborate on his reasons for believing the OSA and PAAS data were unreliable. His hypothesis that only the CIA knew how successful Phoenix had been was disproved a decade after *Phoenix and the Birds of Prey* was first published, when the agency's own account of its activities in Vietnam was declassified. Its official historian, Thomas L. Ahern Jr., concluded that Phoenix had failed for the very same reasons cited by the PSAs, including that, at least as late as July 1970, "attrition of the VCI still depended too heavily on the adventitious results of military activity and too little on Phung Hoang operations aimed at identified members of the apparatus."[23] Ahern noted that dependence on American initiative and expertise was another fundamental weakness in Phoenix that was never overcome. In January 1972 the CIA's regional officer in charge in III Corps, Donald B. Gregg, "found it ironic that, even 'at this late date, it is still Americans who are spearheading an effort so crucial to the survival' of the GVN."[24]

Aggregated HES data can also be of some use in determining whether the insurgency had been defeated. The following graph depicts overall population control from July 1969 through January 1973, as calculated by three different versions of HES. First, there was the original HES, which scored hamlets based on the ratings CORDS advisors assigned to eighteen different indicators. Then there was HES-70, which automatically calculated indicator ratings based on advisors' responses to a series of objective questions about conditions in each hamlet. And finally, there was HES-71, which assigned greater weight to terrorism and VCI presence, and devalued socioeconomic indicators. Richard Hunt argued that these repeated upgrades necessarily called HES's accuracy into question, since "each iteration of HES seemed to raise questions about the validity of the preceding version. Ultimately, it was hard to reconcile the changes with the general notion that security was continually improving."[25] The implicit assumption that even HES-71 might be unreliable is borne out by a PAAS survey conducted in January 1971. No less than 44 percent of the respondents described their hamlet as being less secure than its HES rating suggested, while only 2 percent described it as being more secure. Moreover, respondents who lived in A and B hamlets were far more likely to report that security was overrated than those residing in C, D, and E hamlets.[26]

Many PSAs and deputy PSAs who served during these years were also dubious about HES's reliability—particularly after the system began to be

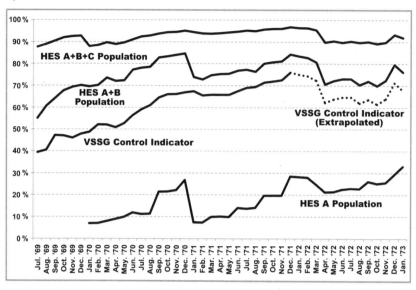

HES & VSSG Control Indicator Data (Jul 1969–Jan 1973). *Source:* Kevin M. Boylan (based on data from HES Summary Reports, various dates, MACV Command Historian's Collection, U.S. Army Heritage and Education Center; and "A Systems Analysis View of the Vietnam War 1965-1952: Volume 9 [Population Security]," 159, 226, 231-232, 241-249, 258, 265, 268, 275-276).

"Vietnamized" in mid-1971.[27] In January 1972 CORDS warned General Abrams about a "HES Data Validity Crisis" in I Corps, where dozens of enemy-initiated incidents (including rocket attacks on provincial capitals) went unreported, guerrilla and VCI strengths were deleted from entire districts, and roads too insecure to travel were reported as "open." When queried about these discrepancies, GVN officials admitted that their superiors had pressured them "to show maximum improvement in year-end HES reports."[28] Colonel Robert S. McGowan, who served in I Corps during this period as Quang Ngai's PSA, reported: "The HES is a good example of command pressure being exerted to upgrade the status of all hamlets, particularly 'V' hamlets. A former [Vietnamese] I Corps Commander is reportedly [*sic*] to have said, 'Any province chief who reports V hamlets goes to jail.' The result: 'V' hamlets rapidly disappeared in this region."[29]

The most conservative estimate of GVN control is therefore invariably the most accurate. In this case, that is provided by the VSSG control indicator, for which data were found covering only the period from mid-1969 through December 1971. However, as is readily discernible on the graph, the VSSG control indicator closely tracked the HES A+B population starting in 1971, averaging 8.4 percent lower over the course of the year. The extrapolated VSSG control indicator trend line was produced by applying this average reduction to A+B population figures onward through January 1973. Needless to say, the extrapolated data are speculative, but it seems clear that even at its peak, the GVN briefly controlled just three-quarters of the rural population and generally controlled only about two-thirds from mid-1970 onward.

The other lines on the graph are misleading, which is not surprising, given that HES was designed to show that pacification was succeeding. The A+B+C line gives an altogether false impression of the extent of GVN control because it lumps contested hamlets with those where the government truly exerted predominant influence. It also proved remarkably resistant to change. Even in the darkest days of 1972, when the Nguyen Hue Offensive had overrun all or most of four provinces and caused declines in security nationwide, the A+B+C population continued to hover around 90 percent. The A+B line is also deceptive, since HES and HES-70 both greatly exaggerated the size of the "secure" population, and the extent of the error was revealed only when the adoption of HES-71 caused the A+B population to plummet by 12 percent between December 1970 and February 1971 (and the A population by nearly 20 percent).[30] About 1,750 hamlet chiefs (roughly a third of the total) still were not sleeping in their hamlets during January 1971.[31] Surges of guerrilla and terrorist attacks in the first quarter of 1971 set HES ratings back three months nationwide, four months in southern IV Corps, six months in northern II Corps (including Binh Dinh), and seven months in I Corps.[32] The A and A+B populations grew for the rest of 1971, but this was largely due to "grade inflation" as HES was Vietnamized.

The Baker's Dozen

While some valuable insights can be gained by scrutinizing quantitative data aggregated for all of South Vietnam, painting with such a broad brush is problematic. If bottom-up analyses are impossible due to the paucity of detailed province studies, one can at least view quantitative data through the prism of individual provinces. The insurgency had always been weakest in those containing large ethnic or religious minority populations that were hostile to the Communists for reasons other than loyalty to the GVN. Thus, An Giang was invariably the most secure province in South Vietnam because its inhabitants overwhelmingly belonged to the Hoa Hao religion—an offshoot of Buddhism that had been implacably hostile to the Communists since 1947, when they murdered its founding prophet, Huynh Phu So. The insurgency tended to be strongest in provinces that had been Vietminh strongholds during the earlier war against the French. The following map depicts areas

AREAS DOMINATED BY THE VIET MINH (1949)

Hue •

• Da Nang

LIEN KHU V

Bong • Son

☆ Saigon

Source: Kevin M. Boylan

of Vietminh domination as of 1949, but in fact, the revolutionaries held sway in most of them throughout the entire First Indochinese War.[33] This map was the palimpsest for the Second Indochinese War, since the GVN never became firmly established in these regions, and all of them emerged as NLF bastions in the 1960s. The Vietminh-dominated areas north and west of Saigon, for example, became the infamous "Iron Triangle" and War Zone C.

Even in the early 1970s, a "baker's dozen" of provinces located in these former Vietminh strongholds still contained over half of all VCI. Not surprisingly, there was a strong correlation between VCI strength and insecurity. In September 1971 eight of the baker's dozen were included among South Vietnam's ten least secure provinces.[34] This was nothing new, since these same thirteen provinces generally had the lowest A+B populations in the country throughout 1969–1971—with Binh Dinh usually coming in dead last after Operation Washington Green ended. The insurgency's continuing strength and vitality in these thirteen provinces suggest that many (if not most) of their inhabitants remained committed to the NLF.

Table 9.4 The Baker's Dozen

Province	VCI, Mar. 1971	Share of Total VCI, Mar. 1971	A+B Population, Sep. 1971
Quang Nam	5,427	7.6%	61.2%
Quang Tin	2,422	3.6%	—
Quang Ngai	3,289	4.9%	62.1%
Binh Dinh	4,333	6.5%	33.6%
Phu Yen	2,183	3.3%	55.8%
Binh Thuan	1,646	2.5%	—
Tay Ninh	2,048	3.1%	—
Dinh Tuong	1,782	2.7%	—
Kien Hoa	3,359	5.0%	59.8%
Vinh Long	1,913	2.8%	—
Vinh Binh	1,683	2.5%	60.0%
Chuong Thien	1,485	2.3%	47.6%
An Xuyen	3,052	4.6%	63.0%
Total	34,622	51.4%	N/A

Source: "A Systems Analysis View of the Vietnam War 1965–1952: Volume 10 (Pacification)," 108, DTIC Online, http://www.dtic.mil/dtic/tr/fulltext/u2/a039317.pdf (accessed 17 April 2015).

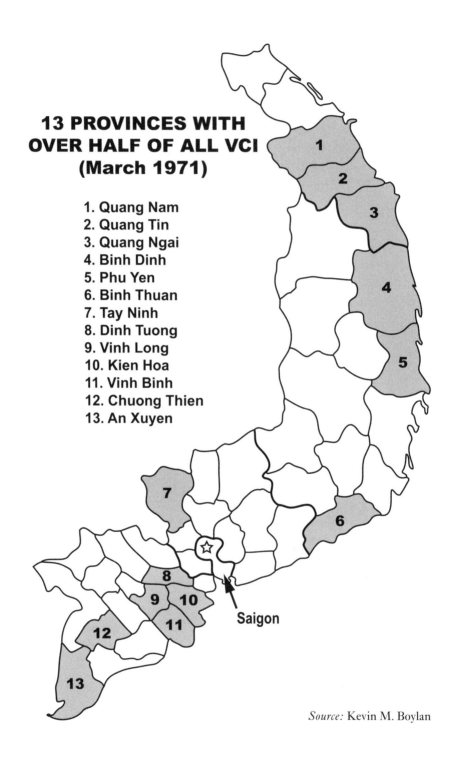

13 PROVINCES WITH OVER HALF OF ALL VCI (March 1971)

1. Quang Nam
2. Quang Tin
3. Quang Ngai
4. Binh Dinh
5. Phu Yen
6. Binh Thuan
7. Tay Ninh
8. Dinh Tuong
9. Vinh Long
10. Kien Hoa
11. Vinh Binh
12. Chuong Thien
13. An Xuyen

Saigon

Source: Kevin M. Boylan

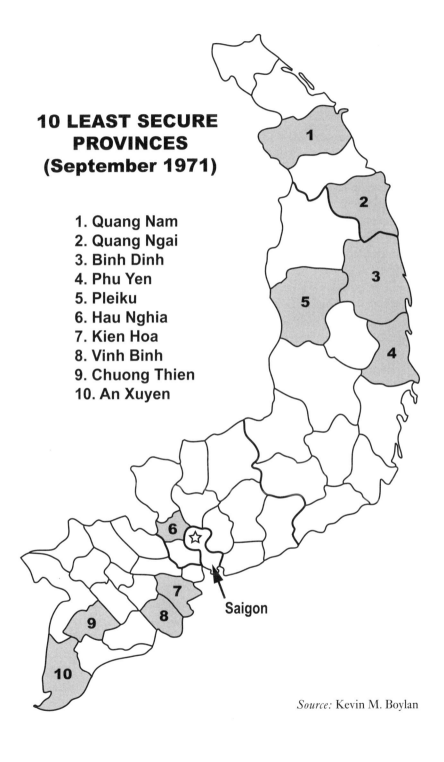

10 LEAST SECURE PROVINCES (September 1971)

1. Quang Nam
2. Quang Ngai
3. Binh Dinh
4. Phu Yen
5. Pleiku
6. Hau Nghia
7. Kien Hoa
8. Vinh Binh
9. Chuong Thien
10. An Xuyen

Saigon

Source: Kevin M. Boylan

The insurgency therefore remained potent in at least a quarter of South Vietnam's provinces even when GVN control was nearing its statistical peak, as measured by HES-71. And even if all thirty-one of the other provinces had been firmly under GVN control (which was not the case), the baker's dozen could not be dismissed as inconsequential because it included many provinces of great military, political, and demographic importance. This was particularly true of those in the former Vietminh *Liên-Khu 5*:

> The three provinces named are among the most populous in South Vietnam and play key roles politically as well as militarily. Quang Nam, with the contiguous autonomous city of Danang, accounts for 1.0 million people [and] has been the scene of some of the heaviest main force clashes of the war. Quang Ngai, as the home province of many of North and South Vietnam's key leaders [such as North Vietnamese prime minister Pham Van Dong], has always been politically active. Binh Dinh, with 0.9 million people, is by far the most important population center between Danang and Saigon.[35]

The GVN *could not* win the war without subduing these three key provinces, which it never did. Instead, they took turns leading the country in enemy ground attacks every year from 1965 to 1971, and they lost that distinction in 1972 only because the Nguyen Hue Offensive focused elsewhere. They all stubbornly resisted pacification, despite benefiting from a massive American military presence, "including some of the best examples of US forces in a pacification role (the US Marines [Combined Action Program] in Quang Nam, and the 173rd Brigade in Binh Dinh)."[36]

The insurgency's survival in key provinces in the Mekong Delta, South Vietnam's most populous and agriculturally productive area, was even more significant. This region of open, densely populated plains had always been a challenging theater of operations for Communist regulars because it generally lacked the jungle and mountain refuges that were readily available in other parts of the country. The decimation of NLF Main and Local Forces during 1968 gravely weakened the "umbrella of protection" they normally provided for the guerrillas and VCI, and "fast and thin" pacification drove most of them into remote base areas and cross-border sanctuaries by undermining their logistical support system. Vietcong bases survived in the Plain of Reeds, Kien Hoa and Vinh Binh Provinces (Base Areas 487 and 490), the isolated peaks of the Seven Mountains (*Bảy Núi*) in Chau Doc Province, and the primeval U Minh Forest at the heart of the Camau Peninsula. Throughout the rest of the Mekong Delta, the NLF's liberated areas were fragmented or eliminated outright, and the surviving VCI and guerrillas were forced to shelter in densely booby-trapped "mini-bases" (often only a few acres in extent) constructed in whatever scraps of tree cover they could find.

Even under these trying circumstances, however, the insurgents were able to keep pressure on the GVN by means of terrorism and waves of ambushes, attacks-by-fire, and sapper raids. During the November 1970–April 1971 dry season (which differed from Binh Dinh's), the monthly tally of enemy-initiated incidents in IV Corps rose to nearly the same level as during the 1968 Tet Offensive. And although they included few large-scale ground attacks, by June 1971, the number of outposts overrun in IV Corps had already matched the total for all of 1970.[37] The PAVN's official history claims the insurgency in the Mekong Delta was revitalized during this period (thanks in part to the absence of many ARVN units operating on the Cambodian border), and the "umbrella of security" provided by Communist regular units was restored:

> Revolutionary organizations were organized in 57 villages in central Cochin China and in 500 hamlets in western Cochin China. Our guerrilla forces at the village and hamlet level grew to 3,000 personnel, and in western Cochin China alone these forces increased from 40 teams in 1969 to 180 teams in 1971. Province and district Local Forces, reinforced with cadre and soldiers who were natives of North Vietnam or drawn from units at the military region level, again began to work in their assigned areas of operations. The rural areas of Cochin China had survived their most difficult period.[38]

Although these accomplishments may have been exaggerated, there can be no doubt that Vietcong activity increased substantially in the southern Mekong Delta during 1971 and caused a marked decline in security. In September CORDS concluded that, based on a comparison of the number of enemy- and GVN-initiated incidents, the Communists enjoyed a "tactical advantage" in all but one of the provinces in the lower delta.[39] Yet, Revisionist historians claim that the allies were well on their way to destroying the insurgency by that point and had finished the job by the time the Paris Accords were signed in January 1973.

The following maps suggest otherwise, since they reveal that more than half of South Vietnam's provinces still had significant security problems when the cease-fire took effect. Some of these resulted from the enemy's eleventh-hour "Land-Grab Offensive," but many of them had arisen much earlier. For example, the regions overrun during the Nguyen Hue Offensive had never been properly secured after being retaken. Nearly all the hamlets in Quang Tri and Binh Long Provinces, and in the northern halves of Binh Dinh and Kontum, had been enemy controlled (V rated) since the spring of

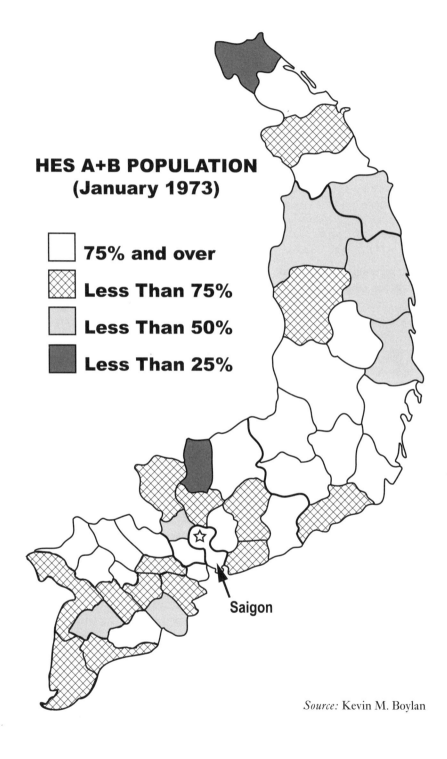

HES A+B POPULATION
(January 1973)

☐ 75% and over

▨ Less Than 75%

▧ Less Than 50%

▨ Less Than 25%

Saigon

Source: Kevin M. Boylan

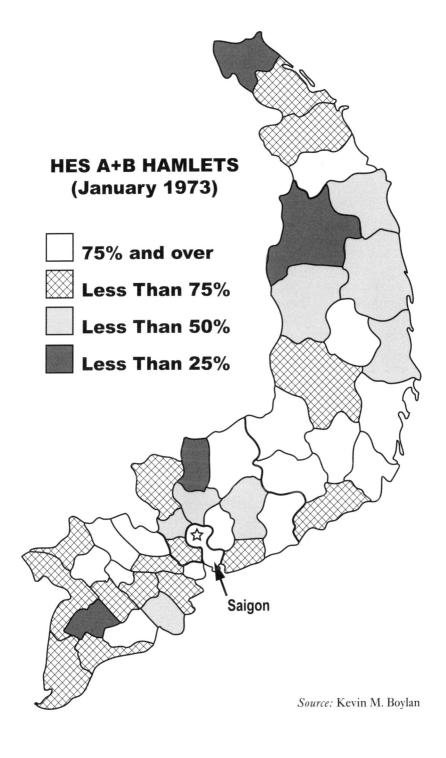

HES A+B HAMLETS
(January 1973)

- ☐ 75% and over
- ▨ Less Than 75%
- ▨ Less Than 50%
- ■ Less Than 25%

Saigon

Source: Kevin M. Boylan

1972. Furthermore, Quang Tri and Binh Long had been so thoroughly devastated that they remained mostly depopulated; in January 1973 the former retained only a tenth of its pre-offensive population, and the latter just over a third.[40]

There was also significant insecurity in many areas remote from the Nguyen Hue Offensive's principal battlefronts. The Revisionists attribute this to the presence of entire NVA units and NVA fillers in Vietcong units operating in those provinces, and there is some truth to this claim. Still, Communist regular units operating away from cross-border sanctuaries depended on the VCI for much of their sustenance. And, no matter where they were, Vietcong and NVA regulars relied on the VCI to provide guides, intelligence, and communications and to mobilize civilians to transport supplies, construct fortifications, and emplace mines and booby traps. If the VCI had been destroyed and the insurgency defeated, it would have been impossible for Communist regulars to operate in most of South Vietnam, with the exception of its border provinces. Spectacular HES statistics showing A+B populations well above 80 percent implied that this was indeed the case in many provinces. Yet the enemy's ability to launch a pair of Land-Grab Offensives just three months apart across the entire length and breadth of the country proved that reports of the insurgency's demise had been exaggerated. Lieutenant Colonel John M. McDonald, who was Phu Yen's PSA during this period, observed: "After reviewing MR II overall HES ratings and the provinces' January 73 monthly reports, I would think serious doubts would exist [about the accuracy of earlier reporting]. Several of the alleged 'more pacified' provinces experienced a sizable amount of enemy action and the VC-NVA there possessed considerable more strength than the pacification program reports would have predicted."[41]

The NLF had gradually rebuilt its Main and Local Force units from their nadir in 1969–1970 but refrained from major offensive activity until the decisive moment came. In the interim, the Communists were content to keep the war's intensity at a low simmer while they waited for enough American troops to withdraw to hopefully ensure the success of their own slowly maturing offensive plans. Some observers mistook this period of relative quiescence as proof that the insurgency had been defeated—or chose to do so because it was politically expedient.

What is most striking about these two maps is how closely the insecure areas of 1973 align with the Vietminh strongholds of 1949. This is particularly true of the one that depicts secure hamlets (i.e., territory) as opposed to secure population, which was skewed by the massive emigration of rural villagers to the safer towns and cities. The legacy of *Liên-Khu 5* is readily visible, as are the old Vietminh haunts north and west of Saigon, in the Camau

Peninsula, and at the mouth of the Mekong Delta. Overall, twelve of the thirteen provinces in the baker's dozen had major security problems in January 1973, and this was no coincidence. Except during the brief interwar period, the Communists had dominated these provinces since the end of World War II. Over the decades, there had been occasions when French, GVN, and US military pressure had weakened the enemy's grip on them, but it had never been broken, and at no point had the GVN won the willing support of more than a fraction of their inhabitants.

Hearts and Minds

In other words, the GVN failed to "win the hearts and minds" of the people residing in these venerable Communist strongholds. But "fast and thin" pacification was founded on the premise that winning the population's active support was unnecessary, since the insurgency would wither away if the allies could "secure" the population militarily and improve its standard of living. The underlying assumption was that rural Vietnamese were essentially apolitical and would passively accept the authority of whichever side dominated their community militarily and controlled the machinery of local government. Many senior allied officials, including Thomas Polgar, the last CIA station chief in Saigon, shared in this belief.[42] It is also the keystone of Mark Moyar's Revisionist scholarship, which argues that loyalties were determined chiefly by popular perceptions of relative military strength at the village level:

> Like their ancestors, the villagers of 1960 looked at the power of the opposing forces when deciding which side held the mandate of heaven, and they almost invariably threw their support to the strongest, though they might reserve some support for the other side as a hedge against unforeseen changes. Military power and success and the sustained presence of troops in the village bestowed prestige, while military weakness and defeat and the sustained absence of troops from the village removed it.[43]

Interest in political issues above the village level was minimal, Moyar says, because abstractions such as nationalism, communism, and democracy meant little to the locals, who also took it for granted that any government would routinely suppress its political opponents, even in peacetime.[44] It therefore did not matter that the GVN was undemocratic, oppressive, and dominated by a small urban elite, because the villagers expected nothing better. If this were true, then the allies could hope to wean the rural population away from the Communists and win the war without having to reform the GVN.

But are these sweeping generalizations about the political culture of rural South Vietnam accurate? If the Vietnamese peasantry was truly so apathetic, how can one account for the eight-year war against the French or, for that matter, the Tay Son Rebellion against the corrupt Nguyen and Trinh warlords? PAAS surveys conducted during the war seem to offer the best source of data on villagers' political attitudes, but Moyar rejects them as unreliable. Nor does he cite any studies of rural South Vietnam produced by social scientists, although this topic clearly falls more within their area of expertise than that of historians. Most scholars who have examined the war from the perspective of the social sciences have concluded that the rural population was not an inert, apolitical mass. Political scientists Jeffrey Race and David Elliott wrote detailed studies of Long An and Dinh Tuong Provinces and concluded that, despite the parochial character of rural Vietnamese society, the NLF succeeded in politically mobilizing a critical segment of the population with its antiforeign message and program of revolutionary socioeconomic change.[45] Economist Robert L. Sansom came to similar conclusions in *The Economics of Insurgency in the Mekong Delta of Vietnam*, which also focused on Dinh Tuong but was supplemented by a study of conditions in Bac Lieu Province and economic surveys of the entire Mekong Delta region.[46]

This consensus about the political culture of the Mekong Delta is echoed in the work of another political scientist, James W. Trullinger, who produced a detailed study of My Thuy Phuong village in Thua Thien Province at the other end of the country. He found that "the [National Liberation] Front imbued its followers with ideas of anti-imperialism, class struggle, nationalism, and mutual cooperation. By 1964–1965, about 80 to 85 percent of the local populace supported the Front, and about 5 percent the Government."[47] There was a significant shift in loyalties in 1968, when the GVN secured military control of the village after the US 101st Airmobile Division established a base camp within its boundaries. But even though the VCI and guerrillas were almost entirely excluded from the village, half the inhabitants still backed the NLF, while support of the GVN rose to only about 15 percent.[48]

Social scientists conclude that the GVN *did* need to win the active support of rural villagers in order to triumph, yet it was often its own worst enemy in its dealings with them. The NLF enjoyed more support, they found, because it gave villagers opportunities for personal advancement that the GVN did not; it offered hope for revolutionary change, which the GVN resisted; and it promised to rid the country of a disruptive foreign presence to which the GVN was beholden. The vast majority of Vietnam War historians have reached similar conclusions, and many of them do not fit the stereotype of the liberal, academic Orthodox school. For example, CIA historian Thomas L. Ahern Jr. was a career operations officer in the agency with a record of service in Indochina, Africa, Europe, and Iran (including 444 days as a hostage at the US embassy in Tehran). He argues that nationalism was a major factor contributing to the NLF's success and rejects the notion that shifting loyalties among villagers was simply "a matter of running city hall."

> [Americans] who saw the Vietnamese peasant as little more than an apolitical pack animal overlooked that the VC were concerned, not with the irredeemably passive element . . . but with those peasants capable of becoming self-motivated servants of the cause. Neither [George] Carver [the CIA's special assistant for Vietnam affairs] nor any other American observer seems to have noticed that the two sides had chosen different targets for their respective efforts to engage the peasantry. For the United States and the GVN, the object was the population at large, to be secured, protected, or controlled. For the VC, the object was the potential leadership cadre, the villager whose energy and dedication would ensure the cooperation of his less-determined fellow villagers.[49]

The contrast between the goals of mobilizing an "active minority" and controlling the entire population explains how the insurgents managed to preserve their influence even in communities where the GVN had an overwhelming military advantage. The NLF could keep its *psychological* grip on a hamlet's population with a few self-motivated VCI backed by a handful of guerrillas. Since the GVN generally did not "win hearts and minds"—and effectively stopped trying to do so after the switch to "fast and thin" pacification—it had to settle for exercising *military* control using at least a platoon of often poorly motivated Territorial Forces and many more even less enthusiastic PSDF militia. And whereas the guerrillas were usually supported by only a single NLF regular company per district, the GVN needed many RF companies (not to mention artillery and aviation units) to bolster the PF and PSDF. Frederick the Great warned, "He who defends everything defends nothing," and the GVN was trying to place South Vietnam's entire populated region under military occupation. In March 1970 Willard E. Chambers, a retired US Army colonel serving as II Corps' assistant deputy for CORDS, observed:

> For the immediate future, it would seem clear to me that we are approaching the limits of what is possible without the active emotional support of the people. We have gone about as far as we can go in turning this country into an armed camp and yet there is not positive security. . . . In this connection, it might be well to re-state a definition of pacification. I define a pacified area as being one in which the VC can do nothing

because the people won't allow them to do anything. It is an area where the VC cannot move without the people reporting their movements. . . . By this definition we have very few pacified areas in Vietnam and we are not apt to have such areas until we involve the people emotionally in the war effort.[50]

If the GVN won the active, emotional support of a hamlet's inhabitants, the VC could no longer operate there because they would have lost their cloak of invisibility. Then, as foreseen by the "oil spot" technique, the GVN could have withdrawn the bulk of its troops and redeployed them elsewhere. This is what the British had done during the Malayan Emergency of 1948–1960. When they eliminated the insurgents of the Malayan Races Liberation Army in a particular district or province, they would declare it a "White Area," rescind the emergency regulations within its boundaries, and restore the normal processes of law and order.[51] Nothing like this was ever done in South Vietnam because the insurgency there was merely suppressed, not defeated. And because the insurgency survived, the GVN was forced to maintain permanent garrisons in thousands of hamlets whose inhabitants either were not actively committed to it or favored the NLF.

Ahern argues that suppression was the best that could be hoped for, since the GVN had already lost the political struggle for villagers' loyalties by 1965.[52] Even if he was mistaken in believing that nothing could be done to retrieve the situation, "fast and thin" pacification was not the solution because it eschewed fundamental reforms and political institution building in favor of the more straightforward task of securing the rural population militarily. If the GVN was to have any chance of winning active popular support in the countryside, its ruling elites would have to be willing to create both a more equitable socioeconomic system and a far more honest, efficient, and democratic government in which the common people truly had a voice. Nothing in the history of South Vietnam suggests that they would have been willing to do so.

Why Don't Our Vietnamese Fight Like Their Vietnamese?

I was born in 1962 and grew up listening to my adult relatives discussing the frustrating war in Vietnam around the Sunday dinner table. The question that came up again and again over the years was: "Why don't our Vietnamese fight like their Vietnamese?" I even heard it asked by a priest who taught at the Catholic school I attended. Thus, although neither he nor my relatives had a deep understanding of what was occurring in Southeast Asia, they had all put their finger on the key issue, for South Vietnam ultimately lost the war because its armed forces' hearts were not in it. Instead of fighting

Table 9.5 RVNAF Desertions (Net) versus NVA and VC Defections (Military), 1967–1971

Statistic	1967	1968	1969	1970	1971
RVNAF desertions	77,714	116,064	107,942	126,753	140,177
NVA/VC defections	16,572	12,569	28,405	17,145	10,914

Source: Guenter Lewy, *America in Vietnam* (New York: Oxford University Press, 1978), 174.

as hard and effectively as they could have, a great many ARVN troops and commanders were content to play it safe by hunkering down in their defensive perimeters, cutting deals with the enemy, or conducting pantomime operations that merely created the illusion of offensive activity. The Vietcong and NVA, in contrast, did not fake ambushes or mount elaborately staged "search-and-avoid" operations, and they generally fought with fierce determination and aggressiveness despite the great risks involved. Nor did they defect in anything close to the numbers that deserted from the ranks of the Republic of Vietnam Armed Forces (RVNAF), even though they faced much greater hardships. I suspect that almost any American who lived through the Vietnam War and was old enough to remember the experience was at least dimly aware of this decisive asymmetry in the conflict. Certainly my friends and I had all recognized it by the time we reached our teen years, and I do not believe we were unusual in this regard.

This is not to say that ARVN units never fought bravely, for they sometimes did, and elite formations such as the Airborne, Marine, and 1st Infantry Divisions almost always did so. However, these were exceptions to the rule, in the same way that elite Bersaglieri, Alpini, parachute, and mechanized units did not fit the dominant pattern of weak morale and combat ineffectiveness that characterized the Italian army of World War II. Taken as a whole, however, there was something fundamentally wrong with the ARVN that went far beyond quantifiable shortcomings that could be rectified by American money, training, equipment, supplies, and air support. Precisely what qualitative factors accounted for its poor performance is open to debate, although it is probably no coincidence that Italy likewise had a weak sense of nationalism, extreme social divisions (including between officers and enlisted men), and a government whose legitimacy was very much in dispute. What is clear is that the rot began at the top, in the corrupt and politicized officer corps that dominated South Vietnam's armed forces, government, and economy. Its own poor motivation was reflected in the generally inferior leadership it provided to the rank and file, and this was the insurmountable hurdle that blocked every improvement necessary for the nation to become self-sufficient. In effect, before the GVN could win the war, it first had to "win the hearts and minds" of its own leadership cadre, whose commitment was disturbingly weak even though it had the most to gain from the regime's continued existence. Lieutenant General Arthur S. Collins, commander of I Field Force from February 1970 to January 1971, recalled:

> Frankly, after a year in country on my second Vietnam tour, I didn't think there was any way that South Vietnam could survive, no matter what we did for them. What put the final nail in the coffin, from my point of view, was when I learned from questioning [ARVN] general officers that almost without exception their sons were in school in France, Switzerland, or the U.S. If they weren't going to fight for South Vietnam, who was?[53]

If, as many Revisionists claim, South Vietnam resolved its leadership problems after 1968, there is precious little evidence of it. The need to sack so many incompetent and psychologically shattered senior commanders during the Nguyen Hue Offensive proves that leadership in ARVN regular units, including at the division and corps levels, was often subpar, even in 1972. Reports written by PSAs and deputy PSAs—including those who served at the very end of the US pacification advisory mission in February 1973— demonstrate that GVN leadership at the province and district levels and in the Territorial Forces was generally no better.[54] A few of their critiques will suffice to demonstrate the extent of the persistent command problems in the countryside. Lieutenant Colonel John L. Keefe, who was deputy PSA of Chau Doc Province in IV Corps at the time, noted that although the Territorial Forces were better trained, better fed, better equipped, and better supplied than their foes, they never achieved their potential due to a lack of aggressive leadership. "This greatest of all shortcomings stems from selection of leaders from the wealthy and politically influential rather than from those who have demonstrated competence in command. Greatly compounding this is corruption which appears to permeate all levels of Vietnamese society and every GVN agency. . . . Frankly and unfortunately, I believe that it is too late in the game to influence a change through advisory efforts."[55] That same month, Vinh Binh Province's last PSA, Lieutenant Colonel Robert C. Hallmark, complained, "RF soldiers can buy assignments and/or less hazardous duty. PF must pay to even join and then with additional money can be assigned to preferable jobs in the more secure areas. Accommodation with the VC is common—only following the practice of village, district and higher officials."[56]

Even former ARVN officers admitted that South Vietnam's leadership problems were never resolved. One of them was Lieutenant General Ngo Quang Truong—probably the best senior commander in the entire ARVN. He took over I Corps from the ineffectual General Hoang Xuan Lam during the Nguyen Hue Offensive, swiftly put an end to mounting panic and disorder in Hue, halted the enemy drive toward the city, and organized the counterattack that retook Quang Tri. Five years after escaping the fall of Saigon in 1975, he wrote:

> There remains though a fundamental question regarding the Vietnam conflict. Why was there a failure to produce strong leadership and motivation? This was, in the final analysis, what plagued the RVNAF the most. To be able to answer this question requires a thorough knowledge of the nature of the war, the kind of political system that directed the war effort, and the circumstances that affected leadership and motivation. A full answer to why there was such a profound lack of strong leadership and adequate motivation lies in these characteristics of the war, its politics, and its circumstances. It can be said though that good leadership and motivation were definitely not developed to an adequate extent and that this failure had a disastrous effect on the eventual outcome of the war.[57]

Lost Victory?

The keystone of the Revisionist "lost victory" hypothesis is the claim that the NLF insurgency was destroyed by its own recklessness during the general offensive–general uprising of 1968 and by the Phoenix program and relentless allied pacification operations in subsequent years. Harry Summers writes:

> After 1968 the guerrilla movement withered away to the point where in the North Vietnamese Army's 1975 final offensive they had almost no role to play. That twenty-two division cross-border blitzkrieg had more to do with the fall of France in 1940 than to any notions of guerrilla warfare. It was a Soviet-supplied T-54 main battle tank, not a black-pajama-clad guerrilla, that broke down the gates of the Presidential Palace in Saigon on April 30, 1975.[58]

Lewis Sorley quotes General Michael Davison, commander of II Field Force Vietnam, who argued, "It is fair to say that by the winter of 1970–1971 the VC had virtually been exterminated."[59] Mark Moyar contends that "from 1969 to 1971 the reinvigorated South Vietnamese forces and their American allies eliminated the remaining South Vietnamese insurgents by killing them, capturing them, or driving them to defect through the national amnesty program. The war ceased to have a significant component of insurgency by the end of 1971, becoming purely a conventional war between the armed forces of North Vietnam and South Vietnam."[60]

Once the insurgency was out of the way, Revisionists suggest that the Vietnamized ARVN, with its improved leadership, training, firepower, and mobility, was capable of defending South Vietnam indefinitely, as long as it continued to receive generous American financial and material assistance and could rely on massive US air support. This added up to victory, they say, and it was only the decline in American aid and the denial of US air support in 1974–1975 that doomed South Vietnam to defeat. Yet, even if these accomplishments were real, this definition of victory is divorced from the larger Cold War strategy objectives that led the United States into Vietnam in the first place. Had Americans really spent a decade fighting in Indochina at the cost of billions of dollars and the lives of 58,000 of their fellow citizens merely to leave South Vietnam locked in an endless stalemate with masses of North Vietnamese troops ensconced within its borders!?

A more meaningful definition of victory was presented in the Vietnam Policy Options study produced by the Rand Corporation in December 1968 (see chapter 2). It defined victory as "the destruction or withdrawal of all NVA units in South Vietnam, the destruction, withdrawal, or dissolution of all (or most) VC forces and apparatus, the permanent cessation of infiltration, and the virtually unchallenged sovereignty of a stable, non-Communist regime."[61] In other words, the goal was to restore the integrity of containment in Southeast Asia by ending the NLF insurgency and expelling the North Vietnamese from South Vietnam. In the larger context of Cold War grand strategy, only this would truly constitute victory. Anything less would mean that containment had failed and call into question the United States' commitment to its other allies in the region. Moreover, Clausewitz would remind the Revisionists that war is "an act of violence to compel our opponent to fulfil our will." In Vietnam, it was the will of the United States that the Vietcong lay down their arms and the North Vietnamese cease their aggression against the South. By this standard, the war clearly had not been won when the United States bowed out in 1973, since the Paris Accords allowed more than 100,000 NVA troops to remain in South Vietnam, and the lingering insecurity and persistent VCI strength in many provinces proved that the insurgency had not been destroyed. The latter point was brought to public attention in November 1972 by Willard E. Chambers, who had spent a dozen years in Vietnam, most recently as assistant deputy for CORDS in I Corps. Amidst all the euphoria prompted by the imminent cease-fire, Chambers resigned from his lucrative, $42,000-a-year job and released his letter of resignation to the press. It opened with this statement: "I am no longer willing to remain patient with the parade of overranked nonentities whose actions reflect their own ignorance of Vietnam, of the peculiarities of a people's war, and of the requirements of counterinsurgency."[62]

Having observed that the war in many provinces exhibited the same unchanging, cyclical pattern that this author discovered in Binh Dinh, Chambers openly challenged the Nixon administration's optimism about pacification: "After all these years of war, I read the newspaper and think 'This is where I came into this war.' Binh Duong, Hau Nghia, Cu Chi, Bien Hoa—the same names we were fighting over then we're fighting [over] now. We're bombing the same places all over again."[63] Three things had to happen, he argued, before pacification would succeed and the war could be won—and none of them had yet been accomplished. First, the GVN needed to give the people a "dream"—a cause worth fighting for that would convince them to support the government actively. Anticommunism was a negative goal that failed to motivate the uncommitted. Second, major tactical reforms were needed in the ARVN, which Americans had created in their own image but had proved even more inept at revolutionary warfare than the US Army on which it was modeled. Finally, somehow the South Vietnamese had to be given hope of ultimate victory. "The only thing that we offer the soldier out there in his outpost is 'If you fight hard enough and aggressively enough, you'll be able to keep on fighting until someday, somehow, in God's own time—and we don't know how or when—the other guy is going to get tired and go home.'"[64]

The Revisionists' definition of victory sentenced the South Vietnamese to many years or even decades of constant warfare, with no end in sight. The Communists faced the same prospect, but at least they could take heart from the fact that, by requiring the withdrawal of all US combat troops and advisors, the Paris Accords represented a great step toward final victory. The South Vietnamese, in contrast, naturally felt abandoned by their ally and could only wonder how they were supposed to finish off the insurgency and expel the North Vietnamese on their own when they had been unable to do so with the aid of half a million American troops. Political window dressing aside, Vietnamization was never really intended to make South Vietnam's armed forces capable of standing on their own against the NVA—and it did not. If some Americans deluded themselves on this score, the South Vietnamese themselves were never fooled. Douglas Blaufarb, a former senior CIA operations officer with extensive wartime experience in Vietnam and Laos, wrote: "When the American soldiers were gone and the Congress sharply reduced its logistic support, panic set in—panic caused, one can only surmise, by the realization of the Vietnamese officer corps that it was really not up to its job. In the final analysis, those who had played out the charade had never been fooled by it. Only the foreigners had been deceived."[65]

The "lost victory" hypothesis is therefore mistaken, since neither pacification nor Vietnamization succeeded, and the GVN was left "holding the bag"—confronted by a weakened but still extant insurgency and an undiminished North Vietnamese military threat. Even the NVA alone would have been enough to make a mockery of any claim of victory, since it is perfectly obvious that the ARVN on its own was *never* going to drive it out of the country. The continuing insurgency and the legacy of "fast and thin" pacification made South Vietnam's prospects even bleaker because hundreds of thousands of RF and PF troops remained tied down guarding semipacified hamlets. Thus, while the GVN was obliged to keep its troops dispersed, the Communists were free to mass theirs. They needed two years to rebuild their forces after the cease-fire, but once they did, it is hard to see how South Vietnam could have survived unless the United States had once again intervened on a large scale. The presence of American troops on the ground might have been necessary because it is uncertain that ARVN commanders could have effectively controlled their units or coordinated US airpower without the aid of advisors.

In Binh Dinh, constant prodding by advisors was needed to get most ARVN, RF, and PF units to perform even routine tasks such as training and daily patrol and nightly ambush missions. In times of crisis, American advisors became the "glue" that held the ARVN together. Only their presence, coordinating US air and naval gunfire support and seizing the reins of command from psychologically defeated ARVN officers, had prevented South Vietnam from being conquered in 1972. The year before, however, US law had prohibited American advisors from accompanying the ARVN units that invaded Laos to cut the Ho Chi Minh Trail in Operation Lam Son 719. Although the participating South Vietnamese troops often fought well, the operation ended in a near rout largely because ARVN commanders could not handle the challenges of modern combined-arms warfare without advisory support. According to James H. Willbanks, who served as an advisor in Vietnam and currently heads the Department of Military History at the US Army's Command and General Staff College, they proved incapable of coordinating infantry, armor, and artillery; employing reserve units effectively; or organizing air support and resupply. On several occasions, ARVN division commanders lost control of their units. In general, "the South Vietnamese had grown far too dependent on US advisers and American support. Many of the things that the ARVN commanders had routinely relied upon their US advisers to accomplish were not done or were done poorly."[66] Thus, it could be argued that the Paris Accords of January 1973 doomed the ARVN by permanently stripping away its advisors. Having proved themselves unready to deal with large enemy combined-arms offensives on their own in 1971 and 1972, it comes as no surprise that senior ARVN commanders still were not up to the task when confronted by a third such offensive in 1975.

Revisionist historians suggest that the enemy's switch to conventional, combined-arms operations proves that the insurgency had been eliminated, but this is a faulty inference. The Communists relied on tanks and artillery to overthrow the GVN because both sides' Cold War patrons had flooded Indochina with modern heavy weaponry, escalating the war's intensity far above its humble guerrilla war origins. And while Americans can fairly argue that South Vietnam would have survived if it had not been for massive North Vietnamese military intervention, the GVN almost certainly would have fallen in 1965 had it not been for massive US military intervention. But despite its escalating intensity, the war was stalemated throughout the period of direct US involvement and remained so when the Americans left in 1973. Their departure broke the deadlock and virtually ensured that South Vietnam's defeat was only a matter of time.

Despite "lost victory" mythmaking in their postwar memoirs, Nixon and Kissinger were both fully aware that the GVN was doomed. By the latter half of 1972, it had become clear that the North Vietnamese would not agree to withdraw their troops from the south, and if the GVN had only reasonable odds of surviving a continuing struggle against the NLF alone, it had no hope whatsoever of prevailing against the NVA as well. The best Nixon and Kissinger could hope for was that the collapse of South Vietnam would be delayed long enough to obfuscate the fact that the United States had been defeated—and their strategy had failed. White House tapes released by the Nixon Presidential Library prove that they were now thinking in terms of a "decent interval" of perhaps only a year's duration. At a meeting in August 1972 Kissinger said, "We've got to find some formula that holds the thing together a year or two, after which—after a year, Mr. President, Vietnam will be a backwater. If we settle it, say, this October, by January '74 no one will give a damn."[67] Two months later, Nixon made it clear that his principal aim was to ensure that there was a face-saving "decent interval" between the American withdrawal and South Vietnam's collapse: "Call it cosmetics or whatever you want. This [the cease-fire] has got to be done in a way that will give South Vietnam a chance to survive. It doesn't have to survive forever. It's got to survive for a reasonable time. Then everybody can say 'goddamn we did our part.' . . . I don't know that South Vietnam can survive forever."[68]

The failure of Operation Washington Green was therefore no anomaly. Both in Binh Dinh and throughout South Vietnam, the GVN never overcame the crippling political and psychological weaknesses that ultimately doomed it to extinction. A volume in the official history of the US Army states:

> South Vietnam's military defeat tended to obscure the crucial inability of this massive military enterprise to compensate for South Vietnam's political shortcomings. Over a span of two decades, a series of regimes had failed to mobilize fully and effectively their nation's political, social, and economic resources to foster a popular base of support. North Vietnamese conventional units ended the war, but insurgency and disaffection among the people of the South made that outcome possible.[69]

Whatever responsibility the US government and its armed forces bear for other aspects of the Vietnam debacle, it is no stain on their reputations that they failed to find a solution to these fundamental dilemmas. "The failure was not that the Americans were unable to solve these problems; they could hardly be expected to do so. Deeply embedded in the very social system the United States was committed to saving, these problems were simply not amenable to an American solution and perhaps could be solved by nothing short of a revolution in South Vietnam itself."[70]

The situation in Vietnam bears disturbing similarities to those currently existing in Iraq and Afghanistan, where the United States is again trying to prop up weak regimes whose legitimacy is widely disputed, and relying on poorly motivated allied militaries whose combat effectiveness remains alarmingly low despite extensive training, material and logistical assistance, and continuing US advisory and air support. Indeed, the "story arc" of Operation Washington Green and its aftermath is strikingly similar to events in Iraq during and after the 2007 "troop surge." There, Multi-National Force–Iraq commander General David H. Petraeus employed a strategy that focused on securing the people by means of population-centric COIN and organizing, training, and equipping local militias known as the "Sons of Iraq." His success in reducing violence allowed the last US troops to be withdrawn in 2011, since it seemed that the enlarged and upgraded Iraqi military would be able to maintain security on its own. Violence began to surge even before the last Americans withdrew, but the Iraqi security forces were able to preserve a tenuous equilibrium because the insurgents, unlike the Communists in South Vietnam, did not have regular military forces that could be thrown into the fray. That changed in June 2014 when thousands of Islamic State of Iraq and the Levant (ISIL) fighters openly attacked across the border from Syria. Although the invaders were lightly armed and badly outnumbered, the poorly led security forces displayed a shocking lack of will to fight. In a virtual replay of the Nguyen Hue Offensive, they collapsed almost immediately, routing in panic, deserting in droves (one estimate put the figure as high as 90,000), and often switching sides.

Within a few weeks, one-third of Iraq had been overrun, and the United States has had to send advisors and Special Operations troops back into the country and provide extensive air support to halt ISIL's advance and start retaking lost ground. It remains to be seen whether ISIL can be defeated and Iraq's unity and territorial integrity restored, but success will depend less on US actions than on the Iraqi government's actions. Only it can give its troops a cause for which they are willing to fight wholeheartedly, and only it can carry out the political and economic reforms necessary to convince its disaffected Sunni citizens to return to the fold. In the wake of the 13 November 2015 terrorist attacks in Paris, some are currently urging that major US ground combat formations be deployed in Iraq and Syria. This could merely inflame passions in the region even more, although it may turn out that nothing else will suffice to break ISIL's overt territorial control. Yet, if and when that is accomplished, only indigenous regimes can pacify the retaken areas and restore the normal processes of law and order (which would be particularly difficult in Syria, since, for all intents and purposes, it has no national government). In that crucial phase of the campaign, there would be little American troops could do to ensure success. Like the 173rd Airborne Brigade in Binh Dinh, they could only provide training, equipment, and financial, logistical, and fire support—and hope for the best, knowing that it was unlikely to occur.

Abbreviations

AAR	after-action report
CAAR	combat after-action report
CICV	Combined Intelligence Center–Vietnam
CMH	US Army Center of Military History, Fort McNair, Washington, DC
CORDS	Civil Operations and Revolutionary Development Support
COSVN	Central Office for South Vietnam, Vietnamese Workers (Communist) Party
CTZ	Corps Tactical Zone
DTIC	Defense Technical Information Center
I FFV	I Field Force Vietnam
HES	Hamlet Evaluation System
HQ	headquarters
HRB	Historical Records Branch
MACV	Military Assistance Command–Vietnam
MAT	Mobile Advisory Team
NARG	National Archives Records Group
OPORD	Operation Order
ORLL	Operational Report on Lessons Learned
PERINTREP	Periodic Intelligence Report
PSG	Pacification Studies Group
RVN	Republic of Vietnam
RVNAF	Republic of Vietnam Armed Forces
Saunders Papers	John W. Saunders, Private Research Collection
SEAB	Southeast Asia Branch
USAHEC	US Army Heritage and Education Center, Carlisle, PA
VNIT	Vietnam Interview Tapes
VSSG	Vietnam Special Studies Group

Introduction: Verlorene Siege

1. Mark Moyar, *Phoenix and the Birds of Prey: Counterinsurgency and Counterterrorism in Vietnam* (Lincoln: University of Nebraska Press, 2007), 312.

2. Lewis Sorley, *A Better War: The Unexamined Victories and Final Tragedy of America's Last Years in Vietnam* (New York: Harcourt Brace, 1999), 217.

3. Mark Moyar, Donald Kagan, and Frederick Kagan, *A Question of Command: Counterinsurgency from the Civil War to Iraq* (New Haven, CT: Yale University Press, 2009), 163.

4. Sorley, *A Better War*, 218–219.

5. Moyar et al., *A Question of Command*, 161.

6. Ibid., 162.

7. The other two were turning against Ngo Dinh Diem and fighting an "American-style" war that focused on military rather than political objectives.

8. William Colby and James McCargar, *Lost Victory: A Firsthand Account of America's Sixteen-Year Involvement in Vietnam* (New York: Contemporary Books, 1989), 363–364.

9. Sorley, *A Better War*, 382.

10. Jeffrey P. Kimball, "The Stab-in-the-Back Legend and the Vietnam War," *Armed Forces and Society* 14, 3 (Spring 1988): 433–458.

11. Harvey Meyerson, *Vinh Long* (Boston: Houghton Mifflin, 1970), xii.

12. VSSG, The Situation in the Countryside, 10 January 1970, 98, John Vann Papers, USAHEC.

13. Status of Pacification Reports—National 1969, 26 September 1969, 1, safe 53, drawer 3, SEAB, CMH.

14. George L. MacGarrigle, *Combat Operations: Taking the Offensive, October 1966 to October 1967, the United States Army in Vietnam* (Washington, DC: US Army Center of Military History, 1998), 8.

15. See, for example, interview with Col. Jared C. Bates, 3 May 1985, 28, Senior Officer Oral History Program, Company Command in Vietnam series, USAHEC.

Chapter One. The "Pacified" Province

1. Ronald J. Cima, ed., *Vietnam: A Country Study* (Washington, DC: Government Printing Office, 1987).

2. Nguyen Nhac and Nguyen Hue were not related to the Nguyen warlords. That surname is the most common in Vietnam and is shared by about 40 percent of the population.

3. Cima, *Vietnam*.

4. Keith W. Taylor, *A History of the Vietnamese* (Cambridge: Cambridge University Press, 2013), 365–393.

5. Bernard B. Fall, *Hell in a Very Small Place: The Siege of Dien Bien Phu* (Philadelphia: J. B. Lippincott, 1966), 46; PSG, Binh Dinh: The Challenge—1971, annex K, A Short History of Binh Dinh Province, 2, Saunders Papers.

6. Roger Trinquier, *Le Premier Battalion de Berets Rouges: Indochine, 1947–1949* (Paris: Editions Plon, 1984), 209–218.

7. Charles W. E. Koburger Jr., *The French Navy in Indochina: Riverine and Coastal Forces, 1945–1954* (New York: Praeger, 1991), 73–74.

8. Ibid., 73–79; Fall, *Hell in a Very Small Place*, 46–47; Phillip B. Davidson, *Vietnam at War: The History, 1946–1975* (New York: Oxford University Press, 1988),

204–213; Michel Grintchenko, *Atlante-Arethuse: Une Operation de Pacification en Indochine* (Paris: Economica, 2001).

9. Fall, *Hell in a Very Small Place*, 47.

10. PSG, Binh Dinh: The Challenge—1971, annex K, 2.

11. Douglas Pike, Binh Dinh: The Anatomy of a Province, October 1972, 6, 29, Province Reports II CTZ—Binh Dinh/Kontum box, SEAB, CMH.

12. Douglas Pike, *Vietcong: The Organization and Techniques of the National Liberation Front of South Vietnam* (Cambridge, MA: MIT Press, 1966), 78–91; Col. Walter F. Choinski, *Republic of Vietnam: Country Study* (US Department of Defense, Military Assistance Institute/American Institutes for Research, 1965), 85; PSG, Binh Dinh: The Challenge—1971, annex K, 2.

13. Merle L. Pribbenow, trans., *Victory in Vietnam: The Official History of the People's Army of Vietnam, 1954–1975* (Lawrence: University Press of Kansas, 2002), 17; Wilfred Burchett, *Vietnam: Inside Story of the Guerrilla War* (New York: International Publishers, 1965), 150–152.

14. Pike, Binh Dinh: Anatomy of a Province, 7.

15. Ibid., 2; Shelby L. Stanton, *Anatomy of a Division: The 1st Cav in Vietnam* (Novato, CA: Presidio Press, 1987), 69; PSG, Binh Dinh: The Challenge—1971, 1–3; CORDS, Fact Book: Binh Dinh, February 1972, 1, Province Reports II CTZ—Binh Dinh/Kontum box, SEAB, CMH.

16. CORDS, Fact Book: Binh Dinh, 1; Pike, Binh Dinh: Anatomy of a Province, 4–5; PSG, Binh Dinh: The Challenge—1971, 3.

17. Pike, Binh Dinh: Anatomy of a Province, 5.

18. Ibid., 1.

19. American Consulate Hue, GVN Operations in Binh Dinh Province, 19 November 1961, 1, Provinces II CTZ box, SEAB, CMH.

20. Pike, *Vietcong*, 100–101; Burchett, *Vietnam*, 189; CORDS, Fact Book: Binh Dinh, 3.

21. CORDS, Fact Book: Binh Dinh, 3.

22. William C. Westmoreland, *A Soldier Reports* (New York: Doubleday, 1976), 125.

23. "Interview with General Theodore C. Mataxis, 1967," 11–12, Vietnam Virtual Archive, item 139010500, http://www.virtualarchive.vietnam.ttu.edu/starweb /virtual/vva/servlet.starweb (accessed 22 October 2015); Pribbenow, *Victory in Vietnam*, 135.

24. Gen. Bruce Palmer Jr., *The 25-Year War: America's Military Role in Vietnam* (New York: Simon & Schuster, 1985), 180.

25. Arthur J. Dommen, *The Indochinese Experience of the French and Americans: Nationalism and Communism in Cambodia, Laos and Vietnam* (Bloomington: Indiana University Press, 2002), 636.

26. RVN, Ministry of Armed Forces, High Command, RVNAF, J-2, Assessment of Enemy Situation in Binh Dinh Sector, 2, Provinces II CTZ—Binh Dinh/Kontum box, SEAB, CMH.

27. Pribbenow, *Victory in Vietnam*, 142.

28. "Interview with Mataxis, 1967," 13–16.

29. "Qui Nhon, 1965: Terrorism Takes a Toll," VFW Magazine Online (February 2015), http://digitaledition.qwinc.com/article/Qui+Nhon,+1965:+Terrorism+Takes+A+Toll/1903942/0/article.html (accessed 22 October 2015).

30. Mark Clodfelter, *The Limits of Airpower: The American Bombing of North Vietnam* (New York: Free Press, 1989), 58–59.

31. Theodore C. Mataxis, "War in the Highlands: Attack and Counter-attack on Highway 19," *Army*, October 1965, 50–52.

32. "Interview with Mataxis, 1967," 16a.

33. RVNAF, J-2, Assessment of Enemy Situation in Binh Dinh Sector, 1.

34. Mataxis, "War in the Highlands," 53–54.

35. Ibid., 54–55.

36. "Interview with Mataxis, 1967," 16.

37. Mataxis, "War in the Highlands," 55.

38. "Interview with Mataxis, 1967," 17.

39. Jack Shulimson and Major Charles M. Johnson, USMC, *U.S. Marines in Vietnam: The Landing and the Buildup—1965* (Washington, DC: US Marine Corps, History and Museums Division, 1978), 53–55.

40. Jeffrey Clarke, *Advice and Support: The Final Years, 1965–1973* (Washington, DC: US Army Center of Military History, 1988), 252–253.

41. Stanton, *Anatomy of a Division*, 23–43.

42. Robert J. Destatte, trans., "The Yellow Star Division: A History" (unpublished, n.d., CMH), 5.

43. Stanton, *Anatomy of a Division*, 45–67; Westmoreland, *Soldier Reports*, 203–205; Lt. Col. Albert N. Garland, ed., *Infantry in Vietnam: Small Unit Actions in the Early Days, 1965–1966.* (Nashville, TN: Battery Press, 1982), 254.

44. Chester L. Cooper, Judith Corson, et al., *The American Experience with Pacification in Vietnam*, 3 vols., Report R-185 (Arlington, VA: Institute for Defense Analysis, 1972), 3:241.

45. Stanton, *Anatomy of a Division*, 72.

46. Ibid., 70–76; Edward Hymoff, *The First Air Cavalry Division—Vietnam* (New York: M. W. Lads, 1967), 71–75.

47. Andrew Krepinevich, *The Army and Vietnam* (Baltimore: Johns Hopkins University Press, 1986), 222.

48. Ibid., 79–81; Hymoff, *First Air Cavalry Division*, 82–88.

49. See, for example, Gen. Van Tien Dung, *After Political Failure, the US Imperialists Are Facing Military Defeat in South Vietnam* (Hanoi: Foreign Languages Publishing House, 1966), 54–59; Ministry of National Defense, Viet Nam Institute of Military History, *Operations in the US Resistance War* (Hanoi: The Gioi Publishers, 2009), 26–33; Pribbenow, *Victory in Vietnam*, 178.

50. Destatte, "Yellow Star Division," 51.

51. Stanton, *Anatomy of a Division*, 83.

52. Ibid., 84–89; George L. MacGarrigle, *Combat Operations: Taking the Offensive, October 1966 to October 1967, the United States Army in Vietnam* (Washington,

DC: US Army Center of Military History, 1998), 85–92; Krepinevich, *Army and Vietnam*, 223.

53. MacGarrigle, *Combat Operations*, 179.

54. Stanton, *Anatomy of a Division*, 92; 1st Cavalry Division, ORLL for the Period Ending 31 July 1967, 17, MACV Command Historian's Collection, USAHEC.

55. MacGarrigle, *Combat Operations*, 322.

56. Dale Andrade, *Ashes to Ashes: The Phoenix Program and the Vietnam War* (Lexington, MA: Lexington Books, 1990), 67.

57. MacGarrigle, *Combat Operations*, 180–189; Stanton, *Anatomy of a Division*, 97.

58. Pike, Binh Dinh: Anatomy of a Province, 8.

59. MacGarrigle, *Combat Operations*, 191.

60. VSSG, Binh Dinh: Control and Security Overview, 1967–1969, undated, 1–3, Saunders Papers.

61. PSG, Binh Dinh: The Challenge—1971, 5.

62. VSSG, Binh Dinh: Control and Security Overview, 3.

63. Lt. Col. William A. Donald, 41st ARVN Regiment in Support of Pacification, 16 February 1968, 5, Province Reports II CTZ—Binh Dinh/Kontum box, SEAB, CMH. Subsequent references to this source are cited parenthetically in the text by page number.

64. Stanton, *Anatomy of a Division*, 110.

65. Interview with Gen. John W. Barnes and Gen. Lu Mong Lan, 27 December 1991, author's research collection.

66. Destatte, "Yellow Star Division," 75–76.

67. Shelby L. Stanton, *Green Berets at War: U.S. Army Special Forces in Southeast Asia, 1956–1975* (New York: Dell, 1985), 174–175; Advisory Team 42, Binh Dinh Province Report for the Period Ending 29 February 1968, Province Reports II CTZ—Binh Dinh/Kontum box, SEAB, CMH.

68. James H. Willibanks, *Vietnam War: The Essential Reference Guide* (Santa Barbara, CA: ABC-CLIO, 2013), 214.

69. Lewis Sorley, *Westmoreland: The General Who Lost Vietnam* (Boston: Houghton Mifflin Harcourt, 2011), chap. 15.

70. Davidson, *Vietnam at War*, 237.

71. Quoted in Harry G. Summers, *On Strategy: A Critical Analysis of the Vietnam War* (New York: Dell, 1984), 137–138.

72. Lewis Sorley, *A Better War: The Unexamined Victories and Final Tragedy of America's Last Years in Vietnam* (New York: Harcourt Brace, 1999), 68.

73. Abrams MAC 7391 to Admiral McCain, General Wheeler, and Ambassador Bunker, Updated Analysis of the Enemy's So-called June "High Point," 2–4, General Creighton Abrams Messages files, HRB, CMH.

74. Sorley, *Better War*, 68–69.

75. CICV, Order of Battle Summary, 1 August–31 October 1968, vol. II, IV-2–IV-3, MACV Command Historian's Collection, USAHEC.

76. CICV, Monthly Order of Battle Summary, 1 May–31 May 1968; CICV, Order of Battle Summary, 1 November–31 December 1968, II-7; CICV, Order of Battle

Summary, 1 September–30 September 1968, vol. I, II-8, MACV Command Historian's Collection, USAHEC.

77. Davidson, *Vietnam at War*, 548.

78. Harvey Meyerson, *Vinh Long* (Boston: Houghton Mifflin, 1970), 192–193.

79. David W. P. Elliott, *The Vietnamese War: Revolution and Social Change in the Mekong Delta 1930–1975*, concise ed. (Armonk, NY: M. E. Sharpe, 2007), 322.

80. Destatte, "Yellow Star Division," 77.

81. Advisory Team 42, Binh Dinh Province Report for the Period Ending 29 February 1968, 6–8.

82. CORDS, Fact Book: Binh Dinh, 3.

83. MAC CORDS-RE, Status of Pacification—Binh Dinh Province (Tet Offensive), 27 March 1968, 1–2, Province Reports II CTZ—Binh Dinh/Kontum box, SEAB, CMH.

84. CORDS, Fact Book: Binh Dinh, 3.

85. 173rd Airborne Brigade: A Brief History, 30 April 1968, 2, MACV Command Historian's Collection, USAHEC; Shelby L. Stanton, *World War II Order of Battle* (New York: Galahad Books, 1984), 263; James H. Belote and William M. Belote, *Corregidor: The Saga of a Fortress* (New York: Harper & Row, 1967).

86. 173rd Airborne Brigade: A Brief History, 3.

87. Ibid., 1; Shelby L. Stanton, *Vietnam Order of Battle* (New York: Galahad Books, 1987), 52.

88. Stanton, *Vietnam Order of Battle*, 158.

89. F. Clifton Berry Jr., *Sky Soldiers: The Illustrated History of the Vietnam War*, vol. 2 (New York: Bantam Books, 1987), 18–33; "Jump into War Zone C," in *A Distant Challenge: The US Infantryman in Vietnam, 1967–1972*, ed. Lt. Col. Albert N. Garland (Nashville, TN: Battery Press, 1983), 3.

90. Shelby L. Stanton, *The Rise and Fall of an American Army: U.S. Ground Forces in Vietnam, 1965–1973* (Stevenage, UK: Spa Books, 1989), 168–178; Edward F. Murphy, *Dak To: The 173d Airborne Brigade in South Vietnam's Central Highlands, June–November 1967* (Novato, CA: Presidio Press, 1993).

91. 173rd Airborne Brigade, ORLL, 15 May 1968, 29–33, MACV Command Historian's Collection, USAHEC.

92. Ibid., 32.

93. Ibid., 29–33.

94. Ibid., 32.

95. Ibid., 30–32; 1st Battalion, 50th Infantry, Combat Operations After Action Report, 25 September 1968, NARG 472, 1st Battalion, 50th Infantry files, S-3 AARs box 4.

96. Clarke, *Advice and Support*, 362.

97. 173rd Airborne Brigade, ORLL, 15 May 1968, 33.

98. 173rd Airborne Brigade, ORLL, 15 November 1968, 38, MACV Command Historian's Collection, USAHEC.

99. Ibid.

100. 173rd Airborne Brigade, Combat After Action Report: HAWK Team Oper-

ations, 4 November 1968–4 January 1969, NARG 472, 173rd Airborne Brigade files, S-3 Brigade AARs 1965–1970 box.

101. 173rd Airborne Brigade, OPORD 3-69, Washington Green, 10 April 1969, annex B, appendix 3, tab C, B-2, NARG 472, 173rd Airborne Brigade files, S-3 Command Reports box 3; 173rd Airborne Brigade, ORLL, 15 November 1968, 37.

102. MACV, Memorandum for the Record: MACV Commanders' Conference, 11 January 1969, tab 11, 13, MACV Command Historian's Collection, USAHEC.

103. MACV and RVNAF, Joint General Staff, AB-144 Combined Campaign Plan 1969, October 1968, annex M, 1–2, MACV Command Historian's Collection, US-AHEC.

104. Clarke, *Advice and Support*, 396 n.

105. Ibid., 396–397; Ngo Quang Truong, *RVNAF and US Operational Cooperation and Coordination*, Indochina Monographs (Washington, DC: US Army Center of Military History, 1980), 135–141.

106. Clarke, *Advice and Support*, 397.

107. Department of the Army, Office of the Adjutant General, Senior Officer Debriefing Report: LTG W. R. Peers, 23 June 1969,10, MACV Command Historian's Collection, USAHEC.

Chapter Two. Fast and Thin

1. CICV, Order of Battle Summary, February 1972, vol. II, I-19, MACV Command Historian's Collection, USAHEC; MACV, Memorandum for the Record: MACV Commanders' Conference, 11 January 1969, tab 10, 1, MACV Command Historian's Collection, USAHEC; Chester L. Cooper, Judith Corson, et al., *The American Experience with Pacification in Vietnam*, 3 vols., Report R-185 (Arlington, VA: Institute for Defense Analysis, 1972), 3:275.

2. Gareth Porter, *Vietnam: The Definitive Documentation of Human Decisions* (Stanfordville, NY: E. M. Coleman Enterprises, 1979), 2:516.

3. MACV J-2, Strategic Research and Analysis Division, Communist Strategy as Reflected in Lao Dong Party and COSVN Resolutions (SRAP 1569), undated, 6, MACV Command Historian's Collection, USAHEC.

4. "Speech by an Official of COSVN to a Cadres' Conference, October 1968," excerpted in Porter, *Vietnam*, 2:516.

5. Ibid., 517.

6. Ibid., 532.

7. Lewis Sorley, *Thunderbolt: General Creighton Abrams and the Army of His Times* (New York: Simon & Schuster, 1992), 233–234.

8. Cooper, Corson, et al., *American Experience with Pacification*, 2:283.

9. Commander MACV, COMUSMACV Commanders Conference: Operational Guidance—4th Quarter CY 68, 1, Miscellaneous Documents from Microfilm, MACV-SJS on Pacification/Phoenix box, MACV Command Historian's Collection, USAHEC.

10. Ibid.

11. Andrew Krepinevich, *The Army and Vietnam* (Baltimore: Johns Hopkins University Press, 1986), 254.

12. Sorley, *Thunderbolt*, 235.

13. MACV, One War: MACV Command Overview, 1968–1972, chap. I, 15, SEAB, CMH.

14. MACV and RVNAF, Joint General Staff, AB-144 1969 Combined Campaign Plan, October 1968, 7, MACV Command Historian's Collection, USAHEC.

15. Phillip B. Davidson, *Vietnam at War: The History, 1946–1975* (New York: Oxford University Press, 1988), 613–614.

16. MACV, One War: MACV Command Overview, 1968–1972, chap. III, 18.

17. Ibid., 19–20.

18. Cooper, Corson, et al., *American Experience with Pacification*, 3:269.

19. Guenter Lewy, *America in Vietnam* (New York: Oxford University Press, 1978), 23.

20. Cooper, Corson, et al., *American Experience with Pacification*, 2:220.

21. David W. P. Elliott, *The Vietnamese War: Revolution and Social Change in the Mekong Delta, 1930–1975*, 2 vols. (Armonk, NY: M. E. Sharpe, 2001), 2:800.

22. Cao Van Vien, *The U.S. Adviser*, Indochina Monographs (Washington, DC: US Army Center of Military History, 1980), 131.

23. Cooper, Corson, et al., *American Experience with Pacification*, 3:287.

24. Ibid., 288.

25. Merle L. Pribbenow, trans., *Victory in Vietnam: The Official History of the People's Army of Vietnam, 1954–1975* (Lawrence: University Press of Kansas, 2002), 237–238.

26. Robert J. Destatte, trans., "The Yellow Star Division: A History" (unpublished, n.d., CMH), 91.

27. Richard H. Schultz Jr., "The Vietnamization-Pacification Strategy of 1969–1972: A Quantitative and Qualitative Reassessment," in *Lessons from an Unconventional War: Reassessing U.S. Strategies for Future Conflicts*, ed. Richard A. Hunt (New York: Pergamon Press, 1982), 61–62.

28. William Colby and James McCargar, *Lost Victory: A Firsthand Account of America's Sixteen-Year Involvement in Vietnam* (New York: Contemporary Books, 1989), 263.

29. Cooper, Corson, et al., *American Experience with Pacification*, 3:288.

30. Lewy, *America in Vietnam*, 91–92.

31. Harvey Meyerson, *Vinh Long* (Boston: Houghton Mifflin, 1970), 196.

32. RVN, Central Pacification and Development Council, Basic Directive on the 1969 Pacification and Development Plan, 15 December 1969, 2, Miscellaneous Documents from Microfilm, MACV-SJS on Pacification/Phoenix box, MACV Command Historian's Collection, USAHEC.

33. John Paul Vann, Thoughts on GVN/VC Control, 2 April 1969, 2, John Vann Papers, USAHEC.

34. Assistant DEPCORDS Williard E. Chambers, ARVN Support of APC, un-

dated, inclosure 1, tab A, NARG 472, MACV Advisory Team 42 files, General Records box 6, Civil Affairs Info '69 folder.

35. James Megellas (I FFV DEPCORDS), Pacification in Binh Dinh Province, 27 March 1969, 1, Province Reports II CTZ—Binh Dinh/Kontum box, SEAB, CMH.

36. Chambers, ARVN Support of APC, 1.

37. 173rd Airborne Brigade, Intelligence Bulletin 20-69: 18th NVA Regiment, 1, NARG 472, 173rd Airborne Brigade files, S-2 Command Reports box; Abrams MAC 7391 to Admiral McCain, General Wheeler, and Ambassador Bunker, Updated Analysis of the Enemy's So-called June "High Point," 2–4, General Creighton Abrams Messages files, HRB, CMH.

38. I Field Force, Vietnam, Operational Report of Headquarters, I FFORCEV for Quarterly Period Ending 30 April 1969, 27–30, I FFV ORLL 68–69 box, SEAB, CMH; Advisory Team 42, Binh Dinh Province Report for the Period Ending 31 March 1969, 1–3, Province Reports II CTZ—Binh Dinh/Kontum box, SEAB, CMH.

39. Megellas, Pacification in Binh Dinh Province, 1.

40. LTG Corcoran, CG I FFORCEV to Gen Abrams COMUSMACV, Utilization of RF/PF, General Creighton Abrams Messages files, HRB, CMH.

41. Megellas, Pacification in Binh Dinh Province, 4.

42. Interview with Gen. John W. Barnes and Gen. Lu Mong Lan, 28 December 1991, author's research collection.

43. Advisory Team 42, Binh Dinh Province Report for the Period Ending 31 August 1969, 5, Province Reports II CTZ—Binh Dinh/Kontum box, SEAB, CMH.

44. 173rd Airborne Brigade, OPORD 3-69, Washington Green, 10 April 1969, 3, NARG 472, 173rd Airborne Brigade files, S-3 Command Reports box 3.

45. James B. Moore, "Impressions of a Third Tour," in *A Distant Challenge: The US Infantryman in Vietnam, 1967–1972*, ed. Lt. Col. Albert N. Garland (Nashville, TN: Battery Press, 1983), 262.

46. 173rd Airborne Brigade, OPORD 3-69, inclosure 2, 1.

47. Interview with Col. Jared C. Bates, 3 May 1985, 35, Senior Officer Oral History Program files, Company Command in Vietnam series, USAHEC.

48. Brig. Gen. John W. Barnes, Operation Washington Green Briefing, 27 July 1969, 5, John W. Barnes Papers, USAHEC.

49. Ibid., 3–4.

50. US Army Combat Developments Command, Debriefings of Returnees from Vietnam, General John W. Barnes Debriefing, 11 March 1970, 12 (from a presentation given at Fort Belvoir, MD, 19 November 1969), John W. Barnes Papers, USAHEC.

51. Barnes, Operation Washington Green Briefing, 3.

52. Ibid., 6.

53. 173rd Airborne Brigade, ORLL, 15 May 1968, 31; 173rd Airborne Brigade, ORLL, 15 August 1968, 29, 173rd Airborne Brigade ORLL box 1, MACV Command Historian's Collection, USAHEC.

54. Department of the Army, Senior Officer Debriefing Report: BG H. S. Cun-

ningham, GC, 173rd Airborne Brigade, Period 9 August 1969 to 10 August 1970, 8, Senior Officer Oral History Program files, USAHEC.

55. Barnes, Operation Washington Green Briefing, 2.

56. Ibid., 6.

57. 173rd Airborne Brigade, OPORD 3-69, 4.

58. Ibid., inclosure 2, 2.

59. Ibid., inclosure 1, 1.

60. Michael E. Peterson, *The Combined Action Platoons: The U.S. Marines' Other War in Vietnam* (New York: Praeger Publishers, 1989), 41.

61. Ibid., 43.

62. Interview with Col. Donald F. Bletz, 22 August 1991, author's research collection.

63. Ibid.

64. 173rd Airborne Brigade, OPORD 3-69, inclosure 2, 6.

65. Interview with Bletz.

66. Jeffrey Kimball, *Nixon's Vietnam War* (Lawrence: University Press of Kansas, 1998), 91.

67. Ibid., 95.

68. William Burr and Jeffrey Kimball, *Nixon's Nuclear Specter: The Secret Alert of 1969, Madman Diplomacy, and the Vietnam War* (Lawrence: University Press of Kansas, 2015), 72.

69. Ibid., 74–79.

70. Jeffrey Clarke, *Advice and Support: The Final Years, 1965–1973* (Washington, DC: US Army Center of Military History, 1988), 294–301; Krepinevich, *Army and Vietnam*, 251.

71. Clarke, *Advice and Support*, 347–352.

72. Phillip B. Davidson, *Secrets of the Vietnam War* (Novato, CA: Presidio Press, 1988), 145.

73. Quoted in Lewis Sorley, *A Better War: The Unexamined Victories and Final Tragedy of America's Last Years in Vietnam* (New York: Harcourt Brace, 1999), 137.

74. Clarke, *Advice and Support*, 350.

75. Ibid., 355.

76. Ibid., 357.

Chapter Three. The Balance of Forces

1. Allan E. Goodman, *Politics in War: The Bases of Political Community in South Vietnam* (Cambridge, MA: Harvard University Press, 1973), 1–5.

2. Paul Berman, *Revolutionary Organization: Revolutionary Institution Building within the People's Liberation Armed Forces* (Lexington, MA: Lexington Books, 1974), 4.

3. Department of the Army, Office of the Adjutant General, Senior Officer Debriefing Report: LTC Robert E. Wagner, Senior Advisor, Quang Tin Province, Dec 70–July 72, 3, NARG 472, NND 972624, box 291.

4. Raymond D. Gastil, *Four Papers on the Vietnamese Insurgency* (Croton-on-Hudson, NY: Hudson Institute, 1967), I-18; Chester L. Cooper, Judith Corson, et al., *The American Experience with Pacification in Vietnam*, 3 vols., Report R-185 (Arlington, VA: Institute for Defense Analysis, 1972), 3:26.

5. Mark Moyar, *Triumph Forsaken: The Vietnam War, 1954–1965* (Cambridge: Cambridge University Press, 2006), 169–170.

6. Ellen J. Hammer, *A Death in November: America in Vietnam, 1963* (New York: E. Dutton, 1987), 130–132, 154–156.

7. William J. Duiker, *The Communist Road to Power in Vietnam* (Boulder, CO: Westview Press, 1981), 160–165.

8. Edward G. Lansdale, *In the Midst of Wars: An American's Mission to Southeast Asia* (New York: Harper & Row, 1972), 340–343; Goodman, *Politics in War*, 23–26.

9. Berman, *Revolutionary Organization*, 4.

10. Jeffrey Race, *War Comes to Long An: Revolutionary Conflict in a Vietnamese Province* (Berkeley: University of California Press, 1972), 56, 91.

11. Gastil, *Four Papers*, III-121.

12. Race, *War Comes to Long An*, 167.

13. Ibid., 251.

14. Ibid., 168.

15. Cooper, Corson, et al., *American Experience with Pacification*, 3:25.

16. Jeffrey Clarke, *Advice and Support: The Final Years, 1965–1973* (Washington, DC: US Army Center of Military History, 1988), 255.

17. Guenter Lewy, *America in Vietnam* (New York: Oxford University Press, 1978), 177–179.

18. Berman, *Revolutionary Organization*, 42.

19. Harvey Meyerson, *Vinh Long* (Boston: Houghton Mifflin, 1970), 106.

20. William R. Corson, *The Betrayal* (New York: W. W. Norton, 1968), 97.

21. Gastil, *Four Papers*, I-20.

22. Ibid., II-122; Corson, *Betrayal*, 159.

23. Shelby L. Stanton, *Vietnam Order of Battle* (New York: Galahad Books, 1987), 13; Brig. Gen. John W. Barnes, Operation Washington Green Briefing, 27 July 1969, 2, John W. Barnes Papers, USAHEC.

24. Clarke, *Advice and Support*, 56, 158.

25. Interview with Brig. Gen. John W. Barnes and Gen. Lu Mong Lan, 28 December 1991, author's research collection.

26. James W. Trullinger, *Village at War: An Account of Revolution in Vietnam* (New York: Longman, 1980), 168.

27. PSG, Binh Dinh: The Challenge—1971, 12 June 1971, annex C, tab B, 3, Saunders Papers.

28. James Megellas (I FFV DEPCORDS), Pacification in Binh Dinh Province, 27 March 1969; Advisory Team 42, Binh Dinh Province Report for the Period Ending 31 May 1969, Province Reports II CTZ—Binh Dinh/Kontum box, SEAB, CMH.

29. Cooper, Corson, et al., *American Experience with Pacification*, 3:213.

30. Ibid., 2:171.

31. Goodman, *Politics in War*, 2, 11.

32. Republic of Vietnam, Central Pacification and Development Council, Basic Directive on the 1969 Pacification and Development Plan, 15 December 1969, annex VII, 2, Miscellaneous Documents from Microfilm, MACV-SJS on Pacification/Phoenix box, MACV Command Historian's Collection, USAHEC.

33. Advisory Team 42, Binh Dinh Province Report for the Period Ending 31 December 1969, 5, NARG 472, MACV Advisory Team 42 files, box 48.

34. PSG, Binh Dinh: The Challenge—1971, annex D, 2; Advisory Team 42, Binh Dinh Province Report for the Period Ending 30 April 1969 and 31 May 1969, Province Reports II CTZ—Binh Dinh/Kontum box, SEAB, CMH.

35. Ngo Quang Truong, *Territorial Forces*, Indochina Monographs (Washington, DC: US Army Center of Military History, 1981), 66–67.

36. Ibid., 70.

37. Advisory Team 42, Binh Dinh Province Reports for the Periods Ending 31 May 1969, 30 June 1969, and 31 July 1969, Province Reports II CTZ—Binh Dinh/Kontum box, SEAB, CMH.

38. Ronald G. Spector, *Advice and Support: The Early Years of the U.S. Army in Vietnam, 1941–1960* (Washington, DC: US Army Center of Military History, 1983), 320–321.

39. Ngo Quang Truong, *Territorial Forces*, 72.

40. PSG, Binh Dinh: The Challenge—1971, annex E, tab B.

41. Ibid., tab C; Cooper, Corson, et al., *American Experience with Pacification*, 2:82.

42. Race, *War Comes to Long An*, 85.

43. Ibid., 171–173.

44. Bernard B. Fall, "The Theory and Practice of Insurgency and Counterinsurgency," *Naval War College Review*, April 1965, 21–38.

45. "A Systems Analysis View of the Vietnam War 1965–1952: Volume 9 (Population Security)," 125, DTIC Online, http://www.dtic.mil/dtic/tr/fulltext/u2/a039316.pdf (accessed 17 April 2015).

46. Berman, *Revolutionary Organization*, 113.

47. Douglas Pike, *Vietcong: The Organization and Techniques of the National Liberation Front of South Vietnam* (Cambridge, MA: MIT Press, 1966), 186–287.

48. Race, *War Comes to Long An*, 167–168.

49. Ibid., 170.

50. Wilfred Burchett, *Vietnam: Inside Story of the Guerrilla War* (New York: International Publishers, 1965), 153.

51. Berman, *Revolutionary Organization*, 75.

52. Cooper, Corson, et al., *American Experience with Pacification*, 2:63.

53. Goodman, *Politics in War*, 13; David G. Marr, *Vietnamese Tradition on Trial, 1920–1945* (Berkeley: University of California Press, 1981), 4; Gabriel Kolko, *Anatomy of a War: Vietnam, the United States, and the Modern Historical Experience* (New York: Pantheon Books, 1985), 14.

54. Pike, *Vietcong*, 166–193.

55. David W. P. Elliott, *The Vietnamese War: Revolution and Social Change in the Mekong Delta, 1930–1975*, 2 vols. (Armonk, NY: M. E. Sharpe, 2001), 2:1240–1242.

56. Thomas L. Ahern Jr., *Vietnam Declassified: The CIA and Counterinsurgency* (Lexington: University Press of Kentucky, 2010), 374.

57. Pike, *Vietcong*, 210.

58. Ibid., 166.

59. Ibid., 234.

60. Untitled document, April 1969, 5, NARG 472, MACV Advisory Team 42 files, General Records box 6, Civil Affairs Info '69 folder.

61. MACV, Vietnam Documents and Research Notes 93: Viet Cong Political Geography of South Viet-Nam, January 1971, 9–15, MACV Command Historian's Collection, USAHEC.

62. Ibid., 4–5; 173rd Airborne Brigade, OPORD 3-69, annex B, appendix 3, tab C; 173rd Airborne Brigade, Intelligence Bulletin 20-69: 18th NVA Regiment, NARG 472, 173rd Airborne Brigade files, S-2 Command Reports box.

63. Untitled document, April 1969, 2–4.

64. 173rd Airborne Brigade, OPORD 3-69, Washington Green, annex B, appendix 3, tab A.

65. APC Status Report, undated, inclosure 6, NARG 472, MACV Advisory Team 42 General Records, box 12, JUSPAO Activities 1970.

66. Stanton, *Vietnam Order of Battle*, 52.

67. 173rd Airborne Brigade, ORLL for the Period Ending 30 April 1971, inclosure C, CAAR Washington Green, inclosure 2, NARG 472, 173rd Airborne Brigade files, S-3 ORLL 69–71 box.

68. Lewy, *America in Vietnam*, 124.

69. Advisory Team 42, Binh Dinh Province Report for the Period Ending 31 May 1969.

70. Cao Van Vien, *The U.S. Adviser*, Indochina Monographs (Washington, DC: US Army Center of Military History, 1980).

71. Barnes, Operation Washington Green Briefing, 6.

72. Dale Andrade, *Ashes to Ashes: The Phoenix Program and the Vietnam War* (Lexington, MA: Lexington Books, 1990), 59–89.

73. Ibid., 87–88.

74. Ibid., 39–41, 176.

75. Ahern, *Vietnam Declassified*, 353.

Chapter Four. Growing Dependency

1. Advisory Team 42, Binh Dinh Province Report for the Period Ending 30 April 1969, 1, Province Reports II CTZ—Binh Dinh/Kontum box, SEAB, CMH.

2. Ibid., 2; 173rd Airborne Brigade, ORLL, 15 August 1969, 14, NARG 472, 173rd Airborne Brigade files, S-3 ORLL 69–71 box.

3. Advisory Team 42, Binh Dinh Province Report for the Period Ending 30 April 1969, 3; I Field Force Vietnam, PERINTREP 18-69, 27 April–5 May 1969, and

PERINTREP 19-69, 5–10 May 1969, NARG 472, I Field Force Vietnam files, G-2 PERINTREPs (1968–69) box.

4. MACV J-2, Strategic Research and Analysis Division, Communist Strategy as Reflected in Lao Dong Party and COSVN Resolutions (SRAP 1569), undated, 7–8, MACV Command Historian's Collection, USAHEC.

5. MACV, Vietnam Documents and Research Notes 64, Summer 1969: A Vietcong Study of the Situation and Prospects, 6, MACV Command Historian's Collection, USAHEC.

6. MACV, Vietnam Documents and Research Notes 61, "Decisive Victory": Step by Step, Bit by Bit, 7, MACV Command Historian's Collection, USAHEC.

7. MACV J-2, Communist Strategy as Reflected in Lao Dong Party and COSVN Resolutions, 7.

8. I Field Force Vietnam, PERINTREP 22-69, 25–31 May 1969, annex H, NARG 472, I Field Force Vietnam files, G-2 PERINTREPs (1968–69) box.

9. I Field Force Vietnam, PERINTREP 27-69, 29 June–5 July 1969, annex K, NARG 472, I Field Force Vietnam files, G-2 PERINTREPs (1968–69) box; Advisory Team 42, Binh Dinh Province Report for the Period Ending 30 June 1969, 2, Province Reports II CTZ—Binh Dinh/Kontum box, SEAB, CMH.

10. 173rd Airborne Brigade, ORLL, 15 August 1969, 68.

11. Brig. Gen. John W. Barnes, Operation Washington Green Briefing, 27 July 1969, 8, John W. Barnes Papers, USAHEC.

12. Advisory Team 42, Binh Dinh Province Report for the Period Ending 30 April 1969, 5; James Megellas (I FFV DEPCORDS), Pacification in Binh Dinh Province, 27 March 1969, 4, Province Reports II CTZ—Binh Dinh/Kontum box, SEAB, CMH.

13. Advisory Team 42, Binh Dinh Province Report for the Period Ending 30 April 1969, inclosure 8, Tam Quan Monthly District Report for the Period Ending 30 April 1969, 1, Saunders Papers; 4th Battalion, 503rd Infantry, Quarterly Historical Report, 1 April–30 June 1969, 2, NARG 472, 4th Battalion, 503rd Infantry files, Organizational History files.

14. VNIT 482-42, interview with Tam Quan district senior advisor, 7 August 1969, synopsis 2, CMH.

15. Ibid., synopsis 1.

16. VNIT 482-4, interview with Binh Dinh Province S-2 advisor, 8 and 25 August 1969, synopsis 2, CMH.

17. VNIT 482-15, interview with Binh Dinh Province Chieu Hoi advisor, 9 August 1969, synopsis 1, CMH.

18. VNIT 482-35, interview with Hoai An district senior advisor, 23 August 1969, synopsis 3, CMH; 4/503rd, Quarterly Historical Report, 1 April–30 June 1969, 2, NARG 472, 4th Battalion, 503rd Infantry files, Organizational History files; 173rd Airborne Brigade, Monthly Unified Mission Progress Report, 8 July 1969, I-2, MACV Command Historian's Collection, USAHEC.

19. Advisory Team 42, Binh Dinh Province Reports for the Periods Ending 30 April 1969, 3, 7, and 31 May 1969, 4, Saunders Papers; Tam Quan Monthly District

Report for the Period Ending 30 April 1969, 3; 173rd Airborne Brigade, Monthly Unified Mission Progress Report, 8 July 1969, I-3.

20. Advisory Team 42, Binh Dinh Province Report for the Period Ending 30 April 1969, 7.

21. Chester L. Cooper, Judith Corson, et al., *The American Experience with Pacification in Vietnam*, 3 vols., Report R-185 (Arlington, VA: Institute for Defense Analysis, 1972), 2:171; Advisory Team 42, Binh Dinh Province Report for the Period Ending 31 May 1969, 1, Province Reports II CTZ—Binh Dinh/Kontum box, SEAB, CMH.

22. Advisory Team 42, Binh Dinh Province Report for the Period Ending 31 May 1969, 6.

23. 4/503rd, Quarterly Historical Report, 1 April–30 June 1969, Roster of Personnel Wounded Due to Hostile Action.

24. 173rd Airborne Brigade, ORLL for the Period Ending 30 April 1971, inclosure C, CAAR Washington Green, 11, NARG 472, 173rd Airborne Brigade files, S-3 ORLL 69–71 box.

25. James R. McDonough, *Platoon Leader* (Novato, CA: Presidio Press, 1985), 137.

26. 4/503rd, Quarterly Historical Report, 1 April–30 June 1969, 20; Tam Quan Monthly District Report for the Period Ending 30 April 1969, 1; Advisory Team 42, Binh Dinh Province Report for the Period Ending 31 May 1969, inclosure 8, Tam Quan Monthly District Report for the Period Ending 31 May 1969, 1.

27. Advisory Team 42, Tam Quan Monthly District Report for the Period Ending 30 April 1969, 1.

28. Barnes, Operation Washington Green Briefing, 8.

29. Ibid., 9; VNIT 482-48, interview with platoon leader, Thien Chanh hamlet, Tam Quan district, Binh Dinh Province, 9 July 1969, synopsis 2, CMH.

30. VNIT 482-39, interview with S-3, 4th Battalion, 503rd Airborne Infantry, 9 July 1969, synopsis 1, CMH; Advisory Team 42, Binh Dinh Province Report for the Period Ending 31 May 1969, 2.

31. VNIT 482-39, synopsis 1.

32. 173rd Airborne Brigade, CAAR Washington Green, 8.

33. 173rd Airborne Brigade, ORLL, 15 May 1969, 68, NARG, 173rd Airborne Brigade files, S-3 ORLL 69–71 box; 173rd Airborne Brigade, ORLL, 15 August 1969, 8.

34. 173rd Airborne Brigade, ORLL, 15 May 1969, 74–77.

35. 173rd Airborne Brigade, ORLL, 15 August 1969, inclosure 4, 3/319th Artillery, Combat After Action Report, Operation Red Thrust VI, 18 May 1969.

36. VNIT 482-47, interview with deputy district senior advisor, Hoai Nhon district, 30 July 1969, synopsis 1, CMH.

37. Advisory Team 42, Binh Dinh Province Report for the Period Ending 30 April 1969, inclosure 5, Hoai Nhon Monthly District Report for the Period Ending 30 April 1969, 1; 173rd Airborne Brigade, ORLL, 15 May 1969, 87; VNIT 482-13, interview with S-3, 2nd Battalion, 503rd Infantry, 15 July 1969, synopsis 1, CMH; VNIT

482-20, interview with CO, 2nd Battalion, 503rd Infantry, 12 July 1969, synopsis 1, CMH.

38. John S. Figueira, Memorandum for L. Craig Johnstone, Chief, CORDS-PSG, Subject: Contra-Productive Activities of the 173rd Airborne Brigade, 10 July 1969, 1, Saunders Papers.

39. John S. Figueira, Memorandum for record, Subject: Continuing Contra-Productive Activities of the 173rd Airborne Brigade, undated, 1, Saunders Papers.

40. I Field Force Vietnam, PERINTREP 19-69, 5–10 May 1969, annex I, NARG 472, I Field Force Vietnam files, G-2 PERINTREPs (1968–69) box; Advisory Team 42, Binh Dinh Province Report for the Period Ending 30 April 1969, 9; VNIT 482-15, inclosure 1 (chart); VNIT 482-49, interview with deputy district senior advisor, Hoai Nhon district, synopsis 1, CMH.

41. Advisory Team 42, Binh Dinh Province Report for the Period Ending 31 May 1969, inclosure, Hoai Nhon Monthly District Report for the Period Ending 31 May 1969, 1; Barnes, Operation Washington Green Briefing, 10.

42. Advisory Team 42, Binh Dinh Province Reports for the Periods Ending 31 May 1969, 9, and 30 June 1969, 8, Province Reports II CTZ—Binh Dinh/Kontum box, SEAB, CMH.

43. Advisory Team 42, Hoai Nhon Monthly District Report for the Period Ending 31 May 1969, 3.

44. Barnes, Operation Washington Green Briefing, 10.

45. Advisory Team 42, Binh Dinh Province Reports for the Periods Ending 30 April, 31 May, and 30 June 1969.

46. Advisory Team 42, Hoai Nhon Monthly District Report for the Period Ending 31 May 1969, 2.

47. 173rd Airborne Brigade, Monthly Unified Mission Progress Report, 8 July 1969, I-2.

48. 2/503rd, ORLL, 2nd Quarter 1969, 8, appendices D and E, NARG 472, 2nd Battalion, 503rd Infantry files, Organizational History files.

49. Douglas Pike, Binh Dinh: Anatomy of a Province, October 1972, 11, Province Reports II CTZ—Binh Dinh/Kontum box, SEAB, CMH.

50. 173rd Airborne Brigade, OPORD 3-69, Washington Green, 10 April 1969, annex B, appendix 3, tab C, 3, NARG 472, 173rd Airborne Brigade files, S-3 Command Reports box 3.

51. Advisory Team 42, Binh Dinh Province Report for the Period Ending 30 April 1969, inclosure 7, Phu My Monthly District Report for the Period Ending 30 April 1969, 4; 173rd Ariborne Brigade, CAAR Washington Green, 7; Shelby L. Stanton, *Vietnam Order of Battle* (New York: Galahad Books, 1987), 151; Anthony B. Herbert and James D. Wooten, *Soldier* (New York: Holt, Rinehart & Winston, 1973), 387.

52. 173rd Airborne Brigade, CAAR Washington Green, 7; Stanton, *Vietnam Order of Battle*, 53; 1st Battalion 50th Infantry Association website, www.ichiban1.org (accessed 12 March 2015).

53. "Short Range Ambush Platoon, 1968–1969," 1st Battalion 50th Infantry Association online, http://www.ichiban1.org/html/cs_srap.htm (accessed 8 July 2015).

54. APC Target Hamlets Progress, April 1969, inclosure 3, NARG 472, MACV Advisory Team 42 files, General Records box 12, JUSPAO Activities 1970 folder.

55. VNIT 482-25, interview with district senior advisor, Phu My district, 23 and 24 July 1969, synopsis 3–4, CMH.

56. Advisory Team 42, Binh Dinh Province Report for the Period Ending 31 May 1969, inclosure 7, Phu My Monthly District Report for the Period Ending 31 May 1969, 3.

57. VNIT 482-24, interview with senior advisor, 41st ARVN Regiment, 24 July 1969, synopsis 2, CMH.

58. US Army Combat Developments Command, Debriefings of Vietnam Returnees: General John W. Barnes Debriefing, 11 March 1970 (from a presentation given at Fort Belvoir, MD, 19 November 1969), 18, John W. Barnes Papers, US-AHEC.

59. VNIT 482-25, synopsis 4.

60. Advisory Team 42, Phu My Monthly District Report for the Period Ending 31 May 1969, 1.

61. Ibid., 1–2; I Field Force Vietnam, ORLL for the Period Ending 31 July 1969, 17, I FFV ORLL 68–69 box, SEAB, CMH.

62. Advisory Team 42, Phu My Monthly District Report for the Period Ending 31 May 1969, 3.

63. VNIT 482-25, synopsis 5.

64. "Plan of Activity to Carry out the Order 'Rapidly Disintegrate Enemy People's Self-Defense Forces,'" in *The History of the Vietnam War*, ed. Douglas Pike (Ann Arbor, MI: University Microfilms International, 1987), Indochina archives unit 1, series 1, section 2, fiche 555.

65. VNIT 482-25, synopsis 6; Advisory Team 42, Phu My Monthly District Report for the Period Ending 31 May 1969, 4; 173rd Airborne Brigade, Monthly Unified Mission Progress Report, 8 July 1969, I-3.

66. Advisory Team 42, Binh Dinh Province Report for the Period Ending 30 April 1969, 5.

67. APC Target Hamlets Progress, inclosure 4; 173rd Airborne Brigade, OPORD 3-69, annex B, appendix 11, tab D.

68. 173rd Airborne Brigade, OPORD 3-69, annex H; 173rd Airborne Brigade, OPORD 10-69 (Washington Green II), undated, annex H, NARG 472, 173rd Airborne Brigade files, S-3 Command Reports box 3; Advisory Team 42, Binh Dinh Province Report for the Period Ending 30 April 1969, inclosure 4, Hoai An Monthly District Report for the Period Ending 30 April 1969, 2.

69. Advisory Team 42, Hoai An Monthly District Report for the Period Ending 30 April 1969, 1–2.

70. Ibid., 5.

71. Advisory Team 42, Binh Dinh Province Report for the Period Ending 31 May 1969, inclosure 4, Hoai An Monthly District Report for the Period Ending 31 May 1969, 2.

72. Barnes, Operation Washington Green Briefing, 11.

73. Advisory Team 42, Hoai An Monthly District Report for the Period Ending 31 May 1969, 1.

74. Advisory Team 42, Hoai An Monthly District Report for the Period Ending 30 April 1969, 1, 6; VNIT 482-30, interview with district senior advisor, Hoai An district, 16 July 1969, synopsis 2, CMH.

75. 1/503rd, Quarterly Historical Report, April–June 1969, 27, NARG 472, 1st Battalion, 503rd Infantry files, Organizational History files.

76. VNIT 482-39, synopsis 1; 173rd Airborne Brigade, Monthly Unified Mission Progress Report, 8 August 1969, I-1, MACV Command Historian's Collection, US-AHEC.

77. Advisory Team 42, Hoai An Monthly District Report for the Period Ending 31 May 1969, 1–4.

78. Ibid., 2–3.

79. VNIT 482-30, synopsis 3.

80. Advisory Team 42, Binh Dinh Province Report for the Period Ending 30 April 1969, 2.

81. Advisory Team 42, Binh Dinh Province Reports for the Periods Ending 31 May 1969, 2, and 31 December 1969, 3, NARG 472, MACV Advisory Team 42 files, box 48.

82. VNIT 482-35, synopsis 2.

83. Advisory Team 42, Binh Dinh Province Report for the Period Ending 31 July 1969, 2, Province Reports II CTZ—Binh Dinh/Kontum box, SEAB, CMH; 173rd Airborne Brigade, Monthly Unified Mission Progress Report, 8 July 1969, III-1; 173rd Airborne Brigade, Monthly Unified Mission Progress Report, 8 August 1969, III-1.

84. Advisory Team 42, Binh Dinh Province Reports for the Periods Ending 30 April, 31 May, and 31 July 1969; Barnes, Operation Washington Green Briefing, 13.

85. Advisory Team 42, Binh Dinh Province Report for the Period Ending 30 June 1969, 4; Barnes, Operation Washington Green Briefing, 7.

86. Barnes, Operation Washington Green Briefing, chart 6; Advisory Team 42, Hoai An District Report for the Period Ending 31 July 1969, NARG 472, MACV Team 42 files, box 48, District Monthly Report files, 1970 folder; Advisory Team 42, Hoai Nhon Monthly District Report for the Period Ending 31 May 1969; HES Monthly Pacification Status Reports, 31 March, 31 May, and 31 July 1969, Pacification Status maps, MACV Command Historian's Collection, USAHEC.

87. Barnes, Operation Washington Green Briefing, chart 1; VNIT 482-15, chart.

88. "PRP Central Committee Assessment of Situation in Binh Dinh Province, January–June, 1969," in Pike, *History of the Vietnam War,* Indochina archives unit 1, series 1, section 2, fiche 522, 2-B.

89. Ibid., 2-11–2-12.

90. Ibid., 2-11.

91. CORDS, Phung Hoang Problem Areas in II CTZ, undated, last page, NARG 472, MACV Team 42 files, General Records box 6, Civil Affairs Info '69 folder.

92. Dale Andrade, *Ashes to Ashes: The Phoenix Program and the Vietnam War* (Lexington, MA: Lexington Books, 1990), 62.

93. VNIT 482-26, interview with DIOCC advisor, Phu My district, 3 August 1969, synopsis 2, CMH; Advisory Team 42, Phu My Monthly District Report for the Period Ending 31 May 1969, 4.

94. Barnes, Operation Washington Green Briefing, 12; Advisory Team 42, Binh Dinh Province Reports for the Periods Ending 30 April, 31 May, and 30 June 1969.

95. VNIT 482-2, interview with Phoenix coordinator, Binh Dinh Province, 8 August 1969, 21–22, CMH.

96. Phung Hoang Problem Areas in II CTZ, undated, 2, NARG 472, MACV Team 42 files, General Records box 6, Civil Affairs Info '69 folder.

97. Advisory Team 42, Binh Dinh Province Reports for the Periods Ending 31 May 1969, 2, and 30 June 1969, 3; Advisory Team 42, Hoai Nhon Monthly District Reports for the Periods Ending 30 April 1969, 4, and 31 May 1969, 4; VNIT 482-50, interview with DIOCC advisor, Hoai Nhon district, 30 July 1969, synopsis 2, CMH.

98. VNIT 482-2, 27.

99. Ibid., 15.

100. VNIT 482-35, synopsis 2.

101. Analysis of Chieu Hoi Program—Binh Dinh Province, undated, 2, NARG 472, MACV Advisory Team 42 files, General Records box 6, Civil Affairs Info '69 folder.

102. VNIT 482-2, 12.

103. VNIT 482-16, interview with chief, pacification and development, and chief, new life development, 8 August 1969, synopsis 2, CMH.

104. VNIT 482-3, interview with Binh Dinh Province deputy province senior advisor, 9 August 1969, 55, CMH.

105. Advisory Team 42, Binh Dinh Province Reports for the Periods Ending 31 May 1969, 6; 30 June 1969, 4–5; and 31 July 1969, 3–6.

106. Advisory Team 42, Binh Dinh Province Report for the Period Ending 31 July 1969, 6.

107. VNIT 482-3, 51–52; VNIT 482-16, synopsis 3.

108. VNIT 482-9, interview with Binh Dinh Province deputy senior advisor for plans and operations, 53–54.

109. VNIT 482-7, interview with Binh Dinh Province psy/ops and S-5 psy/war advisors, 23 August 1969, synopsis 2–3, CMH; VNIT 482-26, synopsis 2.

110. Advisory Team 42, Binh Dinh Province Report for the Period Ending 30 April 1969, 6.

111. Cooper, Corson, et al., *American Experience with Pacification*, 2:189–190.

Chapter Five. Overextension

1. Chester L. Cooper, Judith Corson, et al., *The American Experience with Pacification in Vietnam*, 3 vols., Report R-185 (Arlington, VA: Institute for Defense Analy-

sis, 1972), 3:297–299; MACV, One War: Command Overview, 1968–1972, chap. III, 32–33, SEAB, CMH.

2. 1/503rd, Quarterly Historical Report, July–September 1969, 4–5, NARG 472, 1st Battalion, 503rd Infantry files, Organizational History files; 2/503rd, Quarterly Historical Report, July–September 1969, 7, NARG 472, 2nd Battalion, 503rd Infantry files, Organizational History files; 4/503rd, Quarterly Historical Report, July–September 1969, appendix 1, NARG 472, 4th Battalion, 503rd Infantry files, Organizational History files; 173rd Airborne Brigade, ORLL for the Period Ending 31 October 1969, 3, Saunders Papers.

3. VNIT 482-9, interview with Binh Dinh Province deputy senior advisor for plans and operations, 28 August 1969, 17, CMH.

4. VNIT 482-25, interview with Phu My district senior advisor, 23 and 24 July 1969, synopsis 3, CMH.

5. VNIT 482-16, interview with chief, pacification and development, and chief, new life development, 8 August 1969, synopsis 2, CMH.

6. Ngo Quang Truong, *Territorial Forces* (Washington, DC: US Army Center of Military History, 1981), 63; RVN, Central Pacification and Development Council, Guidelines for the 1969 Pacification Campaign, 12 December 1968, Miscellaneous Documents from Microfilm, MACV-SJS on Pacification/Phoenix box, MACV Command Historian's Collection, USAHEC; Advisory Team 42, Binh Dinh Province Report for the Period Ending 31 July 1969, 3, Province Reports II CTZ—Binh Dinh/Kontum box, SEAB, CMH.

7. 173rd Airborne Brigade, ORLL for the Period Ending 30 April 1969, 22, NARG 472, 173rd Airborne Brigade files, S-3 ORLL 69–71 box; "Company D (Airborne) 16th Armor, 173rd Airborne Brigade," http://www.d16armor173rd.org /uploads/2/6/4/0/26400706/very_short_history_of_d16th.pdf. (accessed 13 March 2015).

8. 173rd Airborne Brigade, ORLL for the Period Ending 31 July 1969, 69, 82, NARG 472, 173rd Airborne Brigade files, S-3 ORLL 69–71 box; 173rd Airborne Brigade, Special Intelligence Bulletin 6-69, 13 October 1969, annex D, NARG 472, 173rd Airborne Brigade files, S-2 Command Reports box.

9. COSVN, Resolution 9, July 1969, 68, MACV Command Historian's Collection, USAHEC. Subsequent references to this resolution are cited parenthetically in text by page number.

10. James W. McCoy, *Secrets of the Viet Cong* (New York: Hippocrene Books, 1992), 320–331.

11. Douglas Pike, *PAVN: People's Army of Vietnam* (Novato, CA: Presidio Press, 1986), 228.

12. 173rd Airborne Brigade, ORLL for the Period Ending 30 April 1971, inclosure C, CAAR Washington Green, 12, NARG 472, 173rd Airborne Brigade files, S-3 ORLL 69–71 box.

13. Brig. Gen. John W. Barnes, autobiographical essay, undated, 28, SEAB, CMH.

14. "Obituary: Hubert Cunningham, 75, Clarkston High Graduate," Lewiston Tribune Online, http://lmtribune.com/obituaries/hubert-cunningham-clarkston-high

-graduate/article_1fcc8c13-36a0-5003-a179-337bba64c46e.html (accessed 17 March 2015).

15. MACV, One War: Command Overview, 1968–1972, chap. IV, 56.

16. Advisory Team 42, Binh Dinh Province Report for the Period Ending 31 August 1969, 1, Province Reports II CTZ—Binh Dinh/Kontum box, SEAB, CMH.

17. I Field Force Vietnam, PERINTREP 19-69, 5–10 May 1969, annex I; PERINTREP 22-69, 25–31 May 1969, annex H; PERINTREP 27-69, 19 June–5 July 1969, annex K; PERINTREP 31-69, 27 July–2 August 1969, annex Q, all from NARG 472, I Field Force Vietnam files, G-2 PERINTREPs (1968–69) box; I Field Force Vietnam, PERINTREP 36-69, 31 August–6 September 1969, annex I; PERINTREP 40-69, 28 September–4 October 1969, annex I, both from ibid., G-2 PERINTREPs (1969) box; I Field Force Vietnam, ORLL for the Period Ending 31 July 1969, 18, NARG 472, HQ-USARV ORLL box 3, I FFV thru I FFV Prov. Arty. Group; Advisory Team 42, Binh Dinh Province Report for the Period Ending 31 August 1969, 1.

18. 1/503rd, Quarterly Historical Report, July–September 1969, 5; I Field Force Vietnam, ORLL for the Period Ending 31 October 1969, 20, I FFV ORLL 68–69 box, SEAB, CMH.

19. 1/503rd, Quarterly Historical Report, July–September 1969, 9; Advisory Team 42, Binh Dinh Province Report for the Period Ending 31 October 1969, 1, Province Reports II CTZ—Binh Dinh/Kontum box, SEAB, CMH.

20. Advisory Team 42, Binh Dinh Province Report for the Period Ending 31 October 1969, 3.

21. Shelby L. Stanton, *Vietnam Order of Battle* (New York: Galahad Books, 1987), 86; 3/503rd, Quarterly Historical Report, July–September 1969, 4, NARG 472, 3rd Battalion, 503rd Infantry files, Organizational History files.

22. 173rd Airborne Brigade, ORLL for the Period Ending 31 October 1969, 4; 3/503rd, OPORD 1-69, undated, 1–3, NARG 472, 3rd Battalion, 503rd Infantry files, Operational Planning 1969–1971 box, S-3 OPORD Sept 69–Dec 70 file.

23. 173rd Airborne Brigade, ORLL for the Period Ending 31 October 1969, 4.

24. Stephen J. Piotrowski questionnaire, 1991, author's research collection.

25. 1/503rd, Quarterly Historical Report, July–September 1969, 11–12; I Field Force Vietnam, ORLL for the Period Ending 31 October 1969, 26, I FFV ORLL 68–69 box, SEAB, CMH.

26. 1/503rd, Quarterly Historical Report, July–September 1969, 6–16.

27. I Field Force Vietnam, ORLL for the Period Ending 31 October 1969, 25.

28. PSG, Binh Dinh Province: The Challenge—1971, 12 June 1971, annex H, Saunders Papers.

29. Douglas Pike, *Vietcong: The Organization and Techniques of the National Liberation Front of South Vietnam* (Cambridge, MA: MIT Press, 1966), 257–258.

30. "Speech by Ranking DRV Cadre: November 1969," in Douglas Pike, *The History of the Vietnam War* (Ann Arbor, MI: University Microfilms International, 1987), Indochina archives unit 1, series 1, section 2, fiche 583, 2.

31. 173rd Airborne Brigade, OPORD 10-69 (Washington Green II), undated, an-

nex H, 2–3, NARG 472, 173rd Airborne Brigade files, S-3 Command Reports box 3; 2/503rd, Quarterly Historical Report, July–September 1969, 7.

32. HQ, MACV, Lessons Learned 80: US Combat Forces in Support of Pacification, undated, 9, SEAB, CMH; 4/503rd, Quarterly Historical Report, October–December 1969, inclosure 1, CAAR Operation Olympia, November 3, 1969, 1–2, NARG 472, 4th Battalion, 503rd Infantry files, Organizational History files; 173rd Airborne Brigade, OPORD 10-69, annex H.

33. Advisory Team 42, Binh Dinh Province Reports for the Periods Ending 31 August 1969, 5, and 31 October 1969, 2, 9.

34. 3/503rd, Quarterly Historical Report, October–December 1969, 22, NARG 472, 3rd Battalion, 503rd Infantry files, Organizational History files.

35. 4/503rd, Quarterly Historical Report, July–September 1969, 1–3.

36. 1/503rd, Quarterly Historical Report, July–September 1969, 3.

37. 173rd Airborne Brigade, ORLL for the Period Ending 31 July 1969, 131.

38. 1/503rd, Quarterly Historical Report, October–December 1969, 22, NARG 472, 4th Battalion, 503rd Infantry files, Organizational History files.

39. 173rd Airborne Brigade, CAAR Washington Green, 14.

40. PSG, 173rd Airborne Brigade Participation in Pacification in Northern Binh Dinh Province, 28 July 1969, 3, Saunders Papers.

41. Advisory Team 42, Binh Dinh Province Reports for the Periods Ending 31 July 1969, 1, and 31 October 1969, 1.

42. George W. Ashworth, "All-out Pacification: Viet Area Sharpens Its Plowshare," *Christian Science Monitor*, 13 September 1969; Joseph Alsop, "Need to Defend VC Structure Puts Hanoi's Forces in Bind," *Los Angeles Times*, 24 September 1969.

43. George W. Ashworth, "Binh Dinh Pacification Praised and Blamed," *Christian Science Monitor*, 7 October 1969.

44. Barnes, autobiographical essay, 29.

45. Orr Kelly, "Binh Dinh Province: General Tells of Pacification Success," *Washington Post*, 11 October 1969, 1.

46. Barnes, autobiographical essay, 29.

47. Ibid.

48. Ibid., 29–30.

49. William E. Colby, DEPCORDS/MACV, Memorandum to MACJ01R, Subject: Role of US Combat Forces in Support of Pacification, undated, 1, MACV Command Historian's Collection, USAHEC.

50. John S. Figueira, Continuing Contra-Productive Activities of the 173rd Airborne Brigade, undated, 2, Saunders Papers.

51. Advisory Team 42, Hoai An Monthly District Report for the Period Ending 31 July 1969, 1, NARG 472, MACV Advisory Team 42 files, box 48.

52. 1/503rd, Quarterly Historical Report, July–September 1969, 4–5; 173rd Airborne Brigade, ORLL for the Period Ending 31 October 1969, 3, Saunders Papers; Advisory Team 42, Hoai An Monthly District Report, 2 September 1969, 1, NARG 472, MACV Advisory Team 42 files, box 48.

53. Advisory Team 42, Hoai An Monthly District Report, 2 September 1969, 1.

54. Advisory Team 42, Binh Dinh Province Reports for the Periods Ending 31 July 1969, 2; 30 September 1969, 2; and 30 November 1969, 2, all from Province Reports II CTZ—Binh Dinh/Kontum box, SEAB, CMH; Advisory Team 42, Binh Dinh Province Report for the Period Ending 31 December 1969, 2, NARG 472, MACV Advisory Team 42 files, box 48.

55. Advisory Team 42, Hoai An Monthly District Report, 25 December 1969, 1, NARG 472, MACV Advisory Team 42 files, box 48.

56. Advisory Team 42, Hoai An Monthly District Report, 2 September 1969, 1.

57. Sir Robert Thompson, *No Exit from Vietnam* (New York: David McKay, 1969), 167.

58. Advisory Team 42, Binh Dinh Province Report for the Period Ending 31 October 1969, 15.

59. VNIT 546, Engineer Activities in Binh Dinh Province, 29 December 1969, synopsis 3, CMH.

60. Ibid., synopsis 2.

61. Ibid., synopsis 3.

62. 173rd Airborne Brigade, ORLL for the Period Ending 31 October 1969, 4.

63. 2/503rd, Quarterly Historical Report, October–December 1969, 5, NARG 472, 2nd Battalion, 503rd Infantry files, Organizational History files.

64. MAT II-90, Weekly Activity Reports, 17 August and 21 September 1969; MAT II-7, Weekly Activity Report for the Period 18–25 January 1970, NARG 472, MACV Advisory Team 42 files, General Records box 9.

65. MAT II-90, Weekly Activity Report, 20 December 1969, ibid.

66. Advisory Team 42, Binh Dinh Province Report for the Period Ending 31 October 1969, 1.

67. MAT II-90, Weekly Activity Report, 13 December 1969, NARG 472, MACV Advisory Team 42 files, General Records box 9.

68. "Senior Officer Debriefing Report: BG C. M. Hall, CG, I Field Force Vietnam Artillery, Period 23 October 1969 to 17 October 1970, 4 March 1971," DTIC Online, http://www.dtic.mil/dtic/tr/fulltext/u2/514360.pdf (accessed 16 April 2015).

69. Ibid.

70. MAT II-90, Weekly Activity Report, 7 December 1969, NARG 472, MACV Advisory Team 42 files, General Records box 9.

71. MAT II-7, Weekly Activity Report for the Period 28 September–5 October 1969, ibid.

72. MAT II-90, Weekly Activity Report, 20 December 1969.

73. MAT II-90, Weekly Activity Report, 23 November 1969, NARG 472, MACV Advisory Team 42 files, General Records box 9; Advisory Team 42, Mobile Advisory Team (MAT) Senior Advisor Debriefing, no date, 4, NARG 472, MACV Advisory Team 42 files, box 50, MAT II-44 file.

74. MAT II-90, Weekly Activity Report, 21 September 1969.

75. Ibid.

76. MAT II-90, Weekly Activity Report, 10 January 1970, NARG 472, MACV Advisory Team 42 files, General Records box 9.

77. VSSG, Binh Dinh: Control and Security Overview, 1967–1969, undated, 6, Saunders Papers.

78. Robert J. Destatte, trans., "The Yellow Star Division: A History" (unpublished, n.d., CMH), 102.

79. US Army Combat Developments Command, Debriefings of Vietnam Returnees: General John W. Barnes Debriefing, 11 March 1970 (from a presentation given at Fort Belvoir, MD, 19 November 1969), 12, MACV Command Historian's Collection, USAHEC.

80. Ibid., 20–21; I Field Force Vietnam, ORLL for the Period Ending 31 October 1969, 15–16, 31; 2nd Brigade, 4th Infantry Division, CAAR-PUTNAM COUGAR, 27 November 1969, 1–5, NARG 472, 2nd Brigade, 4th Infantry Division files, S-3 AARs box 1.

81. 173rd Airborne Brigade, ORLL for the Period Ending 31 October 1969, 2, 4; 3/503rd, Quarterly Historical Report, October–December 1969, 4.

82. 3/503rd, Quarterly Historical Report, October–December 1969, 4.

83. 173rd Airborne Brigade, Intelligence Bulletin 20-69, undated, 3, NARG 472, 173rd Airborne Brigade files, S-2 Command Reports box, Intelligence Bulletins 69 folder; 2nd Brigade, 4th Infantry Division, CAAR-PUTNAM WILDCAT, 15 February 1970, 3, NARG 472, 2nd Brigade, 4th Infantry Division files, S-3 AARs box 1.

84. 172nd Military Intelligence Detachment, Preliminary Interrogation Report 172-060-70, 2, NARG 472, 173rd Airborne Brigade files, S-2 Interrogation Reports Jan–June 1970 box; I Field Force Vietnam, ORLL for the Period Ending 31 January 1970, 20, NARG 472, HQ-USARV, ORLL box 3, I FFV file; F. Clifton Berry Jr., *Sky Soldiers: The Illustrated History of the Vietnam War*, vol. 2 (New York: Bantam Books, 1987), 137–140.

85. 2nd Brigade, 4th Infantry Division, CAAR-PUTNAM WILDCAT, 4; 173rd Airborne Brigade, CAAR Washington Green, 14.

86. 173rd Airborne Brigade, CAAR Washington Green, 14.

87. Shelby L. Stanton, *Rangers at War: Combat Recon in Vietnam* (New York: Ballantine Books, 1992), 182, 186–188.

88. 173rd Airborne Brigade, ORLL for the Period Ending 31 October 1969, 6.

89. 2nd Brigade, 4th Infantry Division, CAAR-PUTNAM WILDCAT, 1–7; 173rd Airborne Brigade, Intelligence Bulletin 20-69, 3–4.

90. 4th Infantry Division, ORLL for the Period Ending 31 January 70, 1–6, NARG 472, 4th Infantry Division files, G-3 ORLL 8/69–1/70 box 6.

91. 173rd Airborne Brigade, ORLL for the Period Ending 31 January 1970, 2, NARG 472, 173rd Airborne Brigade files, S-3 ORLL 69–71 box.

92. I Field Force Vietnam, ORLL for the Period Ending 31 January 1970, 2; Stanton, *Vietnam Order of Battle*, 159.

93. 1/503rd, Quarterly Historical Report, October–December 1969, 25.

94. CICV, Order of Battle Summaries, February 1972, vol. II, I-19; 1–31 March 1969, vol. I, I-3; 1–31 May 1969, vol. I, I-3; 1–31 August 1969, vol. I, I-3; 1–31 December 1969, vol. I, I-3, MACV Command Historian's Collection, USAHEC.

95. Alan D. Weathers, "Western Nam Bo: The War in the Lower Mekong Delta" (Ph.D. diss., University of Maine, 2000), 63.

96. HES, Monthly Pacification Status Report, 31 December 1969, MACV Command Historian's Collection, USAHEC.

97. Advisory Team 42, Binh Dinh Province Report for the Period Ending 31 December 1969, 3–4, NARG 472, MACV Advisory Team 42 files, box 48.

98. James Sterba, "U.S. Brigade Uses Unusual Methods to Stress Hamlet Security," *New York Times*, 1 January 1970, 6.

99. "Speech by Ranking DRV Cadre: November 1969," 2.

100. James B. Moore, "Impressions of a Third Tour," in *A Distant Challenge: The US Infantryman in Vietnam, 1967–1972*, ed. Lt. Col. Albert N. Garland (Nashville, TN: Battery Press, 1983), 260–261.

101. Merle L. Pribbenow, trans., *Victory in Vietnam: The Official History of the People's Army of Vietnam, 1954–1975* (Lawrence: University Press of Kansas, 2002), 246.

102. Cooper, Corson, et al., *American Experience with Pacification*, 3:299–300; MACV, One War: Command Overview, 1968–1972, chap. III, 40–41.

103. CORDS, II Corps Tactical Zone, End of Tour Report: James Megellas, Deputy for CORDS, I FFV, II CTZ, 19 May 1970, 26, NARG 472, NND 994025, box 9.

104. Alfred Friendly, "British Expert Predicts Secure Vietnam by 1972," *Washington Post*, 16 December 1969; Joseph Alsop, "Briton's Report on Vietnam Must Have Heartened Nixon," *Washington Post*, 5 December 1969.

105. Robert G. Kaiser, "The New Optimists II: Pacification (1969 Style) Seems to Be Working," *Washington Post*, 30 October 1969, A-23.

106. Ibid.

107. National Security Council, National Security Decision Memorandum 23, 16 September 1969; US State Department, Telegram 188646, 7 November 1969, both from VSSG files, cabinet 53, SEAB, CMH.

108. As quoted in Richard H. Schultz Jr., "The Vietnamization-Pacification Strategy of 1969–1972: A Quantitative and Qualitative Reassessment," in *Lessons from an Unconventional War: Reassessing U.S. Strategies for Future Conflicts*, ed. Richard A. Hunt Jr. (New York: Pergamon Press, 1982), 56.

109. "A Systems Analysis View of the Vietnam War 1965–1952: Volume 9 (Population Security)," 234–237, DTIC Online, http://www.dtic.mil/dtic/tr/fulltext/u2/a039316.pdf (accessed 17 April 2015).

110. VSSG, The Situation in the Countryside, 10 January 1970, 60–63, John Vann Papers, USAHEC.

111. Ibid., 63–64.

112. Samuel Lipsman and Edward Doyle, *Fighting for Time, The Vietnam Experience* (Boston: Boston Publishing Company, 1983), 70.

113. VSSG, Situation in the Countryside, 97.

Chapter Six. Slowdown

1. I Field Force Vietnam, ORLL for the Period Ending 31 January 1970, 31, NARG 472, HQ-USARV, ORLL box 3, I FFV file.

2. Gen. Elmer R. Ochs questionnaire, 1991, author's research collection; Advisory Team 42, Tam Quan Monthly District Report, 25 January 1970, 1, NARG 472, MACV Advisory Team 42 files, General Records box 10; 4/503rd, Quarterly Historical Report, January–March 1970, NARG 472, 4th Battalion, 503rd Infantry files, Organizational History files.

3. Advisory Team 42, Tam Quan Monthly District Report, 25 January 1970, 1; MAT II-90, Weekly Activity Report, 24 January 1970, and MAT II-7, Weekly Activity Report, 25 January 1970, NARG 472, MACV Advisory Team 42 files, General Records boxes 9–10.

4. MAT II-94, Weekly Activity Reports for the Periods 7–11 and 19–23 January 1970, NARG 472, MACV Advisory Team 42 files, General Records box 9.

5. For example, see 4/503rd, OPLAN/OPORD 2-70 Quick Relief, NARG 472, 3rd Battalion, 503rd Infantry files, Operational Planning 1969–1971 box, S-3 OPORD Sept 69–Dec 70 file, which postulated a multicompany NVA ground assault on Tam Quan's district headquarters.

6. 3/503rd, Quarterly Historical Report, January–March 1970, 3, 15, NARG 472, 3rd Battalion, 503rd Infantry files, Organizational History files.

7. I Field Force Vietnam, ORLL for the Period Ending 30 April 1970, 11–12, I FFV ORLL 68–69 box, SEAB, CMH; 4th Infantry Division, ORLL for the Period Ending 31 January 1970 , NARG 472, 4th Infantry Division files, G-3 ORLL 8/69–1/70 box 6; 1st Brigade, 4th Infantry Division, ORLL for the Period 1 February–30 April 1970, 1, 5, NARG 472, 1st Brigade, 4th Infantry Division files, S-3 ORLL 67–70 box.

8. Ochs questionnaire; 173rd Airborne Brigade, ORLL for the Period Ending 30 April 1970, 2, NARG 472, 173rd Airborne Brigade files, S-3 ORLL 69–71 box.

9. 3/506th, CAAR Operation Washington Green (Hill 474), 2, NARG 472, 3rd Battalion, 506th Infantry files, S-3 ORLL 69–70 box.

10. Ibid., tab E to inclosure 1.

11. Ochs questionnaire, 2–3; 3/506th, CAAR Hill 474, 28–29.

12. 3/506th, CAAR Hill 474, 28, inclosure 5; Department of the Army, Office of the Adjutant General, Senior Officer Debriefing Report: Brigadier General E. R. Ochs, CG 173rd Airborne Brigade, 26 March 1971, 13, Saunders Papers.

13. 172nd Military Intelligence Detachment, Preliminary Interrogation Report 172-041-70, 6 February 1970, 2, NARG 472, 173rd Airborne Brigade files, S-2 Interrogation Reports Jan–June 1970 box.

14. 3/506th, CAAR Hill 474, 27–28; Department of the Army, Senior Officer Debriefing Report: Ochs, 10–11.

15. Robert J. Destatte, trans., "The Yellow Star Division: A History" (unpublished, n.d., CMH), 104–105.

16. 172nd Military Intelligence Detachment, Preliminary Interrogation Report

172-054-70, 24 February 1970, 2, NARG 472, 173rd Airborne Brigade files, S-2 Interrogation Reports Jan–June 1970 box.

17. 3/506th, CAAR Hill 474, 26; F. Clifton Berry Jr., *Sky Soldiers: The Illustrated History of the Vietnam War*, vol. 2 (New York: Bantam Books, 1987), 144.

18. 172nd Military Intelligence Detachment, Preliminary Interrogation Report 172-041-70, 2–3, inclosure 1.

19. 1st Brigade, 4th Infantry Division, ORLL for the Period 1 Feb to 30 April 1970, 5, NARG 472, 1st Brigade, 4th Infantry Division files, S-3 ORLL box 1; I Field Force Vietnam, ORLL for the Period Ending 30 April 1970, 15, I FFV ORLL 68–69 box, SEAB, CMH.

20. Advisory Team 42, Tam Quan Monthly District Report, 26 February 1970, 1; Hoai An Monthly District Report, 24 February 1970, 1; and Phu My Monthly District Report, February 1970, 1, all from NARG 472, MACV Advisory Team 42 files, General Records box 10.

21. Merle L. Pribbenow, trans., *Victory in Vietnam: The Official History of the People's Army of Vietnam, 1954–1975* (Lawrence: University Press of Kansas, 2002), 250.

22. 172nd Military Intelligence Detachment, Preliminary Interrogation Report 172-060-70, 9 March 1970, 2, NARG 472, 173rd Airborne Brigade files, S-2 Interrogation Reports Jan–June 1970 box.

23. 172nd Military Intelligence Detachment, Translation of an ARVN Preliminary Interrogation Report, 22 March 1970, 3, NARG 472, 173rd Airborne Brigade files, S-2 Interrogation Reports Jan–June 1970 box.

24. VSSG, Binh Dinh Province: Control Assessment, 28 October 1970, 6, Saunders Papers.

25. 172nd Military Intelligence Detachment, Preliminary Interrogation Report 172-060-70, 2.

26. MACV, One War: Command Overview, 1968–1972, chap. III, 42, SEAB, CMH.

27. Ibid., chap. II, 16.

28. Ibid., 17.

29. Chester L. Cooper, Judith Corson, et al., *The American Experience with Pacification in Vietnam*, 3 vols., Report R-185 (Arlington, VA: Institute for Defense Analysis, 1972), 3:310–311.

30. Ibid., 308–309.

31. Ibid., 320–321.

32. Advisory Team 42, 1970 Pacification and Development Plan, Binh Dinh Province, First Phase, 1 March 1970, 1, NARG 472, MACV Advisory Team 42 files, General Records box 6.

33. Advisory Team 42, Binh Dinh Province Report for the Period Ending 31 March 1970, 4, NARG 472, MACV Advisory Team 42 files, box 48.

34. 2/503rd, Quarterly Historical Report, January–March 1970, 1–17, annex D, NARG 472, 2nd Battalion, 503rd Infantry files, Organizational History files.

35. MAT II-94, Weekly Activity Report for the Period 16–20 February 1970, 7, NARG 472, MACV Advisory Team 42 files, General Records box 9.

36. MAT II-94, Weekly Activity Reports for the Periods 23–28 February and 1–7 March 1970, NARG 472, MACV Advisory Team 42 files, General Records box 9.

37. MAT II-94, Weekly Activity Report for the Period 16–20 February 1970.

38. 173rd Airborne Brigade, ORLL for the Period Ending 30 April 1971, inclosure C, CAAR Washington Green, 15, NARG 472, 173rd Airborne Brigade files, S-3 ORLL 69–71 box.

39. Advisory Team 42, 1970 Pacification and Development Plan, Binh Dinh Province, First Phase, 3.

40. 3/506th, Quarterly Historical Report, January–March 1970, inclosure 1, NARG 472, 3rd Battalion, 506th Infantry files, S-3 ORLL 69–70 box; 3/503rd, Quarterly Historical Report, January–March 1970, 23, 26, NARG 472, 3rd Battalion, 503rd Infantry files, Organizational History files; 2/503rd, Quarterly Historical Report, January–March 1970, 1–17, annex D.

41. 3/503rd, Sniper and Night Observation Techniques Report—February 1970, 3 March 1970; 3/503rd, Sniper Progress Report, 31 March 1970, both from NARG 472, 3rd Battalion, 503rd Infantry files, S-3 Command Report 69–71 files.

42. 4th Infantry Division, ORLL for the Period Ending 30 April 1970, 11–16, NARG 472, 4th Infantry Division files, G-3 ORLL box 7; 2nd Brigade, 4th Infantry Division, CAAR Operation Earhart White, 9 April 1970, 4, NARG 472, 2nd Brigade, 4th Infantry Division files, S-3 AARs box 1; 1st Brigade, 4th Infantry Division, CAAR Operation Eichelberger Black, 22 April 1970, NARG 472, 1st Brigade, 4th Infantry Division files, S-3 AARs box 3.

43. COSVN, Resolution 9, July 1969, 32, MACV Command Historian's Collection, USAHEC.

44. "Counterpacification Directive, Binh Dinh Province Party Committee, Region V, 5 August 1969," in Douglas Pike, The History of the Vietnam War (Ann Arbor, MI: University Microfilms International, 1987), Indochina archives unit 1, series 1, section 2, fiche 570.

45. Destatte, "Yellow Star Division," 105.

46. Ibid., 108–109.

47. "Combined Document Exploitation Center, U.S. Element, Communist Document Analysis Report 146/70, 11 December 1970," 1–2, Vietnam Virtual Archive, item 2310908008, http://www.virtualarchive.vietnam.ttu.edu/starweb/virtual/vva/servlet.starweb (accessed 15 March 2015).

48. Pribbenow, Victory in Vietnam, 249.

49. Advisory Team 42, Binh Dinh Province Report for the Period Ending 31 May 1970, 1, NARG 472, MACV Advisory Team 42 files, box 48.

50. Advisory Team 42, Tam Quan Monthly District Reports, 25 January 1970, 1; 26 February 1970, 2; and 25 March 1970, 2, NARG 472, MACV Advisory Team 42 files, General Records box 10.

51. Destatte, "Yellow Star Division," 109.

52. PSG, Binh Dinh Province: The Challenge—1971, 12 June 1971, annex H, Saunders Papers.

53. "Resolution on the Mission of People's Revolutionary Committee, VC Binh Dinh Province Committee, VC Region 5," in Pike, *History of the Vietnam War*, Indochina archives unit 5, section 1, fiche 143.

54. 172nd Military Intelligence Detachment, Preliminary Document Readout 172-220A-70: Translation of a Partially Coded Directive, 25 April 70, 2, NARG 472, 173rd Airborne Brigade files, S-2 Interrogation Reports Jan–June 1970 box.

55. Destatte, "Yellow Star Division," 109.

56. Advisory Team 42, Tam Quan Monthly District Report, 25 April 1970, 1, NARG 472, MACV Advisory Team 42 files, General Records box 10; I Field Force Vietnam, ORLL for the Period Ending 30 April 1970, 23; 3/503rd, Quarterly Historical Report, April–June 1970, 4, NARG 472, 3rd Battalion, 503rd Infantry files, Organizational History files; 1/503rd, Quarterly Historical Report, April–June 1970, 1, NARG 472, 1st Battalion, 503rd Infantry files, Organizational History files.

57. MAT II-94, Weekly Activity Report for the Period 4–9 April 1970, NARG 472, MACV Advisory Team 42 files, General Records box 9.

58. Destatte, "Yellow Star Division," 106–107; "Lessons Learned: Headquarters, 7th Battalion, 15th Artillery, 4 September 1970," 6, DTIC Online, www.dtic.mil /docs/citations/AD0511157 (accessed 27 March 2015).

59. I Field Force Vietnam, ORLL for the Period Ending 30 April 1970, 23, I FFV ORLL 68–69 box, SEAB, CMH; "Lessons Learned: Headquarters, 7th Battalion, 15th Artillery, 4 September 1970," 5–6.

60. Advisory Team 42, Hoai Nhon Monthly District Report, 25 April 1970, 2, NARG 472, MACV Advisory Team 42 files, General Records box 10.

61. Destatte, "Yellow Star Division," 107.

62. Advisory Team 42, Phu My Monthly District Report, April 1970, 1, NARG 472, MACV Advisory Team 42 files, General Records box 10.

63. Ibid., 4–5; I Field Force Vietnam, ORLL for the Period Ending 30 April 1970, 22–23.

64. 173rd Airborne Brigade, CAAR Washington Green, 16; RVN, Ministry of Interior, Office of Undersecretary of State, Field Trip Report 207-BNV/VPTT Binh Dinh Province, 30 December 1970, 2, NARG 472, MACV Advisory Team 42 files, box 48.

65. 3/503rd, Quarterly Historical Report, April–June 1970, 3; 2/503rd, Quarterly Historical Report, April–June 1970, 5–6, NARG 472, 2nd Battalion, 503rd Infantry files, Organizational History files; 1/503rd, Quarterly Historical Report, April–June 1970, 5; 173rd Airborne Brigade, CAAR Washington Green, 16.

66. "A Systems Analysis View of the Vietnam War 1965–1952: Volume 9 (Population Security)," 182, DTIC Online, http://www.dtic.mil/dtic/tr/fulltext/u2/a039316 .pdf (accessed 17 April 2015).

67. Keith W. Nolan, *Into Cambodia: Spring Campaign, Summer Offensive, 1970* (Novato, CA: Presidio Press, 1990), chap. 19; I Field Force Vietnam, ORLL for the

Period Ending 31 July 1970, 10–13, NARG 472, HQ-USARV, ORLL box 3, I FFV file; 4th Infantry Division, ORLL for the Period Ending 31 July 1970, 8–9, NARG 472, 4th Infantry Division files, G-3 ORLL 2/70–7/70 box 7.

68. Advisory Team 42, Tam Quan Monthly District Report, 25 May 1970, 1, NARG 472, MACV Advisory Team 42 files, General Records box 10.

69. Advisory Team 42, Phu My Monthly District Report, May 1970, 1, NARG 472, MACV Advisory Team 42 files, General Records box 10.

70. Advisory Team 42, Binh Dinh Province Report for the Period Ending 31 May 1970, 1.

71. MAT II-94, Weekly Activity Report for the Period 2–8 May 1970, NARG 472, MACV Advisory Team 42 files, General Records box 9.

72. 2/503rd, Quarterly Historical Report, April–June 1970, 6.

73. 1/503rd, After Action Report, Sapper Attack on LZ Graham, 15 May 1970, NARG 472, 1st Battalion, 503rd Infantry files, S-3 AARs.

74. 1/503rd, Quarterly Historical Report, April–June 1970, 4–9; Advisory Team 42, Phu My Monthly District Report, May 1970, 1.

75. 3/503rd, Quarterly Historical Report, April–June 1970, 3; 173rd Airborne Brigade, ORLL for the Period Ending 31 July 1970, 1, NARG 472, 173rd Airborne Brigade files, S-3 ORLL 69–71 box.

76. Advisory Team 42, Tam Quan Monthly District Report, 25 June 70, 1, NARG 472, MACV Advisory Team 42 files, General Records box 10; Advisory Team 42, Binh Dinh Province Report for the Period Ending 30 June 1970, 1, NARG 472, MACV Advisory Team 42 files, box 48.

77. VSSG, Binh Dinh Province: Control Assessment, 28 October 1970, 1.

78. Advisory Team 42, Binh Dinh Province Report for the Period Ending 30 June 1970, 1.

79. Jeffrey Race, *War Comes to Long An: Revolutionary Conflict in a Vietnamese Province* (Berkeley: University of California Press, 1972), 147.

80. VSSG, Binh Dinh Province: Control Assessment, 28 October 1970, 7.

81. Ibid., 6.

82. Advisory Team 42, Hoai An Monthly District Report, January 1970, 1, NARG 472, MACV Advisory Team 42 files, General Records box 10.

83. MAT II-90, Weekly Activity Report, 24 January 1970.

84. MAT II-90, Weekly Activity Report, 31 January 1970; MAT II-44, Weekly Activity Report, 18 January 1970, both from NARG 472, MACV Advisory Team 42 files, General Records box 9.

85. MAT II-90, Weekly Activity Reports, 7 and 14 February 1970, NARG 472, MACV Advisory Team 42 files, General Records box 9.

86. MAT II-90, Weekly Activity Report, 21 February 1970, ibid.

87. MAT II-90, Weekly Activity Report, 28 February 1970, ibid.

88. MAT II-7, Weekly Activity Report, 22 February 1970, ibid.

89. MAT II-90, Weekly Activity Report, 7 February 1970.

90. I Field Force Vietnam, ORLL for the Period Ending 30 April 1970, 17; Advi-

sory Team 42, Hoai An Monthly District Reports, January 1970, 1, and 24 February 1970, 2.

91. MAT II-7, Weekly Activity Report, 17 April 1970, NARG 472, MACV Advisory Team 42 files, General Records box 9; I Field Force Vietnam, ORLL for the Period Ending 30 April 1970, 17.

92. MAT II-90, Weekly Activity Report, 17 April 1970, NARG 472, MACV Advisory Team 42 files, General Records box 9.

93. Advisory Team 42, Hoai An Monthly District Report, 25 April 1970, 3, NARG 472, MACV Advisory Team 42 files, General Records box 10.

94. MAT II-94, Weekly Activity Report for the Period 25–30 May 1970, NARG 472, MACV Advisory Team 42 files, General Records box 9.

95. 173rd Airborne Brigade, ORLL for the Period Ending 31 July 1970, 2; Advisory Team 42, Phu My Monthly District Report, June 1970, 1, NARG 472, MACV Advisory Team 42 files, General Records box 10; I Field Force Vietnam, ORLL for the Period Ending 31 July 1970, 13.

96. Advisory Team 42, Phu My Monthly District Report, June 1970, 1, NARG 472, MACV Advisory Team 42 files, General Records box 10.

97. Advisory Team 42, Phu My Monthly District Report, July 1970, 1, ibid.

98. 173rd Airborne Brigade, CAAR Washington Green, 16–17; 173rd Airborne Brigade, Circular 350-8, 1 May 1970, NARG 472, USARV Command Historian's Collection, box 136; 173rd Airborne Brigade, ORLL for the Period Ending 31 July 1970.

99. Advisory Team 42, Hoai Nhon Monthly District Report, 25 June 1970, NARG 472, MACV Advisory Team 42 files, General Records box 10.

100. Ibid.; 3/503rd, Quarterly Historical Report, April–June 1970, 2–3.

101. 3/503rd, Quarterly Historical Report, April–June 1970, 25.

102. Ibid., 3; Advisory Team 42, Hoai An Monthly District Reports, 25 July 1970, 1, and 25 June 1970, 1, NARG 472, MACV Advisory Team 42 files, General Records box 10.

103. Advisory Team 42, Hoai An Monthly District Report, 25 July 1970, 1.

104. MAT II-90, Weekly Activity Report, 29 May 1970, NARG 472, MACV Advisory Team 42 files, General Records box 9.

105. Ibid.

106. Ibid.

107. MAT II-94, Weekly Activity Reports for the Periods 25–29 January, 8–13 June, and 22–26 June 1970, NARG 472, MACV Advisory Team 42 files, General Records box 9.

108. Letter from Senior RD Cadre Advisor—Binh Dinh Province to DEP-CORDS CTZ (AVFA-CORDS-ODO-RDC), 20 July 1970, NARG 472, MACV Advisory Team 42 files, box 50.

109. MAT II-90, Weekly Activity Report, 29 May 1970.

110. Advisory Team 42, Phu My Monthly District Report, April 1970, 3.

111. MACV, One War: Command Overview, 1968–1972, chap. III, 44; Advisory

Team 42, Binh Dinh Province Reports for the Periods Ending 31 March 1970, 3, and 31 January 1970, 3, NARG 472, MACV Advisory Team 42 files, box 48.

112. Advisory Team 42, Binh Dinh Province Report for the Period Ending 31 May 1970, 3.

113. Advisory Team 42, Binh Dinh Province Reports for the Periods Ending 30 June 1970, 4, and 31 July 1970, 4, NARG 472, MACV Advisory Team 42 files, box 48.

114. Binh Dinh Sector, PD Plan Achievement Report: 1st Phase from Jan 1 to June 30, 1970, 2, NARG 472, MACV Advisory Team 42 files, General Records box 12.

115. PSG, Binh Dinh Province: The Challenge—1971, annex E.

116. Advisory Team 42, Tam Quan Monthly District Report, 25 July 1970; Advisory Team 42, Hoai An Monthly District Report, 25 June 1970, both from NARG 472, MACV Advisory Team 42 files, General Records box 10.

117. PSG, Binh Dinh Province: The Challenge—1971, annex E.

118. Dale Andrade, *Ashes to Ashes: The Phoenix Program and the Vietnam War* (Lexington, MA: Lexington Books, 1990), 221; Advisory Team 42, Binh Dinh Province Reports for the Periods Ending 30 April 1970, 1, and 30 June 1970, NARG 472, MACV Advisory Team 42 files, box 48.

119. Andrade, *Ashes to Ashes*, 221.

120. Advisory Team 42, Phu My Monthly District Report, May 1970.

121. PSG, Binh Dinh Province: The Challenge—1971, annex E.

122. Advisory Team 42, Tam Quan Monthly District Report, 25 May 1970; Advisory Team 42, Hoai An Monthly District Reports, 24 February and 25 March 1970, NARG 472, MACV Advisory Team 42 files, General Records box 10.

123. "Political Indoctrination and Postal-Transportation and Communication, VC Binh Dinh Prov, VC Region 5," in Pike, *History of the Vietnam War*, Indochina archives unit 5, section 1, fiche 144.

Chapter Seven. The Red Queen's Race

1. MACV, One War: Command Overview, 1968–1972, chap. III, 44, SEAB, CMH.

2. Lewis Sorley, *Vietnam Chronicles: The Abrams Tapes, 1968–1972* (Lubbock: Texas Tech University Press, 2004), 331.

3. "A Systems Analysis View of the Vietnam War 1965–1952: Volume 9 (Population Security)," 132, DTIC Online, http://www.dtic.mil/dtic/tr/fulltext/u2/a039316.pdf (accessed 17 April 2015).

4. David W. P. Elliott, *The Vietnamese War: Revolution and Social Change in the Mekong Delta, 1930–1975*, 2 vols. (Armonk, NY: M. E. Sharpe, 2001), 2:1169.

5. HES, Summary Reports, 30 April and 30 June 1970, MACV Command Historian's Collection, USAHEC.

6. Headquarters, I Field Force Vietnam, Status of Pacification Effort, 14 February 1970, inclosure 1, 7, CORDS Overviews 1969–1970 box, SEAB, CMH.

7. VSSG, Final Copy of Panel 2 Work, Ceasefire Outcomes, 24 June 1970, 13, VSSG files, cabinet 53, SEAB, CMH.

8. VSSG, Ceasefire Study, Province Summaries, 5, VSSG files, cabinet 53, SEAB, CMH.

9. MACV, One War: Command Overview, 1968–1972, chap. III, 45.

10. Advisory Team 42, Binh Dinh Province Report for the Period Ending 30 September 1970, 4, NARG 472, MACV Advisory Team 42 files, box 48; MAT II-90, Weekly Activity Report, 7 September 1970, NARG 472, MACV Advisory Team 42 files, General Records box 9.

11. MAT II-50, Weekly Activity Report, 24 October 1970, NARG 472, MACV Advisory Team 42 files, General Records box 9.

12. MAT II-90, Weekly Activity Report, 29 August 1970, ibid.

13. MAT II-91, Weekly Activity Report, 19 September 1970, ibid.

14. Advisory Team 42, Memorandum—Subject: Village/Hamlet Defense Plans, 19 October 1970, NARG 472, MACV Advisory Team 42 files, box 50, Office General Management (70) files.

15. MAT II-50, Weekly Activity Report, 29 May 1970, NARG 472, MACV Advisory Team 42 files, General Records box 9.

16. 1st Brigade, 4th Infantry Division, ORLL for the Period Ending 31 October 1969, NARG 472, 1st Brigade, 4th Infantry Division files, S-3 ORLL 67–70 box 1.

17. MAT II-94, Weekly Activity Report, 26 June 1970, NARG 472, MACV Advisory Team 42 files, General Records box 9.

18. MAT II-7, Weekly Activity Report, 26 November 1970, ibid.

19. Advisory Team 42, Combat After Action Report, 20 August 1970, 3, NARG 472, MACV Advisory Team 42 files, box 47, After Action Reports (70) file.

20. Advisory Team 42, Combat After Action Report, 22 March 1970, 1–2, ibid.

21. MAT II-47, Weekly Activity Report, 29 August 1970, NARG 472, MACV Advisory Team 42 files, General Records box 9.

22. Department of the Army, Senior Officer Debriefing Report: Brigadier General R. Ochs, CG, 173rd Airborne Brigade, Period 10 August 1970 through 15 January 1971, 26 March 1971, 4, Saunders Papers; Shelby L. Stanton, *Vietnam Order of Battle* (New York: Galahad Books, 1987), 327.

23. 173rd Airborne Brigade, ORLL for the Period Ending 31 July 1970, 2, NARG 472, 173rd Airborne Brigade files, S-3 ORLL 69–71 box.

24. 2/503rd, Quarterly Historical Report, April–June 1970, 7, NARG 472, 2nd Battalion, 503rd Infantry files, Organizational History files; Advisory Team 42, Hoai Nhon Monthly District Report, 25 September 1970, 2, NARG 472, MACV Advisory Team 42 files, General Records box 10; Department of the Army, Senior Officer Debriefing Report: Ochs, 1–4.

25. 4/503rd, Combat After Action Report: Operation Facelift (Phase II), 21 October 1970, 5, NARG 472, 4th Battalion, 503rd Infantry files, Command Reporting files box, S-3 AAR, 4/69–12/70 file.

26. Department of the Army, Senior Officer Debriefing Report: Ochs, 3–4; Advisory Team 42, Binh Dinh Province Report for the Period Ending 31 October 1970, 2, NARG 472, MACV Advisory Team 42 files, box 48.

27. Advisory Team 42, Binh Dinh Province Report for the Period Ending 31 Oc-

tober 1970, 2; Advisory Team 42, Hoai Nhon Monthly District Report, 24 October 1970, 1; Advisory Team 42, Tam Quan Monthly District Report, 25 September 1970, 1, NARG 472, MACV Advisory Team 42 files, General Records box 10.

28. Advisory Team 42, Binh Dinh Province Report for the Period Ending 31 October 1970, 2.

29. James R. McDonough, *Platoon Leader* (Novato, CA: Presidio Press, 1985), 80–91.

30. Ibid., 102–112.

31. Advisory Team 42, Tam Quan Monthly District Report, 25 October 1970, 1, NARG 472, MACV Advisory Team 42 files, General Records box 10.

32. Department of the Army, Senior Officer Debriefing Report: Ochs, 7–8.

33. Ibid., 8; Lt. Col. Jack B. Farris Jr., "The Fire Surveillance Support Base," in *A Distant Challenge: The US Infantryman in Vietnam, 1967–1972*, ed. Lt. Col. Albert N. Garland (Nashville, TN: Battery Press, 1983), 285–291.

34. Department of the Army, Senior Officer Debriefing Report: Ochs, 8.

35. Farris, "Fire Surveillance Support Base," 289.

36. Ibid., 290.

37. 3/503rd, Quarterly Historical Report, October–December 1970, 21, NARG 472, 3rd Battalion, 503rd Infantry files, Organizational History files.

38. Department of the Army, Senior Officer Debriefing Report: Ochs, 5.

39. 173rd Airborne Brigade, ORLL for the Period Ending 31 October 1970, 1, NARG 472, 173rd Airborne Brigade files, S-3 ORLL 69–71 box.

40. Department of the Army, Senior Officer Debriefing Report: Ochs, 5.

41. Ibid.; Advisory Team 42, Binh Dinh Province Report for the Period Ending 30 November 1970, 3, NARG 472, MACV Advisory Team 42 files, box 48.

42. Advisory Team 42, Binh Dinh Province Reports for the Periods Ending 30 September 1970, 4, and 30 November 1970, 3, NARG 472, MACV Advisory Team 42 files, box 48.

43. Advisory Team 42, Binh Dinh Province Reports for the Periods Ending 30 September 1970, 4; 31 October 1970, 4–5; 30 November 1970, 3; and 31 December 1970, 5–6, NARG 472, MACV Advisory Team 42 files, box 48.

44. Advisory Team 42, Phu My Monthly District Report, 26 December 1970, 2, NARG 472, MACV Advisory Team 42 files, General Records box 10.

45. Advisory Team 42, Hoai Nhon Monthly District Report, 24 October 1970.

46. Advisory Team 42, Binh Dinh Province Report for the Period Ending 30 November 1970, 3.

47. Advisory Team 42, Phu My Monthly District Report, 24 August 1970, 2, NARG 472, MACV Advisory Team 42 files, General Records box 10.

48. Ibid.

49. Advisory Team 42, Hoai Nhon Monthly District Reports, 25 August 1970, 3, and 25 September 1970, 4, NARG 472, MACV Advisory Team 42 files, General Records box 10.

50. Advisory Team 42, Hoai An Monthly District Report, 26 November 1970, 2, NARG 472, MACV Advisory Team 42 files, General Records box 10.

51. Ibid., 1.

52. Advisory Team 42, Hoai An Monthly District Report, 25 October 1970, 1, NARG 472, MACV Advisory Team 42 files, General Records box 10; Shelby L. Stanton, *Rangers at War: Combat Recon in Vietnam* (New York: Ballantine Books, 1992), 192–193.

53. Tad Szulc, "Expert Now Gloomy in Report to Nixon on Vietcong Power," *New York Times*, 3 December 1970, 9.

54. 4th Infantry Division, ORLL for the Period Ending 31 October 1970, 8–9, NARG 472, 4th Infantry Division files, G-3 ORLL box 7; 173rd Airborne Brigade, ORLL for the Period Ending 31 July 1970, 2; Advisory Team 42, Phu My Monthly District Report, 25 September 1970, 1, NARG 472, MACV Advisory Team 42 files, General Records box 10.

55. Advisory Team 42, Binh Dinh Province Reports for the Periods Ending 31 October 1970, 1, and 31 July 1970, 1, NARG 472, MACV Advisory Team 42 files, box 48; Advisory Team 42, Tam Quan Monthly District Report, 25 July 1970, 1; Hoai Nhon Monthly District Report, 25 July 1970, 1; Hoai An Monthly District Report, 25 July 1970, 1; and Phu My Monthly District Report, 24 July 1970, 1, all from NARG 472, MACV Advisory Team 42 files, General Records box 10.

56. VSSG, Binh Dinh Province: Control Assessment, 28 October 1970, Percent Rural Population Control Chart, Saunders Papers.

57. 1/503rd, Quarterly Historical Report, July–September 1970, 1, NARG 472, 1st Battalion, 503rd Infantry files, Organizational History files.

58. Robert J. Destatte, trans., "The Yellow Star Division: A History" (unpublished, n.d., CMH), 114–115.

59. Ibid., 115.

60. 173rd Airborne Brigade, Intelligence Bulletin 5-70: Disbandment of 3d NVA Div, 6, NARG 472, 173rd Airborne Brigade files, S-2 Command Reports box.

61. VSSG, Binh Dinh Province: Control Assessment, 10; Advisory Team 42, Binh Dinh Province Report for the Period Ending 31 August 1970, 2, NARG 472, MACV Advisory Team 42 files, box 48.

62. Advisory Team 42, Binh Dinh Province Report for the Period Ending 30 September 1970, 1–3.

63. Advisory Team 42, Tam Quan Monthly District Report, 25 September 1970, 1.

64. Advisory Team 42, Binh Dinh Province Report for the Period Ending 30 September 1970, 1.

65. Ibid., 2; I Field Force Vietnam, PERINTREP 38-70, 13–19 September 1970, and PERINTREP 39-70, 20–26 September 1970, MACV Command Historian's Collection, USAHEC.

66. Advisory Team 42, Hoai An Monthly District Reports, 25 July and 25 August 1970, NARG 472, MACV Advisory Team 42 files, General Records box 10; 3/503rd, Quarterly Historical Report, July–September 1970, NARG 472, 3rd Battalion, 503rd Infantry files, Organizational History files.

67. Advisory Team 42, Hoai An Monthly District Report, 25 September 1970, 1, NARG 472, MACV Advisory Team 42 files, General Records box 10.

68. 3/503rd, Quarterly Historical Report, October–December 1970, 4, 20; 173rd Airborne Brigade, ORLL for the Period Ending 30 April 1971, inclosure C, CAAR Washington Green, 18, NARG 472, 173rd Airborne Brigade files, S-3 ORLL 69–71 box.

69. 173rd Airborne Brigade, Combat After Action Interview Report—FSB Washington, 15 October 1970, NARG 472, 173rd Airborne Brigade files, Named Operation CAAR files.

70. 3/503rd, Quarterly Historical Report, October–December 1970, 4, 21.

71. Advisory Team 42, Hoai An Monthly District Reports, 25 September 1970, 1, and 25 October 1970, 1; MAT II-90, Weekly Activity Report, 6 November 1970, NARG 472, MACV Advisory Team 42 files, General Records box 9.

72. Advisory Team 42, Binh Dinh Province Report for the Period Ending 30 November 1970, 1; MAT II-50, Weekly Activity Report, 31 October 1970, NARG 472, MACV Advisory Team 42 files, General Records box 9.

73. MAT II-44, Weekly Activity Report, 5 November 1970, NARG 472, MACV Advisory Team 42 files, General Records box 9.

74. Advisory Team 42, Combat After Action Report, 19 November 1970, 1–2, NARG 472, MACV Advisory Team 42 files, box 47, After Action Reports.

75. Ibid., 2.

76. Advisory Team 42, Hoai An Monthly District Report, 26 November 1970, 2.

77. Advisory Team 42, Binh Dinh Province Report for the Period Ending 30 November 1970, 2; 173rd Airborne Brigade, CAAR Washington Green, 18; MAT II-101, Weekly Activity Report, 6 December 1970, and MAT II-90, Weekly Activity Report, 24 December 1970, NARG 472, MACV Advisory Team 42 files, General Records box 9.

78. Advisory Team 42, Binh Dinh Province Report for the Period Ending 31 December 1970, 7.

79. Advisory Team 42, Tam Quan Monthly District Report, 25 May 1970, 2, NARG 472, MACV Advisory Team 42 files, General Records box 10.

80. Advisory Team 42, Binh Dinh Province Reports for the Periods Ending 31 August 1970, 3, and 30 November 1970, 5.

81. VSSG, Binh Dinh Province: Control Assessment, 10.

82. Advisory Team 42, Binh Dinh Province Report for the Period Ending 31 March 1970, 4, NARG 472, MACV Advisory Team 42 files, box 48.

83. Advisory Team 42, Binh Dinh Province Report for the Period Ending 30 November 1970, 5.

84. Advisory Team 42, Binh Dinh Province Reports for the Periods Ending 31 January 1971, 5, and 28 February 1971, 4, Saunders Papers.

85. Advisory Team 42, Binh Dinh Province Report for the Period Ending 31 December 1970, 1.

86. Commanding General, 173rd Airborne Brigade, Subject: Off Limits Area, 8 December 1970, NARG 472, MACV Advisory Team 42 files, box 50, Office Message Reference (70) files.

87. PSG, Anti-American Demonstrations in Qui Nhon, 18 April 1971, 5, Saunders Papers.

88. Nhon Hoa Village Chief to District Chief, Inform: Sub-Sector, S-2, 12 June 1970, NARG 472, MACV Advisory Team 42 files, box 50, Territorial Security Program file; National Police Service Chief of Binh Dinh Province to Province Chief of Binh Dinh Province, Subject: US Army Searched the People's Houses and Seized Their Money and Gold, 15 May 1970, NARG 472, MACV Advisory Team 42 files, General Records box 14, Major Serious Incident (70) file.

89. Maj. Errol E. Clark, District Senior Advisor, Hoai An District, Report of Serious Incident, 8 May 1970, NARG 472, MACV Advisory Team 42 files, General Records box 14, Major Serious Incident (70) file.

90. American Embassy Saigon, Operations Memorandum to Department of State, 21 March 1970, NARG 472, MACV Advisory Team 42 files, box 50, Office General Management (70) files; Binh Dinh Province Chief to Chief of National Police Station Binh Dinh, Lieutenant, Squad Leader of the 22nd Judicial Investigation Military Police Squad, Qui Nhon, 9 November 1970, NARG 472, MACV Advisory Team 42 files, General Records box 14, Major Serious Incident (70) file.

91. Advisory Team 42, Serious Incident Report, 24 February 1970, NARG 472, MACV Advisory Team 42 files, box 50.

92. Ron Baker Jr. questionnaire, 1991, author's research collection.

93. PSG, Anti-American Demonstrations in Qui Nhon, 4.

94. McDonough, *Platoon Leader*, 165.

95. Interview with Lt. Col. Richard F. Timmons, 9 April 1984, 3, Senior Officer Oral History Program, Company Command in Vietnam Series, USAHEC.

96. Interview with John D. Waghelstein, 17 July 1991, author's research collection.

97. Advisory Team 42, Hoai An Monthly District Report, December 1970, 2, NARG 472, MACV Advisory Team 42 files, General Records box 10.

98. 4th Infantry Division, ORLL for the Period Ending 31 October 1970, 8–11; Stanton, *Vietnam Order of Battle*, 75–76.

99. 173rd Airborne Brigade, ORLL for the Period Ending 30 April 1971, 4, NARG 472, 173rd Airborne Brigade files, S-3 ORLL 69–71 box; 173rd Airborne Brigade, CAAR Washington Green, 18.

100. Advisory Team 42, Binh Dinh Province Report for the Period Ending 31 December 1970, 3.

101. PSG, Binh Dinh Province: The Challenge—1971, 12 June 1971, 11, Saunders Papers.

102. Ibid., annex F (Phung Hoang), tab C.

103. Advisory Team 42, Binh Dinh Province Report for the Period Ending 31 December 1970, 5.

104. Col. William J. Mendheim, PSA Briefing, 25 November 1970, Binh Dinh Province, NARG 472, MACV Advisory Team 42 files, box 50, Reference Paper files.

Chapter Eight. Aftershocks

1. Shelby L. Stanton, *Vietnam Order of Battle* (New York: Galahad Books, 1987), 87, 155–156; 173rd Airborne Brigade, ORLL, April 1971, 1–4 NARG 472, 173rd Airborne Brigade files, S-3 ORLL 69–71 box.

2. Telegram, Confidential SPECAT Exclusive for Adm McCain and Adm Moorer from Gen Abrams, 31 January 1971, Miscellaneous and Drug Abuse box, MACV Command Historian's Collection, USAHEC.

3. PSG, Anti-American Demonstrations in Qui Nhon, 18 April 1971, attachments 2, 3, 4, 5, 7, 8, Saunders Papers.

4. Ibid., 17–18.

5. Michael W. Hopson questionnaire, 1991, author's research collection.

6. PSG, Binh Dinh Province: The Challenge—1971, 12 June 1971, 14, Saunders Papers.

7. Brig. Gen. John W. Barnes, Autobiographical Essay, undated, 26–27, SEAB, CMH.

8. Anthony B. Herbert and James T. Wooten, *Soldier* (New York: Holt, Rinehart & Winston, 1973), 312–313, 349, 401.

9. Ibid., 225–229, 363–368; "Lasting Pain, Minimal Punishment," LA Times Online, http://www.latimes.com/news/la-na-vietside20aug20-story.htmlpage=1 (accessed 12 July 2015).

10. Herbert and Wooten, *Soldier*, 279, 396–399.

11. Lee Ewing, "Col. Anthony Herbert: The Unmaking of an Accuser," *Columbia Journalism Review*, September–October 1973, 9.

12. Ibid., 8–9; Barry Lando, "The Herbert Affair," *Atlantic Monthly*, May 1973, 74.

13. "No Case Colonel: A New Twist in a Long Libel Suit, June 21, 2005," Time Magazine Online, http://content.time.com/time/magazine/article/0,9171,1075027,00.html (accessed 21 July 2015).

14. Deborah Nelson and Nick Turse, "A Tortured Past: Documents Show Troops Who Reported Abuse in Vietnam Were Discredited Even as the Military Was Finding Evidence of Worse," *Los Angeles Times*, 20 August 2006.

15. Advisory Team 42, Binh Dinh Province Report for the Period Ending 31 January 1971, 2, Saunders Papers.

16. Robert J. Destatte, trans., "The Yellow Star Division: A History" (unpublished, n.d., CMH), 119–121.

17. Advisory Team 42, Binh Dinh Province Report for the Period Ending 28 February 1971, 2, Saunders Papers.

18. Advisory Team 42, Binh Dinh Province Report for the Period Ending 31 March 1971, 2, Saunders Papers.

19. Advisory Team 42, Binh Dinh Province Report for the Period Ending 30 April 1972, 2, Saunders Papers.

20. Merle L. Pribbenow, trans., *Victory in Vietnam: The Official History of the People's Army of Vietnam, 1954–1975* (Lawrence: University Press of Kansas, 2002), 279.

21. Advisory Team 42, Binh Dinh Province Report for the Period Ending 31 May 1971, 1, Saunders Papers; Destatte, "Yellow Star Division," 121.

22. Advisory Team 42, Binh Dinh Province Report for the Period Ending 31 May 1971, 1.

23. PSG, Binh Dinh Province: The Challenge—1971, 27.

24. John Vann, Senior Advisor II Corps and MR2, Downgrading of HES Reports in Binh Dinh Province, 8 September 1971, 1–4, Saunders Papers.

25. Advisory Team 42, Binh Dinh Province Report for the Period Ending 31 August 1971, 1, Saunders Papers.

26. Advisory Team 42, Binh Dinh Province Report, 3 June 1971, 1, Saunders Papers.

27. Phillip B. Davidson, *Vietnam at War: The History, 1946–1975* (New York: Oxford University Press, 1988), chap. 24; Ngo Quang Truong, *The Easter Offensive of 1972*, Indochina Monographs (Washington, DC: US Army Center of Military History, 1980).

28. Neil Sheehan, *A Bright Shining Lie: John Paul Vann and America in Vietnam* (New York: Random House, 1988), 760.

29. Advisory Team 42, Binh Dinh Province Report for the Period Ending 30 April 1972, 1.

30. Advisory Team 42, Binh Dinh Province Report for the Period Ending 31 May 1972, 1.

31. Advisory Team 42, Binh Dinh Province Report for the Period Ending 30 June 1972, 2, Saunders Papers.

32. Ibid., 1; Advisory Team 42, Binh Dinh Province Report for the Period Ending 31 May 1972, 1.

33. Advisory Team 42, Binh Dinh Province Report for the Period Ending 30 June 1972, 1.

34. Advisory Team 42, Binh Dinh Province Report for the Period Ending 30 April 1972, 1.

35. Davidson, *Vietnam at War*, chap. 24.

36. Destatte, "Yellow Star Division," 177–178.

37. Advisory Team 42, Binh Dinh Province Report for the Period Ending 31 July 1972, 1, Saunders Papers.

38. Advisory Team 42, Binh Dinh Province Report for the Period Ending 30 June 1972, 1.

39. Mark Moyar, Donald Kagan, and Frederick Kagan, *A Question of Command: Counterinsurgency from the Civil War to Iraq* (New Haven, CT: Yale University Press, 2009), 161–162.

40. Dale Andrade, *Trial by Fire: The 1972 Nguyen Hue Offensive—America's Last Vietnam Battle* (New York: Hippocrene Books, 1995), 532.

41. James H. Willbanks, *The Battle of An Loc, April 1972* (Bloomington: Indiana University Press, 2005); Col. G. H. Turley, *The Easter Offensive: The Last American Advisors, Vietnam 1972* (Novato, CA: Presidio Press, 1985).

42. Sheehan, *Bright Shining Lie*, 778–780.

43. Background Information—Binh Dinh Province (Narrative), no date, 1–2, Miscellaneous CORDS files box, SEAB, CMH.

44. Ngo Quang Truong, *Easter Offensive of 1972*, 172.

45. Destatte, "Yellow Star Division," 189.

46. Advisory Team 42, Binh Dinh Province Reports for the Periods Ending 31 August 1972, 1–2, and 30 September 1972, 1, Saunders Papers.

47. Jeffrey Kimball, *Nixon's Vietnam War* (Lawrence: University Press of Kansas, 1998), 323–346.

48. Davidson, *Vietnam at War*, 641–649.

49. Advisory Team 42, Binh Dinh Province Reports for the Periods Ending 31 October 1972, 1–2, and 30 November 1972, 1, Saunders Papers.

50. William Burr and Jeffrey Kimball, *Nixon's Nuclear Specter: The Secret Alert of 1969, Madman Diplomacy, and the Vietnam War* (Lawrence: University Press of Kansas, 2015), 321–325; Cao Van Vien, *The Final Collapse*, Indochina Monographs (Washington, DC: US Army Center of Military History, 1983), 16–26; Davidson, *Vietnam at War*, 649–656.

51. Col. William E. Le Gro, *Vietnam from Cease-fire to Capitulation* (Washington, DC: US Army Center of Military History, 1985), 24.

52. Advisory Team 42, Binh Dinh Province Report for the Period Ending 31 January 1971, 1, Saunders Papers.

53. Pribbenow, *Victory in Vietnam*, 335.

54. Ibid., 335–337.

55. Le Gro, *Vietnam from Cease-fire to Capitulation*, chaps. 4–14.

56. Ibid., 147–149.

57. Ibid., 150–161; Cao Van Vien, *Final Collapse*, 88–95.

58. Le Gro, *Vietnam from Cease-fire to Capitulation*, 161–163; Cao Van Vien, *Final Collapse*, 117–118.

Conclusion: Triumph Mistaken

1. Chester L. Cooper, Judith Corson, et al., *The American Experience with Pacification in Vietnam*, 3 vols., Report R-185 (Arlington, VA: Institute for Defense Analysis, 1972), 2:71.

2. PSG, Binh Dinh Province: The Challenge—1971, 12 June 1971, 25, Saunders Papers.

3. Mark Moyar, *Phoenix and the Birds of Prey: Counterinsurgency and Counterterrorism in Vietnam* (Lincoln: University of Nebraska Press, 2007), 322.

4. Advisory Team 42, Binh Dinh Province Report for the Period Ending 31 December 1970, 4, NARG 472, MACV Advisory Team 42 files, box 48.

5. James R. McDonough, *Platoon Leader* (Novato, CA: Presidio Press, 1985), 136–137.

6. Stephen J. Piotrowski questionnaire, 1991, author's research collection.

7. Interview with John D. Waghelstein, 17 July 1991, author's research collection.

8. Richard A. Hunt Jr., *Pacification: The American Struggle for Vietnam's Hearts and Minds* (Boulder, CO: Westview Press, 1995), 227.

9. Jeffrey Race, *War Comes to Long An: Revolutionary Conflict in a Vietnamese Province* (Berkeley: University of California Press, 1972), xix; Eric M. Bergerud, *The Dynamics of Defeat: The Vietnam War in Hau Nghia Province* (Boulder, CO: Westview Press, 1991), xiii; David W. P. Elliott, *The Vietnamese War: Revolution and Social Change in the Mekong Delta, 1930–1975*, 2 vols. (Armonk, NY: M. E. Sharpe, 2001); Alan D. Weathers, "Western Nam Bo: The War in the Lower Mekong Delta" (Ph.D. diss., University of Maine, 2000).

10. PSG, Binh Dinh Province: The Challenge—1971, annex C, 1.

11. Ibid., 5.

12. Ibid., 6.

13. Moyar, *Phoenix and the Birds of Prey*, 360.

14. Office of the Deputy Assistant Secretary of Defense for Systems Analysis, Southeast Asia Analysis Report, September 1972, 1–2, MACV Command Historian's Collection, USAHEC.

15. Tad Szulc, "Expert Now Gloomy in Report to Nixon on Vietcong Power," *New York Times*, 3 December 1970, 1, 9.

16. Office of the Deputy Assistant Secretary of Defense for Systems Analysis, Southeast Asia Analysis Report, June/July 1971, 2, MACV Command Historian's Collection, USAHEC.

17. Ibid., 6.

18. "A Systems Analysis View of the Vietnam War 1965–1952: Volume 9 (Population Security)," 258, DTIC Online, http://www.dtic.mil/dtic/tr/fulltext/u2/a039316.pdf (accessed 17 April 2015).

19. Kevin M. Boylan, "Goodnight Saigon: American Provincial Advisors' Final Impressions of the Vietnam War," *Journal of Military History* 78, 1 (January 2014): 243–247.

20. Moyar, *Phoenix and the Birds of Prey*, 428n.

21. Ibid., 240.

22. Ibid., 246.

23. Thomas L. Ahern Jr., *Vietnam Declassified: The CIA and Counterinsurgency* (Lexington: University Press of Kentucky, 2010), 338.

24. Ibid., 349.

25. Hunt, *Pacification*, 260.

26. "A Systems Analysis View of the Vietnam War 1965–1952: Volume 9 (Population Security)," 231–232.

27. Boylan, "Goodnight Saigon," 238–242.

28. "The Hamlet Evaluation System (HES) Reports, 21 January 1972," 3, Virtual Vietnam Archive, item 2160103005, http://www.virtualarchive.vietnam.ttu.edu/starweb/virtual/vva/ servlet.starweb (accessed 12 August 2015).

29. Department of the Army, Office of the Adjutant General, Senior Officer Debriefing Report: Colonel Robert S. McGowan, Senior Advisor, Quang Ngai Province, Nov 71–Jul 72, 4, NARG 472, NND 972624, box 291.

30. HES Summary Reports, 31 December 1970 and 28 February 1971, MACV Command Historian's Collection, USAHEC.

31. "A Systems Analysis View of the Vietnam War 1965–1952: Volume 9 (Population Security)," 240.

32. Ibid., 248–251.

33. Ibid., 191.

34. Ibid., 278.

35. Ibid., 272.

36. Ibid., 273.

37. "A Systems Analysis View of the Vietnam War 1965–1952: Volume 1 (The Situation in Southeast Asia)," 95, DTIC Online, http://www.dtic.mil/dtic/tr/fulltext/u2/a039313.pdf (accessed 17 April 2015).

38. Merle L. Pribbenow, trans., *Victory in Vietnam: The Official History of the People's Army of Vietnam, 1954–1975* (Lawrence: University Press of Kansas, 2002), 282.

39. Weathers, "Western Nam Bo," 115.

40. HES Summary Reports, 31 March 1972 and 31 January 1973, MACV Command Historian's Collection, USAHEC.

41. CORDS, Province Advisor's Completion of Tour Report, LTC John M. McDonald, 15 February 1973, 3, safe 75, drawer 2, folder 10 Phu Yen, SEAB, CMH.

42. Ahern, *Vietnam Declassified*, 350.

43. Mark Moyar, *Triumph Forsaken: The Vietnam War, 1954–1965* (Cambridge: Cambridge University Press, 2006), 93–94.

44. Moyar, *Phoenix and the Birds of Prey*, 315–316.

45. Race, *War Comes to Long An*; Elliott, *Vietnamese War*.

46. Robert L. Sansom, *The Economics of Insurgency in the Mekong Delta of Vietnam* (Cambridge, MA: MIT Press, 1970).

47. James W. Trullinger, *Village at War: An Account of Revolution in Vietnam* (New York: Longman, 1980), 111.

48. Ibid., 143.

49. Ahern, *Vietnam Declassified*, 362.

50. Office of the Assistant Deputy for CORDS, I Field Force Vietnam, A Personal Mid-Tour Report, Willard E. Chambers, 10 March 1970, 2, NARG 472, NND 994025, box 11.

51. Richard Clutterbuck, *Riot and Revolution in Singapore and Malaya, 1945–1963* (London: Faber & Faber, 1973), 195.

52. Ahern, *Vietnam Declassified*, 374.

53. Interview with Lt. Gen. Arthur S. Collins, 1982, 2:363, Senior Officer Oral History Program, USAHEC.

54. Boylan, "Goodnight Saigon," 265–269.

55. Headquarters MACV, Senior Officer Debriefing Report of LTC John L. Keefe, Deputy Province Senior Advisor, Chau Doc Province, 8 February 1973, 5, Senior Officer Oral History Program files, USAHEC.

56. CORDS Advisory Team 72, Province Senior Advisor Completion of Tour

Report, LTC Robert C. Hallmark, 12 February 1973, 7, NARG 472, NND 927624, box 280.

57. Ngo Quang Truong, *RVNAF and US Operational Cooperation and Coordination*, Indochina Monographs (Washington, DC: US Army Center of Military History, 1980), 183.

58. Harry G. Summers Jr., foreword to Moyar, *Phoenix and the Birds of Prey*, xii.

59. Lewis Sorley, *A Better War: The Unexamined Victories and Final Tragedy of America's Last Years in Vietnam* (New York: Harcourt Brace, 1999), 217–218.

60. Mark Moyar, Donald Kagan, and Frederick Kagan, *A Question of Command: Counterinsurgency from the Civil War to Iraq* (New Haven, CT: Yale University Press, 2009), 163.

61. Jeffrey Kimball, *Nixon's Vietnam War* (Lawrence: University Press of Kansas, 1998), 91.

62. Associated Press, "U.S. Pacification Aide Quits Post," *Chicago Tribune*, 16 November 1972, 18.

63. Ibid.

64. Ibid.

65. Douglas Blaufarb, *The Counterinsurgency Era: U.S. Doctrine and Performance, 1950 to the Present* (New York: Free Press, 1977), 304–305.

66. James H. Willbanks, *A Raid Too Far: Operation Lam Son 719 and Vietnamization in Laos* (College Station: Texas A&M University Press, 2014), 169.

67. "Oval Office Conversation 760-6, Nixon and Kissinger, 3 August 1972," Nixon Presidential Library, http://www.nixonlibrary.gov/forresearchers/find/tapes/finding_aids/august1972.php (accessed 6 October 2015).

68. "EOB Conversation no. 371-19, Nixon and Haig, 23 October 1972," Nixon Presidential Library, http://www.nixonlibrary.gov/forresearchers/find/tapes/finding_aids/october1972.php (accessed 6 October 2015).

69. Richard W. Stewart, ed., *American Military History*, vol. 2, *The United States Army in a Global Era, 1917–2003* (Washington, DC: US Army Center of Military History, 2005), 364.

70. Samuel Lipsman and Edward Doyle, *Fighting for Time: The Vietnam Experience* (Boston: Boston Publishing Company, 1983), 67.

Bibliography

Archives
Defense Technical Information Center (DTIC) Online
National Archives and Records Administration (NARA), Archives II, College Park, MD
US Army Center of Military History (CMH), Fort McNair, Washington, DC
US Army Heritage and Education Center (USAHEC), Carlisle, PA
Vietnam Center and Virtual Archive, Texas Tech University, Lubbock, TX, http://www.vietnam.ttu.edu/virtualarchive/

Books, Articles, and Dissertations
Ahern, Thomas L., Jr. *Vietnam Declassified: The CIA and Counterinsurgency.* Lexington: University Press of Kentucky, 2010.
Alsop, Joseph. "Briton's Report on Vietnam Must Have Heartened Nixon." *Washington Post*, 5 December 1969.
———. "Need to Defend VC Structure Puts Hanoi's Forces in Bind." *Los Angeles Times*, 24 September 1969.
Andrade, Dale. *Ashes to Ashes: The Phoenix Program and the Vietnam War.* Lexington, MA: Lexington Books, 1990.
———. *Trial by Fire: The 1972 Nguyen Hue Offensive—America's Last Vietnam Battle.* New York: Hippocrene Books, 1995.
Ashworth, George W. "All-Out Pacification: Viet Area Sharpens Its Plowshare." *Christian Science Monitor,* 13 September 1969.
Associated Press. "U.S. Pacification Aide Quits Post." *Chicago Tribune,* 16 November 1972, 18.
Belote, James H., and William M. Belote. *Corregidor: The Saga of a Fortress.* New York: Harper & Row, 1967.
Bergerud, Eric M. *The Dynamics of Defeat: The Vietnam War in Hau Nghia Province.* Boulder, CO: Westview Press, 1991.
Berman, Paul. *Revolutionary Organization: Revolutionary Institution Building within the People's Liberation Armed Forces.* Lexington, MA: Lexington Books, 1974.
Berry, F. Clifton, Jr. *Sky Soldiers: The Illustrated History of the Vietnam War,* vol. 2. New York: Bantam Books, 1987.
Birtle, Andrew J. "PROVN, Westmoreland and the Historians: A Reappraisal." *Journal of Military History* 72 (October 2008): 1213–1247.

Blaufarb, Douglas. *The Counterinsurgency Era: U.S. Doctrine and Performance, 1950 to the Present.* New York: Free Press, 1977.

Boylan, Kevin M. "Goodnight Saigon: American Provincial Advisors' Final Impressions of the Vietnam War." *Journal of Military History* 78, 1 (January 2014): 233–270.

Brigham, Robert K. *ARVN: Life and Death in the South Vietnamese Army.* Lawrence: University Press of Kansas, 2006.

Burchett, Wilfred. *Vietnam: Inside Story of the Guerrilla War.* New York: International Publishers, 1965.

Burr, William, and Jeffrey Kimball. *Nixon's Nuclear Specter: The Secret Alert of 1969, Madman Diplomacy, and the Vietnam War.* Lawrence: University Press of Kansas, 2015.

Cao Van Vien. *The Final Collapse.* Indochina Monographs. Washington, DC: US Army Center of Military History, 1983.

———. *The U.S. Adviser.* Indochina Monographs. Washington, DC: US Army Center of Military History, 1980.

Choinski, Col. Walter F. *Republic of Vietnam: Country Study.* US Department of Defense, Military Assistance Institute/American Institutes for Research, 1965.

Cima, Ronald J., ed. *Vietnam: A Country Study.* Washington, DC: Government Printing Office, 1987.

Clarke, Jeffrey. *Advice and Support: The Final Years, 1965–1973.* Washington, DC: US Army Center of Military History, 1988.

Clodfelter, Mark. *The Limits of Airpower: The American Bombing of North Vietnam.* New York: Free Press, 1989.

Clutterbuck, Richard. *Riot and Revolution in Singapore and Malaya, 1945–1963.* London: Faber & Faber, 1973.

Colby, William, and James McCargar. *Lost Victory: A Firsthand Account of America's Sixteen-Year Involvement in Vietnam.* New York: Contemporary Books, 1989.

Cooper, Chester L., Judith Corson, et al. *The American Experience with Pacification in Vietnam.* 3 vols. Report R-185. Arlington, VA: Institute for Defense Analysis, 1972.

Corson, William R. *The Betrayal.* New York: W. W. Norton, 1968.

Daddis, Gregory. *No Sure Victory: Measuring U.S. Army Effectiveness and Progress in the Vietnam War.* New York: Oxford University Press, 2011.

Davidson, Phillip B. *Secrets of the Vietnam War.* Novato, CA: Presidio Press, 1988.

———. *Vietnam at War: The History, 1946–1975.* New York: Oxford University Press, 1988.

Destatte, Robert J., trans. "The Yellow Star Division: A History." Unpublished, n.d. US Army Center of Military History, Washington, DC.

Dommen, Arthur J. *The Indochinese Experience of the French and Americans: Nationalism and Communism in Cambodia, Laos and Vietnam.* Bloomington: Indiana University Press, 2002.

Duiker, William J. *The Communist Road to Power in Vietnam.* Boulder, CO: Westview Press, 1981.

Elliott, David W. P. *The Vietnamese War: Revolution and Social Change in the Mekong Delta, 1930–1975.* 2 vols. Armonk, NY: M. E. Sharpe, 2001.

Ewing, Lee. "Col. Anthony Herbert: The Unmaking of an Accuser." *Columbia Journalism Review,* September–October 1973, 8–14.

Fall, Bernard B. *Hell in a Very Small Place: The Siege of Dien Bien Phu.* Philadelphia: J. B. Lippincott, 1966.

———. "The Theory and Practice of Insurgency and Counterinsurgency." *Naval War College Review,* April 1965, 21–38.

Friendly, Alfred. "British Expert Predicts Secure Vietnam by 1972." *Washington Post,* 16 December 1969.

Garland, Lt. Col. Albert N., ed. *A Distant Challenge: The US Infantryman in Vietnam, 1967–1972.* Nashville, TN: Battery Press, 1983.

———. *Infantry in Vietnam: Small Unit Actions in the Early Days, 1965–1966.* Nashville, TN: Battery Press, 1982.

Gastil, Raymond D. *Four Papers on the Vietnamese Insurgency.* Croton-on-Hudson, NY: Hudson Institute, 1967.

Goodman, Allan E. *Politics in War: The Bases of Political Community in South Vietnam.* Cambridge, MA: Harvard University Press, 1973.

Grintchenko, Michel. *Atlante-Arethuse: Une Operation de Pacification en Indochine.* Paris: Economica, 2001.

Hammer, Ellen J. *A Death in November: America in Vietnam, 1963.* New York: E. Dutton, 1987.

Herbert, Anthony B., and James T. Wooten. *Soldier.* New York: Holt, Rinehart & Winston, 1973.

Herrington, Stuart. *Silence Was a Weapon: The Vietnam War in the Villages.* Novato, CA: Presidio Press, 1982.

Hickey, Gerald C. *Village in Vietnam.* New Haven, CT: Yale University Press, 1964.

Hunt, Richard A., Jr. *Pacification: The American Struggle for Vietnam's Hearts and Minds.* Boulder, CO: Westview Press, 1995.

———, ed. *Lessons from an Unconventional War: Reassessing U.S. Strategies for Future Conflicts.* New York: Pergamon Press, 1982.

Hymoff, Edward. *The First Air Cavalry Division—Vietnam.* New York: M. W. Lads, 1967.

Kaiser, Robert G. "The New Optimists II: Pacification (1969 Style) Seems to Be Working." *Washington Post,* 30 October 1969, A-23.

Kelly, Orr. "Binh Dinh Province: General Tells of Pacification Success." *Washington Post,* 11 October 1969, 1.

Kimball, Jeffrey. *Nixon's Vietnam War.* Lawrence: University Press of Kansas, 1998.

———. "The Stab-in-the-Back Legend and the Vietnam War." *Armed Forces and Society* 14, 3 (Spring 1988): 433–458.

Koburger, Charles W. E., Jr. *The French Navy in Indochina: Riverine and Coastal Forces, 1945–1954.* New York: Praeger, 1991.

Kolko, Gabriel. *Anatomy of a War: Vietnam, the United States, and the Modern Historical Experience.* New York: Pantheon Books, 1985.

Krepinevich, Andrew. *The Army and Vietnam*. Baltimore: Johns Hopkins University Press, 1986.

Lando, Barry. "The Herbert Affair." *Atlantic Monthly*, May 1973, 73–81.

Lansdale, Edward G. *In the Midst of Wars: An American's Mission to Southeast Asia*. New York: Harper & Row, 1972.

Le Gro, Col. William E. *Vietnam from Cease-fire to Capitulation*. Washington, DC: US Army Center of Military History, 1985.

Lewy, Guenter. *America in Vietnam*. New York: Oxford University Press, 1978.

Lind, Michael. *Vietnam—The Necessary War: A Reinterpretation of America's Most Disastrous Military Conflict*. New York: Free Press, 1999.

Lipsman, Samuel, and Edward Doyle. *Fighting for Time: The Vietnam Experience*. Boston: Boston Publishing Company, 1983.

Logevall, Fredrik. *Embers of War: The Fall of an Empire and the Making of America's Vietnam*. New York: Random House, 2012.

MacGarrigle, George L. *Combat Operations: Taking the Offensive, October 1966 to October 1967, the United States Army in Vietnam*. Washington, DC: US Army Center of Military History, 1998.

Marr, David G. *Vietnamese Tradition on Trial, 1920–1945*. Berkeley: University of California Press, 1981.

Mataxis, Theodore C. "War in the Highlands: Attack and Counter-attack on Highway 19." *Army*, October 1965, 49–55.

McCoy, James W. *Secrets of the Viet Cong*. New York: Hippocrene Books, 1992.

McDonough, James R. *Platoon Leader*. Novato, CA: Presidio Press, 1985.

McNamara, Robert S. *In Retrospect: The Tragedy and Lessons of Vietnam*. New York: Times Books, 1995.

Meyerson, Harvey. *Vinh Long*. Boston: Houghton Mifflin, 1970.

Ministry of National Defense, Viet Nam Institute of Military History. *Operations in the US Resistance War*. Hanoi: The Gioi Publishers, 2009.

Moyar, Mark. *Phoenix and the Birds of Prey: The CIA's Secret Campaign to Destroy the Viet Cong*. Annapolis, MD: Naval Institute Press, 1997.

———. *Phoenix and the Birds of Prey: Counterinsurgency and Counterterrorism in Vietnam*. Lincoln: University of Nebraska Press, 2007.

———. *Triumph Forsaken: The Vietnam War, 1954–1965*. Cambridge: Cambridge University Press, 2006.

Moyar, Mark, Donald Kagan, and Frederick Kagan. *A Question of Command: Counterinsurgency from the Civil War to Iraq*. New Haven, CT: Yale University Press, 2009.

Murphy, Edward F. *Dak To: The 173d Airborne Brigade in South Vietnam's Central Highlands, June–November 1967*. Novato, CA: Presidio Press, 1993.

Nelson, Deborah, and Nick Turse. "A Tortured Past: Documents Show Troops Who Reported Abuse in Vietnam Were Discredited Even as the Military Was Finding Evidence of Worse." *Los Angeles Times*, 20 August 2006.

Ngo Quang Truong. *The Easter Offensive of 1972*. Indochina Monographs. Washington, DC: US Army Center of Military History, 1980.

———. *RVNAF and US Operational Cooperation and Coordination.* Indochina Monographs. Washington, DC: US Army Center of Military History, 1980.

———. *Territorial Forces.* Indochina Monographs. Washington, DC: US Army Center of Military History, 1981.

Nguyen Truong Giang, Military History Institute of Vietnam. *Tổng kết những trận then chốt chiến dịch trong kháng chiến chống Mỹ* [Summary of the key battles in the campaign of resistance against the American invasion]. Hanoi: People's Army Publishing House, 2009.

Nolan, Keith W. *Into Cambodia: Spring Campaign, Summer Offensive, 1970.* Novato, CA: Presidio Press, 1990.

Palmer, Gen. Bruce, Jr. *The 25-Year War: America's Military Role in Vietnam.* New York: Simon & Schuster, 1985.

The Pentagon Papers: The Defense Department History of United States Decision-making on Vietnam. Senator Gravel ed. 4 vols. Boston: Beacon Press, 1971.

Peterson, Michael E. *The Combined Action Platoons: The U.S. Marines' Other War in Vietnam.* New York: Praeger Publishers, 1989.

Pike, Douglas. *The History of the Vietnam War.* Ann Arbor, MI: University Microfilms International, 1987. Microform.

———. *PAVN: People's Army of Vietnam.* Novato, CA: Presidio Press, 1986.

———. *Vietcong: The Organization and Techniques of the National Liberation Front of South Vietnam.* Cambridge, MA: MIT Press, 1966.

Porter, Gareth. *Vietnam: The Definitive Documentation of Human Decisions.* Stanfordville, NY: E. M. Coleman Enterprises, 1979.

Prados, John. *Vietnam: The History of an Unwinnable War, 1945–1975.* Lawrence: University Press of Kansas, 2009.

Pribbenow, Merle L., trans. *Victory in Vietnam: The Official History of the People's Army of Vietnam, 1954–1975.* Lawrence: University Press of Kansas, 2002.

Race, Jeffrey. *War Comes to Long An: Revolutionary Conflict in a Vietnamese Province.* Berkeley: University of California Press, 1972.

Sansom, Robert L. *The Economics of Insurgency in the Mekong Delta of Vietnam.* Cambridge, MA: MIT Press, 1970.

Sheehan, Neil. *A Bright Shining Lie: John Paul Vann and America in Vietnam.* New York: Random House, 1988.

Shulimson, Jack, and Major Charles M. Johnson, USMC. *U.S. Marines in Vietnam: The Landing and the Buildup—1965.* Washington, DC: US Marine Corps, History and Museums Division, 1978.

Sorley, Lewis. *A Better War: The Unexamined Victories and Final Tragedy of America's Last Years in Vietnam.* New York: Harcourt Brace, 1999.

———. *Thunderbolt: General Creighton Abrams and the Army of His Times.* New York: Simon & Schuster, 1992.

———. *Vietnam Chronicles: The Abrams Tapes, 1968–1972.* Lubbock: Texas Tech University Press, 2004.

———. *Westmoreland: The General Who Lost Vietnam.* Boston: Houghton Mifflin Harcourt, 2011.

Spector, Ronald G. *Advice and Support: The Early Years of the U.S. Army in Vietnam, 1941–1960.* Washington, DC: US Army Center of Military History, 1983.

Stanton, Shelby L. *Anatomy of a Division: The 1st Cav in Vietnam.* Novato, CA: Presidio Press, 1987.

———. *Green Berets at War: U.S. Army Special Forces in Southeast Asia, 1956–1975.* New York: Dell, 1985.

———. *Rangers at War: Combat Recon in Vietnam.* New York: Ballantine Books, 1992.

———. *The Rise and Fall of an American Army: U.S. Ground Forces in Vietnam, 1965–1973.* Stevenage, UK: Spa Books, 1989.

———. *Vietnam Order of Battle.* New York: Galahad Books, 1987.

———. *World War II Order of Battle.* New York: Galahad Books, 1984.

Starry, General Donn A. *Mounted Combat in Vietnam.* Vietnam Studies. Washington, DC: US Army Center of Military History, 1978.

Sterba, James. "U.S. Brigade Uses Unusual Methods to Stress Hamlet Security." *New York Times,* 1 January 1970, 6.

Stewart, Richard W., ed. *American Military History,* vol. 2, *The United States Army in a Global Era, 1917–2003.* Washington, DC: US Army Center of Military History, 2005.

Summers, Harry G. *On Strategy: A Critical Analysis of the Vietnam War.* New York: Dell, 1984.

Szulc, Tad. "Expert Now Gloomy in Report to Nixon on Vietcong Power." *New York Times,* 3 December 1970, 1, 9.

Taylor, Keith W. *A History of the Vietnamese.* Cambridge: Cambridge University Press, 2013.

Thompson, Sir Robert. *No Exit from Vietnam.* New York: David McKay, 1969.

Thompson, W. Scott, and Donaldson D. Frizzell. *The Lessons of Vietnam.* New York: Crane, Russak, 1977.

Tran Dinh Tho. *Pacification.* Indochina Monographs. Washington, DC: US Army Center of Military History, 1980.

Trinquier, Roger. *Le Premier Battalion de Berets Rouges: Indochine, 1947–1949.* Paris: Editions Plon, 1984.

Trullinger, James W. *Village at War: An Account of Revolution in Vietnam.* New York: Longman, 1980.

Turley, Col. G. H. *The Easter Offensive: The Last American Advisors, Vietnam 1972.* Novato, CA: Presidio Press, 1985.

Van Tien Dung. *After Political Failure, the US Imperialists Are Facing Military Defeat in South Vietnam.* Hanoi: Foreign Languages Publishing House, 1966.

Weathers, Alan D. "Western Nam Bo: The War in the Lower Mekong Delta." Ph.D. diss., University of Maine, 2000.

Westmoreland, William C. *A Soldier Reports.* New York: Doubleday, 1976.

Wiest, Andrew A., and Michael Doidge, eds. *Triumph Revisited: Historians Battle for the Vietnam War.* New York: Routledge, 2010.

Willbanks, James H. *Abandoning Vietnam: How America Left and South Vietnam Lost Its War.* Lawrence: University Press of Kansas, 2004.

————. *The Battle of An Loc, April 1972.* Bloomington: Indiana University Press, 2005.

————. *A Raid Too Far: Operation Lam Son 719 and Vietnamization in Laos.* College Station: Texas A&M University Press, 2014.

————. *Vietnam War: The Essential Reference Guide.* Santa Barbara, CA: ABC-CLIO, 2013.

Online Documents

"Company D (Airborne) 16th Armor, 173rd Airborne Brigade." http://www.d16armor 173rd.org/uploads/2/6/4/0/26400706/very_short_history_of_d16th.pdf (accessed 13 March 2015).

"EOB Conversation no. 371-19, Nixon and Haig, 23 October 1972." Nixon Presidential Library. http://www.nixonlibrary.gov/forresearchers/find/tapes/finding _aids/october1972.php (accessed 6 October 2015).

"Lasting Pain, Minimal Punishment." LA Times Online. http://www.latimes.com /news/la-na-vietside20aug20-story.htmlpage=1 (accessed 12 July 2015).

"No Case Colonel: A New Twist in a Long Libel Suit, June 21, 2005." Time Magazine Online. http://content.time.com/time/magazine/article/0,9171,1075027,00 .html (accessed 21 July 2015).

"Obituary: Hubert Cunningham, 75, Clarkston High Graduate." Lewiston Tribune Online. http://lmtribune.com/obituaries/hubert-cunningham-clarkston-high-graduate /article_1fcc8c13-36a0-5003-a179-337bba64c46e.html (accessed 17 March 2015).

"Oval Office Conversation 760-6, Nixon and Kissinger, 3 August 1972." Nixon Presidential Library. http://www.nixonlibrary.gov/forresearchers/find/tapes/finding _aids/august1972.php (accessed 6 October 2015).

"Qui Nhon, 1965: Terrorism Takes a Toll." VFW Magazine Online (February 2015). http://digitaledition.qwinc.com/article/Qui+Nhon,+1965:+Terrorism+Takes +A+Toll/1903942/0/article.html (accessed 22 October 2015).

"Short Range Ambush Platoon, 1968–1969." 1st Battalion 50th Infantry Association online. http://www.ichiban1.org/html/cs_srap.htm (accessed 8 July 2015).

"A Systems Analysis View of the Vietnam War 1965–1952: Volume 1 (The Situation in Southeast Asia)," 95. DTIC Online. http://www.dtic.mil/dtic/tr/fulltext/u2 /a039313.pdf (accessed 17 April 2015).

"A Systems Analysis View of the Vietnam War 1965–1952: Volume 9 (Population Security)," 125. DTIC Online. http://www.dtic.mil/dtic/tr/fulltext/u2/a039316 .pdf (accessed 17 April 2015).

"A Systems Analysis View of the Vietnam War 1965–1952: Volume 10 (Pacification)," 108. DTIC Online. http://www.dtic.mil/dtic/tr/fulltext/u2/a039317.pdf (accessed 17 April 2015).

Index

Abrams, Creighton W.
  commanding officer, 45
  endorsement of pacification operations,
    45–46, 58
  leadership, 5, 46
  report on "White House" broadcast, 243
  strategic and contingency planning, 47,
    67, 68–69, 160
Accelerated Pacification Campaign (APC)
  achievements of, 52, 53, 54
  Chieu Hoi (open arms) amnesty
    program, 53, 54 (table)
  expansion of the Territorial Forces, 51
  hamlet ratings, 48–50, 51, 52–53
  idea of, 48
  Mobile Advisory Teams (MATs), 51
  Pacification Campaign of 1969, 54–56,
    55 (table)
  recruitment of People's Self-Defense
    Force militiamen, 51–52
  "spreading oil spot" technique, 48, 52
  Third-Party Inducement program,
    53–54
  US troop attitude to, 60–61
  Vietcong strategy, 50–51
Accelerated Phase II Improvement and
  Modernization Plan, 67–68
Advisory Team 42
  on American misconduct, 237
  on Communist advancement in Binh
    Dinh, 249
  on enemy recruiting, 267
  on hamlet ratings, 122
  on ineffectiveness of South Vietnamese
    forces, 189, 241
  objectives of, 94, 130
  on performance of RD cadres, 103

personnel, 92, 135
report on Easter Offensive, 255, 256
reports, 97, 103
role in pacification campaigns, 213
on Vietcong tactic, 184
Ahern, Thomas L., Jr., 86, 275, 288–289, 290
Allen, Richard J., 38
Alsop, Joseph, 147
Andrade, Dale, 257
Area of Operations (AO) Lee
  anti-VCI operations, 226
  April–June 1969, 98 (figure)
  enemy defectors statistics, 147 (table)
  estimated Vietcong forces in, 89 (table)
  January–June 1970, 170 (figure)
  July–December 1969, 134 (figure)
  July–December 1970, 207 (figure)
  North Vietnamese Army in, 90, 162
    (table)
  US military occupation of, 142–143
  Vietcong Infrastructure presence in,
    91–92
  Yellow Star Division's headquarters in,
    158
Area Security Zones, 172 (table)
Army of the Republic of Vietnam (ARVN)
  commanding officers, 30, 77
  dependency on US support, 22–23, 24,
    296–297
  desertions from, 291
  ineffectiveness of, 257, 265, 291
  leadership crisis, 257, 291–293, 296
  military strength, 78
  morale of, 291, 295–296
  Operation Lam Son 719, 296
  operations in Military Region II, 262
    (figure)

Army of the Republic of Vietnam (ARVN),
  continued
  planning to improve firepower and
    mobility, 67
  politicization of, 30, 76–77
  population security and, 265
  Tet Offensive of 1965, 20–21, 23
  training, 264
  See also Republic of Vietnam Armed
    Forces
Army of the Republic of Vietnam (ARVN)
  units
  I Corps, 19, 32, 276
  II Corps, 32, 253, 257, 261, 270–271
  IV Corps, 283
  7th Division, 17
  9th Division, 17
  22nd Division: allied operations, 42;
    Land-Grab Offensive, 261, 263;
    medical care for civilians, 129; Nguyen
    Hue Offensive, 256; pacification duty,
    106, 179; security missions, 115, 116,
    168, 176–177; Tet Offensive, 23
  23rd Division, 141
  40th Regiment: K-8 campaign, 186,
    189, 199; Nguyen Hue Offensive,
    253–254, 257; Operation Dan
    Thang-69, 77–78; Operation Facelift,
    217; Operation Washington Green,
    173, 265; Operation Wayne Span II,
    227; pacification duty, 179; security
    missions, 59, 107, 133, 179; Tet
    Offensive, 20
  41st Regiment: Easter Offensive,
    257; Hawk Teams' tactics, 41;
    K-8 Offensive, 186, 196; Land-
    Grab Offensive, 263; Nguyen
    Hue Offensive, 255; Operation
    Dan Thang-69, 77–78; Operation
    Washington Green, 265; performance
    of, 197; security missions, 30–32, 59,
    113, 115, 116, 133, 179
  42nd Regiment, 263
  47th Regiment, 172
Ashworth, George W., 147
Atatürk, Mustafa Kemal, 74

Baker, Ron, Jr., 237
Bao Dai, emperor of Vietnam, 72
Barnes, John W.
  accusation of covering war crimes,
    244–245, 246, 247
  as commanding officer, 58, 138
  on Operation Washington Green, 58, 59,
    60, 121, 264
  photograph, 139 (figure)
  public relations, 149
  reaction to Figueira's memorandum, 109
  on Sky Soldiers' role in pacification, 61
  as spokesman on Vietnamization, 148–
    149, 246
  on warfare in Binh Dinh Province, 32
Bates, Jared C., 61
Behaine, Pigneau de, 11
Berenzweig, Marvin J., 26
Binh Dinh Province
  balance of forces in, 71
  Campaign 275, 261–263
  cease-fire scenarios, 208
  Communist influence in northern, 141,
    257–258
  Communist offensives, 99–101, 175–176,
    248, 249, 261–263
  Communist redistributive program, 16
  cyclical patterns of military operations
    in, 215–216
  developmental programs, 129
  Easter Offensive, 253–254
  economy, 7–8
  enemy defectors, 127–128, 147 (table)
  first American unit in, 24
  during the First Indochinese War, 12–14
  food shortage, 175–176
  geography, 15–16
  government of Vietnam (GVN) in, 192,
    228, 249, 250, 251, 253
  guerrilla warfare, 15
  hamlet ratings, 56, 163, 191
  hamlet statistics, 57 (table), 145 (table),
    192 (table), 208, 250 (table), 260
    (table)
  impact of Operation Washington Green,
    251

last major battle in, 29
leadership quality, 132
Local Force units, 90–91
map, 21 (figure)
military authority, 77
militia forces, 163
National Police, 81
open arms amnesty program, 127, 128
    (table)
pacification efforts, 12, 57–58, 79, 80,
    127, 264, 269–270
Phoenix (Phung Hoang) Program, 203,
    204, 225
population of, 7, 8, 16, 57 (table), 164–
    165
psychological climate in, 192–193
public health program, 129–130
rebellion against Nguyen warlords, 11
reconstruction projects, 163–164
refugees, 15, 110 (figure), 111
resistance of montagnard tribes, 15
school-building program, 128–129
South Vietnamese counteroffensive,
    260–261
standard of living, 16
strategic importance of, 8
terrorism casualties, 184 (table), 185
transportation routes, 8
US troop withdrawal from, 244
Vietcong Infrastructure, 123–124, 203
Vietcong military strength, 239–241, 240
    (table)
Vietcong offensives, 56–57, 97, 161–162,
    233
Vietnamization process, 264, 269–270
Village and Hamlet Defense Plan
    program, 210–211
Village Self-Development projects, 163
Binh Khe district, 230
Blaufarb, Douglas, 295–296
Bletz, Donald F., 65, 66
Bong Son, battle of, 25
Bong Son Plains, 107, 239
Brady, Phil, 243
Brown, Charles, 213
Bui Trach Dzan, 30

Bumgarner, Roy E., 245–246
Bunker, Ellsworth, 6, 48

Calley, William, 246–247
Camp Radcliffe, 24, 161, 189, 231, 239
Cao Van Vien, 42
Carver, George, 289
Central Office for South Vietnam
    (COSVN), 44–45, 51, 136–138,
    182–183, 229
Chambers, Willard E., 289–290, 294–295
Chieu Hoi (open arms) amnesty program,
    53, 54 (table), 110, 127, 128 (table),
    145–146, 165
China's assistance to North Vietnam, 5
Civil Operations and Revolutionary
    Development Support (CORDS),
    275–276
Clark, John J., 200, 226
Clarke, Jeffrey, 69
Clausewitz, Karl von, 9, 294
Clifford, Clark W., 67
Colby, William, 1, 4, 5–6, 53, 146–147
Collins, Arthur S., 198 (figure), 292
Combined Campaign Plan (1969),
    41–42, 47
Combined Intelligence Center-Vietnam
    (CICV), 272 (table), 273, 273 (table)
Corcoran, Charles A., 58
Corry, Francis B., 239
Cunningham, Hubert S., 138–139, 139
    (figure), 161, 162, 171, 198 (figure),
    216

Daddis, Gregory, 2
Dai Viet (Great Vietnam) political party, 74
Dak To, battle at, 37–38
Davidson, Philip W., 33, 34, 68
Davison, Michael, 293
Diem. See Ngo Dinh Diem, president of
    Republic of Vietnam
District Intelligence and Operations
    Coordination Centers (DIOCCs),
    124, 203–204, 205, 224–225, 226
Doidge, Michael, 2
Donald, William A., 30, 31

Easter Offensive
    B-52 air strikes, 253, 255
    beginning of, 253
    capture of city of Loc Ninh, 253
    casualties, 255
    Communist objectives, 256
    in comparative perspective, 256
    failure of, 257
    government of Vietnam (GVN) forces,
        254, 255
    map, 252 (figure)
    South Vietnamese military performance,
        254, 256–257
    stalemate period, 255–256
    Territorial Forces and militia, 254–255
Elliott, David, 2, 50, 288
Espanol, Onofre C., 102
Esplin, Willard B., 254, 255
Ewing, Eldon E., 135

Fall, Bernard B., 82, 249
Farmers' Liberation Association, 87
Figueira, John S., 108, 109, 149
Fire Support Surveillance Bases (FSSB),
    220–223, 231
First Indochinese War, 12–15
Fitzgerald, Frances, 1
Ford, Gerald, 5
Franklin, Joseph Ross, 60, 64, 65–66, 244–
    245, 246, 247
Friendly, Alfred, 165
Functional Liberation Association, 87

Geneva Agreement of 1954, 14–15
Gia Long, emperor of Vietnam, 12
Gompf, Clayton N., 125, 129, 139, 143, 154
government of Vietnam (GVN)
    assassinations of officials, 249
    association with Western imperialism,
        72–73
    collapse of, 297
    corruption in, 265
    defense plans' preparation, 211–212
    dependence on American support,
        167–168, 264, 268, 294, 295–296
    educated elite in, 76

encounters with the enemy, 265
    guerrilla warfare against, 17
    inefficiency of, 130–131, 249
    lack of discipline, 180, 267
    leadership, 264–266, 292
    media on, 166
    nation-building and, 71
    number of officials, 83
    organizational problems, 72
    pacification campaigns and, 53, 63, 211
    political weakness, 72, 73, 287, 297–298
    public health program, 129
    reform initiatives, 85–86
    Rural Development program, 80
    rural population's support of, 287, 288,
        290
    Vietnam Special Studies Group control
        indicator, 167–168
Green, Gordon, 97
Gregg, Donald B., 275

Hall, C. M., 154
Hallmark, Robert C., 292
Hamlet Evaluation System (HES)
    characteristic of, 48
    data manipulation, 206, 208
    definition of ratings, 49 (table), 50
    on nationwide regression in security, 206
    objectives of, 165
    population control data, 275–278, 276
        (figure), 284 (figure), 285 (figure),
        286
hamlets
    in Area of Operations (AO) Lee, 57
        (table)
    in Binh Dinh Province, statistics of, 57
        (table), 145 (table), 192 (table), 208,
        250 (table), 260 (table)
    control indicator, 167
    definition of, 77
    rating, 56, 163, 191, 206
Herbert, Anthony B., 245, 246, 247
Herbert v. Lando, 247
Hill 262, 173
Hill 474, battle of, 172, 174–175
Hill 875, battle of, 38

Hoai An district
  bridge building across the Kim Son
    River, 152
  civic action projects, 151–152
  Communist penetration into, 232, 258
  decline in Chieu Hoi defectors, 150
  DIOCC advisors, 151
  estimated Vietcong military strength in,
    240 (table)
  Fire Support Surveillance Base, 221
  geography, 117
  hamlets controlled by Vietcong, 117–118
  inefficiency of logistical system, 120
  Mobile Advisory Teams, 153–154, 155,
    156, 157, 194
  neutralization of Vietcong
    Infrastructure, 151, 205, 226
  Operation Washington Green, 118–119,
    121
  pacification campaign, 117, 199, 200, 230
  paddy-level fifth column in, 234
  public health service, 120
  Return-to-Village (RTV) refugee
    resettlement program, 119
  security gains, 121
  shortage of Rural Development Cadre
    Teams, 120–121
  Territorial Forces, 121, 154–156, 157,
    196
  US troop deployment in, 118–119, 121,
    180
  Vietcong offensives, 150–151, 195–196
  Vietnamization, 149–157
  Voluntary Informant Program, 119
Hoai Nhon district
  assault on landing zone English, 109, 110
  casualties during Operation Washington
    Green, 112
  estimated Vietcong military strength in,
    240 (table)
  geography, 105–106, 107
  hamlet ratings, 110–111
  infrastructure rebuilding, 112
  mines and booby traps, 112
  neutralization of Vietcong
    Infrastructure, 205

  pacification efforts, 111–112, 199, 230
  population, 105–106, 107
  prisoners-of-war snatch missions, 106
  "Red Thrust" artillery raids, 106–107
  Return-to-Village (RTV) refugee
    resettlement program, 111
  shortage of Rural Development Cadre
    Teams, 111–112
  Territorial Forces, 179–180
  US–South Vietnamese relations, 108–
    109
  US troop deployment, 107–108, 112,
    179, 180
Hoang Xuan Lam, 293
Ho Chi Minh, 74, 141, 296
Hopson, Michael, 244
Hunt, Richard, 269, 275
Hyle, Archie K., 26

Ia Drang Valley, battle of the, 25
Intelligence Coordination and Exploitation
    (ICEX) program, 94
Islamic State of Iraq and Levant (ISIL),
    298–299

Johnson, Lyndon, 20, 25, 33, 45

K-8 Campaign
  attacks on Tam Quan's district, 186, 191
  casualties, 187–188
  in Hoai Nhon district, 189–190
  impact on Phu My's pacification, 187
  Operation Darby Sweep, 188
  sapper attack on landing zone Graham,
    190
  Suoi Ca operation, 187–188, 190–191
  targets, 185–186
Kaiser, Robert G., 165, 166
Keefe, John L., 292
Kissinger, Henry, 6, 66, 67, 166, 258, 297
Kolko, Gabriel, 1
Komer, Robert, 53

Laird, Melvin R., 68, 69, 148, 243
Landberg, James A., 114, 116, 135
Lando, Barry, 247

League for Independence of Vietnam. *See* Vietminh
Leaty, Daniel L., 249
Le Cau, 263
Le Duc Tho, 258
Le Hien Tong, emperor of Vietnam, 11
Le Truc, 28
Lewy, Guenter, 1
Liên-Khu (Interzone) 5, 12, 52, 90, 266, 277 (figure), 282, 286–287
Lind, Michael, 2
Long An Province, 192
Long-Range Planning Task Group, 45, 46, 47
Lu Mong Lan, 32, 42, 43, 56, 78
Lutzy, Richard C., 125

MacFarlane, Jack, 243
Maguirem, Frank J., 130
Mao Zedong's revolutionary warfare doctrine, 138
Marx, Groucho, 3
Mataxis, Theodore, 20, 23
McCain, John S., 138
McDonald, John M., 286
McDonough, James R., 104, 219–220
McGowan, Robert S., 276
McNamara, Robert S., 1
Megellas, James, 56, 57, 58, 165
Mendheim, William J.
    on advancement of Communists in Binh Dinh, 248–249
    appointment as province senior advisor, 163
    on electricity stealing by government officials, 248
    investigation of Vietcong attacks, 233
    on Phung Hoang program, 225
    report on ambush in Hoai An, 214
    on responsibilities of South Vietnamese forces, 241–242
    on Rome plow operations, 219
    on terrorist attacks, 192, 230
Metzer, Melvin, 194
Meyerson, Harvey, 7
Military Assistance Command–Vietnam (MACV), 19, 45, 48

Mini–Tet Offensive of 1968, 34, 39
Mobile Advisory Teams (MATs), 51, 94, 194
Moorer, Thomas H., 243
Moyar, Mark
    criticism of Orthodox historians, 2
    interpretations of Vietnam War, 4, 5, 293–294
    on leadership of government of Vietnam, 157, 266
    on Phoenix program, 274–275
    on popular perceptions of military strength, 287
    on undemocratic practices in South Vietnam, 74
    on US strategy in Vietnam, 3–4
    works of, 1, 2, 271, 275

National Liberation Front (NLF)
    accountability, 84
    characteristic of, 81–82
    efforts to spark popular uprising, 35
    formation of, 17
    influence on rural population, 288
    interprovincial borders and, 90
    organizational structure of, 86–87
    policy in countryside, 83–84
    political reorientation, 164
    popular support, 278–279, 286, 288
    recruitment and promotion policies, 84
    reform programs, 84–85
    strategy, 82
    See also Vietcong (VC)
National Police Field Force (NPFF), 81, 95, 102–103, 117, 128
National Priority Areas, 8
National Priority Pacification Area, 36
National Security Study Memorandum 1, 67
Navarre, Henri-Eugene, 14
Ngo Dinh Diem, president of Republic of Vietnam
    "Anti-Communist Denunciation Campaign," 15, 73
    assassination of, 17, 19
    confrontation with Buddhist population, 17

defeat of organized crime, 73
formation of Republic of Vietnam, 72
personality of, 74–75
removal from power, 76
Ngo Dinh Nhu, 75
Ngo Dzu, 257
Ngo Quang Truong, 293
Nguyen Anh (Emperor Gia Long), 11–12
Nguyen Be, 79
Nguyen Hue (Emperor Quang Trung), 11, 302n2
Nguyen Hue Offensive. *See* Easter Offensive
Nguyen Huu Tai, 101
Nguyen Huu Thong, 263
Nguyen Nhac, 11, 302n2
Nguyen Van Hieu, 77, 115
Nguyen Van Huan, 118
Nguyen Van Thieu, president of South Vietnam, 48, 51, 133, 209, 257, 258–259
Nixon, Richard
    creation of Vietnam Special Studies Group (VSSG), 166
    criticism of, 295
    on government of Vietnam, 297
    inauguration, 48
    meeting with President Thieu, 68
    postwar memoirs of, 6
    request for aid to South Vietnam, 5
    on troop withdrawal from South Vietnam, 258
    Vietnamization policy, 4, 149
    Vietnam war strategy, 66
North Vietnam. *See* Vietnam, Democratic Republic of
North Vietnamese Army (NVA)
    in Area of Operations Lee, 90, 162 (table)
    desertions from, 291 (table)
    efforts to induce defections in, 174
    Land-Grab Offensive, 259
    Mini–Tet Offensive, 39
    morale of, 174, 291
    operations in Military Region II, 262 (figure)
    organizational structure, 44
    presence in South Vietnam, 4, 87
    strategy, 44
    support to Vietcong, 9
    Z Offensive, 56–57, 97
North Vietnamese Army (NVA) units
    3rd Division (*see* Yellow Star Division)
    14th Engineer Battalion, 256
    18th Regiment, 40–41, 100, 181, 229, 254, 256, 259
    21st Regiment, 253
    22nd Regiment, 38, 161, 162 (table), 172–175, 183, 228–229
    33rd Regiment, 25
    41st Regiment, 30, 31
    90th Engineer Battalion, 162 (table), 230
    95B Regiment, 90, 100, 261
    174th Regiment, 38
    200th Antiaircraft Battalion, 161, 162 (table), 229
    300th Artillery Battalion, 159, 161, 162 (table), 191, 229
    320th Regiment, 25
    325th Division, 19, 24
    400th Sapper Battalion, 159–161, 162 (table), 175, 186, 190, 227, 229
    403rd Sapper Battalion, 253, 254
    406th Sapper Battalion, 253, 254
    450th Sapper Battalion, 253
    500th Transport Battalion, 229

Ochs, Elmer R., 217, 222, 223, 243
OPEC oil embargo, 5
Operation Attleboro, 37
Operation Bolling, 38
Operation Cedar Falls, 37
Operation Cochise, 38
Operation Crazy Horse, 25, 26
Operation Dan Sinh, 40, 41
Operation Darby Maul I, 136
Operation Darby Trail III, 158
Operation Davy Crockett, 25
Operation Earhart White, 182
Operation Eichelberger Black, 182
Operation Facelift, 217–220
Operation Ferret, 223–227
Operation Irving, 26

Operation Jim Bowie, 25
Operation Junction City, 37
Operation Lam Son 719, 296
Operation Masher, 25
Operation Pershing, 27 (figure), 27–28
Operation Putnam Wildcat, 160
Operation Skycourage, 41
Operation Skyhammer II, 41
Operation Skyhawk, 41
Operation Thayer I, 26
Operation Thayer II, 26, 171 (figure)
Operation Velvet Hammer, 38–39
Operation Washington Green
    accomplishments, 163–164
    characteristic of, 8–10
    civic actions, 64
    concept, 59
    difficulties, 202–203
    end of, 239
    engagement rules, 60
    failure of, 251, 264–265, 266, 297–298
    government of Vietnam leadership and,
        265
    lack of progress, 205
    main phases, 97
    National Police Field Force, 95
    objectives, 62–63, 127
    phase III, 180
    phase IV, 197, 199, 202
    phase V, 223
    Regional Forces in, 90
    role of US troops, 62, 92–94
    Territorial Forces, 62, 265
    Yellow Star Division, 266–267
Operation Washington Green: Phase I
    casualties, 103–104, 122
    Communist morale, 122–123
    Communist offensives, 99–101, 100
        (table)
    dependence on American support,
        127–131
    hamlet statistics, 122, 123 (table)
    interrogation of defectors, 127
    neutralization of Vietcong
        Infrastructure, 124–125, 126
    pacification campaign, 131

    practical benefits of, 97
    progress of, 121–123, 125
    role of DIOCCs, 124, 126
    in Tam Quan district, 101–105
    Vietnamization policy, 131–132
Operation Washington Green: Phase II
    1969 High-Point Offensives, 140 (table)
    attack on Camp Radcliffe, 161
    casualties, 144
    civic action projects, 151–152
    Communist activities, 142, 145–146
    danger of mines and booby traps, 143–
        145
    defection rate, 146
    hamlet statistics, 135, 145 (table)
    historians on, 147–148
    initial stage of, 171–172
    military accomplishments, 139–140
    occupation of Area of Operations Lee,
        142–143
    progress assessment, 145–146
    public relations, 149
    September campaign, 141–142
    Territorial Forces, 145, 146 (table)
    terror attacks, 139–140, 142
    turning point of, 162
    Vietcong tactics, 144–145
    Yellow Star Division, 157–163
Operation Wayne Span II, 227–228

pacification
    fast and thin technique, 55, 58, 130, 165,
        166
    historians on, 264, 289–290
    optimism about, 165–166, 295
    outcome, 269–270
    progress of, 223
    role of Territorial Forces, 270
    "spreading oil spot" technique, 48
    US military and, 45–46, 267–268
    See also Accelerated Pacification
        Campaign (APC)
Pacification Attitude Analysis System
    (PAAS), 271–273, 288
pacification campaign of 1969, 133, 135
pacification campaign of 1970

in comparative perspective, 179
features, 176–177
Land-to-the-Tiller (LTTT) program,
    178–179
major operations, 181, 182
objectives, 176–177, 179
security of population, 179
US troops and, 179–181
Village Self-Development (VSD)
    program, 203
Yellow Star Division advancement, 181
Paris Peace Accords, 5, 6, 260, 294–295
Peers, William R., 42, 43, 246
People's Liberation Committees, 45–46
People's Self-Defense Force (PSDF)
in Binh Dinh Province, statistics of, 235
    (table)
combat strength, 122
desertion from, 103
ineffectiveness of, 194, 234
Key Inter-Teams (KITs), 178, 234
mission of, 8
problem of reliability of, 233–234, 235
recruitment, 51–52, 80–81, 165
training, 234–235
weapons distribution, 234
Petraeus, General David H., 298
Pham Van Dong, 282
Pham Van Phu, 261
Phan Dinh Niem, 261
Phan Minh Tho, 77, 97
Phoenix (Phung Hoang) program
analysis of, 125
ineffectiveness of, 123, 124–125, 126,
    165, 205
inspection teams' report, 204
negative opinions about, 274–275
objectives, 96, 117
organizational structure, 94–95
outcome of, 132, 226–227, 265, 273–274,
    275
shortcomings, 203–204
Phoenix program in reverse, 142
Phu Cat Airbase, 8, 22 (figure), 175, 234,
    263
Phu My district

communist movement in, 112
estimated Vietcong military strength,
    240 (table)
geography, 112–113
hamlets controlled by Vietcong, 114
K-8 Campaign, 187
murder of civilians, 237
National Police Field Force, 117
neutralization of Vietcong
    Infrastructure, 225–226
pacification campaign, 113, 115–116, 230
People's Self-Defense Force (PSDF),
    116–117
population attitude to government of
    Vietnam, 114–115
withdrawal of American forces, 161–162
Phung Hoang Centers, 204
Phung Hoang program. See Phoenix (Phung
    Hoang) program
Phu Yen Province, 14, 16, 26
Pike, Douglas, 16, 83, 142
Piotrowski, Stephen J., 141
Piper, Curtis D., 121, 150
Polgar, Thomas, 287
Popular Forces (PF) units, 31
81 platoons, 79
222nd platoon, 169
231st platoon, 232
269 platoons, 78
population-centric counterinsurgency
    (COIN) operations, 9
Porterfield, Jack B., 115
Prados, John, 1
Prisoners-of-war interrogation (IPW) teams,
    223–224
Project In-Depth II, 147
propaganda campaigns, 222
province senior advisors (PSAs), 274–275
Provincial Reconnaissance Units (PRUs),
    96
Provisional Revolutionary Government
    (PRG), 99
psychological warfare, 222

Quang Ngai Province, 16, 20, 29
Quang Trung, emperor of Vietnam, 11

Qui Nhon City
  anti-American demonstrations, 235–237,
    243–244
  guerrilla war, 20
  murder of civilians, 237
  population, 16
  terror attacks, 140
  transportation hub, 8

Race, Jeffrey, 192, 288
Red Queen's Race paradox, 213–214, 251
Regional Forces (RF) units, 91
  24th Group, 201, 232–233, 239
  25th Group, 232
  45th Group, 119
  48th Group, 119, 232
  215th Battalion, 256
  217th Company, 102
  540th Company, 102
  943rd Company, 214
  945th Company, 195
  972nd Company, 195
  981st Company, 195
Republic of Vietnam Armed Forces
    (RVNAF), 42, 291 (table)
Resor, Stanley R., 228
Revisionist historiography
  on advantage of allied forces, 283, 286,
    297
  definition of victory, 295
  "lost victory" hypothesis, 3–4, 8, 205,
    264, 271, 293, 296
  main works, 2
  on Phoenix program, 274–275
  top-down analyses of Vietnam war, 6–7
  on US aid to South Vietnam, 5–6, 294
  on Vietnamization policy, 5
Revolutionary Development Support
    (CORDS)
  American advisors and, 92, 94
  creation of, 48, 50
  formation of Mobile Advisory Teams,
    63
  organizational structure, 94, 95 (figure)
  strategy, 99
Riley, Wilmot T., 102

Roberts, Thomas C., 124, 125, 126, 127, 128
Robnett, Anthony C., 187, 197
Rome plow operations, 216–219, 218
    (figure), 219–220
Roosevelt, Franklin, 34
Rural Development (RD) Cadre Teams,
    36, 79–80, 103, 111–112, 120–121,
    135, 202
Rural Pacification Program, 40

Sansom, Robert L., 288
Schmucker, Roland L., 130
Schnoor, Dean F., 101, 102
Schorr, David, 253
Schultz, Richard H., Jr., 52
Second Indochinese War, 17–19
Shafer, Stuart G., 147
Sheehan, Neil, 253
Sky Soldiers. See US Army units: 173rd
    Airborne Brigade
Soldier (Herbert), 245
Sorley, Lewis, 1–2, 3, 4, 5–6, 34, 205
Southeast Asia Treaty Organization
    (SEATO), 37
South Korean troops, 172, 176
South Vietnam. See Vietnam, Republic
    of
Special Pacification and Development
    Campaign (1969), 133
Special Pacification and Development Plan
    (1970), 209–210, 211
Stanton, Shelby, 31
Summers, Harry, 1, 3–4, 293
Sutton, Elwood, 112

Tam Quan, battle of, 29
Tam Quan district
  estimated Vietcong military strength,
    240 (table)
  geography, 101
  hamlet statuses, 101, 104
  North Vietnamese offensive, 169, 174
  Operation Washington Green, 101–105
  pacification efforts, 230
  paddy-level fifth column, 234
  population, 101, 104–105

programs for civilians, 105
terrorism casualties, 184
Vietcong activity, 103, 104, 169
Vietcong Infrastructure, 91–92
Ten Eyck, Earnest L., 150, 154, 156, 157,
    194
Territorial Forces
    ammunition requisitions, 202
    expansion of, 51
    ineffectiveness of, 189, 194–195, 200–
        201, 210, 289
    lack of cooperation between units,
        211–212
    leadership, 156, 196, 265, 270–271, 292
    media on, 166
    misconduct, 237
    misuse of, 57–58
    pacification and Vietnamization work,
        265, 270
    performance of, 78–79, 154–156, 197,
        211–212, 265, 270–271
    recruitment, 78
    training, 197–198, 199–201, 213
terrorism
    as Communist tactic, 230, 267, 283
    statistics, 184 (table), 185, 268 (table)
    in the twenty-first century, 298–299
Tet Offensive of 1965, 19–23
Tet Offensive of 1968
    casualties, 32, 35
    characteristic of, 33–34
    civilian casualties, 32–33
    conspiracy theory, 34
    contemporary accounts, 33, 36
    impact on American public, 33
    intelligence reports, 34–35
    outcome, 35, 36
    planning, 32
    rural uprisings, 35–36
Thangh, Captain, 155
Thieu. See Nguyen Van Thieu, president of
    South Vietnam
Tho. See Phan Minh Tho
Thompson, Robert, 165, 227, 273
Tran Hieu Duc, 253
Tropical Storm Louise, 232

Trullinger, James W., 288
Turley, Gerald, 257

Undercoffer, John T., 118, 119–120
US Air Force
    AH-1 Cobra helicopter, 106
    B-52 Bombers, 159 (figure)
    B-57 Bombers, 22
    Cessna O-1G "Bird Dog," 92
    CH-47 Chinook helicopters, 92, 143–
        144, 172
    CH-54 "Tarhe" helicopters, 92
    F-100 Fighter-Bombers, 22
US Army
    cases of misconduct, 237–238
    civilian population and, 235–238, 244
    fragging incidents, 238
    one war strategy, 45–47
    tactics, 39–40, 46
    Task Force South, 42–43
US Army units
    1st Cavalry Division (Airmobile), 8,
        24–25, 27–30, 31–32, 108, 113, 146
    4th Infantry Division: Cambodian
        incursion, 189; departure from
        Vietnam, 239, 244; deployment in
        Area of Operations Lee, 161, 172;
        operations in Base Area 226, 176,
        181; Operation Wayne Span II, 227;
        pacification duty, 113, 158; Pair Off
        operations, 42; report on enemy
        engagement, 211–212
    5th Special Forces Group, 136
    8th Cavalry (Airmobile Infantry)
        Regiment, 29
    9th Cavalry Regiment, 29
    11th Air Assault Division, 24, 37
    12th Cavalry Regiment, 29
    12th Infantry Regiment, 158, 160, 189
    17th Cavalry Regiment, 106, 118, 152,
        160, 193
    22nd Infantry Division, 160
    25th Infantry Division, 27, 37
    36th Sapper Battalion, 35
    50th Infantry (Mechanized), 29, 38, 101,
        107, 113, 141

US Army units, *continued*

52nd Combat Aviation Battalion, 20

75th Infantry Regiment (Ranger), 106, 136, 160, 221

82nd Airborne Division, 37

101st Airborne Division, 161, 288

140th Transportation Detachment, 20

173rd Airborne Brigade (Sky Soldiers): attacks on guerrillas, 40; battle at Dak To, 37–38; battle of Hill 875, 38; beginning of Vietnam mission, 37–38; bridge across the Kim Son River, 152; Brigade Advisor Teams (BATs), 63; "Bushmaster" operations, 39–40; civilian population and, 65, 237–238, 268–269; combined operations, 42, 61; commanding officer, 38, 138; Company D, 16th Armor, 135–136; composition of, 93–94 (table); deployment in Area of Operations Lee, 58, 63, 181; deployment in Binh Dinh, 36, 38, 133; Dufflebag data, 220–221; field interviews with personnel, 147; Hawk (Hunter-Killer) Team, 40–41; headquarters, 138; in Hoai An district, 150, 156; intelligence, 220–221; K-8 Campaign, 187–188; "kill ratio," 122; last operation in Vietnam, 243; memorandum on Contra-Productive Activities, 109; misconduct of personnel, 149, 236–238; neutralization of Vietcong Infrastructure, 225; offensive plans, 41; Operation Attleboro, 37; Operation Cedar Falls, 37; Operation Dan Sinh, 40, 41, 59; Operation Darby Trail III, 158; Operation Junction City, 37; operations in Hoai Nhon, 106; Operation Velvet Hammer, 38–39; Operation Washington Green, 8–10, 59, 62–64, 77–78, 103–104, 144, 267–269, 268 (table); order of battle, 92; pacification duty, 60–61, 62–64, 244, 267–268; Pair Off program,

42–43; psychological warfare, 222; public image, 149; reorganizations, 141, 189; road building, 112; Rome plow operations, 216–217; security missions, 62, 122, 127, 128, 180–181, 268; Short-Range Ambush Platoon, 113; tactics, 39–40; VIP guests, 228

173rd Provisional Tank Company, 135

503rd Infantry Regiment of the 173rd Airborne Brigade: attachment to Task Force South, 141; battle of Hill 875, 38; casualties, 144; deployment in Area of Operations Lee, 181; deployment in Vietnam, 36–37; Fire Support Surveillance Bases, 221, 231; Hill 474, 172; in Hoai An district, 118, 133, 199–200, 230–231, 239; in Hoai Nhon district, 107, 108 (figure), 109, 164; Operation Darby Sweep, 188; Operation Darby Trail III, 158; Operation Greene Lightning, 243; Operation Greene Storm, 243; Operation Greene Sure, 243; Operation Washington Green, 101–102; pacification duty, 193–194, 199, 239; in Phu My district, 133, 161, 231; reorganizations, 37; security missions, 101, 107, 133, 142–143, 219–220, 221; Suoi Ca operation, 188, 191; training missions, 197–198, 201

506th Infantry (Airborne) Division, 161, 172

525th Military Intelligence Detachment, 126

US Defense Department's Office of Systems Analysis (OSA), 274

US Marine Corps, 24, 29, 62, 64–65

Vann, John Paul, 55–56, 253, 257

Vietcong (VC)
attacks-by-fire, 137–138
booby trap planting, 217–218
civilian population and, 29
defection statistics, 291 (table)
estimated forces in Area of Operations Lee, 89 (table)

government of Vietnam and, 265, 292
hamlets controlled by, 117–118
in Mekong Delta, 282–283
military strength, 239–241, 240 (table)
morale of, 291
offensives, 56–57, 97, 150–151, 161–162, 195–196, 233
reinforcement, 183–184
resistance to Rome plow operations, 219–220
strategy, 44, 50–51, 229
tactics, 9, 138, 144–145, 182–183, 184
in Tam Quan district, 103, 104, 169
terrorism, 184
underground facilities, 219
Z Offensive, 56–57, 97
Vietcong Infrastructure (VCI)
in Area of Operations Lee, 91–92
government of Vietnam and, 185
influence of rural population, 83
number of officials, 83
objectives, 82–83
role in defeating Operation Washington Green, 266, 267
strength estimate, 91–92, 271–274, 272 (table), 273 (table)
Vietcong (VC) units, 9, 91
2nd Main Force Regiment, 35
2nd Regiment: 506 Valley battle, 221; in Area of Operations Lee, 162 (table), 229–230; Hill 474, 174; K-8 Offensive, 186, 187; Operation Washington Green, 158, 160–161, 172; Operation Wayne Span II, 227; reorganization, 229; Suoi Ca Valley operation, 187–188, 190–191; Tet Offensive, 23, 32, 39, 175
36th Sapper Battalion, 35
300th Sapper Battalion, 90, 230
Local Force Battalions, 90–91
XC-11 Infantry Battalion, 35, 90
Vietminh
areas controlled by, 13 (figure), 277 (figure), 278–279
seizure of power, 12

Vietnam (before 1955)
Chinese invasion, 11
First Indochinese War, 12–15, 13 (figure), 75
first unification of, 11
French colonial rule, 12
Geneva Conference declaration, 15
Japanese invasion, 12
Jesuit missions, 11
Tay Son rebellion, 11–12
See also Second Indochinese War
Vietnam, Democratic Republic of (1945–1975), 5, 12, 71, 72
Vietnam, Republic of (1955–1975)
collapse of, 76
Communist influence in administrative areas of, 88 (table)
formation of, 72
government officials, 75–76
nation building, 73–74
political culture of rural population, 76, 287–289
political parties, 74, 75
reforms in countryside, 75
Vietnam, State of (1949–1955), 71–72
Vietnamese Nationalist Party, 74
Vietnamization policy
characteristic of, 68, 69–70, 295
historians on, 4
objectives, 264
planning, 162
progress and outcome, 131–132, 269–270, 296
US strategy, 4, 67
Vietnam Policy Options study, 294
Vietnam provinces
Communist advantage in, 283
population security data, 278–279, 279 (table), 280 (figure), 281 (figure), 283, 284 (figure), 285 (figure), 286–287
Vietnam Special Studies Group (VSSG)
cease-fire scenarios, 208–209
creation of, 7, 166
population control indicator, 167, 191–192, 192 (table), 276–278

Vietnam Special Studies Group (VSSG), *continued*
  report on population control in Binh Dinh, 193
  tasks, 167–168
Vietnam War
  American society and, 1, 5, 47
  cease-fire agreement, 258–259
  civilian casualties, 25–26
  in comparative perspective, 298–299
  in context of the Cold War, 294
  cost of, 294
  diplomatic efforts to end, 258–259
  errors of American performance in, 5, 302n7
  historiography of, 1–4, 183–184, 294–295, 298 (*see also* Revisionist historiography)
  one war strategy, 45–47
  Rand Corporation study on prospects for victory, 66–67
  statistics about, 165–166
  US strategy, 5–6, 52, 67
  war crimes investigations, 245–248
  "White House" broadcast, 243–244

Waghelstein, John D., 238, 269
Walker, Glenn D., 181
War Comes to Long An (Race), 192
weapons
  2.75-inch rockets, 144
  8-inch artillery shells, 143
  .30-caliber machine guns, 113
  .50-caliber machine guns, 113, 164
  60 mm mortars, 214
  75mm recoilless rifles, 159
  82mm mortars, 159
  105mm artillery shells, 143
  122mm rockets, 175
  155mm howitzer, 173
  B-40 rockets, 109, 138, 142
  M-16 assault rifles, 51, 116, 118, 121, 214
  M-21 sniper rifles, 181

  M-56 Scorpion (a 90mm antitank gun), 136
  M-60 machine guns, 121
  M-72 LAW (light antitank weapon), 109
  M-79 40mm grenade launchers, 121, 202, 214
  M-113 armored cavalry assault vehicles (ACAVs), 113, 114 (figure), 136
  M-132s flamethrower turret, 113
  M-551 Sheridan light tanks, 219
  nonlethal chemicals, 173
  Soviet RPG-2 rocket-propelled grenade, 109
  T-54/55 tanks, 253
Westmoreland, William C., 3, 18 (figure), 19, 22, 24, 25, 228
Weyand, Frederick C., 33
Wheeler, Earle G., 68
Wheeler, Neil W., 270–271
Wiest, Andrew, 2
Willbanks, James, 2, 257, 296
Winship, David L., 195, 201
Wood, Chalmers, 92, 103
Woodall, James R., 113, 115

Yellow Star Division (3rd NVA Division)
  1970 Tet Offensive, 169
  attack on landing zone English, 159
  campaign in Binh Dinh, 159, 261
  casualties, 263
  disbandment of, 228
  Easter Offensive, 253, 256
  headquarters, 158
  Hill 474, 173
  in Hoai An district, 180
  regiments, 24
  response to Operation Washington Green, 157–158, 162, 266–267
  support from civilian population, 26
  training, 136

Zimmerman, Lawrence E., 107, 108, 112
Z Offensive, 97